"Kent and Calishain have written **an easy-to-follow book** (with nice touches of humor thrown in). The authors go into great detail as they discuss search engine registration, giving and getting online awards, places to announce your e-zine, both paid and free sources of press release distribution and a lot more. Especially helpful are the liberal lists of web resources included in every chapter."
—*Quick Tips For Creative People* newsletter

"After demolishing the concept that success on the Internet is a no-effort proposition our intrepid co-authors take on the idea that e-commerce sites are like bricks-and-mortar stores. Kent and Calishain argue that they are more like mail-order catalogs. Why? Because you have to reach a large number of people to make a sale. **Recommended.**"
—*Low Tech Internet Marketing Tips* newsletter

[The authors] explain how you can deploy the fluorescent dye pouch of low-budget advertising to attract attention to your pages. Their advice isn't complicated—it mostly amounts to identifying your audience, providing them with what they want, and taking good care of the customers you have—but reading their advice is **inspirational**."
—*Amazon.com Delivers General Computing* newsletter

"There is so much to do so don't hesitate. **Go now as fast as you can and get this book** and soon your Web site will reach the heights of the well known."
—Linda Roeder, About.com

"This book offers readers the ability to discipline themselves and the resources they need to succeed. It's loaded! The gripping writing style of these two authors contribute to an **enjoyable** time of reading and learning. They are **first-rate** teachers! **Highly recommended!**"
—Jim Moran, The Web Reviewer

"The level of information contained within these pages is **positively brilliant**...simply astounding. [This book] should be read by any businessman or woman worth their salt."
—*Buzz Review News* newsletter

"This is not a 'how to get rich quickly and with little effort by setting up your own web site' type of book. Nor will the book recommend that you pay exorbitant amounts of money to 'Internet Marketing Experts.' Rather [this book] will give you the basics you need to get started promoting your site effectively. It will help prevent making basic errors that will cost you time and money."
—Entrepreneur Books

"I've recommended the predecessor to this book, *Poor Richard's Web Site*, frequently enough that it should surprise no one to see me **heartily approve** of the latest from Peter Kent and company."
—*Small Office TECH* newsletter

"**Full of ideas** and suggested actions . . . a very stimulating read, and the most useful one of its kind that I have come across."
—*Internet Resources Newsletter*

Praise for other books in the Poor Richard's Series . . .

Poor Richard's Web Site

"Makes it possible for ordinary people to set up effective business websites without going broke or spending forever online. It's a great read for anyone who wants to build a business site, and it becomes a part of our recommended library."
—CMPnet's Techweb

"A good source with easy step-by-step directions." —*Publishers Weekly*

"Offers clear advice to help you defend against jargon-happy sales people and computer magazines." —Fortune.com

"If you really want to build a functional Web site [this] might just be the book for you." —CNN Interactive

Poor Richard's E-mail Publishing

"The single most authoritative and helpful guide an entrepreneur can turn to when it's time to move beyond a Web site." —*The Newsletter on Newsletters*

"Unites commonsense advice with clear explanations of e-mail technology . . .The book is packed with marketing know-how and tells you how to make money with your newsletter . . .Don't click Send without [this book]." —*PC World*

"Transforms what could be boring technical jargon into an easy-to-understand tutorial on the ins and outs of Email publishing."
—*Website Success Monthly* newsletter

Poor Richard's Building Online Communities

"An extensive course on creating a vital Web community." —Entrepreneur.com

"Create a web community for a business or family using the power of the Internet and this *Poor Richard's* guide, which focuses on inexpensive methods of achieving such a goal. From locating and participating in mailing lists to joining web-based communities for business and pleasure, this imparts the basics of understanding how such groups function." —Review's Bookwatch

"Another great book from the *Poor Richard's* Series. This book will help the novice or expert build a online community that will make the most out of the different components that turn a Web site into a community."
—Nathan Allan, Community Development Manager, Sausage Software

POOR RICHARD'S INTERNET MARKETING AND PROMOTIONS

How to Promote Yourself, Your Business, Your Ideas Online

SECOND EDITION

by

Peter Kent and Tara Calishain

TOP FLOOR
PUBLISHING

Poor Richard's Internet Marketing and Promotions:
How to Promote Yourself, Your Business, Your Ideas Online, Second Edition

SAN#: 299-4550
Top Floor Publishing
8790 W. Colfax #107
Lakewood, CO 80215

Feedback to the author: feedback@topfloor.com
Sales information: sales@topfloor.com
The Top Floor Publishing Web Site: http://TopFloor.com/
The Poor Richard Web Site: http://PoorRichard.com/
Cover design/illustration by Marty Petersen, http://www.artymarty.com

Library of Congress Catalog Card Number: 00-105953

ISBN: 1-930082-00-2

03   02   01   6 5 4 3 2 1

For my wife, Debbie.
—Peter Kent

Dedicated to my husband, Phil.
—Tara Calishain

ACKNOWLEDGMENTS

I'd like to thank everyone involved in creating this book. Tara Calishain, of course. I'd also like to thank Sydney Jones, copyeditor; Jerry Olsen, development editor; Joann Woy, proofreader; Liz Cunningham, indexer; and last but certainly not least, layout whiz and publisher Missy Ramey.

—Peter Kent

Thanks very much to Syd Jones (who put up with my silly comments during author review) and Jerry Olsen (who put up with everything else). Missy and Peter were great to work with, as always.

—Tara Calishain

ABOUT THE AUTHORS

Peter Kent is the author of over 40 business and computer books. His work has appeared in a variety of publications, from the *Manchester Guardian* to *Internet World*, *Computerworld* to *Smart Partner*. He is also the founder of BizBlast.com, an e-business service provider.

Tara Calishain is the owner of CopperSky Writing & Research and the co-author of several computer books. She distributes a weekly newsletter about Internet research resources at http://www.researchbuzz.com/.

CONTENTS AT A GLANCE

PART IV: E-MAIL PR

PART V: OUTSIDE THE INTERNET

TABLE OF CONTENTS

PART III: GETTING THE WORD OUT

INTRODUCTION

We all know the Internet is paved with gold; we've heard that enough from the press over the last seven years. "Just set up shop on the Internet, and you'll be inundated with orders. So you don't really need this book …"

Of course reality is very different from the Internet hype we've been fed. You may have heard that a Web site is a billboard on the Information Superhighway; it's not. A Web site sits in the darkness of cyberspace, waiting for people to visit. Unlike a billboard, which is seen by anyone who glances up as they drive or walk by, a Web site is only seen if the viewer has *chosen* to see it. A conscious decision must be made. And the competition for attention is stiff, too. There are far more Web sites to choose from—many thousands of times more—than billboards lined along your daily drive to work or school.

So in the real Internet, as opposed to the media-created myth, the Internet most certainly is not paved with gold, or even with silver. That's the bad news. The good news is that you really can benefit from the Internet, either in a direct financial manner or a more indirect way. You've just got to work at it.

That's where this book comes in. Tara and I have been using the Internet for real. This isn't a book written by a writer who's been given an assignment. It's not a "find out as much about marketing and promotions on the Internet and write a book for us" sort of thing. We actually market and promote real products and services on the Internet.

Here's an example. I promoted the first book in this series—*Poor Richard's Web Site: Geek-Free Commonsense Advice on Building a Low-Cost Web Site*—on the Internet. Despite the fact that my publishing company, Top Floor Publishing, is a small company with very limited resources, that book became probably the most widely reviewed title in computer-book history. Top Floor Publishing grossed around $35,000 in Web site sales in the first 12 months of the book's life, and thousands of copies were sold through bookstores. Around 10,000 copies were sold in the first year, a decent number for any publisher, let alone one working on a shoestring budget. And at the time of writing sales of that book seem to be accelerating, as it becomes more well-known and appears in the press over and over again.

How was this publicity achieved? I used many of the techniques you'll learn about in this book to get *Poor Richard's Web Site* into the hands of journalists, to drive people to my Web site, and to sell the book at the site. But there's more. Tara Calishain has added many other things to the mix, little techniques that I was unaware of. Tara's specialty is research; she's written a book about Internet research, does a weekly newsletter on new Internet research resources (http://www.researchbuzz.com), and has worked in public relations (out in the "real world"). She has also used many of the techniques you'll find in this book to promote her work online.

In fact, one problem you may run into is that you'll find *too many* techniques in this book. I received an e-mail message the other day from an entrepreneur asking how he could "apply all of this dynamite information to two (as yet unpublished) Web sites, run one business, start the second, learn FrontPage while simultaneously designing both Web Sites, …" Good question. Sometimes you just have to pick and choose what you're going to do. You can't do everything, so you have to decide what you think might work for you. And don't imagine that everyone else out there on the Internet is working a 40-hour week. Someone once said that an entrepreneur is someone who works 18 hours a day for himself, so that he doesn't have to work 8 hours a day for someone else. The Internet is a new entrepreneurial arena; there are plenty of us working 18-hour days!

Read the entire book, and then pick and choose the techniques you want to use. But do *something*. If you're trying to promote a product, service, or idea on the Internet, you can't afford to just set up a Web site and wait for something to happen. You've got to *make it happen*, and this book will show you how.

—*Peter Kent*

PART I
PREPARATION

CHAPTER ONE

What Are You Promoting and Who Are You Targeting?

The first thing you need to do before beginning your marketing and promotion campaign is to decide exactly what you are promoting, what you want to achieve, and who you are targeting. Before we begin, though, we need to explain a little shortcut that we use throughout this book. We talk about how you can promote your *product* or *service,* but in fact you can use the techniques in this book to promote just about anything. You can promote a physical item you're selling, your political ideas, your religious beliefs, a charitable institution, a sports team, a hobby, a club or association...just about anything you want to get into the public eye. The principles are the same.

Perhaps most readers of this book have something to sell; but a great deal of activity on the Internet—possibly most, depending on how you measure it—is noncommercial. So those of you promoting something other than a product or service will, we hope, forgive us if we sound a little too commercial...and should understand that these techniques can be used for many different purposes.

Let's begin, then. We'll start with three premises—let's call them *Poor Richard's Laws of Promotions*:

1. No one knows as much about you and your product or service as you do.
2. No one cares as much about you and your product or service as you do.
3. That's as it should be.

Whether you have a million-dollar company or a dog-walking service (or even a million-dollar dog-walking service) no one's ever going to feel the drive and enthusiasm for your product or service that you do. Even if you hire someone to advertise and promote your company, you'll never be able to impart to them everything you know about your company or industry. Nor will you be able to infect anyone else with your enthusiasm and knowledge. (Remember, every parent thinks his or her child is beautiful...but other people may have a quite different view!)

If you've picked up this book, it's quite possible that you're on your own and you need to do some online marketing and promotion. Poor Richard's laws are good news for you! You have the knowledge to effectively promote your product; now all you need are the tools. And here's a little more good news: the tools we're going to describe in this book, the various Internet systems and techniques, provide a very low-cost and effective way to promote your products and services. (We'll be looking at a few expensive tools, such as banner advertising, but it's quite possible to create an effective Internet-promotion campaign without getting involved with those sorts of things.) But maybe you're a little suspicious of this whole promotion and marketing thing. Who needs it, anyway?

WHY PROMOTE?

Long ago, when everyone lived within the confines of a small town, promotion wasn't an issue. If you ran the only grocery store, people *had* to buy their groceries from you. Hanging out your shingle pretty much ensured some business when you were the only game in town.

As cities got bigger, of course, more options became available. Suddenly grocers had to compete; but there was still a limit; people would drive only so far for groceries. Grocers for the most part had to be concerned with other grocery stores only within a limited area.

With the Internet, the limitation on geography is virtually eliminated—in some cases, at least. Perhaps not so much for grocery stores, but certainly for stores of other kinds. Customers can order from music and bookstores all over the world, for instance. We have only just begun to see this kind of "worldwide demand" for goods and services online, since up until the last year or so North America and Europe contained most of the people on the Web. Now, more and more people from more and more countries are being represented. To get an up-to-the-minute idea of which countries are getting more people online, and whether they're buying anything, check out the **Nua Internet Surveys** site, e-commerce section, at http://www.nua.ie/surveys/index.cgi?f=FS&cat_id=14. From the marketing point of view, this is a double-edged sword. Yes, you may be able to sell your products on the other side of the world; but perhaps people on the other side of the world can now sell products in *your* neighborhood, too. Unless you're selling specialty items for left-handed yak herders whose favorite color is mauve (and perhaps not even then), you're not the only game in town! You have the whole world, potentially, to compete with.

So this Internet thing is both good and bad news. We hear a lot about the good news, but don't underestimate the bad; online *sales* are cutting into real-world sales. For example, in a June 2000 survey of French Internet users, more than 40 percent said that the Internet had changed their shopping habits.

(Details: http://www.nua.ie/surveys/?f=VS&art_id=905355821&rel=true.) Still, from the marketing and promotion point of view, it's pretty good news. You also have the whole world full of potential customers; but to reach them you're going to have to market and promote your product or service. You're going to have to get the word out, rise above the crowd, shout above the storm, and all those other clichés.

You've probably heard the maxim that if you "build a better mousetrap, the world will beat a path to your door." Well...it's not true. It doesn't matter how good your product is; if nobody knows about it, nobody will buy it. This is not news to people who have been in sales, promotions, and marketing in the real world. Many people on the Internet don't understand this concept, though, for two main reasons:

1. Because it's relatively cheap and easy to set up a business on the Internet, many people who have never been in business before are setting up shop online. Many of these people don't understand basic principles of sales and promotions.
2. The media has hyped the Internet terribly. You've probably heard that a Web site is like a billboard on the Information Superhighway. It's not. If it were true, all you'd need to do is set up a Web site and take orders; but a Web site sits in the darkness of cyberspace, seen by nobody...until you convince someone to visit your site.

Promoting on the Internet really does work; but of course that's what this book is all about. You're going to discover *how* to make it work. Now that you're converted (we hope), let's take a look at what promotion and marketing actually involve.

WHAT ARE PROMOTION AND MARKETING?

There's a little confusion about these two terms, *promotion* and *marketing*. So let's look at a couple of dictionary definitions. The term *marketing* has been used for more than 400 years. It's variously defined as the process of selling a product or service; as the process of promoting, selling, and distributing a product or service; and as the entire process of moving goods and services from a producer to a consumer. So *promotion* (or *promotions*) is a subset of marketing; it's the process of encouraging people to accept or buy your goods or services.

This book is titled *Poor Richard's Internet Marketing and Promotions* because the two processes are interlinked, because they overlap, and because in many people's minds they tend to mean similar things. To make clear what this book covers, then, here's what we plan to explain in this book:

This book covers how to let people know about your products and services using newsletter ads, how to give away products at other people's Web sites, how to use reciprocal links, how to answer questions and participate in discussion groups, how to use free and paid banner ads, and other methods. It will teach you how to use a Web site to provide information and take sales—how to find a shopping-cart system, for instance, how to take orders, and even how to find a fulfillment company (a company that can ship your products for you). This book is an overview of the entire process of marketing and promotions.

PROMOTION AND MARKETING REQUIRE STEADY WORK

You have to promote and market over time because...

- Getting an idea into people's minds and keeping it there takes a lot of time and effort. It's not something that's done once and sticks; you have to keep working at it. Call it "mindshare." These days we're getting bombarded with ads. They're everywhere from on elevators to wrapped around cars. We're getting better and better at subconsciously filtering out all this advertising noise. You as a marketer have to do a lot—and do it cleverly—in order to maintain mindshare.

- More people get on the Internet every day. (The Internet population was at one point increasing exponentially and has only recently slowed. Now the focus is on more countries besides the United States getting on the Internet. Remember, the Internet is becoming truly global.)

- More competition gets on the Internet every day (unless you're catering to those left-handed yak herders, of course).

- There is still time to brand yourself. Yes, everyone thinks of Amazon when it comes to buying books online—but who do they think of when shopping for a car? Looking for a real-estate service? Trying to buy videos online? When it comes to buying and selling, the Internet is still young, and by marketing and promoting yourself you can establish your dominance in an unclaimed niche.

As you can see, there are several reasons to promote online, several ways to do it, and a strong impetus to continue your effort over time; but enough about the whys and wherefores of this book—let's talk about *you*.

YOUR WEB SITE AS A MARKETING AND PROMOTIONS CENTER

We believe that a Web site is a great way to start your marketing and promotions. Your Web site can be your center of operations, your headquarters.

About the URLs—*We're going to be mentioning a lot of URLs—Internet addresses—in this book. You can view a Web page containing all these address links at a Web site associated with this book: http://PoorRichard.com/promo/. Copy the page to your hard disk and then create a bookmark to the page stored on your hard disk, so it will be easily accessible.*

It's possible to promote products and services without ever creating a Web site. Many consultants promote themselves in newsgroups and mailing-list discussion groups, a subject we discuss in Chapter 9, *Promoting in the Newsgroups and Mailing Lists.* In the late eighties and early nineties, for example, Peter promoted his technical-writing services in CompuServe's discussion groups. At that time there was no Web, so having a Web site was not an option. Still, he was able to find literally tens of thousands of dollars in business by promoting his services online.

We really believe that these days, however, it makes sense to have a Web site, if only because Web sites are so cheap and easy to create. So we're working under the assumption that you will have a Web site, and that your Web site will be your center of operations. And indeed that's what most people do. If the Web had been available to Peter during his CompuServe-promotion days, he would have created a Web site to hold a résumé, samples of his work, a list of clients, and so on. However, most people don't think of their Web site as the center of their operations. Here's what most people do:

1. Set up a Web site.
2. Register the Web site with the search engines.
3. Wait for people to visit.

That's not making the Web site the *center* of operations. In this case, the Web site is the entirety of the operations.

Here's what we think you should do:

1. Set up a Web site.
2. Register the Web site with the search engines.
3. Do lots and lots of other things to bring people to your site.

We'll be talking about #1 in Chapter 3. We'll be talking about #2 in Chapters 5 and 6. And as for #3, that's what the bulk of this book is all about.

In effect your Web site becomes an intermediate step. You go out and promote your Web site to bring people to the site, so that they will learn about your products and services and, we hope, buy something.

PROMOTING YOUR WEB SITE, PRODUCTS, AND SERVICES

There's an important principle to consider here. Your Web site has to serve you, and it has to serve your visitors. If it doesn't serve you, it has no purpose, of course; but if it doesn't serve your visitors...you won't have any visitors.

If you use your Web site as an intermediate step—bringing people to the site to promote your products and services—then you have to think carefully about what you have to offer at your Web site. Just as there are good products and bad products to sell, there are good and bad Web sites to promote. When you are out there promoting your products and services directly, you should also consider what you are saying, and whether people are likely to care. Let's look at the bad stuff first.

The Bad Stuff

While we want to focus on the good stuff, of course, we also need to take a few minutes and tell you about what your Web site shouldn't look like—the bad stuff.

YOUR WEB SITE AS A BROCHURE

Let's get something clear. We have no objections to brochures as instruments of marketing; a photograph on slick paper really is worth a thousand words. However, sometimes you'll see someone who puts up a Web site that is, essentially, only a brochure. It has a price, and lots of marketing copy, and a couple of snazzy photographs. And they try to promote it. There's nothing to promote! Nobody cares about a Web site that's a brochure any more than they'd care about a plain old brochure. A Web site needs community, case histories, support, good ideas, examples, testimonials, or any of a dozen other elements to be attractive. It's not attractive just because it's got a cool photograph and features your price list. One of the big keywords on the Web (and the Internet in general) is content. You want to give people a reason to visit. You don't do that with a brochure. You do that by sharing your knowledge, your expertise—in short, the information you gained while working in the business or cause that you're promoting in the first place. You have to have content.

There's an exception to this rule, though. It's what Peter calls the *résumé* or *business card* Web site. You direct people to the site to get information about you, your products, or your services. So people aren't just wandering around the Web looking for a type of product or service. They've already learned about you and want to know about *your* products and services. Here's how it works. You set up a simple Web site, perhaps just a single page. The purpose of the site is really to get people to call you; you include all your contact info—business name, phone number, e-mail address, and so on. Then you put the URL to your Web site wherever you can. (CNBC anchor Ted David has a good example of a business card site at http://www.teddavid.com/.)

For instance, let's say you're a house painter. You put the URL on the sign that you post outside houses you're painting. Of course you want a distinctive URL, something like BostonPainters.com, PaintPaintPaintNow.com, WePaintQuick.com, or whatever. (By the way, all those URLs were available at the time of writing. With a little imagination, it's still possible to find a distinctive URL that will work on a sign.) You don't have to use a domain name that is the same as your company name—the important thing is to pick a memorable and descriptive domain name.

Now, as people drive by your sign, they'll see a phone number (you *do* put your phone number on your signs, don't you?) and a URL. They won't remember the phone number, but if they see the URL a few times, there's a good chance they'll remember it. They'll be able to reach your site; in effect, you passed out a business card, without either you or the recipient realizing it at the time. The URL can be displayed on everything—the side of your trucks and cars, the employees' uniforms, your windows...anything you know people will see. People don't go online to look for a house painter, or a lawn service, or a plumber; they use the Yellow Pages. But if they've seen a memorable URL a few times, they'll remember it and may go to the business-card Web site.

Business-card Web sites can work well for delivery services, carpet-cleaning services, plumbers, house cleaners, kids cutting lawns, milk-delivery services, diaper services, window cleaners you...get the idea.

***Make Your URL Distinctive**—Use this little trick to make your URL more distinctive when you use it in signs, brochures, business cards, e-mail, and so on. Uppercase some of the letters to make it easier to read. Instead of writing paintpaintpaint.com or bostonpainters.com, write PaintPaintPaint.com or BostonPainters.com—you see how it's easier to read that way? You don't really need the www. bit at the front, either; at least you shouldn't have to include it, but this depends on how your Web site is set up. Make sure people can reach your site using www.BostonPainters.com or simply BostonPainters.com. (Don't fool around with the capitalization of the rest of the URL, the directory and file names—only the domain name can be modified.)*

Consider using colors where possible, too: in Web pages, brochures, business cards, and so on. By using different colors for each word in the URL, you make it easier still to read. Look at what the Tom Peters' site does. It has the name Tom in red, with the word Peters in black. Often the .com isn't even used after the site name, but when it is, it is red, so the URL goes like this: tom(red) peters(black) .com (red again.) The URL is broken up visually and is much easier to remember.

ANCIENT WEB SITES

You're just getting around to promoting a site that's so out of date it's got dust bunnies in the source code? Don't bother. Do something, add something to the site, before you start talking about it. Ask yourself this: Is my Web site useful to people *today* (forget about how useful it *used* to be). If you have a plan to make it useful tomorrow, and keep it useful forever, you're ahead of the game.

Please, please, please don't fall into the trap of thinking, "Well, I can do a little bit of promotion before I update the site." *No you can't!* You don't want one single person to visit your moldy old site. You want everyone to see your nice fresh sparkly site. We admit we have been guilty of this a couple of times—being so excited about a new site that we've promoted it before the update was completely finished—and we always regret it.

MINOR DETAILS

If you're in charge of promotion for a publicly held company, there are things you have to announce in the interest of disclosure; but even that has its limits. You don't need to trumpet the fact that you're now using Doodad 3.1 instead of Doodad 3.0 to maintain your Web site. Nobody except your maintenance people needs to know that you've upgraded to stain-free carpet. These may seem like silly examples to you, but you'd be amazed what people consider grounds for a press release!

When you spend a lot of time focusing on minor events, you're conditioning people to respond as if all your news is minor—and your major news loses a lot of its impact. Save your loudest voice for the biggest news and mention the minor stuff in passing, if at all.

If you must announce that stuff, write a press release and put it in a corner of your Web site—preferably a far corner.

VAPORWARE

If it hasn't happened yet, don't get noisy about it. If you've used computers for any length of time, you've probably heard the term *vaporware*. Vaporware is software that's been announced (usually with much fanfare) but over time doesn't appear on the store shelves. It's delayed, and delayed, and delayed, and eventually it's quietly cancelled. This not only costs a company money, it costs credibility; anyone familiar with your company will look askance at future announcements.

Vaporware applies not only to products but also to services. If you're preparing to offer a three-leash dog-walking service, make sure you have all the leashes ready and your license upgraded to triple-leashing; a delay could cause you trouble.

LOUSY PRODUCTS

There are many people searching for the pavements of gold on the Internet. The Internet hype has been so intense that people are desperate to get involved in some way. They're scared of missing the boat. So what do they do? They run out and find a product—any product—and set up shop on the Internet.

Many of those products are trash. There's enough trash being sold on the Internet today to fill half the landfills in North America.

It really is possible to sell trash. You can promote the hell out of a product, and you'll sell some of it; but it's far better to have a *good* product, as we'll explain in a moment.

The Good Stuff

Okay, that's the bad stuff. In contrast, there's really good stuff to market and promote.

CONSISTENTLY UPDATED RESOURCES

If you've put together a Web site containing a list of links that deals with your industry, product, or service, and you update it regularly (that is, check for new resources and remove old ones that no longer work), you're providing an invaluable service to the Internet community. Likewise, if you publish a listing of resources on paper, or in some other way publish a list that provides value, that's something worth promoting. If you have information of any kind that your target market will find useful, it's worth promoting. Here's an example. Visit one of Peter's sites at http://PoorRichard.com/freeinfo/special_reports.htm and you'll find a number of special reports, such as the *Shopping-Cart Software & Services Directory* and a report called *Places to Register Your Email Newsletter*. Recently someone posted a message about this Web page to a discussion group about newsletter publishing:

> *This is a GREAT site!!! It will keep you busy for days with places to register your ezine and resources on promoting your ezine. There are a TON of links...*

Comments like this lead visitors to Peter's site...and some of them buy his books.

Niches Are Cool!—Worried about maintaining a list for your product or service because you're niche oriented? Worry not; niches are cool! The nichier the better, within reason. Although lots of sites have the broad categories covered, there has been less excursion into the niche side of things. Niche sites are also easier to maintain and update because you have to cover less ground.

FREE TRAINING AND SUPPORT

You make WidgetWare and on your Web site, you have free training units that teach how to use WidgetWare in certain vertical markets, as well as a technical support site that helps beginners with frequent WidgetWare problems. If you're offline, you have a newsletter called *WidgetWare for the Bemused* that assists beginners with your product. You have an extensive faxback service and update your documentation regularly, sending out free updates as necessary. You're not only providing super customer service, but you also have a great service to promote. Anything that falls in the line of free training and support—maybe it's a housecleaning service giving out a database of tips on cleaning household items, or a business realtor offering seminars on readying retail stores for hurricanes—is a good thing to promote.

SAMPLES AND DEMONSTRATIONS

Samples are great. On the Internet, software is easily distributed as a sample or demonstration (often called trialware). But there are other things you can provide as online samples, too—for example books, issues of newsletters, stock photography, and so on. If you cannot physically provide the sample online, provide an order form for a visitor to request one to be sent by mail. (Keep things in perspective—no one is going to get too excited about the ability to order a sample of dishwashing liquid online. However, if you've just completed a major upgrade to a $600 product, and you're making a free trial available online, you're going to attract some interest.)

Here's another real-life example. When Peter published *Poor Richard's Web Site: Geek-Free, Commonsense Advice on Building a Low-Cost Web Site,* he posted several sample chapters at his Web site (see http://PoorRichard.com/sample_chapt/). Do these benefit him? Absolutely; people often buy the book after reading these chapters, and journalists often contact him for review copies.

COMMUNITIES AND DISCUSSIONS

A well-moderated discussion is a beautiful thing. You may have noticed that in open forums like newsgroups and mailing-list discussion groups, chaos does occasionally reign in the form of inappropriate messages, fights (also called *flame wars*), new users asking the same question over and over again, and so on. Taking the time and trouble to create and moderate a discussion that answers questions about your product and industry, provides answers and support, and facilitates discussion among your customers will really pay off. You're getting ideas for your customers and content for your Web site, and potential customers will see your community as a sign that you stand behind your product or service.

A word of caution, though; please don't start communities and discussions without adequate resources to keep them going. A slaphappy community or a discussion group you sponsor that's completely out of control could do more harm than good to your image.

GOOD PRODUCTS

When you're promoting a good product, here's what happens:

1. You convince people to buy the product.
2. They love the product, so...
3. They tell friends, family, and colleagues.
4. Their friends, family, and colleagues buy the product.

If you have a bad product, you miss out on steps 2, 3, and 4. The best product to promote is one that can promote itself. Then, in effect, what you are doing is priming the pump. Your initial promotional efforts are multiplied several times, perhaps many times, by the effects of steps 2, 3, and 4.

We've mentioned only a few examples here; we haven't mentioned things like announcing new products, new services, the appointment of new executives, and other things that traditionally call for marketing or promotion. If you're not sure whether the thing you want to promote is a good thing or a bad thing, look at it from your customers' viewpoint and ask yourself, "So what? Who cares? What's in it for me?" If the answer is, "I don't know what, not me, nothing much," you should think twice about promoting it. On the other hand, if you do have a good solid answer, make sure it's incorporated into your marketing and promotion materials.

Now that you have an idea of what makes a good (and bad) marketing or promotion push, you need to think about who needs to see the push.

WHAT DO YOU WANT TO HAPPEN?

If you're simply selling a product or service, this question might strike you as the king of no-brainers. You want people to go out and grab your product or sign up for your service, of course! However, if you're promoting a cause or you're trying to build recognition for your company, the question is not that easy to answer. There are a few ways it might be answered.

I want people to buy my product (join my cause, use my service, sample my new brand of cheese dip, etc.)

If you want people to buy your product, you'll need to concentrate on *visibility*—making sure people hear about your product or service—with a secondary focus on *credibility*—making sure that they hear, from a third party, that your product or service is good. Visibility can be obtained through both promotional and advertising efforts, while credibility can best be obtained through promotional efforts like reviews, newspaper articles, and case studies. Don't neglect credibility in your search for visibility, however; customers will have questions about your product that strong credibility will help answer.

I want to build recognition for my company, product, or service

If you want to build recognition, it follows that you want to concentrate on visibility. To a much lesser extent, you want to build credibility. Recognition should not be the first and last goal of your campaign, however; you should aim for a critical mass of recognition (via visits to your Web sites, sales calls, orders, whatever) and then concentrate on another goal, such as sales. You can also use this goal to build recognition for individual happenings within the company—a product upgrade, a new service, or a significant shift in personnel.

I want to build credibility for my company, product, or service

This is the flip side of building visibility. Once a lot of people have heard about your product or service, you want to concentrate on giving them a good reason to buy, which calls for concentrating on credibility. Editorial coverage of your product or service is much more credible to a reader than an advertisement; you want to try to get *other* people to say nice things about your products and services. People do pay attention to ads, to some degree, but they don't necessarily trust them. They know the person paying for the ad is biased, after all; but if someone who isn't apparently linked with your company says good things, that counts for a lot.

You can also combine these two goals into one. You can build visibility and credibility at the same time. In this case, you'll want to split your resources between generating both visibility and credibility. (It should be noted that if you have a bad or marginal product, no amount of promotional effort is going to keep the truth from eventually coming out. We're assuming that you have a good product that you're proud to sell.)

If you ever have to make a decision between where to invest your resources, always put credibility before visibility. Guard your credibility like your most treasured possession—because, on the Internet, that's exactly what it is. You can always work to build up your visibility. It's far more difficult and time-consuming to repair damaged credibility.

I want to diffuse a rival's efforts

Are competitors promoting that they have better prices than you do? That the quality of their service is superior to yours? What you'll need to focus on depends on what claim you're trying to deflect. If they're saying you have a shoddy product, you want to build credibility. If they're trumpeting their service and you know yours is better, you want to concentrate on visibility. If they're merely making vague claims that their product is the best around or the only service of its type and you know that's not true, you want to concentrate on the following:

- Building visibility for you and your product (so that the only service of its type claim is put to rest)
- Building credibility (so that the best around is at least put to a challenge)

So think carefully about what you are trying to achieve. What do you have to promote or market? Is there something you can do to improve it before you begin your marketing or promotion campaign? What do you want to happen? Do you want people to rush out and buy your product? Do you want them to get a warm fuzzy feeling when they think of you? Do you want them to think of you immediately when the need arises for a certain service? Knowing the outcome you want will help you decide your program.

WHO ARE YOU AIMING AT?

Who are you aiming your promotion at? The short answer is, of course, customers. A longer answer will serve you better. Consider whether you are aiming at...

Consumers in general—Do I have a product as ubiquitous as pencils that everyone needs to have, or is it at least fit for a large group of people? (We're not saying there won't be some demographic group that's most appropriate for your product or service, just that it will be a large group or several groups.)

Businesses—Is it more a business-to-business product or service, like a retail accounting form?

Vertical markets—Vertical markets are markets that are oriented to one particular specialty. For example, plastics manufacturing is a vertical market. Transportation engineering is a vertical market. Medical supply companies need to deal only with healthcare customers; therefore a press release to the *Small Town Gazette* isn't going to do much good. A press release to *Medical Supply Monthly* would be far more appropriate.

Very specific, smaller markets—If your product or service deals with a particular niche—a particular specialty occupation, a specific age group, or a specific locale (like a catering service)—you need to focus very specifically on those people.

It may seem like those products and services related to consumers in general might have an advantage. After all, there are many more outlets available for their advertising, more places they can send press releases, etc.

On the other hand, having so many outlets available tends to diffuse efforts. One can't contact every newspaper in the country to deliver a promotional pitch without expending a lot of time and money. In addition, when you try for coverage in those media outlets, you're competing with a lot of other products and services. If you're in a specialized niche, you have less competition, and fewer media outlets on which you can focus more attention.

Take a little time now and think about at whom your product is aimed. In some cases, it'll be really obvious; in other cases, some thought will be necessary. Who are you selling your product or service to now? Who helps you develop it? Into what markets do you hope to expand? What new products or services are you developing and for what markets have you developed them?

It's extremely important to decide whom you are trying to reach, or your efforts won't be concentrated in the best way possible. If you have a product or service with a wide prospect base, take some time and think about how you can break down the prospects into different segments and focus on one segment at a time. For example, maybe you sell an educational toy. You could break your focus down into several segments:

- Teachers
- Child-development experts
- Parents
- Grandparents and other family members
- Professional caregivers

Breaking down your prospect base into segments like this will keep you from becoming overwhelmed when you're searching for your marketing and promotional targets. (We'll get into that in Chapter 4, *Finding Your Targets*.)

Be creative when identifying these groups. For instance, when Peter was promoting the first book in the Poor Richard's series, *Poor Richard's Web Site*, he wanted to find periodicals to publish reviews of the book. He could have focused solely on the computer press—computer magazines, technology columnists in newspapers, computer papers, and so on; but he also realized that the book would be of interest to many people who might not consider themselves "geeks" or even particularly computer literate. After all, everyone these days seems to want to create a Web site. So he also approached the business press and a variety of other niches. The book has been reviewed or mentioned in a wide range of periodicals, such as *The Philadelphia Inquirer, The New England Non-Profit Quarterly, Home Office Computing, Keyboard Magazine,* the *USA Today* Web site, *Marketing Technology,* and so on. (In fact, this may be the most widely reviewed computer book ever.)

When computer-book publishers send out review copies, they generally focus on the computer press. A computer subject should be reviewed in the computer press, right? But Peter thought about whom he wanted to read the book, and why they would read it, and realized that he could reach these people through a wide variety of periodicals.

Tara's done the same thing with an Internet-related book she co-authored She approached editors at business publications, educational publications—any group that she felt would need to find information on the Web regularly. And it did pay off, as her book was reviewed in several business- and education-related publications. Tara also publishes a newsletter on search engines that's gotten coverage in publications as general as newspapers and as specific as magazines about banking! Sometimes it's surprising to find out who might be interested in your product or service.

To summarize, before you can promote a product or service you have to think about what it is you are trying to promote, to whom you are promoting it, and what you want the outcome to be. This may sound obvious, but when you look at the way in which many companies promote themselves, their products, and their services, it's clear that they've spent little or no time thinking through this process. A few hours spent on this process early on will save you a great deal of time, money, and effort later.

Once you know what you want to do, it's time to prepare the tools and materials. Chapter 2, *What You Need Before You Start,* will show you what you need to get started.

ABOUT THE URLs

I will mention in this book literally hundreds of links to all sorts of useful resources that will help you in your marketing and promotions. To save typing all those links, I suggest you visit the Web site associated with this book (http://PoorRichard.com/promo/). You'll find a Web page with all the links sorted according to chapter and alphabetically within each chapter. You can save that page on your hard disk or simply bookmark the page; then you'll be able to go to the sites that we've mentioned in this book with a quick click.

This book's publisher, Top Floor, will be checking those links periodically so that we can update them as they change—as any group of hundreds of Web links surely will over time. Also, let us quickly explain a simple trick for using links that appear to be broken—a handy little trick you can use whenever you're traveling around the World Wide Web. Let's say, for instance, that you see a URL like this (or a link containing this URL):

http://www.heyneat.com/firstdirect/seconddirect/this.html

Now, you type this URL (or click the link), and you get a browser error telling you that the requested item has not been found. What can you do? Well, if you typed the link, make sure you typed it correctly; in particular, make sure you used the correct file extension (.html and not .htm in this case). If you did type it correctly, or if you clicked a link, it may be the file has been moved or deleted. What next? Do you just give up?

No, you can work your way up the directory path to see whether you can find another Web page that might contain information that will help you find the page you're looking for. Remove the filename from the URL in the browser's Location bar and try again:

http://www.heyneat.com/firstdirect/seconddirect/

Press Enter, and one of three things will happen. Your browser may display a document that is the default document for that directory, or it may display a listing showing all the files in that directory. You can then click the different .htm and .html files shown in the directory to display them. Or it may display another error, telling you that nothing was found or that the "virtual directory could not be displayed." If so, try moving up to the next directory. Type this:

http://www.heyneat.com/firstdirect/

Again, you may see a Web page, a directory listing, or an error. If you see an error, move back to the next directory. In this example you'd type the following:

http://www.heyneat.com/

Now you'll almost always find something, assuming the domain name is correct. You may find a page that indicates where you can find the information you want...or that the information is no longer present at that server. Using this technique, you can often find the information you need, even if it's been moved to a new location at the Web site.

CHAPTER TWO

What You Need Before You Start

You need to do several things before you set to work. This book doesn't describe in detail the beginner's stuff—the basic things you need to know to work effectively on the Internet. We explain what to do once you understand all the basics; but we will at least explain the sort of background information and the tools that you need before you start.

Even if you already have Internet access and think you're ready to jump in and get started, please don't skip this chapter. Many Internet users don't understand the relationship between their Internet service, their e-mail system, and their Web site, for instance, and to work efficiently you must know how these three systems hook together. At least skim through and see what we have to say.

Later in the chapter we'll be looking at a number of tools that most people don't know about, yet which are useful when promoting a product or service online; so, here's a quick rundown of what you need to effectively promote online. This is a basic list—the things a small business needs as a minimum to get started:

- A computer
- Hardware connecting the computer to the Internet
- Internet access through an Internet service provider
- A POP e-mail account
- Somewhere to put your Web site
- Basic Internet-access software
- Basic Internet knowledge
- Advanced research and marketing software
- Text-automation tools
- Offline browsers
- Web page archives
- Contact-management software
- Full-blown databases

We'll take a look at each of these things one by one.

YOUR COMPUTER

This almost goes without saying: you need a computer. Pretty much any recent PC or Mac computer—one that was built since, say, 1997—will work okay. Older computers may have problems; while you'll probably be able to get by with a basic Pentium PC, for instance, you'll have trouble finding good software that will run well on a 486 PC.

Access Doesn't Mean All-Access—*Just because your computer is good enough to get on the Internet doesn't mean it's good enough to run all the programs on the Internet. Multimedia programs, especially those that allow you to play video or audio off the Internet, also take up a lot of system resources. Bear that in mind if you get on the Internet with a very basic computer.*

PC owners are lucky in that they have a huge selection of software to choose from; if you own a Mac, you'll find that you can get hold of good programs for some tasks, but may have a severely limited choice of software for other things. For instance, if you look at the list of search-engine registration software in Chapter 6, *Registering with the Search Sites*, you'll see that there are loads of Windows programs...but we've only managed to find one of these programs that runs on the Mac. In some cases there may be no Macintosh equivalents, either, so it's not merely a matter of picking another brand of software. (Please, don't write and complain that we're being unfair to Macs. We're not saying that Windows machines are better, just that there's more software available.)

You need a fast computer with lots of RAM (Random Access Memory). RAM is cheap these days; so don't skimp. You could easily spend hours each day with multiple programs running: your browser, word processor, e-mail program, some kind of clipboard or text-automation program, a contact-management program, and so on. All this uses a lot of memory. Don't believe the nonsense about how Windows 95 or Windows 98 can run in 16MB of RAM; the simple truth is, it can't, even if you're only using one or two programs. Rather, it uses "virtual memory." That's a euphemism for storing information on your hard disk instead of in memory. Hard-disk space is much, much slower than RAM, so your computer will run much, much more slowly. Virtual memory made sense in the old days, when memory was expensive. These days memory's dirt cheap, so buy plenty; 64MB on a PC is not too much...128MB is better. In fact RAM is more important than processor speed. If you buy a new computer, for instance, it's far better to buy a 450 MHz Pentium with 128MB of RAM than a 600 MHz Pentium with 64MB of RAM. (Better still is a 450 MHz Pentium with 128MB of RAM. You can never have too much RAM!) If you have just a little extra money when you come to choosing your computer, consider increasing the RAM before going for a faster processor.

CONNECTING YOUR COMPUTER TO THE INTERNET

The other piece of critical hardware is the line-access hardware. This could be one of these things:

- A modem
- A cable modem
- An ISDN terminal adapter (often known as an ISDN modem)
- A DSL (Digital Subscriber Line) service
- A satellite connection
- Something horribly expensive and probably unnecessary (T1 and a router)

Modems

A modem connects your computer to normal phone lines. It takes the signal from your computer, modulates it—that is, converts the digital computer data into analog phone data—then sends it across the phone lines to the computer you've connected to. When data is sent across the phone lines to your computer, the modem demodulates it—that is, converts it from analog to digital data—and sends it to your computer. The word *modem* is a contraction of *mo*dulate/*dem*odulate.

You can buy external modems—boxes that you connect to your computer's serial port—and internal modems, which are the same as external modems except the processor card is installed inside the computer. We recommend that you buy a 56K modem, that is, one that runs at a speed of 56 Kbps (bits per second, a measure of how fast the modem can send data). That rating is only theory; the modem will actually run more slowly than that (though still faster than other, slower-rated modems). 56K modems are reasonably cheap these days, and if you're working on a phone line you'll find the Internet frustratingly slow anyway...so you'll need to squeeze whatever speed you can out of it.

There's been a lot of confusion about 56K modems because for two years there were two competing, and incompatible systems: 3Com/US Robotics' X2 system and Rockwell/Lucent's K56Flex. There is now a standard, though, known as V.90. In theory, then, all 56K modems should be able to operate with all others. In practice, the modem you buy may not yet have the V.90 programming, though it's probably upgradeable. Also, many service providers have not yet converted to V.90; they may still be using one or another of the old methods.

If you buy a 56K modem, make sure that it's already V.90 compatible, or that it's going to be easy to upgrade it. (The manufacturer may have placed upgrade software at its Web site.) Also make sure that you'll be able to use the modem with your Internet service provider.

If you'd like to find more information about the two main 56K manufacturers, check the **3Com/USRobotics** Web site (http://www.3com.com/ or http://www.3com.com/56k/) and the **Rockwell** Web site (http://www.rockwell.com/) where you'll also find lists of service providers using the respective modem standards.

By the way, if you're really short of money, it's perfectly possible to work on the Internet with a 28,800 bps or 33,600 bps modem. However, you wouldn't want to go much slower than that! 14,400 bps modems are irritatingly slow, and anything below that feels positively glacial, especially if you want to do things such as access online audio and video.

Cable Systems

You might also be able to connect to the Internet through your local cable-TV company. Call and ask—many cable companies already have Internet service, but may not be promoting it heavily because they know they don't have the staff or equipment to keep up with the demand if they advertised the service. It can take two or three installers several hours to get one of these things up and running...if they're lucky. Cable-TV access has had some serious teething problems—remember, the cable companies were promising this service back in 1994; but it really wasn't until late in 1998 that they started to roll out cable access on a large scale.

Peter connects to the Internet through cable, and loves it. It's fast, and quite reliable; during a few periods, it was close to unusable, but overall it's been more reliable than his other Internet access accounts. Cable access typically costs around $150 to install and $30–$40 a month. Sometimes cable companies offer specials where the installation fee is waived, so keep an eye out for that.

Cable speeds vary from system to system, somewhere between 200Kbps and 2mbps (2000Kbps). A few cable systems are only unidirectional; you have to use a phone line at the same time that you are connected through the cable modem. The data coming from the Internet flows along the cable, while information from your computer back to the Internet goes along the telephone line. The better systems are fully bi-directional—no need for a phone line.

For more information, see the **Cable Modem Resources** on the Web page at http://rpcp.mit.edu/~gingold/cable/, and the **Yahoo Cable Modems** page at http://dir.yahoo.com/computers_and_internet/hardware/peripherals/cable_modems/. Or call your local cable company.

A quick warning about the cable companies' dirty little secret—security. Security on these cable systems is *very* bad. Every cable modem is connected to a local neighborhood network "node." For instance, you may have 240 computers connected together in one neighborhood. If those individual computers are not configured properly, it may be possible for other people on the network to access data on the computers. Peter estimates that 10 percent or more of the computers in his neighborhood node are open to the outside—that is, anyone else can view the data on their hard disks, So, if you get one of these systems, make sure you ask the installers exactly how to disable file sharing, or at least password protect your data. You can also go to Steve Gibson's **Shields Up!** page at https://grc.com/x/ne.dll?bh0bkyd2/ to test the your computer's connection to the Internet and discover how much it reveals.

View These Links Online—*Remember, you can view a Web page containing these links at* http://PoorRichard.com/promo/.

ISDN

Another option available in many areas, though not all, is to install an ISDN (Integrated Services Digital Network) phone line. This is a digital phone line and can carry data more quickly than an ordinary analog phone line; you can transmit and receive data at either 64Kbps or 128Kbps, depending on the type of line you select. (Yes, the faster line is more expensive.) In the United States, ISDN typically costs around $60 to install and $60 a month to run—more if you use it extensively because there are per-minute charges—and that's if you can get it. (ISDN prices can vary greatly between regions, though; the installation price may be two or three times that, and in some cases, you won't pay per-minute charges.) In many areas you'll find it impossible to obtain ISDN service at present. In fact the unofficial definition of ISDN is: It Still Doesn't Work. At least that's the U.S. definition; in some other parts of the world, ISDN is much more easily available.

Internet Service Provider (ISP)—*An Internet service provider (ISP) is a company that provides access to the Internet. Your computer connects to one of the company's computers, allowing your computer to communicate with the Internet. ISPs are also known as Internet Access Providers (IAP).*

You'll also have to pay more to get ISDN Internet access. That is, not only will you pay the phone company $60 or more a month to use the line, but you'll also pay a special fee to the ISP. On top of that you'll pay around $250 to $300 for an ISDN terminal adapter. Though often called an ISDN modem, a terminal adapter doesn't actually modulate or demodulate.

You can find more information about ISDN at the **ISDN Tutorial** (http://www.ralphb.net/ISDN) or your local phone company's Web page. However, here's a warning. ISDN is not for the technically timid. It can be very difficult to install an ISDN line and get it running properly, partly because the phone companies seem to be technically incompetent. Horror stories about ISDN abound.

Don't Forget about Narrowband*—While you're reading about all these options, you may get the idea that everyone's connecting to the Internet with high-speed access—also called fat pipes or broadband. That isn't true; in fact, access through wireless phones and handheld devices is proliferating just as rapidly. This kind of access is called narrowband. When you're developing your Web pages, remember that someone might be looking at them through a cable modem or a mobile phone. Don't overload your pages, but don't be too skimpy with your design, either. Aim for a happy medium.*

DSL

The phone companies, and sometimes your local ISP, also have a system called DSL (Digital Subscriber Line). It may be available in your area, or perhaps not; but if it isn't, you may be lucky. Horror stories about DSL are almost as common as horror stories about ISDN.

DSL comes in various flavors: HDSL (High-Rate DSL), ADSL (Asymmetric DSL), RADSL (Rate Adaptive DSL), VDSL (Very High Data-Rate DSL), and so on. These lines will range in speed from 128Kbps to 700Kbps. We have seen rates from $30 to $50 a month. Peter recommends getting a cable system if possible over DSL or ISDN; he's had too many problems with the phone company, and heard too many complaints from others. Of course *your* phone company may be better, and since ISPs are now offering DSL, you have more options. See **dslreports** at http://www.dslreports.com/ for more information about who's offering DSL and discussion about who the good (or bad!) providers are.

ISDN Hype*—Sales people from ISDN-hardware companies often tout the phenom-enal speeds possible through ISDN. If data is compressed, you can actually transmit at several times the 128Kbps limit we've mentioned here. Don't be fooled, though. You almost certainly won't be able to go above 128Kbps when connecting to the Internet, because most Internet service providers are not set up to compress data.*

Satellite Systems

If you can't get cable, DSL, or ISDN, you might try a satellite connection, using DirecPC from **Hughes Network Systems** (http://www.direcpc.com/). This is available in some areas of North America. You'll have to pay for a satellite dish, plus an installation fee, and you'll still need a modem connection across a phone line, too. It works like this: your software uses the modem connection to send information out onto the Internet. When you want to display a Web page, for instance, you click a link in the Web browser, and a message is sent across the modem to the Web site. When the Web site sends the page back, it's grabbed by a computer at the DirecPC operations center, transmitted up into space, picked up by a satellite, and transmitted down to earth, where it's picked up by your satellite dish. Incoming data—the data coming from the satellite—moves at 400Kbps; outgoing data (along the phone line) moves at normal modem speeds.

You'll pay Hughes anywhere from $20 a month to $110 a month, plus hourly fees over a certain number of hours. For instance, the $110 plan gives you 200 free hours, and charges either $.99 or $1.99 an hour for additional hours, depending on whether you use its ISP.

T1s and Other Stuff

The phone company can provide you with other neat things—special phone lines with names such as 56K lines, T1 lines, fractional T1s, and T3s. These are generally quite expensive and complicated and more than the average small business needs.

Set-Top Boxes—*Since the first edition of this book was written, a new class of Internet access devices called Internet appliances has been developed. It includes already available products like **WebTV** (http://www.webtv.com/) and products that are still in development, such as **FreePad** (http://www.freepad.net/). While these are good ways to access the Internet, they are limited in some ways, for example how they can print, their storage, multimedia, and so on. For the sake of this book, we recommend you connect to the Internet with a PC for now.*

Which Do You Pick?

What should you get? The cheapest and easiest thing is to buy a fast modem, and for most small companies this is fine. It's relatively cheap, and it will be easy to find an ISP that will work with you. Don't cheap out and buy a low-cost or slow modem, however. Get a high-quality, fast modem. It'll make a big difference. If you can get a cable modem, go for it! It's cheap, fast, and probably quite reliable. If you can't get cable access, you may want to try ISDN or DSL, but be prepared for headaches and make sure you are tough on the phone company and force them to live up to their promises. You might consider a satellite system rather than fool with the phone company.

Tara is very jealous of Peter's fast access, but she wants to point out that you can use the Internet efficiently with only a phone line. The trick is to make sure you take advantage of the Internet's slow periods—when not as many people are online. If you access the Internet at one o'clock in the morning, you'll find it a lot faster and easier to use than if you access it at 6 PM. She also recommends you avoid the Internet between 8 and 11 PM; in her experience this is when the Internet is slowest and least responsive.

INTERNET ACCESS

The next thing you need is a connection to the Internet. The Internet is a giant public network. To connect to it, you must connect to a computer that is already connected to the Internet. That's done through what's known as an *Internet service provider (ISP)*. There are more ISPs than you can shake a stick at, ranging from free systems providing very limited service to a few hundred people in a single community, to huge companies providing access to millions of people in several countries. In general, the free services won't be of much use to you; you get what you pay for, and you may find that the free services are overloaded to the extent that you have a hard time getting on, getting your e-mail, and so on. (This might happen with an ISP you pay money for, but at least in that case you feel like you have enough leverage to complain.)

There are several different types of ISPs:

- True ISPs
- Online services
- Phone companies
- Cable-TV companies

True ISPs are companies that are primarily in the business of providing Internet access and associated services—Web-page design, Web-hosting, and so on. These companies range from small local companies with a few hundred subscribers, to national companies with hundreds of thousands of sub-scribers. If you already have some form of Internet access, you can track down service providers in your area using the **Yahoo! Internet Access Provider's** page at http://dir.yahoo.com/Business_and_Economy/Business_to_Business/Communications_ and_Networking/Internet_and_World_Wide_Web/Network_Service_Providers/Internet _Service_Providers__ISPs_/ or **The List** at http://thelist.iworld.com/. You may be able to get to these pages from a computer at your local library, for instance.

Online services are companies such as CompuServe, America Online (AOL), Prodigy, Microsoft Network, and GEnie. These companies are like private clubs. They provide access to all sorts of services: thousands of discussion groups about almost any imaginable subject, chat rooms, news and weather information, and so on. If you want to access these services, you have to join the club; but they also provide Internet access, so if you're a member of the club, you can still get onto the Internet and use the World Wide Web, newsgroups, and other services.

Some phone companies also provide Internet access. Companies such as BellSouth, AT&T (AT&T WorldNet), and MCI (internetMCI) now provide low-cost Internet access throughout North America. Many local phone companies provide Internet access, too. However, the phone companies often "just don't get it," and although they understand how to connect everything together, they don't really understand what people want to do on the Internet. You may find you get better service from a true ISP than from one of the phone companies.

Finally, the cable-TV companies are the next big players in this arena, providing Internet access through the cables they've been using to provide TV shows.

Which of these should you use? Well, that depends partly on the type of access you want. If you want cable access—which is a good choice, if you can get it— then you'll be going with a cable-TV company, of course.

Whatever you choose, we recommend that you have at least two ways to get onto the Internet, from two separate ISPs. For instance, Peter has access through cable TV, but he also has a CompuServe account. In his earlier, pre-cable days, he had several accounts—from Sprint, CompuServe, and EarthLink. He's considering getting rid of his CompuServe account, because the cable connection seems so reliable now; but when he was dependent on ISP connection through a phone line, he found he would often have to switch between accounts. Three different accounts, with three different services, ensured that he could always get online. It's possible to play this multi-account game for as little as $30 a month.

Not only does having two accounts allow you to get on at all times, it also increases your chances of getting to the Internet sites you want to visit. It's quite feasible for network problems to make it impossible for you to access a particular Web site through one Internet service provider, but possible through another service provider. Also, if you use one of the private-club type access providers, such as AOL or CompuServe, you are limited in some of your choices. For example, when you use AOL, you're pretty much stuck with AOL's mail program. You won't be able to use some of the e-mail programs we'll discuss later in the book. On the plus side, local dial-up numbers for AOL and similar services are available practically everywhere, so if you travel a lot it's easy to check your e-mail without incurring long-distance charges.

Unlimited Access?—*Just because a service advertises that it provides unlimited Internet access for $19.95 a month, it doesn't mean it really does so. It may mean $19.95 for as many hours as you're able to connect, if you can get past the busy signals, and if we don't drop you off the system. A few years ago 20 state Attorney Generals threatened to sue AOL for promising unlimited access but providing only busy signals.*

We advise that you talk with other Internet users in your area, check ads in local papers and magazines, and try a few services to find a reliable one. We don't want to recommend or denounce any particular service. We've used many, and found that they all have their ups and downs, and none we've tried so far was completely reliable.

A POP E-MAIL ACCOUNT

You need an e-mail account, but you really need a POP e-mail account. POP means Post Office Protocol, and it's the standard e-mail system used on the Internet. While most true Internet service providers, such as the phone-company Internet service providers and the cable companies will give you a POP account, it's important to understand that the online services generally do not. Rather, they have their own mail systems that were designed before Internet access was important, so they work in a very different manner. If you have a CompuServe account, you *can* have a POP account, but you have to sign up for it—it's not provided automatically.

Why do you need a POP account? Because it's much more flexible than a non-POP account. Ideally you want your own domain name (which you'll learn all about in Chapter 3, *Web Site Basics*) and a POP account. For instance, Peter's domain name is topfloor.com. Because he has his own POP account and his own domain name, he can create as many e-mail addresses as he wants:

- pkent@topfloor.com
- info@topfloor.com
- sales@topfloor.com
- ipn@topfloor.com
- whateveriwant@topfloor.com

Furthermore, with a POP e-mail account, you have your choice of e-mail programs. With an online service's own proprietary system, you get whatever software they give you or, in some cases, you can choose from a limited selection. With POP, you have a huge choice, and some good programs to work with.

For instance, you could pick a POP program that can filter messages (most can, these days). That is, it automatically sorts messages into separate folders. When you send a message, a copy is placed in the appropriate folder, and when you receive a message, it's automatically routed to the correct folder. This capability is essential for anyone serious about doing business on the Internet.

Filters Are Essential—*If you're serious about promoting on the Internet, you'll be flooded with e-mail. At times you'll get scores, even hundreds of messages every day; so it's essential that you get to know your e-mail program's filtering system. You may want to use a special e-mail address while contacting people on the Web. Some mail programs allow you to use various From: addresses. Eudora and AK-Mail, for instance, let you set up separate accounts, each account with a different e-mail address. So you could use different Reply To: addresses for different purposes. Of course to be able to use different addresses, you'll have to have your own domain name. We'll talk about this—and more about working with e-mail—in Chapter 16, Reaching Journalists Online.*

You don't have to get your POP account at the same place you get your Internet access, though. If you wish, you can get a POP account from a completely different company. See, for instance, the **Yahoo! E-mail Providers** page (http://dir.yahoo.com/Business_and_Economy/Business_to_Business/Communications _and_Networking/Internet_and_World_Wide_Web/Email_Providers, where you'll find links to all sorts of e-mail services, and the free e-mail **Providers Guide** (http://fepg.net/), which lists over 1200 free e-mail providers.

So you can have an account with CompuServe or AOL, for instance, and still have a POP e-mail account somewhere else. How will you access your mail? You'll use CompuServe or AOL to connect to the Internet and then start a POP e-mail program (such as Eudora, Netscape Messenger, Microsoft Outlook, AK-Mail, Pegasus, or one of many others). You'll then use this program to connect to your POP account, wherever on the Internet that happens to be, and grab your mail. In the same way that you can start a CompuServe or AOL connection, open a Web browser, and connect to a Web site, you can start a CompuServe or AOL connection, open a POP e-mail program, and connect to an e-mail account hosted on a computer out on the Internet.

When you get your POP account, make sure that you can have unlimited e-mail aliases within that POP account; that is, unlimited e-mail addresses that will be accepted by that account. Some services may set up the POP account to accept e-mail to only one address: pkent@topfloor.com, for instance; but you want to be able to accept e-mail addressed to various addresses—pkent@topfloor.com, info@topfloor.com, sales@topfloor.com, ipn@topfloor.com, whateveriwant@topfloor.com, and so on. So ensure that you're getting the right kind of account before you buy.

Before you run off and buy a POP account, read on. You'll be looking for a place to put your Web site, and most Web-hosting companies will give you a free POP account.

Which Program?—*Peter's currently using an e-mail program called **Eudora**, which is very good. It's available in a freeware or commercial version for Windows and Macintosh—though to use filters you'll have to get the commercial version or the adware version. (It's free and as functional as the commercial version, but you have to look at ads):* http://www.eudora.com/. *Tara also likes Eudora. In the past Peter's used **AK-Mail**, which is also good. It's a Windows 95/NT shareware program, and you can get it from* http://www.akmail.com/ *or from many shareware libraries. It has some filter features that Eudora doesn't have, but all in all Eudora is easier to use, and it seems likely that AK-Mail won't be developed any further. Another very highly rated program is **Pegasus** Mail (*http://www.pegasus.usa.com/), *which is free and available for Windows 3.1 and Windows 95/NT. See the **Yahoo! Electronic Mail** page:* http://www.yahoo.com/Computers_and_Internet/Software/Internet/Electronic_Mail/.

SOMEWHERE TO PUT YOUR WEB SITE

You also need somewhere to put your Web site. We'll go into this subject in detail in Chapter 3, *Web Site Basics*; but for the moment we want to clear up two misconceptions. The first is that when you get Internet access, you get a Web site with it. Some service providers don't give their members Web space, and even if a service provider does, the Web site probably won't be suitable as a business Web site. (Do you really want your Web site address to look like http://www.topfloor.com/somebody/somecompany/?) In Chapter 3, you'll learn about the services you need, and you may, in fact, find that your service provider can provide all the required Web services. You're more likely to discover, however, that your ISP cannot provide what you need, or will provide everything for an additional (exorbitant) fee.

The other misconception is that you have to have a Web site with the same company that you get Internet access from; in other words many people believe that if their service provider doesn't provide Web space, they'll have to leave and find one that does; but Internet access and Web space are two completely different things. As with POP accounts, you can set up your Web site on any Web-hosting service anywhere in the world. You can then connect to your ISP, and connect to your Web site across the Internet.

HOW IT ALL HOOKS TOGETHER

So you need Internet access, a POP account, and a Web site. This confuses people. Aren't these all much the same thing; don't you get all three at once? No, and no. Let us clarify how all these hook together.

Internet access merely allows your computer to communicate with the Internet—nothing more, nothing less. It's like your phone service; having your house connected to the phone system allows you to make calls across the system. It doesn't provide friends and a family for you to call; you have to provide them yourself.

Once you have Internet access, you can connect to computers all over the world. Those computers can provide some of the services you're going to need: your POP account and your Web site. You pay a fee to a company somewhere out there on the Internet, it sets up your POP account and provides space for your Web site, and away you go.

Your business may be in Vancouver, British Columbia in Canada. You may be using a large international ISP head-quartered in, say, Washington, D.C., in the U.S. You may have your Web site on a computer sitting in London, England, and you may have a POP account in Dublin, Ireland. (Actually you'll generally have your Web site and POP account at the same place.)

IAP, ISP, Hosting Companies—*There's a lot of confusion about the term Internet Service Provider (ISP). The problem is that this term was in use long before hosting companies appeared on the scene; it used to mean a company providing access to the Internet. Yet these days many people use the term ISP to mean any company providing any service on the Internet—including hosting companies. Some people use the term to mean a company providing any Internet service other than Internet access (based on the theory that as there's another term for Internet-access businesses—Internet Access Providers (IAP)—that should free up the term ISP). If you want to refer to a Web-hosting company, be specific—don't use the term ISP or you're likely to confuse.*

Geographical location makes little difference, except that the ISP has to have a phone number in your area. You can use services anywhere in the world. What's more important is how reliable those services are. Here's why it's important to look at these things as separate items. You want the best ISP, and the best hosting company (which will also provide you with a POP account). It's not always easy to find those things separately, so the chance of getting both together is slim, and these companies may be good today, but bad tomorrow. You may have a great ISP now, but a few months from now it may be very hard to connect to it, so you'll have to find another...there's no need to switch your Web host at the same time.

BASIC INTERNET-ACCESS SOFTWARE

Before you can do business on the Internet, you need the software that allows you to move around on the Internet. When you sign up with a service provider, that company will generally provide you with software to get started, although you may want to switch to better programs later. Here's what you need:

- Dial-up software
- An e-mail program
- A World Wide Web browser
- A newsreader
- An FTP program

Those are the basic tools you need, but we'll be adding things to that list as we go along. The dial-up software is the software required to make the connection to the Internet. There are loads of options; but generally, an ISP will give you the software you need or tell you how to configure your operating system to make the connection. Windows 95, 98, and NT, for instance, come with built-in dial-up software.

You need an e-mail program to send and receive electronic mail. You need a Web browser to view pages on the World Wide Web. You need a newsreader to read newsgroup messages, and you need an FTP (File Transfer Protocol) program to upload files to your Web site.

***FTP**—FTP (File Transfer Protocol) sounds like one more intimidating abbreviation, but it's not too bad. Basically it's just a way for you to send files back and forth to a remote computer. Since you're sending files back and forth, and not viewing them (as you would with a browser) an FTP interface is much simpler to use than a browser.*

Note that the two major Web browsers, Netscape Navigator and Microsoft Internet Explorer, come bundled with e-mail and newsreader programs. However, you may be better off working with another, more sophisticated program. The bundled programs are fine for getting started, and Outlook—which many ISPs make available and some computer manufacturers include with their computers—has quite a few advanced tools. Still, you may need the tools provided by the specialized programs. Also, most Web browsers, including these two, can work with FTP to some degree; but you really need a true FTP program to work with file transfers quickly and efficiently (which is important for maintaining a Web site).

***FTP Programs**—For Windows users, we'd suggest CuteFTP or WS_FTP, both of which you can find at various shareware libraries. Tara has found CuteFTP easy to use and easy to teach other people to use, which is handy if you want everyone in your office using the Internet. For the Macintosh, Fetch is the most popular program, though there are a number of other FTP programs, including several new ones that are getting good reviews: NetFinder, NetBatch, Mirror, and Download Deputy. For a list of shareware libraries, see "Where Will You Get the Software?" later in this chapter.*

Which browser should you get? Literally scores of different browsers are available. The two most popular are **Netscape Navigator** (http://www.netscape.com/)

and **Microsoft Internet Explorer** (http://www.microsoft.com/ie/). In fact, you'll probably be given one of these when you sign up for Internet service. Actually it's a good idea to have *both* of these on your system; when you create your Web site you want to make sure it looks good in both browsers. There's an open-source browser that might attract your attention, though, especially if you're computer-savvy enough to like to tinker with your programs. (Open source means lots of people are working together to develop it, which means you can too, if you want.) It's called **Mozilla** and it's available at http://www.mozilla.org/.

If you're using an old computer, you might find that Netscape Navigator and Internet Explorer run somewhat sluggishly. Even on a 486, the most recent version of Navigator or IE can use up a lot of memory and processing power. You might want to try working with **Opera**, a back-to-basics browser available at http://www.operasoftware.com/. Opera's designers state that it'll work well even on a 486 with 8MB of memory.

BASIC KNOWLEDGE

You're going to need two forms of basic knowledge. You'll need to understand how to work with your computer, and how to work with the Internet. You'll have to understand how to open compressed files that you've download from the Internet, how to work with your own computer's file-management system, how to move around on the World Wide Web, how to work with e-mail, and lots, lots more.

It's not the purpose of this book to explain these sorts of things. We have plenty to do once you understand how to get around on the Internet. We suggest that, if you don't already understand the Internet, you read a few good books; you might start with Peter's *Complete Idiot's Guide to the Internet* (Que).

If you want computer-related definitions, try the **ComputerUser High Tech Dictionary** at http://www.currents.net/resources/dictionary/index.html, the **AcronymFinder**, at http://www.AcronymFinder.com/, or **NetLingo** at http://www.netlingo.com/. For now, though, in case you are just exploring the idea of setting up a Web site and need to understand some of the basic lingo, here's a mini-glossary with a few basic definitions:

> **The Internet**—A giant computer network connecting millions of computers and millions of people around the world. This is a public network, though many of the computers connected to it are also part of smaller private networks.
>
> **The World Wide Web**—Contrary to popular misconception, the World Wide Web is not a synonym for the Internet. The World Wide Web is a software system running across the Internet. The Internet is the hardware; the Web is just one type of Internet software. You might think of the Internet as a huge highway system, and the Web as a trucking company

moving things hither and thither across these roads. Other software systems include e-mail and FTP.

Web browser—This is a program that displays Web pages. If you want to "go onto the Web," "navigate the Web," "surf the Web," or whatever else you might call it, you need a Web browser.

Web server—This term can refer to a couple of things. It's often used to mean the software that manages one or more Web sites. When a Web browser wants to view a Web page, it sends a message to the Web server, which transmits the page back to the browser. The term also often refers to the whole kit and caboodle involved in this process—not just the Web server software but the computer on which the software is running, too.

Web site—This term generally means a collection of associated Web pages: the Yahoo Web site, the Library of Congress Web site, and so on. A single Web server may administer multiple Web sites—sometimes a few dozen, sometimes hundreds. One Web-hosting company's staff told us that its two servers had almost 1,000 Web sites. You will be creating your own Web site—your own collection of pages.

Web page—This is also known as a Web document. It's a single document stored at a Web site. A single Web browser window generally displays a single Web page at a time, though the window may be split into separate frames with a document in each frame. A Web page is stored in a single computer file, generally with the .htm or .html file extension. (You'll see other file extensions, usually when a page is created on the fly by a program. For example, if a page is generated by using a search engine, its URL is generally huge and doesn't end with HTML.)

URL—A Web "address." It tells your Web browser exactly where to find a particular file. For instance, http://PoorRichard.com/freeinfo/special_reports.htm means open the file named special_reports.htm, which is in the directory named freeinfo at the host computer named PoorRichard.com. In some cases the URL doesn't include a filename, in which case the Web server will send the default file, probably a file named index.html.

Web host—If you don't have your own Web server (and you probably won't), you can find someone else to "host" your Web site for you. Companies, known as Web-hosting companies or Web presence providers, sell space on their Web servers. You'll learn about these companies in Chapter 3, *Web Site Basics*.

Host computer—This simply means a computer connected to the Internet.

Hypertext—A system by which electronically stored documents are linked together. The World Wide Web is the world's largest hypertext system, in which documents are viewed in Web browsers. Links are operated by pointing with the mouse at a picture or underlined text and clicking. Using a link loads the document referenced by the link.

Home page—This term has two meanings. Originally it meant the page that a Web browser displays when you start the program or when you use the browser's Home command. Now it frequently means the main page at a Web site.

E-mail—This is short for electronic mail, a system in which messages can be sent across the Internet to an individual mailbox. Messages may take a few minutes to travel across the world or, when things are getting sluggish, a day or two.

FTP—File Transfer Protocol, one of the earliest software systems running on the Internet. This system allows you to transfer files between computers on the Internet. Although to a great extent it's been superseded by the World Wide Web (which also allows you to transfer files), there are still many FTP sites around the world. More importantly, when you set up a Web site you'll also get an FTP account, so you can transfer files from your computer to your Web site.

Newsgroup—A discussion group. There are tens of thousands of newsgroups around the world, of which almost 30,000 are distributed internationally. Think of a subject, and there's probably a newsgroup dedicated to it, which means that whatever you are trying to sell or promote, there's a newsgroup with people who are interested. To read newsgroup messages, you need a program known as a newsreader. These discussion groups are distributed via a system called Usenet, so you'll often see them referred to as Usenet groups.

Mailing list—Another form of discussion group. To read this type of group, though, you'll need nothing more than your e-mail program. There are tens of thousands of mailing lists, some private, many public.

You should know about a few other terms, though you will probably not actually use these systems:

Archie—This is a system used to search for files at FTP sites.

Gopher—This system was supposed to revolutionize the Internet, taking a complicated command-line system and turning it into a simple menu system. Then came the Web, and Gopher dropped out of the race; but there are still many Gopher sites around, and Web browsers can display Gopher menus and pages.

Telnet—This system allows you to log onto a computer across the Internet and work on that computer, running programs, searching databases, and so on. Fewer and fewer Internet users know how to use Telnet or even what it is.

Chat—You type a message and someone else across the Internet—perhaps a whole lot of people—can read it. They can respond immediately, generally with dross. You can respond to the response, perhaps with dross of your own. Peter can't stand chat; many people love it.

Talk—This is similar to chat, though it's intended as a private system. Programs such as ICQ and AOL Instant Messenger are *talk* systems.

IRC—This stands for Internet Relay Chat, which was the first popular Internet chat system.

VON—Voice On the Net, a way of holding "phone" conversations on the Internet. You'll need a microphone, sound card, VON software, and someone to talk to who has the same setup. Several different systems of this type exist, but they're still in their infancy.

Learn as much as you can about the Internet...we won't be explaining too much about the basics in this book.

ADVANCED RESEARCH AND MARKETING SOFTWARE

So far we've discussed a basic Internet system, but if you're going to set up and promote a Web site, you'll need a variety of programs to help you along the way. You'll need software to help you create your Web pages, for instance. You may want a program that will help you register your site with the Web search engines, programs that you can use to do research, and so on. We'll discuss these programs as we go along. We'll give URLs to lead you to some of these programs. In some cases you may wish to buy commercial software. There are thousands of different Internet programs, and it's impossible to keep up with all of them. We'll mention programs that we use, like, or know about, but you may find equivalents that you prefer.

Where Will You Get the Software?

As we mentioned earlier, when you sign up for Internet service, the ISP will provide you with basic software to get you started. Later you'll want more. You'll see ads for Internet software all over the place, of course—in the computer press, in the software catalogs you get in the mail by the dozen, and so on. You can also find great software at shareware libraries on the Internet. These sites contain several types of software:

Public domain—Free software that belongs to nobody. The program author has given away all rights.

Freeware—This type of software belongs to someone, but the owner is giving away the rights to use it, sometimes in particular circumstances—it's free to individuals, but companies have to pay, for instance.

Shareware—Take it; use it, and if you like it, send money.

Demoware—Take it; use it, and if you like it, send money and they'll send a program that actually works.

Crippleware—A demo that's substantially disabled—the Save function doesn't work, for example, or it won't print. Take it; use it, and if you like it, send money and they'll send a program that has all the features enabled.

Adware—Software that works like the regular version, only it's free or considerably less expensive. In return, while you use the software you have to look at ads.

There are other kinds of 'ware—postcardware, where if you like it you send a postcard, and linkware, where if you like it you link to the developer's site—but the ones previously listed are the main types of 'ware. We'll be talking about all sorts of software in this book. Here are a few addresses of shareware libraries to get you started. We'll point you to particular sites for particular programs as we progress, but if there's ever something you think you need but which we haven't helped you find, check these sites:

Info-Mac HyperArchive
http://hyperarchive.lcs.mit.edu/HyperArchive.html

Jumbo! (Programs of all sorts for Windows, UNIX, and Macs)
http://www.jumbo.com/

Macdownload.com
http://macdownload.com/

Shareware.com (All types of programs for Windows, UNIX, and Macs)
http://www.shareware.com/

Tucows—The Ultimate Collection of Winsock Software (Originally just Windows software, it now carries Mac, Linux, PalmOS, and OS/2 programs)
http://www.tucows.com/

The Ultimate Macintosh Site
http://www.flashpaper.com/umac/

Winfiles (A large archive of 32-bit Windows software)
http://www.winfiles.com/

Winsite (A huge archive of Windows software)
http://www.winsite.com/

You can also search for software at Yahoo and other Web search sites. As you've seen in this chapter, Yahoo has several useful software categories. We've mentioned the e-mail page, but you can also find pages with information about

FTP programs

http://www.yahoo.com/Computers_and_Internet/Software/Internet/FTP/

Usenet newsreaders

http://www.yahoo.com/Computers_and_Internet/Software/Internet/Usenet/

Programs for converting word processing documents to Web (HTML) documents

http://www.yahoo.com/Computers_and_Internet/Software/Internet/World_Wide_Web/HTML_Converters/

Links to Macintosh programs

http://dir.yahoo.com/Computers_and_Internet/Hardware/Personal_Computers/Macintosh/Software/Shareware/

TEXT-AUTOMATION TOOLS

Promoting on the Internet can be hard on your fingers—you'll find you do an awful lot of typing. The frustrating thing is that you seem to be typing the same thing over and over again: your e-mail address, your Web site's URL, a description of what you are promoting, a suggestion for a particular type of cooperative promotion, and so on.

Finding Software at Yahoo!—*To search for Internet software at Yahoo! go to the* ***Internet Software*** *page (http://dir.yahoo.com/Computers_and_Internet/Software/Internet/), select Just This Category from the drop-down list box next to the Search button, and then type the search term. That way you'll limit the search to useful categories.*

Don't do this! It simply doesn't make sense to type this stuff over and over again. You need to spend a little time figuring out how you can work more efficiently. The very simplest method is to set up a boilerplate text file—a file containing all the things you have to type frequently. You can then copy these pieces and paste them in when necessary.

Even that's inefficient. You should seriously think about investing in a few tools to help you. Let's see what's available:

- Clipboard utilities
- Text-replacement tools
- Programmable keyboards

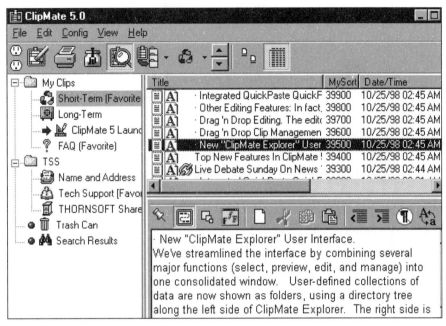

FIGURE 2.1: ClipMate makes it easy for you to work with large amounts of clipboard material.

Clipboard Utilities

One of the annoying things about Windows is its clipboard. Its clipboard can only hold one "clip" at a time. That means if you need to move several clipped items you have to cut the clip out of one application, move to the other application, paste it, and repeat several dozen times or until you get sick of it.

Fortunately this problem bothers lots of people. We say fortunately because many people have come up with programs that address this Windows limitation. Tara's absolute favorite clipboard utility is **ClipMate**, which you can get from http://www.thornsoft.com/. This little program is everything the Windows clipping utility should have been (Figure 2.1).

ClipMate allows you to clip several different file formats—both text and graphics. You can save text that you use often in a long-term collection so you don't have to type it repeatedly. You can use a "glue" feature and clip several things together at one time. You can edit the text clips in ClipMate without having to use a text editor. You can even open a "picker window" and rearrange the clips you've made into different collections, add them together, and so on. ClipMate now includes a cleanup feature that lets you remove quote marks from e-mail conversations, and a neat feature called exploding PowerPaste that allows you to paste fragments of a clip (for example, if you have a clip consisting of tab-delimited text fragments, you could paste in one tab-delimited fragment at a time.)

When you're doing research leading up to your promotional effort, you'll be moving around your data a lot. You'll make that clipping a lot easier if you invest $20 and download a copy of ClipMate. (If you want a disk and a manual, that'll cost you $25 plus shipping.) In addition to ClipMate, several clipboard programs are available for the PC:

APS-EZR
http://www.btsunlimited.com/

Click&Paste
http://bigmeg.net/

CoodClip
http://www.aha.ru/~deep125/

CopyPaste
http://www.scriptsoftware.com/

SmartBoard
http://www.wintools.com/smtbrd/

You can also find these programs at the shareware libraries we mentioned earlier in this chapter.

For a Macintosh, you can use clipboard programs, such as:

CopyPaste
http://www.scriptsoftware.com/)

MultiClip PRO
http://www.olduvai.com/products.html

Text-Replacement Tools

Another way to quickly automate typing is to use a text-replacement tool such as **ShortKeys** (http://www.shortkeys.com/). This Windows program lets you replace a small piece of typing with something longer or more complicated. For instance, if you want to type your mailing address, phone number, and e-mail address, all you need to do is type, say, *adr*, and ShortKeys types it all for you.

It works like this. You create entries and assign keystroke sequences to them. You might, for example, assign your e-mail address to *e-*; whenever ShortKeys sees that you have typed *e-*, it will back up and delete the typed characters, and then type the full e-mail address for you (see Figure 2.2). You can create different files, too. Each file can hold a set of replacement instructions, so you can use files for different purposes. For instance, you might use a file full of replacement texts for when you are replying to journalists after doing a mass mailing (see Chapter

16, *Reaching Journalists Online*), another file for when you are wandering around the Web asking people to link to you (see Chapter 8, *Other Places to Register Your Site*), and so on.

ShortKeys is a $19.95 shareware program; there's also a free version, ShortKeys 98 Lite. The publisher has several other automation tools, too, such as **Keyboard Express** (http://www.wintools.com/smtbrd/) and the SmartBoard clipboard utility we mentioned earlier.

We haven't found many other

FIGURE 2.2: Tell ShortKeys what you'll type— in this case *e-* —then tell it what you want it to type for you.

text-replacement tools, though there probably are others. We have run across a Mac program that's supposed to be good: **TypeIt4Me** ($27 registration— http://www.users.dircon.co.uk/~r-ettore/ or http://www.hebel.net/~rettore/).

Programmable Keyboards

Programmable keyboards are a godsend to the serious computer user. Yet network administrators hate them because the inexperienced computer user often accidentally programs something into the keyboard and ends up getting completely confused. If you know how to use one, though, it can save you scores of hours of work each year.

A programmable keyboard allows you to "record" keystrokes on particular keys. If you have to repeat a process, you can quickly record the process and assign it to a key, and then press that key whenever you want to perform it again. You could record your e-mail address on, say, the F12 key, and then press that key whenever you want to type the address. You could record a product description on F11, and press that rather than typing the entire description.

The problem is, where do you get one of these wonderful things? Peter bought a **Gateway** computer a few years ago (http://www.gateway2000.com/), at a time when all their computers came with a programmable keyboard. He's still using it; but new Gateways don't come with this keyboard—they'll sell them to people who have bought Gateways before, but the keyboards won't work with Pentium II computers. (They'll work with Pentiums, Pentium Pros, or earlier.) If you have a computer earlier than a Pentium II, you might try to find someone who bought a Gateway in the past and get him or her to buy the keyboard for you.

Programmable Mice—*Programmable mice, such as the Kensington Thinking Mouse, are also available. These allow you to assign procedures to a mouse button or a mouse/keyboard combination.*

There are several other programmable keyboards, though it's hard to find them in the stores:

Maxim keyboard, Kinesis Corporation
http://www.kinesis-ergo.com/

MCK-142 Pro, Kbtek America (Their Web sites are awful—at the first you can view product information but not order...then you can order but not view product information.)
http://www.ortek.com/http://www.eagle-touch.com/

Avant Stellar keyboard, Creative Vision Technologies, Inc. (Recommended by Jerry Pournelle in *BYTE* magazine.)
http://www.cvtinc.com/

Datadesk (various keyboards, for Macs and PCs)
http://www.datadesk1.com/

Floating Arms Keyboard, Workplace Designs
http://www.wpdesigns.com/

InterFatron-BBc, Ltd. (This company designs keyboards, but doesn't sell them...they link to sites where you can buy them, though.)
http://www.ifbbc.com/

Grabbing E-Mail Addresses

One procedure we *haven't* found a tool for is the automated saving of e-mail addresses. While you are wandering around the Internet, you'll come across a lot of useful e-mail addresses: newsletter editors, owners of Web pages containing link directories that you want to be listed in, owners of Web pages who are probably interested in your products, and so on. You'll want to collect these e-mail addresses for use later.

We'd really like to be able to point at a mailto: link in a Web page, press a keyboard combination—Ctrl+G, for instance—and have the program grab the e-mail address from the link and save it in a file. So far we haven't found anything like this. The best we've figured out so far is this: if you're out researching something, wandering around the Web grabbing e-mail addresses, you can start a text editor, such as Windows Notepad, and copy mailto: addresses into there quite quickly if you have a programmable keyboard.

So, for instance, here's what you could do: right-click with your mouse on a mailto: link, and up pops the menu. Quickly press the key that's associated with the recording, and the recording plays; it selects the Copy Shortcut command on that pop-up menu and then presses Alt+Tab to switch from the browser to the text editor. It presses Ctrl+End to move the cursor to the end of all the text in the text editor, presses Enter to move down a line, and then presses Ctrl+V to paste the mailto: line into the text editor. Then it presses Alt+Tab to go back to the browser.

That's it; the address is quickly copied with a single mouse click and a single keystroke. All the e-mail addresses captured this way now have the mailto: prefix, but they can be removed in a word-processing program.

We suggest that you build address books while you're doing your research; one could be a list of addresses of people maintaining link directories, another a list of Web-site owners who might be interested in a cooperative promotion of some kind, and so on. Later you'll be able to mail to everyone in an address book very quickly.

If you're contacting several different categories of people, Tara has found it useful to set up a spreadsheet. She sets it up in several columns: one for the URL where the address came from, one for the site name, one for the e-mail address, one for site category (she sets up a list of several categories in advance and assigns each of them a letter from the alphabet) and so on. Having things set up in columns makes it easy to sort them, and having them in a spreadsheet means the information can be exported in useful formats, such as a tab-delimited file.

OFFLINE BROWSERS

Another tool that can be very handy is the offline browser, which is a program that grabs Web pages that you specify. For instance, you tell it to go to a particular Web page, look at all the links on that page, and grab the referenced pages. You can tell it to grab pages referenced by links on those pages and even to grab the pages referenced by links on that set of pages...I'm sure you get the picture. Most of these products allow you to state how many levels down you want to go. One's usually enough—if you do too many, it can take forever and end up filling your hard disk.

Overnight Problems—*Leaving a process to run overnight is often a problem thanks to the unreliability of Internet connections. There's a good chance your connection will drop five minutes after you walk out the door. A better solution may be to let the program run while you're doing something else—filing, talking on the phone, or working on a different computer, for instance. Some of these programs can restart the process if the connection drops—an essential feature.*

This is the sort of thing you set up to work over lunch or overnight. Once it's finished, it stores the Web pages that it's downloaded in a special directory on your hard disk, so your browser can view them very quickly. You can then decide which are useful and which are not.

The following are some ways to use these programs:

- If you find a Web page with a lot of links to pages associated with your business—a link directory, which we'll discuss later in this chapter—you can use the program to download the pages linked to this site and view them to see if they can be useful to you.

- If you use a search engine to find sites of interest to you, you can save the results page on your hard disk. Then you can remove links that are clearly of no use—links pointing back to other areas of the search site, for instance, and links that clearly point to sites that are of no use to you. Then use the offline browser to grab the pages referenced by the links you're interested in learning more about. Some offline browsers make it difficult if not impossible to work on pages stored on your hard disk, so you may have to store the page at your Web site and then continue the operation.

- Do a number of searches, save the results pages on your hard disk, and then merge them, keeping just the links that look as though they might be useful. Then use the program to get the referenced pages.

- Use the program to check links on your own site. There are programs that will check links to make sure they work, but they're "dumb." They can tell you if there's a page at the URL in the link, but not if that page has the information you think it has. So you can use one of these programs to make sure the links on your site really do reference the information you say they do: run the offline browser on your links page, and then you can quickly view each page one by one.

These programs vary in price from free to around $70. Unfortunately, most are not worth anything. Peter used a number of these programs, and had all sorts of problems with them. In general this software category is low quality, so it's hard to find a good one; even the ones highly rated by the computer press are often awful. For instance, FlashSite seems to work well, except that it will pull pages from only a single domain—it won't follow links across to other Web sites, which makes it almost useless for our purposes. Of all that Peter has tried, he's found NetAttaché to be the best of the lot, but perhaps the others will improve over time. Tara finds that Adobe Acrobat makes a handy way to print and save individual pages to files, though for creating several pages she doesn't have a preference. Try a few and see which you prefer. It's worth spending a little time finding one that works for you because these systems can really save you a lot of thumb-twiddling time. Don't sit in front of your computer waiting for things to transfer—let the computer do it for you while you're doing something else. Here's where you'll find a few offline browsers:

FlashSite (Windows 95/NT)
http://www.incontext.com/

NetAttaché (Windows 95/NT, Windows 3.1)
http://www.tympani.com/

Teleport Pro (Windows 95/NT)
http://www.tenmax.com/

Web Buddy (Windows 95, Macintosh)
http://www.dataviz.com/

WebWhacker (Windows 95/NT)
http://www.bluesquirrel.com/

WEB PAGE ARCHIVES

Here's a class of software you may not have heard about, but it can be very handy. A Web-page archive program is one that saves Web pages for you. For instance, you find a page containing useful information, something you want to save for later. Perhaps it's a review of your product, or a competitor's site you want to take a closer look at when you have time. You could set a bookmark on the page. But as you probably know by now, Web pages don't always hang around for long; the next time you try to return to the page it may not be there.

You could use the browser's Save As command, but that's a nuisance; it won't save all the images in the page, and it'll just drop the page into a directory—the browser will provide no tools for retrieving the page later.

A Web-page archive program (we just made up that term, by the way) will save the page for you, images and all. For instance, take a look at Figure 2.3. This is **SurfSaver**, a shareware program that you can find at http://www.askSam.com/.

SurfSaver allows you to create multiple folders so you can categorize your pages, add keywords and notes to help you find and recognize the pages later; see a list of all the pages in a folder; or search by keyword, title, URL, date, or even search the actual Web-page text. It's an easy program to use, too. To save a page into the archive all you have to do is click the button that the installation program placed on your browser's toolbar, and then click QuickSave (to save it in a predetermined folder) or click Save and select the folder where you want to save the page. (One tip, though—SurfSave's documentation doesn't mention this, but if your browser has JavaScript turned off, SurfSaver won't work properly.)

FIGURE 2.3: SurfSaver provides a great way to save and later retrieve Web pages.

Are there other archive programs? We don't know—SurfSaver is the only one we've run across, though there may be more.

Using Online Services for Saving Pages—*Some online services will let you aggregate search results and other Web pages into a single result. Try **Quickbrowse** (http://www.quickbrowse.com/) for a start. It offers a Quickbrowse utility that allows you to combine several single pages into one page. qbSearch allows you to combine several different pages of search engine results into one page. Some online bookmark managers allow you to save pages;* ***iHarvest*** *(http://www.iharvest.com) is one of these.*

CONTACT-MANAGEMENT SOFTWARE

Relationships are what marketing and promotions are all about: making relationships with your customers, prospects, and vendors, and maintaining those relationships to everybody's benefit. To juggle all the details about the people you interact with regularly in an efficient manner, you can use contact-management software.

Contact-management software helps you—that's right—manage contacts. This covers everything from keeping address information all in one place, to tracking when you've made particular calls, to when you need to make a follow-up call, when appointments are scheduled, and so on.

Contact managers have a couple of problems. First of all, one size doesn't fit all. Few people have needs that are likely to be met by many of the contact-management forms. If you have particularly complicated needs, you may find that a free-form database works better than a contact-management program for you. Let's take a look at both.

Standard Contact Managers

You've probably seen standard contact managers. They have forms that you fill out to indicate certain standard information: name, phone number, fax number, e-mail address, and so on. Many of them also have calendars, to-do lists, and other efficiency-boosting features.

Some contact managers are little more than basic address books. Some contact managers can do everything up to and including developing telemarketing scripts and helping you with contact management. Which one you try depends on your needs. Do you simply need to keep track of names and addresses? Do you have a lot of scheduled appointments? You can probably get by with a simple contact manager. Do you use the contact information you have to do many different things—make follow-up sales calls, for example, or send letters? Do you analyze the information or try to break out different groups based on type of contact or where they live? You probably want a contact manager with more features. Do you share contacts across a network at your company? Do you use your contacts for one particular function—sales, for example—and use them very aggressively, constantly making and tracking contacts? You probably want an extensive or specialty contact manager.

There are dozens of contact managers you can choose from. Let's take a look at a couple of them.

SIDEKICK

http://www.sidekick.com/

Sidekick is a basic contact manager that helps you maintain an address book, do basic scheduling, and write letters and memos. And that's pretty much it. You can specify fields, but you can't design your input screen. You can't dial a phone or track your expenses with the latest version of Sidekick. Its main function is to keep your address book.

Tara uses Sidekick extensively and finds it useful. She appreciates the fact that you can export the address books in a variety of formats, and that it's easy to create address labels from within the program. Sidekick also uses little enough memory that you can keep it open while you're running several other different applications. If you have peripheral programs you're happy with, such as e-mail and word processing, and you don't want to spend a lot of money and need a simple address book as your contact manager, Sidekick is a good one to look at.

It also integrates well with a Palm Pilot, which makes it easy for you to keep track of contacts on your computer and carry them around. However, should you ever get into heavy contact management—making lots of contacts, tracking calls, keeping track of client expenses, and so on, Sidekick probably won't be the program for you.

***It Won't Work if You Don't Use It**—You can have the greatest contact-management software in the world and it won't do you any good if you don't use it. When you're shopping for a good PIM, make sure that you look for something you can actually use. Don't get something so simple that you're immediately frustrated by what it can't do. Conversely, don't get something that's so complicated that you're immediately frustrated by what you don't understand. Lots of contact managers offer demos—take advantage of that. Try before you buy.*

ACT!

http://www.symantec.com/act/

ACT! is a powerhouse of a contact-management software package, but you need to make sure you can use everything that it offers—and it'll take a little while to learn. ACT! offers all the features you would expect of a standard contact manager: address book, to-do list, calendars and alarms, and so on; but ACT! also offers configurable contact screens (you can design your own screens and figure out what you want to track); callback reminders; integration with the Internet (you can use Internet search tools to find contact information and download them to ACT!, send e-mail directly from the program, and so on); caller ID, and more. There's even a little feature called SideACT! that allows you to enter information into the program without keeping the entire program open.

All of this would be great for you if you're willing to put most of your contact needs into one program, and you don't rely heavily on external programs to make contact. If you don't need all the bells and whistles, however, you might find this program to be a little more than you bargained for.

GOLDMINE

http://www.goldminesw.com/

Wow. GoldMine will do just about everything but butter your toast. It's a highly rated program with features not available in other programs; but it is expensive, and it's very hard to learn. In fact, Peter rants about this one—he believes it's the epitome of a program created by a software-publishing company that thinks that as long as it creates software with lots of features, it doesn't have to worry about making it easy to use or provide good documentation. The publisher is definitely losing business by making this program so complicated—they lost Peter, for one.

Third-Party Helpers for Your Contact Manager—*ACT!, GoldMine, and many of the bigger contact manager programs have third-party and add-on products available. If you have unique contact needs, or are working in a niche industry, check these add-ons to see if any of them are appropriate to your needs.*

GoldMine is used by many sales people; it can be used to track contacts through sales cycles, schedule follow-ups, work with other people across a company network (GoldMine is perhaps the only full-featured contact-management program with complete network integration), and even go through telemarketing scripts. It also has Internet integration and a built-in e-mail center. If you have to work in a group that shares contact-management data, you might want to look at GoldMine.

But whatever you do, don't buy before you try. Download the software first, and see if you can figure out how to use it. Or, as was the case with Peter, see if you want to spend that much time figuring out how to use it. ACT! is a good alternative—much easier to use—though it doesn't have the network integration.

Not Just Software—*Don't be afraid to mix high-tech and low-tech. Tara uses Sidekick, but she finds it very handy to periodically (every few months or so) print out the addresses in Sidekick and keep them in a Rolodex next to her computer. That way she doesn't open the contact manager every time she needs a phone number or e-mail address and doesn't have to have her Palm Pilot at hand either.*

These three software packages are only a sample of the contact managers available. You can also check out the following to get an idea of the different kinds of contact managers available:

ACE Contact Manager
http://www.goace.com/

SaleSmartz
http://www.eurosmartz.co.uk/

Janna Contact Managers
http://www.janna.com/

Maximizer
http://www.maximizer.com/

Sharkware
http://www.sharkware.com/

Time and Chaos
http://www.isbister.com/

Lotus Organizer
http://www.lotus.com/home.nsf/welcome/organizer

Free-Form Personal Information Managers

The previously mentioned software packages offer very strict forms of information management. They're based around address books that have forms for input, with fields for each piece of information. In some cases you can modify the fields—rename or add fields, but in general there's a limit to the type of modifications you can make.

Sometimes the information you have to manage doesn't fit into these neat little packages. Instead, you might want to save large things—clippings of news stories, lists of URLs, ideas, memos, what-have-you—things that don't fit into neat little packages and that can't be expressed in a form.

In cases like this, you might want to look at free-form information managers. These hold information that can't be categorized well and that may not fit into a standard form. There are two very well-known information managers: AskSam and InfoSelect.

The Web Is All You Need?—*There are free online services that duplicate some of the things that a contact manager will do.* **When.com**, *at* http://www.when.com/, *will set you up with a free Web-based scheduling calendar.* **Yahoo!** *has a free calendar and to-do list at* http://calendar.yahoo.com/. **Dataferret** *(*http://www.dataferret.com/*) can store up to 10 contacts and provide you with a free Web-based calendar service. People who do a lot of group scheduling might want to check out* **JointPlanning** *at* http://www.jointplanning.com/, *which offers free group scheduling, address book, calendar, and to-do list. Some of these products may be handy, but they in no way replace a contact-management program on your computer.*

ASKSAM

http://www.asksam.com/

Sometimes you want to maintain large blocks of text-based information, such as e-mail records or memos. At the same time, you want them to be searchable quickly. In those situations, you could use AskSam, which allows you to dump large chunks of text in one database for quick searching and organization. You can specify form fields to enter data, like you use with standard contact managers, but it isn't required.

Let's take an example of how you'd use AskSam. Say you do media monitoring for your company and a couple of competitors. You want to stash the full text of any magazine or newspaper articles you find in a database. With AskSam, you could simply take the electronic versions of the documents and drop them into a database without specifying any form fields. The articles would be completely searchable and all together in one place. On the other hand, you could specify form fields for the name of the publication in which the article appeared and the publication date. With the form fields added, you would be able to both search the full text of the articles and list the articles by publication name or date. AskSam also has several filters that allow you to import information from various sources—Eudora and Microsoft Word, for instance.

What Should You Track?—*As you evaluate different types of contact-management software, a question might occur to you: what kind of information is essential to track? That's a difficult question to answer; everyone has his or her own idea of what is essential. Name of Web site, URL, and name and e-mail of contact person, surely. Name and postal address of the organization behind the Web site— good to have but not always essential (and not always available). After that you get into details—how often the online publication updates, how the online journalist prefers receiving news releases, fax numbers, a site's policy for reciprocal links. All these details aren't things you'll need immediately, or even often; but the more details you can keep track of, the more effective you can be in promoting your Web site.*

If you handle a lot of free-form information such as articles, you'll appreciate the quick searchability of AskSam and its capacity for a lot of information. However, this system won't work well for normal contact management, and AskSam is a little expensive, ranging from $150 to $400.

INFOSELECT

http://www.miclog.com/

InfoSelect provides contact management, a calendar, free-form information organization, and an easy way to maintain lots of information snippets and organize them over time. It's unusual and will take a little getting used to, but if you do a lot of information gathering, you'll get a lot out of it.

MS Outlook—*Many Windows users have Microsoft Outlook, which can be used as a contact-management program. It can store contact information, tasks, appointments, and so on, but it lacks some of the advanced contact-management features that these other programs have.*

InfoSelect offers an outline format from which you can organize various different types of information: text, calendars, images, outlines, databases, forms, and so on.

In the past, Tara used InfoSelect to organize snippets of information .At one point, she administered two newsletters and several different Web sites. Instead of organizing these in a contact manager (since she needed them within a few days of finding them) she used InfoSelect's outline format to file different snippets under different topics. When she went from two newsletters to three and began sharing her information with several different people, InfoSelect proved to be too limited, but until then it was useful. InfoSelect uses a frame setup to provide access to a huge amount of information. InfoSelect has a few drawbacks. It's an unusual program, so it takes a while to understand. If you need more standard contact management, you'll find it awkward to use for that purpose, and if you already have an external e-mail program you like, you won't have any use for InfoSelect's e-mail features.

Full-Blown Databases

You may find a need for a full-blown database, a program designed to work with large numbers of records. For instance, in Chapter 16, *Reaching Journalists Online*, we'll discuss how you can take a database of media contacts—perhaps 12,000 individuals—and select appropriate ones to receive press releases. Working with large numbers of contacts like this is best done using a full-blown database program, such as **Microsoft Access** (http://www.microsoft.com/), **FileMaker Pro** (http://www.filemaker.com/), or **Alphasoftware's** Alpha Five (http://www.alphasoftware.com/). It'll take you a long time to sift through very large databases using a contact-management program; you really need the features of a database program.

These programs have a couple of problems, though. Because they are specialized—few people use powerful database programs—prices are high, and usability is low. In other words, you pay a lot and get a little. It takes some effort to learn these programs, but it's worth it in the long run if you're working with big contact lists.

More Database Programs—*If you want to investigate database programs further, see the* **Yahoo!** *database page:* http://dir.yahoo.com/Computers_and_Internet/Software/Databases/. *Several Web-based database services might do what you want. Check out* **Bitlocker** *at* http://www.bitlocker.com *or* **Activespace** *at* http://www.activespace.com/.

Gathering Web-site information relevant to you and your promotional activities is one of the most important things you'll do, so it's important that you find tools to help you work efficiently. Building a strong database of people who can help you and people you can help will get your promotional activities off to a great start. Spend a little time working with the different types of software we've recommended—trying different programs, seeing what you like, how it works, and how you like to work with it. Once you're a little more comfortable with all this software and with the Internet in general, it's time to think about putting up a Web site. The next chapter will introduce you to all the Web-site basics.

CHAPTER THREE

Web Site Basics

You don't have to have a Web site to do business on the Internet—but if you don't, you're missing out on a huge opportunity. Most businesses working online have Web sites or are perhaps in the planning stages. Your Web site can be your operational headquarters, the center around which your other promotions are based. It seems, in fact, that many of the businesses that are choosing to work online *without* a Web site are spammers—companies using e-mail spam as their only promotional tool, companies that are to some degree "in hiding" in cyberspace, trying to generate fax and mail orders.

Most people reading this book probably want, or already have, a Web site. That's easy enough, isn't it? Everyone and his dogs seems to have Web sites these days. You get an Internet account with an ISP; the ISP gives you some Web space, and away you...go you set up your site.

The reality is different. Sure, it's easy to set up a Web site with a few pictures of your spouse, kids, and assorted pets, as half of AOL's members have proven; but if you're in business, your needs are more complicated.

Some time ago Peter received a call from a jeweler in Texas who wanted to buy *Poor Richard's Web Site*. The jeweler was having problems, he said, because he couldn't seem to get secure forms set up (that is, Web forms that would transfer credit-card information in an encrypted manner). It turned out he couldn't set up secure forms because his hosting company didn't have a secure server. Of course he should have asked the hosting company if it had one before he ever signed up with them; but, he didn't know enough to ask!

We're going to talk about some issues like that in this chapter, including domain names and hosting companies; but this chapter provides only a cursory introduction to the subject. We strongly recommend that you read *Poor Richard's Web Site: Geek-Free, Commonsense Advice on Building a Low-Cost Web Site*, by Peter (Top Floor Publishing, ISBN: 0-9661032-8-9). This book contains, for instance, an entire chapter explaining the different types of locations for your Web site, an entire chapter on the things to ask a hosting company, an appendix with a check list to help you compare hosting companies, two chapters discussing domain names, and so on.

WHERE TO PUT YOUR WEB SITE

Too many people begin their Internet presence with the idea that there's only one place to put their Web site—on the Web space provided by the company they use for Internet access. In fact there are a number of choices. You can put your Web site at one of these types of locations:

At an ISP's personal-page site—When you sign up for Internet access, you'll probably be given a bit of Web space. This is not appropriate for most businesses; you need your own domain name (which you can't use on personal space), and the personal space probably doesn't have all the services you need.

At a free-page Web site—A number of places, such as **GeoCities** (http://www.geocities.com/), **XOOM** (http://www.xoom.com/), and **Tripod** (http://www.tripod.com/) will allow you to set up a Web site for free. Again, you won't be able to use your own domain name, and you won't get all the services you need. Many of the free Web site services also have restrictions on how you can use their space. Many, for example, frown on commercial sites. Credibility is also an issue; because these pages are so easy to get, they're also easy for spammers and scammers to use. If you try to run a business from a free page Web site, expect a lot of glances askance from potential customers.

At a cybermall—Forget the malls. A mall is a stupid idea—geography is meaningless in cyberspace—and the online malls seem to be stacked with badly designed Web sites. The only time the mall idea even vaguely makes sense is when your business gets a Web store that's attached to some really popular Web property. For example, you can get a store at Yahoo! Stores. The advantage to that is that you are listed in Yahoo!'s directory, and you benefit from their extensive traffic. However, Yahoo! is popular because it's Yahoo!, not because it's a mall.

At a Web store—Some places sell a particular type of product—books, for instance. They'll sell you a generic page or two (a specific size and format). Again, you can't use your own domain name and you'll have limited services.

At a Web host's site in a subdirectory or subdomain—Web-hosting companies sell you space on their server, and you can do whatever you want with it. A subdirectory or subdomain means that you are dependent on the domain; you don't have your own domain name, so if you move, your site will have a new address.

At a Web host's site as a virtual domain—This is the best choice for most small businesses and organizations. You can use your own domain name, and, if you choose the right company, you get all the services you need.

On your own Web server—This is expensive, complicated. and not something the average small business should do. It requires a huge investment of time and resources.

You should understand that there's a lot of overlap. You may find that your local Internet Service Provider, the company you pay to provide you Internet access, is also a good Web-hosting company. You may run across a cybermall that is also a hosting company. Sometimes the free-page sites sell more advanced Web services, such as sites with shopping carts. What we're saying is that it's important for you to pick the right type of service at the right company. We're not implying that if a company provides free space it can't be a good commercial host.

GETTING YOUR OWN DOMAIN NAME

We've just mentioned that some of these services are not suitable because you can't have your own domain name. So what? What's it matter? It matters a lot. If you're serious about doing business or maintaining a long-term Web site, you should register your own domain name.

When we say *domain name,* we're really talking about a second-level domain name. For instance, look at this domain: cnn.com.

The .com bit is what's known as a top-level domain (TLD). The cnn bit is the second-level domain name. So CNN, the cable news channel, registered its own domain name as cnn.com.

If you set up your Web site at your online service or service provider, you'll have to use that company's domain name in your Web address—your URL. So the Web site's URL may be something like http://www.members.aol.com/ acmekites/, or http://ourworld.compuserve.com/ homepages/acmekites/. If you set up with a free service, such as **GeoCities** or **Xoom**, you'll end up with a URL such as http://www.geocities.com/Paris/LeftBank/54312/acmekites.html or http://members.xoom.com/ acmekites/.

Why, then, is it so important to get your own? For a variety of reasons:

- It looks more professional. It's hard to take http://www.geocities.com/ Paris/LeftBank/54312/acmekites.html seriously; this company should use http://acmekites.com/ so that it looks like it plans to stay in business.
- It's shorter. It's easier for your visitors to remember acmekites.com than http://www.geocities.com/Paris/LeftBank/54312/acmekites.html/.

- It won't change when you move your Web site, and one day you *will* move your Web site. If you don't own your own domain name, you'll have to change it...and change your business cards, letterhead, catalogs, and so on. When you move, your old visitors won't know where you've gone, unless you pay to keep a redirection page at the old account.

- Once you have your own domain name and an account set up with a hosting company, you'll also have an e-mail account at that domain name, so you can create multiple e-mail addresses (sales@acmekites.com, fred@acmekites.com, and so on).

- Yahoo!—the single most important search engine on the Web—has a bias against subdomains; they're much less likely to add http://www.geocities.com/Paris/LeftBank/54312/acmekites.html to their index than http://acmekites.com/.

When the first edition of this book was written, it cost $70 to register a domain name for the first two years, with a $35 a year renewal fee after that because you could only go to one place, **Network Solutions** (http://NetworkSolutions.com/), to get a domain. Since the first edition, however, the situation has changed completely; there are now over 60 domain-name registrars (you can find a list here: http://internic.net/regist.html). While the list price for a domain is still $35 a year (you no longer have to pay for two years when you first register), you'll find that some registrars are charging less, sometimes much less.

Top-Level Domain Name Choices

You have a number of choices for top-level domain names. The top level is the first piece of the domain name, on the right side: in cnn.com, for instance, the top level is .com. However, CNN has another top-level domain—.net; try cnn.net, and you'll find it takes you to their Web site, too. They also have the .org domain.

The .com domain was originally intended for commercial enterprises; .net for Internet-related organizations such as ISPs and hosting companies; and .org for non-profit organizations, professional associations, and so on. But these days it's common for companies to register a domain name in all three top-level domains (in fact Network Solutions has encouraged this for some time).

You may have seen or heard advertising encouraging you to register your domain in various other top-level domains. These are generally country domains. For instance, you can register a .cc domain name or a .to domain name, and there's currently a lot of money going into advertising the .tv domain. What's happened in these cases is that an entrepreneur has persuaded the countries that own these top-level domain names to sell them off—.cc belongs to the Cocos Islands, .to to Tonga, and .tv to Tuvalu.

You might have heard that you should register every available variant of your domain name. (For example, if you're Acme Kites, you should register AcmeKites.to, AcmeKites.cc, AcmeKites.tv, and so on.) Do we agree with this? Absolutely not; attempting to register every permutation of your domain name is expensive and includes periodic renewal payments, and most of the new top-level domains aren't as well known. Stick to .com. Sure, get the .net and .org if you want, but if the .com variant that you want has already gone, you probably shouldn't bother to get .net or .org. People simply don't remember top-levels other than .com, so if you promote a domain in a top-level other than .com, you're spending money to help a potential competitor! (A good example: the owners of Rent.Net spend millions to advertise their domain; undoubtedly much of the traffic generated went to Rent.com.)

However, early in 2001 this situation is likely to change. A variety of new top-level domain names will be introduced. (Will *probably* be introduced; these names are a couple of years overdue as it is.) At the time of writing it wasn't clear what names would be available, but probably names such as .shop, .ecology, .biz, .sucks, .banc, .geo, and, eventually, many more. Eventually the predominance and importance of the .com domain will fade, as the top-level domain becomes a more important part of a company's domain name.

Companies that Register Domain Names

We mentioned the list of domain-name registrars earlier (http://internic.net/regist.html), but there are many more places to register a domain name. There are many companies that are not true registrars, but that work in conjunction with a registrar reselling domain names; most Web-hosting companies register domain names for their clients, too. There may be some registrars that haven't been added to the list, as well. In any case, if you want a larger list of places to register domain names, including places to register domains in country top-level domains, try this listing at Yahoo!: http://dir.yahoo.com/Business_and_Economy/Business_to_Business/Communications_and_Networking/Internet_and_World_Wide_Web/Domain_Registration/.

Do It Yourself—*It's a good idea to register domain names yourself, rather than allowing a hosting company to do it for you. We've heard a number of stories of people arguing with hosting companies and then finding their domain names hijacked! That's not to say you shouldn't register using forms at a hosting company, but that you should be listed as one of the main contacts for the domain name (the Administrative contact, for instance).*

What if you have a domain name you want to register—and want to do it right away before someone else grabs it—yet you don't yet have a hosting company you're working with? Domain names have to be "pointed" somewhere—you have to provide the IP numbers of two nameservers that are responsible for keeping information about where the domain name's Web site and e-mail accounts are actually store (on which server). If you haven't yet set up a Web site, you can *park* the domain. Parking the domain means that you're reserving it for yourself, but you haven't created a hosting space for it yet. Most registrars these days will allow you to park the domain name on their servers.

Picking a Domain Name

How do you choose a domain name or domain names? You may want several names for different purposes: one for your company (Peter has http://TopFloor. com/, for instance), one for a particular product (he also has http://PoorRichard. com/), one that identifies your general area of business, and so on. Here are a few guidelines:

- Try to get a domain name that matches your business name, or even create a business name that matches a domain name. CDnow.com, for instance, is the domain name of **CDnow Online, Inc.**; Amazon.com is the domain name of **Amazon.com, Inc.**; BizBlast.com is the domain name of **BizBlast.com, Inc.**

- Try to get a short domain name, though sometimes that's difficult. Barnes and Noble had two major problems, for instance. It's been in business with a long name for a long time. Yet it got into the Internet business too late to pick a domain name such as books.com, so it ended up with barnesandnoble.com. Eventually it wised up and now uses http://www.bn.com/.

- Look for a *keyword*.com domain name if possible, such as http://word.com/, http://football.com/, http://skydiving.com/, or http://scuba.com/. (Sorry, those are all taken, but it's still possible to find keywords for more obscure subjects.) Often users type a plain keyword in their browsers' Location boxes to see where it takes them; in many browsers if you type a single word, the browser will add www. and .com for you, so these keywords can be valuable. On the other hand, Netscape changed the way its browser works, so in many cases the keyword won't work in that manner; rather, the browser searches a database at Netscape's site.

- If you can't get what you want at first, use some imagination to pick a name. If you have a lawn service (or sell hemp products, perhaps), try http://GrassGrassGrass.com/. If you paint houses in Denver, try

http://DenverPainters.com/. If you sell footwear, try http://Sandals
AndSneakers.com/. Sometimes it seems that all the good domain names are
gone, but at the time of writing all these domain names are still available.

Getting Help with Your Domain Name—*Bashing your head against the wall
trying to be creative about your domain name? Try* **NameBoy** *at*
http://www.nameboy.com/. *The site suggests domain names for you. For information
on domain names, including plenty of links to sellers and research tools, check out
the* **Internet Gold** *Rush at* http://igoldrush.com/.

Clarifying Your Domain Name

You'll notice, no doubt, that we've used both uppercase and lowercase in these
domain names. Rather than typing http://grassgrassgrass.com/, we wrote
http://GrassGrassGrass.com/. Many people assume that a domain name has to be
lowercase; it doesn't. Browsers ignore capitalization in the domain name, so you
can capitalize any way you choose when advertising your URL.

Using mixed case is a good way to make a domain name much more readable.
For instance, Peter's Poor Richard's site is http://poorrichard.com/. However, some
people don't notice that there are two r's in the middle of poorrichard, so Peter
writes it http://PoorRichard.com/ to make it clearer.

There are two basic rules for using this little trick.

* You can write the domain name any way you want, it makes no difference
  to a browser or Web site: http://PoorRichard.com/, http://POORRICHARD.COM/,
  http://poorrichard.com/, http://PoOrRiChArD.cOm/. Capitalization of the
  domain name doesn't matter as far as the browser is concerned. (Try these
  URLs and you'll see that they all work.)

* It does matter, though, how you write the rest of the URL—the
  directories and filename. For instance, http://PoorRichard.com/newsltr/
  archive.htm/ will work, but http://PoorRichard.com/Newsltr/Archive.htm/ will
  not. You should not change case of the text that follows the domain-name
  portion of the URL.

By the way, you can generally do the same with e-mail addresses; they are
rarely case sensitive, so if it looks better to use uppercase letters in some positions
(PeterKent@TopFloor.com, for instance), go ahead and try it. Try to send a
message written in that manner. Most e-mail systems will handle it fine; if the
message gets through, then you can start writing your addresses that way.

Here are some other clever ways to clarify URLs. Some sites use different
colors; **BizBlast.com**, for instance, uses blue for Biz, red for Blast, a yellow dot,

and blue for com. **NameBoy**, which we mentioned a little earlier in the chapter, has a single-color URL, but the text is in two different styles—the *name* part of the URL is in a thicker font than the *boy* part. Tara's own site, **ResearchBuzz**, uses two different fonts for the words *Research* and *Buzz*. As long as you can easily tell what the words are, consider dividing them up with fonts, colors, and styles.

Finally, why bother with www. at all? You'll notice that many of the URLs we've shown in this chapter—http://PoorRichard.com/, for instance—completely omit the www. piece. Many other sites seem to have dropped it too, at least in the logo at the top of their Web page. **Amazon.com** doesn't use it in their logo at the top of their page either. (They use Amazon in bold, with .com in a lighter type.) There's one catch here, though. Some Web-server administrators simply haven't caught on, and they set up the servers so that you *must* use www, so before you write your URLs like this, make sure they'll work and if they don't, ask the administrator why not.

.com Getting Tacky?—We've noticed fewer and fewer sites using the .com in their name. Apparently it's getting rather unpopular. Consider that when evaluating whether to include it in your official name.

CHOOSING A HOSTING COMPANY

We said that in most cases the best place for a Web site is at a hosting company. There are now thousands of hosting companies. It's easy to track them down; try one of these sites:

budgetweb.com
http://www.budgetweb.com/budgetweb/

Host Facts
http://www.hostfacts.com/

Host Find
http://www.hostfind.com/

Leasing a Server List at budgetweb.com
http://budgetweb.com/hndocs/list.shtml

Microsoft FrontPage Web-Presence Providers
http://www.microsoft.com/frontpage/

NerdWorld-WWW Servers
http://www.nerdworld.com/nw1642.html

Yahoo!-Web Presence Providers page
http://www.yahoo.com/Business_and_Economy/Companies/Internet_Services/Web
_Services/Hosting/

Checking Domain Names*—If you want to find out if a .com, .net, or .org domain has been registered, use the Whois system at* **Network Solutions***: http://networksolutions.com/cgi-bin/whois/whois/ Type the name you want into the text box (remember to include the .com, .net, or .org bit at the end) and press Enter, and Whois will search to see if the name has been registered.*

If you want more options for checking domain names, visit **AskReggie** at http://www.askreggie.com/. This system makes it easy to search for domain names and for specific companies to see what domain names they own. (You can do all this at the Network Solutions site, but AskReggie simplifies it.) Also remember that most, if not all, domain registration services offer some way to look through the existing domain names and see what's been taken.

What to Ask a Hosting Company

These places will help you find low-cost hosting services—you may end up paying only $15–$30 a month or sometimes even less; but how on earth do you figure out which one to pick? That's a problem. Many different services are available, so before you can choose a host you have to understand what those services are. Here's a quick summary. (Remember, *Poor Richard's Web Site* has an entire chapter on this subject.)

DOES THE COMPANY HAVE MICROSOFT FRONTPAGE SERVER EXTENSIONS?

This is important only if you plan to use Microsoft FrontPage (a popular Web-authoring program). If the hosting company doesn't have the server extensions installed, some of the FrontPage features won't work.

HOW MUCH DOES IT COST?

Most services charge a setup fee, and then a monthly charge. Some don't have a setup fee, and some will waive the setup fee if you are transferring an existing Web site and domain from another location. Even if a service doesn't advertise that it does so, if you are transferring a site it might be worth asking whether it will waive the fee.

MINIMUM CONTRACT AND GUARANTEE?

Some Web-hosting companies want you to pay a year's fee at one time; but you should ask if you can pay for, say, three months. Some simply go month by month; others charge by the month and give the first month free—the ideal situation. Also ask what sort of guarantees the company offers, and get the guarantee in writing if you can; some companies offer a 30-day money-back guarantee. Some hosting companies offer an uptime guarantee, which guarantees its servers will be up and running a certain percentage of the time. Look out for that too.

HOW MUCH DISK SPACE?

Your Web site will be limited to a certain amount of disk space, though you can buy more. Small, low-cost accounts may have only a couple of megabytes of disk space; larger sites will get tens, even hundreds of megabytes. You can actually fit a lot into a megabyte or two, and a huge site will need only a few hundred megabytes unless it includes a lot of multimedia.

HOW MUCH ARE HIT AND DATA-TRANSFER CHARGES?

Some companies charge you for the number of hits—the number of times someone transfers one of your pages to his or her browser. Others charge according to the amount of data transferred out of your Web site. Either way, the busier your site, the more you'll be charged under these pricing schedules. Others have no limit.

Unlimited use may not be so good if it means that all the sites handled by the server are busy, of course. In any case, most companies provide a certain minimum amount of data transfer for free, which is usually plenty for most sites.

HOW MUCH ARE UPGRADES?

If your Web site grows, so will your hosting needs. Check to see how much it'll cost you to add more disk space, transfer more data, create more e-mail accounts, and so on.

HOW MUCH TO HOST MULTIPLE DOMAIN NAMES?

If you have more than one domain name, you can have them all point to the same Web site. For instance, you might have one domain name for your company and other domain names that you are using to promote specific products. There are different ways to handle this. All the domains can point to the same directory, or you can have separate directories for each domain. Of course, companies have different ways to charge, too. You may be allowed two free domains, perhaps, with an additional fee for extra domains, or maybe you'll pay an additional fee for all extra domains.

IS THERE A CHARGE FOR E-MAIL ACCOUNTS?

You'll generally get an e-mail account with your Web site. Sometimes you'll get several accounts even though you may need no more than one. Some companies, however, may charge extra for the accounts.

With a single e-mail account, you can retrieve e-mail that has been sent to various addresses: info@acmesewercover.com, sales@acmesewercover.com, joe@acmesewercover.com, susie@acmesewercover.com, and so on.

HOW MANY MAIL FORWARDING ACCOUNTS?

You may also want to make sure the Web-hosting company allows you to set up mail forwarding—automatically defining certain types of incoming e-mail messages to be forwarded somewhere else. For instance, messages to susie@acmesewercover.com could be forwarded to susiesewer@aol.com. Ask how many accounts can be forwarded.

DO YOU HAVE MAIL RESPONDERS?

A mail responder, or autoresponder, is a program that automatically responds to incoming mail. For instance, if someone sends e-mail to info@acmesewercover.com, an informational message can be sent back. These can be very useful, so we recommend that you use a host that provides them. There are several things a good autoresponder should be able to do:

- Quote the incoming message in the autoresponse.
- Save the incoming message.
- Redirect the incoming message somewhere else (to a mailing-list server, for instance).
- Grab the e-mail address from the incoming message and put it in a text file.

The last of these is particularly important, as it allows you to collect e-mail addresses from messages sent to your autoresponders. Here's the problem: you almost certainly won't find an auto-responder system that does all these things. (This list is really Peter's 'this is the way auto-responders *should* work' list.)

DO YOU HAVE MAILING LISTS?

A mailing list is a discussion group based on the e-mail system. You may want to set one up; they're useful promotional tools, as we'll discuss in Chapter 11, *Creating Newsletters and Discussion Groups*. Even if you don't want to host a discussion group, you can use a mailing-list program to distribute a newsletter. Many companies have mailing-list software available for their clients to use. If your host does, ask whether there's an additional cost, how many mailing lists you are allowed to have, and how many members per list. Sometimes a hosting company will have the capacity for mailing lists available, but they're for small lists or lists that are limited in some other way, so be sure to investigate this one closely.

DO I GET A SHELL ACCOUNT? (TELNET ACCESS)

A shell account allows you to log onto the Web site using Telnet and modify files and directories. This can be useful, and you'll find that most companies provide a shell account. Some don't, though, and this can present problems. For instance, if you want to install your own CGI scripts, you may need Telnet access so you can get to the scripts and modify their permissions, rename files, and so on. Having said that...most FTP programs these days let you change permissions, too; so shell access is becoming less and less important, and as it's also a security risk to Web servers some hosting companies don't provide it.

DO I GET FTP ACCESS?

You'll need FTP (File Transfer Protocol) access. This allows you to transfer files to and from your Web site; so virtually all companies provide this service. Some may provide a different way to transfer files, such FrontPage; but even if you use FrontPage, it's nice to have FTP access too.

CAN I SET UP AN ANONYMOUS FTP SITE?

This is not the same as FTP access to your Web site. Rather, it allows you to set up an FTP site that people can access to download files. You might want to do this if you are distributing software, for instance. While it's possible to transfer files directly from your Web site, it's sometimes handy to have an FTP site, too. People without good Web access can still use the FTP site. Furthermore, some FTP sites can resume interrupted downloads. If users try to transfer a file, get halfway through, and their ISP or phone company drops the line, they can come back and continue the transfer where they left off—a handy feature for large downloads.

DO YOU HAVE A SECURE SERVER?

If you plan to take orders online or transfer sensitive information, you'll need a secure server. (You'll often see it referred to as an SSL server, meaning a Secure Sockets Layer server.) For instance, credit-card information typed into a form will be encrypted before it is sent from the user's Web browser to the server. There may be an additional fee to use the secure server. You don't have to have a secure server to take orders online, but many people won't place orders unless you do.

DO YOU HAVE SHOPPING-CART SOFTWARE?

If you plan to sell products and want to offer users some kind of catalog combined with an order form, you might want to find out whether the Web-hosting company has any shopping-cart software already available and, if so, what its capabilities and costs are. If not, ask whether you can add your own shopping-cart software. We'll discuss this further in a moment.

CAN I USE CGI SCRIPTS?

CGI means Common Gateway Interface. It's a way to provide interactivity to Web pages, in particular to handle the input from forms. For instance, you can use CGI to take information from a form and send it to your e-mail account, and many shopping-cart programs use CGIs. Many Web-hosting companies have libraries of CGI scripts you can use. Some allow you to install your own CGI scripts, but don't provide a library. Others don't allow you to add any CGIs. We recommend that you find a company that at least allows you to add your own.

DO I GET ACCESS REPORTS?

Access reports show you information about visitors to your site. You need this information, as it can show you where visitors are coming from, when they arrive, which pages they view, and so on. Some companies send reports to you automatically via e-mail each day or week. Some create charts to show access information. If you're planning to use your own software, such as WebTrends or Urchin, to review the access reports, you need to find out if you get the raw logs—the plain log files that your hosting company's server generates—in addition to formatted access reports. On the other hand, many hosting companies now provide WebTrends or Urchin reports for you, or perhaps for an additional fee (while others provide basic reports created by public-domain report programs).

CAN I HAVE PASSWORD-PROTECTED PAGES?

If you need to set up a private area at your Web site, some companies will help you create password-protected areas. This is quite easy to do for yourself using Microsoft FrontPage, by the way.

DO YOU HAVE TELEPHONE TECHNICAL SUPPORT?

Ask about the type of technical support available. Can you call and talk with someone? If so, is it a toll-free or local call? This is a significant issue, as you'll almost certainly have to get help at some point. Some Web-hosting services try to handle all their support through e-mail, but the problem with this is that it's too easy to ignore e-mail or delay responses. You must have some way to talk to someone. Toll-free numbers are relatively rare for low-cost Web-hosting companies; you may end up having to use a long-distance number; but a long-distance number is better than no phone support at all. Some companies charge extra for phone support; some don't.

Additionally find out when phone support is available. If your Web site goes down at 9 P.M. on Saturday night, are you out of luck, or is someone going to answer at your hosting company's tech support? If no one's there to answer, is there at least on option to page someone? If you're going to be using your Web site to sell products and services, you don't want to be trapped in a situation where your site has gone down and you have no one to talk to for help.

These are some of the most important issues involved in choosing a hosting company. Other things to consider are...

- Is commercial use allowed?
- Is there a discount for non-profit organizations?
- Is online credit-card and check processing provided?
- Can you resell Web space?
- Are there promotional and design services?
- How many computers does the company have?
- What size is the company?

In addition...

- Ask for references and Check Them.
- Consider the look and feel of the hosting company's own Web site.

CREATING YOUR WEB PAGES

How are you going to create your Web pages? Well, the simplest way is to pay someone else to do it for you. Unfortunately we don't all have that option, and in fact it doesn't have to be terribly complicated to create Web pages.

There are two ways to create Web pages. One is to work with the raw HTML (HyperText Markup Language). Want to see what HTML looks like? Load a Web page in your browser; then use the View|Page Source command (or similar). You'll see something like Figure 3.1.

These little codes tell the browser what to display, and how to display the page. It tells whether the text is a heading or body text; whether a picture should be placed in a table; where the picture comes from; whether to create frames; whether a word is red or blue; and a multitude of other details.

FIGURE 3.1: This is what a Web page looks like behind the scenes. The stuff between < and > are the HTML codes.

If you don't already know HTML, this is all a big hassle. There's a lot to learn. Luckily you don't have to learn it. There are many authoring tools—word processors that create Web pages—you can use. If you can use a word processor, you can create Web pages. Sure, there are a few differences, but it shouldn't take you long to learn how to use one of these programs. These editors are called *WYSIWYG* editors—What You See Is What You Get—and you can see an example in Figure 3.2. (It's pronounced wizzy-wig.)

Peter has often recommended Microsoft FrontPage and the feedback he's gotten has been favorable. There is one important thing to be aware of, though: while Microsoft FrontPage for Windows is a good product, Microsoft FrontPage for the Macintosh is lagging way behind in development, and, it appears, probably won't be updated.

In any case, FrontPage isn't your only choice. Many, many authoring programs are available to you. These are the different types of programs:

Simple HTML Editors—Simple HTML editors display all the codes but help you enter them. Instead of typing a code for something, you can click a button, and the editor drops the code in for you. These are like beefed-up text editors.

Sophisticated HTML Editors—A step up from the simple HTML editor is the sophisticated HTML editor, for people who like to see their tags but

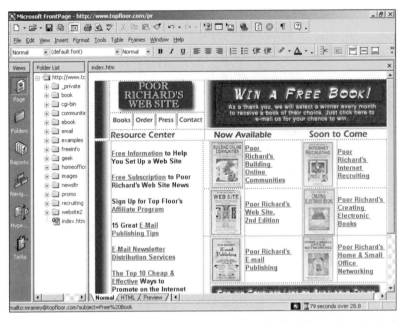

FIGURE 3.2: This is Microsoft FrontPage, a WYSIWYG HTML Editor. On the left you can see the structure of the Web site—the individual directories. On the right is one of the pages being edited.

want to speed up the process of creating pages. These editors have a plethora of tools to help you enter the codes more quickly. Many expert HTML authors use this sort of tool.

WYSIWYG HTML Editors—While creating your pages, you can see, more or less, what a user would see while viewing the page in the Web browser. You don't see the HTML tags. This is like working with a modern word processor, and for nonexperts it is much easier than using a simple or even sophisticated HTML editor. (FrontPage is a WYSIWYG editor.)

HTML Converters—A number of programs are used for converting files into Web pages (converting them from various word-processing and desktop-publishing formats, for instance). This is handy for companies that have a lot of paper documents to convert and put on the Web. You generally use a converter in conjunction with a good HTML editor because converters do little more than convert.

Built-in Converters—Many programs now contain built-in HTML converters; a number of word processors, for instance, allow you to save documents in HTML format.

Here's a sampling of WYSIWYG programs to get you started:

CorelWEB.DESIGNER (Windows 3.1/95/98/NT)
http://www.corel.com/corelweb/webdesigner/

Dreamweaver (Windows 95/98/NT, Macintosh)
http://www.macromedia.com/software/dreamweaver/

Internet Creator (Windows 95/98/NT)
http://www.formaninteractive.com/

Microsoft FrontPage (Macintosh, Windows 95/98/NT)
http://www.microsoft.com/frontpage/

NetObjects Fusion (Windows 95/98/NT, Macintosh)
http://www.netobjects.com/

PageMill (Macintosh, Windows 95/98/NT)
http://www.adobe.com/prodindex/pagemill/main.html

Symantec Visual Page (Windows 95/98/NT)
http://www.symantec.com/vpage/

Symantec Visual Page (Macintosh)
http://www.symantec.com/vpagemac/

WebExpress (Windows 3.1/95/98/NT)
http://www.mvd.com/

Yahoo!-HTML Editors
http://dir.yahoo.com/Computers_and_Internet/Software/Internet/World_Wide_Web/HTML_Editors/

Here are a few sophisticated HTML Editors:

BBEdit (Macintosh)
http://www.barebones.com/

HotMetal Pro (Macintosh, Windows 95/98/NT, UNIX)
http://www.hotmetalpro.com/

Sausage Software's HotDog Pro (Windows 95, 98, NT)
http://www.sausage.com/

Agile (Windows 9x, NT)
http://www.agilic.com/

Yahoo!-HTML Converters
http://dir.yahoo.com/Computers_and_Internet/Software/Internet/World_Wide_Web/HTML_Converters/

Remember that you can also find many, many shareware programs at the software libraries we mentioned in Chapter 2, *What You Need Before You Start.*

SETTING UP A SHOPPING-CART

If you're planning to sell products online, you will need to set up a shopping-cart system. (*Shopping-cart* is the term commonly used to mean the system of forms employed to take orders at a Web site.) It should be simple to do this, but at the time of writing, it's really not so simple, especially if you want a full-featured system.

First, though, a disclaimer on the part of Peter. Sometime after launching Top Floor Publishing, and selling thousands of copies of *Poor Richard's Web Site* and this book, *Poor Richard's Internet Marketing and Promotions* on the Web, Peter started BizBlast.com, an e-Business Service Provider (that's the latest jargon for companies that provide e-business services—such as shopping-cart systems). BizBlast.com is funded by several venture-capital firms, including Softbank Venture Capital, the world's top Internet fund.

Why did he launch this business? Because his experience in setting up an e-commerce site for Top Floor Publishing convinced him that e-commerce is way too difficult for small businesses. There are so many ways to get stuck, or to spend too much money. He decided there had to be a better way. So he began BizBlast.com to supply affordable and easy to use—yet sophisticated—e-commerce tools to small businesses.

There are many shopping-cart systems available, but they have a variety of problems:

- They're often expensive.
- They're often difficult to use.
- They're usually lacking important features.
- They often limit you to a set of templates, not allowing you to customize the look of the Web pages (so you can't get your store to look like your Web site).
- They're often a combination of the above.

First, some background. If you know a little about HTML—the coding required to build Web pages—you probably know that HTML can be used to create forms; but HTML cannot make a form actually *do* anything. To get the form to do something, you need a special program running on the server. That program might be a CGI (Common Gateway Interface) script, Java servlet, or server "extension" installed on the Web server.

When a site has a shopping-cart system, the buyer sees a series of forms. When the user enters information in those forms and submits the forms, the data is taken by the program on the server and manipulated—sales tax, shipping costs, totals, and so on are calculated. Then the information is sent back to the user's browser. So you must understand that a Web store is a combination of Web pages and the program running on the server to which the pages send information. In other words, the two things must match—your Web server must be running the appropriate program.

There are several ways to set up a shopping-cart system:

1. Buy the software and install it on your own server.
2. Buy the software and install it on your hosting company's server.
3. Sign up with a Web-hosting company that has shopping-cart software available.
4. Sign up with a shopping-cart service; the shopping-cart software runs on their server, linked to from your Web site.

As we noted before, option 1 is out of the question for most small businesses—it's way too complicated and expensive. As for option 2, before you buy a product you have to know what you are getting into. Will you be able to install the product on your hosting company's server? Will the hosting company let you? Do you have the skills to do so? (It's not always easy.) In general options 3 or 4 will be your best options. Let's look at options 2 through 4 in turn.

Install Software on Your Hosting Company's Server

When you go looking for shopping-cart software, make sure you ask the following questions; don't rely on the company's product blurbs or declared system requirements:

- How does the system create the program that runs the forms? Does it require special extensions at the server, does it install CGIs, or does it require a particular server?
- Can I use this at any hosting company, or do I have to work with a particular company or choose from a list of companies? (Some products are set up to work at a few dozen companies only, and can't be installed on other hosting servers.)
- If I can use it with any hosting company, which types of Web servers will it run on? (Make sure it's compatible with the one your hosting company uses.)

- Who will install the program on the server? (It's not a simple task to install these programs, so at the least you need good technical support available.)

There are many products that you can install on your host's server. These products generally use CGI (Common Gateway Interface) scripts running on the server. Therefore, you must make sure that you're allowed to use CGIs on your server, that the products you are buying are compatible with the server, and that you're sure that either you are capable of installing those products or that you can find someone to install them for you. These things can be *very* tricky, but some software companies will install the products for you.

Such programs vary widely in cost. Actually some freeware programs are available, but they're generally difficult to set up; perhaps you can hire a consultant to install them for you. Prices go up into the many thousands of dollars.

Use a Hosting Company with Shopping-Cart Software Available

Perhaps the simplest thing is to sign up with a Web-hosting company that already has shopping-cart software available for use. At least you know it's already installed on the server, so it should be relatively easy to get running...well, perhaps. Just because your hosting company chose it doesn't mean it's either easy to use or has all the features you need. Check it out carefully. (We'll discuss this in a moment.)

Use an E-Business Service Provider

There are now many companies operating as *e-Business Service Providers*, companies dedicated to providing e-commerce services. These companies will host your shopping-cart. In most cases these companies provide only shopping-cart systems and, perhaps, some kind of simple tool for creating a few templated Web pages. What they don't generally provide are full Web-hosting services (the ability to use, for instance, FrontPage to create pages, the ability to install other CGI scripts, e-mail accounts, and so on). Peter's company, BizBlast.com, *does* provide full hosting services in addition to the e-commerce services, but that's not the norm.

In other words, you can have your Web site at one location, the shopping-cart at another, and link from one to the other. Most customers won't even realize that they've jumped from one site to another during the order process.

The advantages? You may find a Web-hosting company you really like, with the exception of its shopping-cart system; you can keep your Web site where it is, and pick and choose between shopping-cart services. They're usually relatively easy to set up (*relatively* easy we said, not easy). It's someone else's responsibility to keep the thing going. (If you install your own system, in contrast, you'll have to worry about maintenance.) In addition, they can be quite affordable; but they're often rather weak systems, lacking important features.

In fact there are now many companies providing free e-commerce accounts, companies such as **BigStep** (http://www.BigStep.com/), **eCongo** (http://www.eCongo.com/), and **Freemerchant** (http://www.freemerchant.com/). But there are several major problems with such accounts:

- Customer support is next to nonexistent; these companies aren't making money, after all, so you can't expect support.
- The tools are relatively weak. For instance, BigStep, at least at the time of writing, does not allow merchants to sell and ship products overseas.
- The products allow a minimum of customization, so you can't get your store to match a Web site you may have just created.

Are free e-commerce systems really free? Not if you find they don't suit you and you have to move to a more sophisticated system! You will have spent a lot of time and effort to set up your store *twice*, and you'll end up paying anyway.

Picking a Shopping-Cart

Choosing a shopping-cart system is an exercise in compromise. There's no perfect solution. You'll be juggling features, price, and ease of installation. Here, to help just a little, are a few things to watch for when picking a shopping-cart system:

- Will the program be able to handle as many categories and products as you need?
- Does the program allow the buyer to add products to a basket and then continue shopping and add more products?
- Can you import items? If you have a lot of products, you need to be able to import a list. If you only have a few products, you can enter them by typing in the information.
- Can buyers leave, come back later, and continue shopping where they left off? (This is a nice feature, though not essential.)
- Can buyers search for products? (This is not important if you have a small number of products.)
- Will the program allow you to add fields? For instance, you may want to add a check box that allows buyers to sign up for a free newsletter, or a "where did you hear about this product" drop-down list box. (Of course,

this information must then be included in the order information provided to you by the program.)

- How does the program calculate state sales tax? You should be able to specify sales tax for particular states—ideally for particular cities or ZIP codes. However, some programs don't calculate sales tax well. (For instance, if the user types Colorado instead of CO, the sales tax may not be calculated.)

- Does it allow you to specify all the shipping methods and rates you want to use? Some programs provide little flexibility, or even don't allow the customer to choose a shipping method at all but only tack on a set shipping price, making selling overseas impossible—if you can't differentiate between shipments to Arizona and shipments to Australia, how can you price shipping overseas? (This is a ridiculous situation when you consider that the Internet is an international forum.)

- Will the program verify that credit card numbers and e-mail addresses were entered in the correct format?

- How does the program provide confirmation to the user? It should display a confirmation page; but it should also send an e-mail message.

- Will the program e-mail a message to you letting you know that an order has been taken?

- Does the system require that buyers register before making a purchase? (It probably shouldn't, but some do.)

- How is the order information delivered to you? It should be easy to import into a database, so you need a text-file format (comma- or tab-delimited text) or a database format. Some systems deliver an e-mail message, which is usually inconvenient. (How do you get it into a mailing-label or credit-card processing program?)

- Try entering information in many different ways—foreign phone numbers and provinces, different country names, and so on. Does the program handle different situations well, or does it display error messages?

- Do you like the overall look and feel of the product? Is it confusing, or simple to use? Does it make your customers jump through hoops, or is it quick and easy?

A Quick Word About Transaction Processing

Selling products online involves two basic processes. First, you must take the order. Then, you have to process the financial transaction, which generally means processing a credit-card order, though there are other types of money:

checks, debit cards, and even 900 numbers. (That's right, you can charge transaction to a telephone bill by having the buyer call a 900 number.)

Most small companies take orders online and then do the transaction processing offline. In other words, they download the orders and then use a hardware credit-card terminal to process the orders, or, perhaps, some kind of PC or Mac software that dials into the credit-card network to process the cards. Why? Because they probably already have a credit-card merchant account and the terminal equipment.

A Ban on Offline Transactions?—At the time of writing, there was a rumor that MasterCard and Visa were planning to ban the processing of credit-card numbers acquired on the Internet in any kind of non-Internet method. That is, they will not allow a merchant to take a credit card, and then process it later in some kind of hardware terminal or through a processing program such as PCAuthorize or ICVerify. This ban would come into effect early in 2001. We're not sure of the veracity of this rumor, but even people working in the credit-card merchant-account business claim that there's a good chance it is true. So by the time you read this, if you want to take credit cards you may have to process online.

It is possible to do online transaction processing—to set up a system that takes the order, processes the credit card, and then saves the completed order information. Transaction processing is often expensive to set up, though, $100 to $200, depending on the shopping-cart system you're working with. Shop around, though, and you'll find lower rates. There may also be a monthly "gateway" fee, plus, in some cases, a per-transaction fee—perhaps $1 per transaction, perhaps more (on top of your normal credit-card transaction fees). Here's a common breakdown of monthly fees:

Transaction gateway fee: $19.95

Credit-card merchant account statement fee: $19.95

Credit-card minimum transaction charges: $24.95

Be careful, though, in setting up your credit-card merchant account. First, you must make sure you set up the merchant account with the company that is running your e-commerce software; these programs are generally set up to use merchant accounts from just one credit-card transaction network, so you usually can't get a merchant account first and expect it to work with any kind of software you pick.

Secondly, the merchant-account business is a bit of a scam; it can cost literally thousands of dollars to set up a merchant account, generally in monthly leasing fees. We've even seen companies leasing free gateway software, and then charging a gateway fee on top! Compare prices carefully; it is possible to get accounts at a low cost, though the problem is finding software you want to use *and* that has merchant accounts available at a low cost. (Peter's company, BizBlast.com, sets up accounts for just $19.95, and has low monthly statement fees [$14.95], with no monthly minimums.)

There are now other payment options, though. For instance, PayPal (see sidebar) provides a way for merchants to take credit cards without setting up a credit-card merchant account; buyers can sign up for a PayPal account and pay for the product at the same time. However, at the time of writing, only one sophisticated e-commerce system can work with PayPal (you may have guessed it...Peter's BizBlast.com system). By the way, PayPal currently pays a $5 referral bonus for new accounts, so merchants that take PayPal payments earn $5 each time a buyer signs up for a new account. Yet another advantage—although at the time of writing PayPal only let U.S. residents sign up for accounts, by the time you read this the policies should be changed to allow anyone in the world with a credit card to set up an account, allowing merchants anywhere in the world to accept credit cards payments through PayPal. (It's currently much more difficult for non-U.S. residents to set up credit-card transactions.)

There are other systems available that allow merchants to, in effect, share a merchant account. For instance, **ProPay** (http://www.ProPay.com/), **Planet Payment** (http://www.planetpayment.com/), and **CCNow** (http://www.CCNow.com/) let you set up an account with them fairly easily—in the case of ProPay, for instance, it takes just a few minutes—and they'll process your credit cards for you. There are several problems with such systems. First, the per-transaction fees are higher than with your own merchant account, sometimes considerably higher (though, to be fair, for low-volume merchants still less than with a merchant account overall because there are no monthly statement fees and minimums). In addition, the service may hold your money for some time—Planet Payment holds six percent of your money for six months, for instance. The final problem is...finding a suitable shopping-cart system, with all the features you need, that is set up to work with one of these payment systems.

Making and Getting Payments with PayPal—PayPal *(http://www.paypal.com) is a new kind of electronic transaction processor. It allows you to make and request payments through an online interface without having to use credit cards. In effect you can e-mail money to people. A personal account is free; but a business account (which costs you a percentage of your transaction) allows you to deposit PayPal funds into a checking account daily, gives 24 hour, 7 day customer service, and so on. Yahoo! calls these kinds of services digital money; you can see more of them at* http://dir.yahoo.com/Business_and_Economy/Business_to_Business/Financial_Services/ Transaction_Clearing/Digital_Money/.

Finding Shopping-Cart Systems

Where do you begin your search for a shopping-cart system? Look for a hosting company or e-business service provider. Peter has a special report at the Top Floor Publishing site, **Shopping-Cart Software & Services Directory**, which you can find at http://www.poorrichard.com/freeinfo/special_reports.htm. This currently lists over 70 different programs and services. (Unfortunately the report is rather out of date, though Peter's threatening to update it sometime.) You might also try these Yahoo! categories:

Yahoo!-Electronic Commerce Software

http://dir.yahoo.com/Business_and_Economy/Business_to_Business/Electronic _Commerce/Software/Yahoo!-Electronic Commerce
http://www.yahoo.com/Business_and_Economy/Electronic_Commerce/

Yahoo!-Web Software Companies
http://dir.yahoo.com/Business_and_Economy/Business_to_Business/Computers/
Software/Internet/World_Wide_Web/

Simple Online Transactions

Here's a quick description of a simple order-processing system for Web sites, one that Peter has used. Peter's switched between two transaction systems: one that he used in the early days of his company, and another that his publishing company's staff now uses. Here's the basic process he originally followed, an example of a simple method that small businesses can use to process orders:

1. The shopping-cart grabs the credit-card information.
2. The information is downloaded from the Web server.
3. The information is imported into Microsoft Access.
4. The information is exported to PCAuthorize.
5. The credit-cards are processed.
6. Labels are printed.

Sell It on the Web*—The **Sell It On the Web** (http://www.SellItOnTheweb.com/) site is a good place to go if you want to learn more about setting up shopping carts. It reviews products, examines Web sites that sell products, tells you what reviewers like and don't like about them, and announces new services, and so on.*

Step 1: The Shopping Cart

Peter's publishing business originally used a shopping-cart system called **Hazel** (http://hazel.netsville.com/), a flexible system that he installed on the hosting-company's server himself. Later, he switched to the system created by his other company, the **BizBlast.com Transaction Engine** (http://www.BizBlast.com/). Both these systems save the transaction information—the person's name and shipping address, the credit-card number and expiration date, and so on—in a text file on the Web server, and then send him an e-mail message telling him an order has been taken.

Step 2: Download the Data from the Web Server

Peter transfers the order information from the Web server to his office computer. Some shopping-cart programs and services—such as BizBlast.com's system—provide a secure Web page from which sales data is downloaded.

The data files are comma-delimited text files, so he can quickly and easily import the files into a database program. This is an important feature of a shopping-cart program: the format in which the data is saved should allow for database imports. Peter believes that this is a critical feature; evidently some shopping-cart designers disagree with him.

Note that using his new system, steps 2 through 5 are not essential. Rather than following these steps, Peter's publishing-company staff can do all the processing using the online tools, and just periodically import the data into a database for record-keeping purposes.

Step 3: Import into Access

Peter uses Microsoft Access to save all his transaction data. It's not the easiest program to learn to use; but then he hasn't been able to find any other easy-to-use programs that will do everything he needs yet.

Peter has created an Access macro to process incoming orders. When he double-clicks the macro, it imports the order file that was downloaded from the shopping-cart system. Peter can then view the data in the database to make sure it looks okay—that the buyer provided all the information he needs to process the order.

Creating macros really isn't terribly hard, but if you don't know anything about Access, it may take you a while to figure it all out. Perhaps you can find someone to help you set up a database and create a macro or two. Someone who knows how to use a database program should probably be able to do everything you need in an hour, two hours maximum.

Step 4: Export to PCAuthorize

Peter created another macro to export the information into another text file, this time in the format used by PCAuthorize. PCAuthorize is the program he uses to process credit cards. Setting up an import template took ten minutes, and it allows him to import the data quickly each day.

Step 5: Process the Credit Cards

Next Peter opens PCAuthorize and imports the text file that he's just created. Then he clicks on a button, and PCAuthorize dials into the credit-card network and processes the cards. For every card that is approved, PCAuthorize prints a receipt (which is sent with the book).

(Note that by the time you read this, you may not be allowed to do this type of offline processing of credit cards—see the sidebar, earlier in this chapter. Also, Peter switched to BizBlast's system, which allows him to do online processing. The console provided allows him to view and manage the credit-card transactions. Some merchants using BizBlast's system still process offline, though.)

PCAuthorize is a great little program, and according to Peter, it's really fun to use. Peter's been working with computer programs for almost 20 years, yet this is the first program he's ever worked with that actually takes money from someone else's bank account and moves it into his! By the way, for those of you who don't process credit cards and are wondering what proportion are approved, Peter's found that the vast majority go through. He's experienced around a 1 percent failure rate. Sometimes the problem is an incorrectly entered expiration date, or perhaps the buyer didn't realize the card was over limit. If he e-mails the buyers when there's a problem, a number of them will provide new information—a different expiration date or another card number. There's around a 50 percent chance that a bad order will eventually go through. Your mileage may vary—fraud and failure rates vary between different types of businesses, with computer-book publishing being a relatively safe business.

Step 6: Print Labels

For every order that goes through, Peter needs a mailing label. This is where it gets just a little clunky. The version of Access Peter was using has a bug that prevents it from printing mailing labels. So instead, he creates a report. (Actually, the macro that exports the data to the PC Authorize text file creates this report at the same time.) Then he clicks on a button at the top of the report, and the report is opened in Word for Windows. He then runs a macro in Word that cleans up the formatting in the report, removing tabs from it. (With the BizBlast system that he switched to, Peter's staff can open a browser window displaying a shipping label and print it directly.)

Next, he opens his LabelWriter program. LabelWriter is a little label printer connected to the computer's serial port. He selects the first mailing address in

Word for Windows and copies it to the Clipboard and then clicks a button in LabelWriter and the content of the Clipboard is pasted into a mailing label and printed. And that's it. The sold items can be shipped.

FULFILLMENT SERVICES

So how do you ship? If you don't ship products already, it can be quite a hassle setting up to do so, and processing a few orders each day. If you automate it as much as possible, you may find that it's not so hard; but perhaps you'd rather pay someone to do it for you.

That's where fulfillment companies come into the picture. These companies will ship products for you. They may even take the orders for you. Peter had used a fulfillment company called **Bookmasters** (http://www.bookmasters.com/) in the past, though now Top Floor Publishing handles fulfillment internally. As the name implies, Bookmasters ship mainly books, but will ship almost any small product. Peter had Bookmasters take all his phone orders—it has its own toll-free lines—but still shipped his own Web orders. Occasionally—such as when he was traveling—he'd process Web orders on his computer or laptop and then send the shipping addresses to Bookmasters so that they could ship the products for him.

Internet Fulfillment Companies—Watch for new fulfillment companies coming on the scene specifically directed at helping Web businesses ship products, companies such as *TrueSynergies* (http://truesynergies.com/).

You can find fulfillment companies in a variety of ways. Check your local Yellow Pages, for instance, or use an online system such as **Yahoo!'s Yellow Pages** (http://yp.yahoo.com/) or **US West Dex** (http://www.uswestdex.com/). Perhaps you don't need a fulfillment service in a particular area. Perhaps, for example, you're with a company outside North America looking for a fulfillment company to ship your products for you within North America. In that case, you should check **Yahoo!'s Fulfillment Services** page at http://dir.yahoo.com/ Business_and_Economy/Business_to_Business/Marketing_and_Advertising/Fulfillment_ Services/. Also, if you search for the word *fulfillment* at Yahoo!, you'll find that there are other categories, such as lists of fulfillment services in Canada and Great Britain. Another way to search for fulfillment houses in Great Britain—and soon, perhaps, in North America—is through **Yell.com** (http://www.yell.com/).

When you are looking for a fulfillment service, these are the things to consider:

- Does the service have staff who can take orders by phone 24 hours a day, or does it only ship products to lists of people that you send to it? (Many fulfillment companies ship, but do not process orders.)

- Will the service ship orders you send to it if you process the payment first?
- Does the service have its own toll-free lines, or do you have to provide your own line?
- Do you have to provide your own credit-card merchant account, or will the service process credit cards for you?
- Can it accept orders by fax and mail?
- Can you e-mail orders to the service?
- What are the service's charges? Make sure you understand every little charge, as you'll probably be charged for every touch (that is, every little process involved in taking the order and shipping the product).

Unfortunately fulfillment is often extremely expensive, at least to a small business. You may find it's more cost effective to do it yourself, or pay a part-timer to come in for an hour or so a day to do it for you.

WEB DESIGN—IT'S SOFTWARE, NOT GRAPHIC DESIGN

How do you go about designing a Web site? We believe you should remember that a Web site is a piece of software. Few site owners seem to understand this, and even fewer Web designers do. Web design has become the domain of the graphic designer, which is a big mistake. Consequently there are many thousands of great looking Web sites that load slowly and are difficult to navigate.

A Web site is a piece of software. It has to *do something*. Unlike a piece of graphic design—a billboard or magazine ad, for instance—a Web site is interactive. People click links and buttons to make the site actually do some-thing; so the primary concern should be user-interface design. Does the Web site actually work properly? Does it achieve its aims? (By the way, a good place to visit to learn more about user-interface design, and in particular learn about its application to Web design, is the **User Interface Engineering** Web site: http://www.uie.com/. **Jakob Nielsen** also has a lot of information on user interface design and site usability at his Web site: http://www.useit.com/. Finally, a Web site that deals almost exclusively with a customer's experience on a Web site and what's right (or wrong!) about it is available at **Good Experience**, http://www.goodexperience.com/.)

Long Pages or Short?—*Here's an example of the sort of thing you'll find at the User Interface Engineering site. You may have heard that it's better to create lots of short Web pages, rather than make users scroll through long pages. This is one of those graphic-design myths. User Interface Engineering studied this issue and discovered that in fact users don't mind scrolling, and that, more importantly, long pages often work better. People find it easier to navigate around the site and find what they need.*

Once you have a Web site that *works*, you can make it look good. You shouldn't work the other way around.

Web design is a big subject, one that we have no space for here. However, before we move on, we'd like to point out another important consideration. Your Web site must serve your visitors, but it must also serve *you*. There's a balance to be found here. If your Web site doesn't serve your visitors well, you won't have any visitors (or, at least, few repeat visitors). However, what's the point in having a Web site if it doesn't serve you, too?

You must find a way to make the site easy to move around in for your visitors, and provide the information and services that they need. At the same time, you have to make sure that you get something out of it—for instance, that visitors see the sales blurbs that you want them to see, that they provide you with the information you need, and so on. Again, a Web site is not simply graphic design; it's more complicated than that. In some cases, you may have to make compromises. Sometimes the site won't be as attractive as it could be because you want to make it easier to use in some way; or perhaps a process is not as simple as it could be because you want to make sure the visitor passes through an area of the site. For instance, Peter often mentions his special reports in mailing-list discussion groups or his newsletter. He could provide a link directly to the report he's talking about, but instead he points people to the **Poor Richard's Special Reports** page at his Web site (http://www.poorrichard.com/freeinfo/special_reports.htm). It's still easy for the visitors to find the report for which they're looking; but Peter has made sure that they see a list of other reports, and see links back into the main Poor Richard's site, where they can find more information about the book...and, Peter hopes, buy the book.

CHAPTER FOUR

Finding Your Targets

In Chapter 1, *What Are You Promoting and Who are You Targeting*, we took a look at some essential questions to consider before starting your promotion or marketing campaign and then left you to think over those ideas while we explained what you needed before you got started.

We hope you did take some time to think over those ideas because in this chapter we're going to show you how to find your targets by describing research resources that will help your promotional campaign. These promotional resources will give you an idea of the newspapers, periodicals, and other media outlets available that might have an interest in your product or service.

When you see how many are available—and there are thousands upon thousands—you might be a little intimidated. Don't be. Consider one of the focuses you decided on in Chapter 1, and start from there. Don't try to drink the river in one gulp.

If you have plenty of time, you might want to bypass the focuses and instead go methodically through a checklist that contains information specific and helpful to your Web site. You'll need a checklist, a few tips for using search sites, and possibly some search-site software. We'll be looking at ways to find information related to your promotional campaign in this chapter.

PLANNING YOUR SEARCH

When searching for sites that might be interested in you and your product or service, you can break down the sites for which you search by category. You want to keep your eye out for certain kinds of sites that can help you during your quest for online promotion. (We'll be more specific about how you can contact and use these sites as we continue through the book.)

Specialty indexes—These sites index sites like yours. You want to both pursue links in these indexes and investigate the sites that they index as possible promotional partners. (We'll discuss partnerships in detail in the second part of this book.)

85

Competitors' sites—What are your competitors doing online? Who are they linking to? Who's linking to them? If you know what your competitors are up to, you may get a few good ideas or be able to head them off at the pass in some way...and people linking to your competitors may want to link to you, too.

Industry update sites—These may be formal publications, online newsletters, or simply Web pages that are updated a couple of times a week, but you want to keep an eye out for sites that keep their visitors informed about your industry. For one thing, you'll pick up valuable hints about new Web sites that pertain to your industry. For another thing, you'll have a nice list of media to alert when you offer new services on your site or launch a site overhaul.

Potential partner sites—These sites cover a broad range of possibilities: sites with whom you could swap banner ads, sites whose interests dovetail with yours, sites that could share promotional ideas with you—in other words, sites that don't directly compete with yours but in some way could partner with you for mutual benefit.

In this chapter we're going to cover how you can find media and promotional resources; but since we can't give you exhaustive lists of every type of site you want to find, we're going to kick off this chapter with some tricks for finding Web sites using search sites.

FINDING THE SITES YOU NEED: SOME HINTS

This book can't give you an exhaustive tutorial in Internet research. For that, you might want to check out Tara's online site and newsletter **ResearchBuzz** at http://www.researchbuzz.com/. (She covers developments in the new search engine universe and new and interesting online collections of information.) However, we can give you a few hints that'll make your search easier.

You may know about Boolean searching: using the AND, OR, NOT, and other operators to make very specific queries. For instance, you could search for *rabbits OR hares* to find pages related to either rabbits or hares; or *rabbits AND NOT hares* to find pages related to rabbits but only if those pages are not related to hares; or *rabbits AND hares* to find only pages that are related to both rabbits and hares. Most search systems allow you to use some kind of Boolean logic, but you have to check each one to see how it works. For example, AltaVista doesn't understand *rabbits NOT hares*, while other systems might; in the case of AltaVista this would have to be entered as *rabbits AND NOT hares*.

Perhaps you've used these Boolean operators while searching; but you might not have heard of specialty syntaxes, which allow you to do even more specialized searching.

Special Search Syntax

Many search sites have their own special, advanced search syntaxes—special ways to put together search terms and keywords to create a highly targeted search. You can find information about advanced syntax in a search site's documentation, but as an example we'll look at the special keywords offered by **AltaVista** (http://www.altavista.com/). AltaVista has a variety of keywords that help you do some "fancy" searches, as AltaVista calls them. There's the *anchor:* keyword, *applet:*, *image:*, *title:*, and so on. Let's see how some of these work.

Bugs in AltaVista—*Note that there are, at the time of writing at least, software bugs in AltaVista; a search that find one set of results one time, and one set of results another time. Stay aware of two things: First, Internet research is not an exact science, and secondly, Internet search-engine indexes are changing all the time, just as the Web is changing. Don't expect your search results to stay the same from day to day; there's just too much going on. You can make sure AltaVista does a clean search by going back to the first page each time. Click the AltaVista logo at the top of the page to go back to AltaVista's home page.*

DOMAIN:

The *domain:* keyword is one of Tara's favorites. Adding *+domain:com* to a query ensures that your results will come from a domain that ends with .com, like http://www.poorrichard.com/ or http://www.amazon.com/. That is, AltaVista will only show you pages from .com domains. If you use *-domain:com* instead, AltaVista will only show you pages from domains other than .com domains. This works for any domain, from the ones that are very common (.com, .org, .net, and .edu) to the less common or even downright obscure (.gov, .mil, and country codes like .jp, .us, and .fi). Try it for yourself. If you search for *yak hunting australia*, AltaVista will find literally millions of pages—almost four million when we checked; but if you search for *yak hunting australia +domain:nu* (which means "only find pages from the .nu domain"), you'll get only a relative handful (2,514 when we tried). If you go even further and put a + in front of all the query words (+ works like a Boolean AND, and says to AltaVista, "all these results must be in the search query") you'll get just one page.

When you're looking for sites, you can narrow down your search results by specifying the kind of domain for which you're searching. If you need academic resources, you can use *+domain:edu* to ensure your results are mostly aca-demically oriented. If you want only commercial results, such as online stores, you can use *–domain.edu –domain.org* to make sure you have more commercially oriented results; but remember that such a search strategy won't work perfectly because there are so many different domain suffixes—net, com, org, gov, all the country codes, and Web-site owners don't always pick the type of domain one might expect.

You Can't Judge a Site by Its Country Code—*You can't always determine where a site is by its country code. As we noted earlier in the book, you can register your site for one of many different country codes. Don't assume that just because a site's domain is .to that it's in Tonga or is run by a person from Tonga.*

HOST:

The *host:* keyword allows you to narrow your search to a specific host, or Web site, on the Internet, or avoid finding pages on a particular host. For example, *poorrichard.com* refers to a particular host computer, so if you added *–host:poorrichard.com* to your search query, you would eliminate all the Web pages that are hosted on poorrichard.com. If you added *+host:poorrichard.com*, you would be specifying that only pages hosted on *poorrichard.com* should be included in your search results. This strategy works well when you're searching for information in a particular area; for example, if you were looking for information at a particular college, you could search by specifying its host. Specifying the host is also useful when searching for links to a particular Web site. You can tell AltaVista to show you links to the site but to omit internal links—links from other Web pages within that site.

Be Careful How You Use the Host—*Some sites have subdomains—other ways their site are represented besides www. For example, the* **Library of Congress** *has www.loc.gov, and thomas.loc.gov. These are two very different Web sites. If you search AltaVista and include +host:loc.gov, AltaVista will search all its indexed pages from the loc.gov domain. However, if you include +thomas.loc.gov, AltaVista will search only its indexed pages from the thomas.loc.gov part of AltaVista.*

TITLE:

The *title:* keyword allows you to search *only* the titles of pages for particular keywords. This comes in handy when you're looking for a particular type of resource but the resource has a common keyword. For example, say you were looking for sites pertaining to starfish. If you did a search for starfish in AltaVista, you'd find more than 50,000 results (at the time of writing, at least...these numbers will change, of course). However, if you searched for *starfish* in the title of a Web page (*title:starfish*) you'd find just over 2,500 results. If you narrowed those results down to more academic sites by using the query *+title:starfish +domain:edu*, you'd find only 28 Web pages.

That brings us to another point. You can mix and match these keywords. They don't exist in a vacuum. You can use different ones and add Boolean query modifiers. The Internet has millions and millions of Web pages; use every resource at your disposal to narrow down the number of Web pages you have to search.

AltaVista has these other important keywords:

anchor:*text*—Finds pages with the specified text in a link (links are known to the more geeky of us as anchors). This keyword searches for the link text that appears on the page, not the URL specified by the link.

applet:*name*—Finds pages containing a particular Java applet.

image:*filename*—Finds pages containing a particular image name.

link:*URLtext*—Finds pages with links that contain specified text; unlike the *anchor:* keyword, this one actually looks at the URL specified by the link.

text:*text*—Limits the search to the actual text, ignoring the image tags and links.

url:*text*—Finds pages with a particular word or phrase in the pages' URLs.

You can find more information about these keywords at **AltaVista** http://doc.altavista.com/adv_search/ast_ma_index.shtml.

***Don't Use AltaVista Alone**—Just because we're using AltaVista in these examples doesn't mean you shouldn't explore other search sites and the special syntaxes they have to offer.* **Google** *(*http://www.google.com/*) offers many different types of specialty searching. Be sure to go through the help files of each search engine so you can get an idea of how to use it to its fullest.*

Natural-Language Searching

Maybe you can't be bothered to learn all these keywords. Maybe Boolean searching confuses you. In that case, you should try a newer search technology that's slowly getting better: natural-language searching.

Natural-language searching is just that—stating what you want in English (or, in some cases, a number of other languages—AltaVista claims to be able to work with a couple of dozen) and have the search site get results for you. You can visit **Ask Jeeves** at http://www.askjeeves.com/ or **Subjex** at http://www.subjex.com/ if you want to see search sites that use only natural-language searching, but you can also visit AltaVista and use natural-language searching on that system, too.

Formulating questions when using natural-language searching is an evolving art. You have to make the question simple enough to understand, but thorough enough to get what you want. For example the search string, *Where can I find puppets?* is probably not as good a query as it could be. You haven't specified what kind of puppets you want. The query *Where can I find hand puppets?* may be a better query. Notice that you don't have to specify that you want sites about hand puppets; asking *Where can I find sites about hand puppets* might confuse the search sites. Keep it simple, simple, simple. Figure 4.1 shows you what the Ask Jeeves site looks like. As you can see, it looks a lot like a regular search engine interface.

If you don't get the information you need with the first search, try rephrasing the query. The query *A giraffe is how tall?* won't work well. Rephrased as, *How tall is a giraffe?* the query works much better.

The Right Tool for the Right Occasion—*If you're searching for really general topics, like cancer, use a topic index like Yahoo first. You'll save a lot of time.*

If you're used to going to a search site and typing in only one or two search terms, it's time for an attitude adjustment. It's possible, using Boolean operators, special keywords, natural-language searching, and so on, to perform carefully targeted searches, and to find exactly what you're looking for, and don't forget to check the search engine's help files.

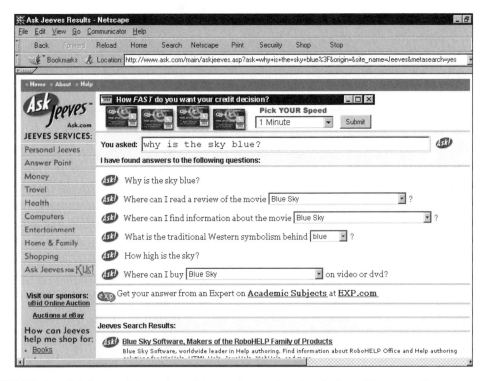

FIGURE 4.1: Ask Jeeves lets you make search queries simply by asking questions.

META-SEARCH ENGINES ONLINE

In this chapter and other parts of the book, we talk about specific search sites—**AltaVista, HotBot, Yahoo!**, and so on. Wouldn't it be great if instead of visiting each of these sites individually, you could search them all at once?

Well, you can. Sites that can help you search several sites at one time are called *meta-search engines*. You can use meta-search engines online, or you can get software packages that offer meta-search features.

Meta-search engines gather the results of several search sites into one big group of results. The more advanced meta-search engines even remove the duplicate results. Meta-search engines can come in handy, since there's less overlap between search sites than you might think. Different search sites will return very different search results, so you probably need to search several of them; you can get a huge list of results all in one place.

The problem with meta-search engines is that when you use one, you get an even larger pool of results from which you can draw information. It's imperative that when you use meta-search engines, you use as specific a query as possible. Otherwise you're going to be drowned in results. You can choose from several search engines, including the following.

INFERENCE FIND

http://www.infind.com/

Inference Find is a fast meta-search. It searches WebCrawler, Yahoo!, Lycos, AltaVista, InfoSeek, and Excite. While Inference Find admits that sometimes Boolean searches don't work properly with its meta-search engine, it's still worth a look. Tara finds that it's one of the fastest meta-search engines she's used, and she usually gets a result from all the search sites that Inference Find queries. (On some meta-search engines, some of the individual search sites time out before returning results.) Inference Find also doesn't overwhelm you with results, so you can use it for general queries without of the risk of drowning in results. (If you do want to use really general searches, though, stick with a topic index like Yahoo! or LookSmart.)

Ixquick

http://www.ixquick.com/

Ixquick meta-searches news, pictures, MP3 directories, and the Web. The interesting thing about Ixquick is that it awards one star for each search engine that places a site in its top ten, so you get relevance-upon-relevance ranking. Ixquick is smart enough to examine your query and send it to certain search engines based on the Boolean modifiers you included, so your query may not use all of the dozen-odd search engines available for general searches.

METAEUREKA

http://www.metaeureka.com/

METAEUREKA has an attitude. It promises no graphics on its pages, no news, and no weather reports. ("...if we need one we usually take a look out of the window.") It searches AltaVista, Google, Northern Light, Alltheweb, and Yahoo, and provides 10–20 results per search engine. All results are dumped on one big page.

Each search result offers the name of the page, the summary (though you can skip that if you like), and what search engines the result appeared on; but the neat thing is the Site Info link. Click that link (with JavaScript activated) and a little window pops up. That window gives you a bevy of information without even going to the site. Say you are doing a search on the Idaho State Fair, but you want information on the upcoming Idaho State Fair, not state fairs of the past, so it is important to you to find a page that's been updated recently. You'd do a search for *Idaho State Fair* and pick a likely candidate from the list of results, but instead of going straight to the page, you'd click *Site Info*. A window would pop up giving you the site's server information, the date on the server, the LAST TIME THE PAGE WAS UPDATED (very important!), and a variety of other information including (if available) title, author, keywords, and description.

***404 Errors and You**—Do 404 (File Not Found) errors drive you crazy when you search the Web? The search engine Google caches Web pages. Even if the page for which you're searching isn't available anymore, if it shows up in your search results you can look at it in the Google cache.*

Several other meta-search engines are available online, including

Dogpile
http://www.dogpile.com/

Profusion
http://www.profusion.com/

Metor
http://www.metor.com/

Mamma
http://www.mamma.com/

byteSearch
http://www.bytesearch.com/

While the meta-search engines are good, sometimes you might find yourself needing something with a little more flexibility—something that resides on your own hard drive, perhaps.

SEARCH SOFTWARE

Search software—programs running on your own computer—can both conduct meta-searches and allow you to build your own databases of searches and results. They can give you a head start on your research, especially when you're doing extremely complicated or esoteric searches. You enter a search term, click a button, and off goes the program, searching the Web for whatever you've specified. It checks a set of search sites—you'll probably be able to add new ones to the list—and retrieves a list of hits. Then the magic begins.

Up to this point, you see, you've simply searched the sites and gotten a list of links back in return. You can do that for yourself—not as quickly as the search program, but reasonably quickly nonetheless. What really takes a long time, though, is checking all of those links. If you find 10,000 links that might refer to something interesting, how do you check them all? There's no way you can; it's just too big of a job; but you can let the search program run overnight and do it for you.

***Mini-Search Engines**—Many of the major search sites offer mini versions of their search technology for download. These are generally not meta-search utilities, however.*

Come back in the morning and what do you find? Something like the window shown in Figure 4.2. This is a screenshot from Copernic, one of these programs. With Copernic, you can do a search and then refine the search still further—and quickly, too, considering that you can go through the pages that have been downloaded your computer. Also, you can search several different categories—including shopping, news, and books—so you can narrow down where you search.

Another nice feature of these programs is that you can use them to repeat searches periodically to find new things that have appeared. Search once or twice a month, and you may be able to keep up with what's going on on the Web.

You can choose from a number of different meta-search–software packages. Here are a couple that Tara likes:

BULLSEYE PRO

http://www.intelliseek.com/

BullsEye Pro can search over 800 search sites and can refine searches, remove redundant results, and generally whittle down the huge ocean of search results

FIGURE 4.2: Copernic is like a search engine on steroids.

to a small list. One of the benefits of BullsEye, indeed with most software packages, is that you can store a particular type of search and do it over and over again. BullsEye also allows you to monitor search sites for changes—a handy feature if you tend to do the same type of research often.

Monitoring Sites for Changes—*If you want to monitor sites for changes, or search engines for new materials that have been added to them, you have several different options. Check out* **Mind-It** *at* http://www.netmind.com/, **Spyonit** *at* http://www.spyonit.com/, *or* **Tracerlock** *at* http://www.trackerlock.com/.

COPERNIC

http://www.copernic.com/

Copernic allows you to search over 600 search engines that are also categorized like BullsEye. Copernic has three levels of BullsEye with different prices: the first level is free, the second level costs $39.95, and the third level is $79.95. Each version has different levels of searchability and little bells and whistles.

Is More Better?—*Sometimes, if you're trying to get an exhaustive overview of what's actually on the Internet, more is better. However, most of the time it isn't. The fact that you get every last scrap of information on the Internet is not as important as getting the most use out of what you* do *have.*

There are many other search programs out there:

Hurricane WebSearch (Windows)
http://www.gatecomm.com/websearch/

Mata Hari (Windows 95/98/NT)
http://thewebtools.com/

BeeLine
http://www.transcomsoft.com/beeline/

WebBandit (Windows 95/98/NT)
http://www.1billionsites.com/webbandit.htm

WebSeeker (Windows 95/98/NT)
http://www.bluesquirrel.com/

Do you have to use a meta-search engine or search software when researching Web sites relevant to your promotional effort? Not really; the better you know how to use the search sites, the less you'll need to use the meta-search engines and software. Tara, who spends a great deal of her time doing online research, actually uses meta-searching very little. She works instead on creating as focused a query as possible and then makes the most of the results she gets. Most of the time, that focus is sufficient to do a good job on her research work. Of course, when you get into esoteric research, you might find that using a meta-search tool is the only way you can get more than a dozen results. For example, this might be the case if you are working for a nonprofit organization that's trying to educate the public on a rare childhood illness that has little exposure on the Web. These specialized tools can also be handy in cases where you have a lot of time available to get into a very extensive and comprehensive promotional campaign, or when you simply have to know *everything* about a particular subject; but in most situations one search site at a time will probably be enough.

PROMOTIONAL RESOURCES

Don't be daunted by the idea of doing all this searching. We know you want to get a jump start on your online promotional activities, and we want to help by getting you started with your research activities. There are some general site types that almost all of you will want to take a look at.

Let's start with promotional resources—Web sites that will help you track down places to promote your products and services. It used to be that if you wanted lists of media, you had to go to the library. That was, however, B.I. (Before Internet.) Nowadays all you have to do is get online and check into these resources. Let's take a look at various resources available to you.

All Types of Media

While many specialty indexes concentrate on one type of media or another, the following indexes are broad enough to encompass all media.

NEWS365

http://www.news365.com/

News365 offers listings of newspapers, magazines, and TV stations—over 10,000 media listings. The listings are broken down by industry, so if you're looking for a vertical market publication this is a good place to start. You can also get media listed by American state or by country, from Albania to Iceland to Zimbabwe.

AJR NEWSLINK

http://ajr.newslink.org/

AJR NewsLink is a service of the American Journalism Review and has been one of the great online reference sites for years now. It features listings of newspapers, magazines, broadcasters (television and radio), and news services worldwide—over18,000 links total. Its newspapers are broken down both by geographic location and by type (dailies, nondailies, alternative, etc.). It also has an excellent collection of college newspapers.

NEWSDIRECTORY.COM

http://www.newsd.com/

NewsDirectory.com (formerly Ecola) lists both newspapers and magazines. It lists over 17,000 categorized information links, with a *what's new* section so you can see what's been added lately. It's another one of the old-timer Internet-reference sites, having been around since 1995. (Within the last year it was bought by Infonautics, the same people who do the Electric Library.) It lists its magazines by type and has a wide variety of industry/vertical-market publications. American magazines are listed first, followed by regional magazines listed by region, and international magazines and their country of origin. Newspapers are listed by continent and country of origin, with business newspapers having their own section broken down geographically.

GEBBIE PRESS

http://www.gebbieinc.com/

Gebbie is specifically designed for promotions people and combines a bevy of free resources with publishable resources to make your work easier. This site lists radio and TV stations, daily newspapers, weekly newspapers, and online magazines. Its more than 20,000 listings are broken up by state (they seem to be mostly U.S. listings) and provide both links to the appropriate Web sites and e-mail addresses when available. In the case of radio listings, programming format is provided. In the case of TV, the network is provided. Magazines are listed by category. This site has a very simple design, so if you have a slow Internet connection or a simple browser, start with this site (see Figure 4.3). If you really like the information here, you can also get the information in print or on disk.

NEWO NEWS

http://newo.com/

NeWo provides not only listings of newspapers and other media outlets, but also information aggregates like InfoJunkie and NewsIndex.com. Sites are listed by geographical area and broken down from country to state or region as appropriate. NeWo's strength lies in its simple interface and the fact that it's easy to tell when listings were last updated. (You don't want to get stuck with a stale listing.) NeWo is decidedly not American-centric; it's a good choice if you're looking for media all over the world.

FIGURE 4.3: Gebbie Press breaks out media by state. Click the state abbreviation for a media list.

KIDON MEDIA LINK

http://www.kidon.com/media-link/index.shtml

Kidon is another good choice if you're looking for media from all over the world. Its listings are broken down by country. Once you've selected a country, you get the name of the media outlet, the language it's in, frequency (this isn't listed all the time), and occasionally an icon representing special features on the site, like streaming media or Adobe PDF availability.

MEDIAINFO LINKS

http://www.mediainfo.com/emedia/

MediaINFO is a service of *Editor & Publisher* and includes links to journalism-related associations, city guides, magazines, newspapers, radio, syndicates and news services, and television. The City Guides are a good browse if you run a retail establishment that needs to focus its promotional efforts in a certain area. The magazine section especially has a lot of listings not found on most sites. It's broken down geographically, so it's another good site to consult if you're focusing on promotion within a certain area.

If you want to get an idea of the range of targets you can have for your promotion campaign, take some time to explore the previous sites. If you want to concentrate on newspapers, magazines, or another specific media, check one of the following listings.

Newspapers

There are thousands of newspapers online from all over the world. The following directories will give you a head start on finding them.

NEWSPAPERLINKS.COM

http://www.newspaperlinks.com/

Hosted by the Newspaper Association of America, NewspaperLinks.com lists only American newspapers. It has an easy-to-use interface that enables you to search for a newspaper by city name or paper name or list newspapers by state. NewspaperLinks.com also provides links to special sections, like election coverage.

COLLEGE NEWSPAPERS ONLINE

http://www.cpnet.com/

CPNet is a lot more than a list of links to college newspapers. It has a list of over 400 college newspapers in its database, which you can search by school name, newspaper name, or city. (It also has several resource listings and an excellent set of links if your product or service is aimed at college students.) You can also get a list of college newspapers at http://beacon-www.asa.utk.edu/resources/papers.html.

Magazines

Just like newspapers, there are magazines available online from all over the world. These directories will give you pointers both to magazines online and newsletters and magazines available, in paper, offline.

PUBLIST

http://www.publist.com/

If you're looking for periodicals appropriate to your promotional campaigns, start here. You can find over 150,000 periodicals in this database, encompassing both online and offline publications. You can search by title, keyword, publisher, or ISSN. It lists both American and international publications. The listings provide a wealth of information, including frequency, publisher's mailing address, phone number, advertising rates, and circulation. (Different publications supply different amounts of information.) Publist also has a list of upcoming publications (updated monthly) that might give you the jump on coverage in publications that haven't been publishing long.

Radio Stations

Radio stations on the Web are representative of offline stations and stations that are wholly online (called *streaming radio* or *streaming media* stations). For purposes of PR, you probably want to stick to offline stations, though there are some popular online-only stations.

RADIODIRECTORY

http://www.radiodirectory.com/Stations/

RadioDirectory lists radio stations by geographic location (and even includes a listing of radio stations that exist solely on the Internet—304 at the time of writing). They're grouped by continent (Africa, North America, and etc.) and then grouped by country and state. There's also a free, monthly newsletter available, so you can keep up with changes to the listings.

'Zines and Newsletters

A 'zine used to be a kind of fringe publication that was published by smaller organizations than publishers of large, slick magazines. (The term *'zine* is commonly used on the Internet to mean any kind of e-mail publication. The term *e-mail newsletter* is also widely used.) With the advent of the Internet, however, 'zines and e-mail newsletters have begun to come in all shapes and sizes, from one person's essays and observations about life (with a readership of about 20) to a biweekly newsletter that's administered by ten people and has a circulation of hundreds of thousands.

Many people shrug off the possibility of promoting to 'zines, but it's wrong to paint them all with so broad a brush. Some of them aren't particularly good; some of them are absolutely fantastic, and most of them fall somewhere in between. There are a number of very influential 'zines, and they can be a great place to get mentioned. When Peter's **Poor Richard** Web site (http://PoorRichard. com/) was mentioned in **Lockergnome** (http://www.lockergnome.com/), for instance, he received thousands of visits to his Web site, a couple of thousand new subscribers to his own e-mail newsletter, a couple of dozen book orders on the Web site, and more orders through bookstores. Lockergnome has around 180,000 subscribers, and despite the fact that Internet users often feel overwhelmed by the quantity of e-mail they receive, many of Lockergnome's readers really do pay attention to what the newsletter recommends.

Unlike large-circulation magazines, there isn't a certain level of quality you can assume with a 'zine. On the other hand, 'zine editors can often devote more time to listening to your pitch, tend to have loyal readers and can give you valuable feedback on the way you're approaching people, and they're not nearly as intimidating as calling up *Business Week*.

Tara's favorite resource for e-mail publications is **John Labovitz's e-zine list** at http://www.meer.net/~johnl/e-zine-list/. At the time of writing, this list listed over 4,000 'zines and newsletters. They run the gamut from the original fringe publications to daily newsletters put out by large computing companies. Unfortunately the list is no longer being updated though it's still available on the Web.

Nowadays many free e-mail list services are used to create weekly newsletters, and you can search for the newsletters at two of the major services, **Topica** (see Figure 4.4) at http://www.topica.com/ and **Egroups** at http://www.egroups.com/. The nice thing about finding newsletters through these outlets is that you can get a subscriber count, and if archives are available, you can browse through them to see if the newsletter has ever covered your type of product or service before.

There are scores of other places to find 'zines and newsletters, including a number of detailed directories that are for sale. Note that some of the directories listing mailing-list discussion groups also include newsletters. Here are a few sites worth checking:

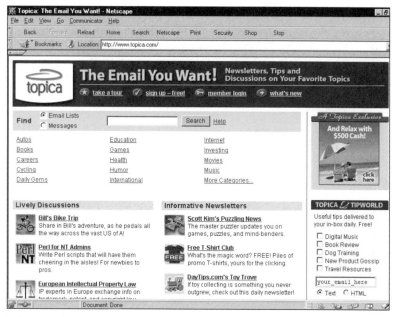

FIGURE 4.4: By searching Topica, you can find a variety of newsletters, from small to huge.

Liszt
http://www.liszt.com/

Publicly Accessible Mailing Lists
http://www.paml.net/

A1 Ezine Directory
http://www.a1co.com/freeindex.html

ARL (Association of Research Libraries) Directory of Electronic Journals, Newsletters and Academic Discussion Lists
http://arl.cni.org/scomm/edir/

Electronic Journal Access
http://www.coalliance.org/ejournal/

Low Bandwidth—This site incorporates the data from Todd Kuiper's E-mail-zines list, a popular list that was closed recently.
http://www.disobey.com/low/

InfoJump
http://www.infojump.com/

The E-ZineZ
http://www.e-zinez.com/

NewJour—A large directory of newsletters (over 9,000)
http://gort.ucsd.edu/newjour/

This should keep you busy for a while; but if you need more, see Peter's free *Places to Register Your E-mail Newsletter* report, which lists literally scores of places to find more information. You can find this report, along with various others, at http://www.poorrichard.com/freeinfo/special_reports.htm.

Most directories provide some kind of background information, so you can figure out what a 'zine or newsletter is about. Before you approach one about advertising or promotion, read a few back issues to get an idea of what it's about and what it offers, and if you do want to advertise, make sure there's some way you can get a circulation statement.

When you first begin to look at all these resources, the sheer number of periodicals available online might overwhelm you. That's why it's important to divide the people who might be interested in your product or service into subgroups. That way you can focus on one group at a time. Take the educational toy example we used in Chapter 1, *What Are You Promoting and Who Are You Targeting*. You could focus on promoting to parents and teachers for three months, and then move on to work with grandparents and child-development. If you rotate through different subgroups, you'll

- Keep your approach fresh.
- Generate new ideas for promoting your product or service.
- Keep yourself from saturating a particular subgroup.

Instead of trying to gather all the contact information together at once, do a little at a time. Surf Web pages for 20 or 30 minutes at a time, as much as you can stand. (You'll be able to do more over time.) If you try to sit down and do too much at one time, you'll find yourself getting distracted, drifting over to the sports pages, checking out RealAudio, and not getting any work done.

Once you have your targets together, you're ready to think about promotion; but before you can really promote effectively, you need to examine your Web site. Is it ready for prime time? Is everything together? Check out the next chapter for information on how to get your Web site in good shape for the search sites.

PART II
WEB SITE
REGISTRATIONS

CHAPTER FIVE

Web Site Checkup: Preparing for Indexing

How long have you had your Web site? Do you have tons of content, millions of guests, and the presidents of huge Internet companies calling you for advice? Well, it doesn't matter; however happy you are with your site, it probably needs tuning up for the search engines. Before you get started doing a big promotional push, you need to examine your site carefully, to make sure it's ready to be indexed.

GET YOUR OWN DOMAIN NAME

A quick word of warning: If you don't have your own domain name, you'll find it harder to register at some search sites, in particular at Yahoo!. For instance, if you have the http://members.aol.com/~rocketry/ URL, you'll find it much harder to register in Yahoo! (which is, after all, one of the most important search sites out there—perhaps *the most* important) than if you were using, say, the following URL: http://Rocketry.com/.

Peter's heard many people complain about this, as if somehow it isn't fair; but look at it from Yahoo!'s point of view. Yahoo! needs a useful directory of Web sites, yet a major problem is that Web sites come and go quickly, so it has to reduce the link attrition rate. It can do that by avoiding sites that are likely to disappear. If you have a URL that clearly states "this is hosted at my ISP...who knows where it'll be next month," Yahoo! is not interested in you. If you have your own domain name, though, you've gone to some trouble to set up the site, so you're less likely to close it down—and even if you move it, you'll be able to take the domain name with you. So think seriously about getting your own domain name!

IS WHAT YOU HAVE WORTH PROMOTING?

Before we get started, we're making some assumptions about your site. We have to assume that what you have really is worth promoting. As we've discussed already, your site has to be worth visiting. Perhaps you can get listed in the search engines—but if your site isn't worth visiting, you'll never get someone to visit you more than once, and you won't get people to recommend your site to others. There's also another reason: in some cases you won't even get listed at some important search sites (in particular Yahoo!) because some search sites evaluate sites before they add them to their directories. Let's consider, then, what makes a good site.

It's More Than One Page

There are a lot of rather sparse Web sites out in cyberspace. It may be possible to create a site that is useful to someone and yet not take up more than one page or so...but it's unlikely. Make sure you have enough information at your site to make it worth visiting. Here's a good rule of thumb: the less unusual your topic, the more content you need. If you've devoted your site to the southeastern aerosol industry, ten information-packed pages could be quite a draw for your prospects. On the other hand, if you're putting up yet another site devoted to small businesses, you're going to need a lot of content—a lot of very good content, considering the competition—to stand out from the pack.

It's More Than Simply a Brochure and an Order Form

Let us reemphasize something we pointed out in Chapter 1, *What Are You Promoting and Who Are You Targeting*. No one cares about your product or service as much as you do. Therefore, it's silly to think you can attract visitors to your Web site with nothing but the electronic equivalent of a brochure and an order form. That might work if you've discovered a foolproof, exercise-free diet or a cure for the common cold—maybe; but for most other products you're going to have to establish your expertise, build credibility, and define to your prospects why they need to buy whatever you're selling—and a brochure and an order form isn't gonna do it.

It's Been Updated Sometime in the Recent Past

Internet time isn't like real time. Time moves a lot faster on the Internet. A week moves like a month. Three months move almost like a year, and a year—wow, you wouldn't believe how a year moves. That means that you probably can't update your site once every three months and think you're keeping up with Internet time.

So how often *should* you update your site? Well, we (the authors) don't completely agree on this point. Tara believes that you should be continually updating your Web site—daily if possible. (Was that the sound of a few of you hitting the floor?) If you can't manage daily, she believes, you should update your site weekly, and if you can't manage weekly, you should definitely update your site no less than once a month.

Why do you want to update frequently? Because it'll affect how often visitors come back. If your visitors come to your site four or five times over a three-month period and nothing's going on, they will stop coming back. You can bring them back later by keeping them updated about you and your business via newsletters (more about that in Chapter 11, *Creating Newsletters and Discussion Groups*), but a better way to keep their attention is to update your pages regularly and condition visitors to expect additions if they visit regularly.

Tara learned this through administering two very different sites. One site she updates almost every business day. Another has been growing for over a year and she has backed off to the point that she's updating it only once every few months. Guess which site gets the most consistent traffic? That's right, the most frequently updated site.

Peter has a different view. He believes that if the information is still up-to-date—still valid today—then it's of value, regardless of whether the information has been changed in a couple of weeks or not. What's important is *timeliness*, not age. Daily changes are, for most people, impractical, and they're probably not necessary. What counts is whether the information is useful to people. If it is, you don't have to keep changing it. It all depends on what you are trying to achieve. If you are selling advertising at your site, you want as many people as possible to come to your site and to come as often as possible. Constant change may be useful in that case. If you are selling a book, however, you don't care how often people come back...as long as they buy your book on their initial visit, so it's not necessarily true that you must be constantly changing your site.

Let People Know Your Site Has Changed—*If you update your site irregularly, consider using a free service like* **Mind-it** *(http://www.netmind.com/) or* **Spyonit** *(http://www.spyonit.com). These services will allow you to put a button on your Web site allowing users to receive an e-mail alert when your page changes.*

The most important thing, though, is something we mentioned in Chapter 1, *What Are You Promoting and Who Are You Targeting*. Your Web site must be useful today. If you have something that's useful today, you can attract viewers.

It's Useful!

More than anything, what really counts is that there's a reason for people to visit your Web site. If you haven't given people a *reason* to visit, there's not much point in trying to get them to visit. Here's an example. CDnow wants to sell you

CDs, but that's not a reason for you to visit its site. After all, do you really care if it makes money? CDnow understands this principle well, so it set out to give people a reason to visit its Web site—lots of reasons, really. The company created a site that's full of information (hundreds of thousands of pages), and full of sound clips (over 250,000 of them). It's created special personalized areas—the *My CDnow* pages—that are Web pages in which people can store information. Visitors can keep a list of music they'd like to buy some time and even allow their friends and family to view the list. (Hey, maybe Gran will buy you that *Beastie Boys* album you want.) It provides links to your favorite bands' pages; it recommends music based on your previous purchases and responses to questions; and so on. The founders of CDnow have given people a reason to visit by building what they call *the better music store*.

Why would anyone want to visit *your* Web page? If you can't come up with a good answer to that, you have problems.

Have you got your stuff together? Do you have a site worth marketing and a page worth promoting? Great. Make sure you have all the details down, and remember this one important idea:

Think about what your visitors care about, not what you *care about.*

Your visitors don't care what you want. They care only about what *they* want. So give it to them, and they will come.

SEVEN STEPS TO WEB-SITE READINESS

While the concepts of why and what are very important, you must also focus on the details that make a site look professional. Don't overlook proofreading and other site housekeeping. You should take these seven steps to make sure your Web page is ready before cranking up your promotions.

1. **Spell check it**—You may have the most beautifully written copy in the world, but if it is not free from spelling errors, it will leave a bad impression on the reader. Nothing cuts into your credibility more than a bunch of typos littering your pages. (Visitors may forgive one or two typos, but don't push your luck.) Many HTML editing programs, like FrontPage, have built-in spell checkers. If you don't have such a program, you can get a spell check online. (See the section on online resources at the end of this list.)

2. **Proofread it**—Spell checking works when words are actually misspelled, but it doesn't point out faulty word choices and grammar errors. Go over your page with a magnifying glass, if you have to, and get rid of those

mistakes. That doesn't mean you have to use the Queen's English, of course. (Substitute proper French or whatever language you're writing in for Queen's English.) If your Web site is oriented towards teenagers or a particular aspect of pop culture, the use of vernacular and not-quite-proper English might be appropriate; but make sure your use of that vernacular is deliberate, and not a result of sloppy proofreading.

3. **Get someone else to proofread it**—When you write something, your eyes are so close to it you will miss mistakes. Go out and find some fresh eyes—preferably someone who's never seen your site before—and get that person to proofread it. Not only will this help you find mistakes you might have missed; but your reader might be able to point out where your copy is confusing or difficult to understand. Ideally this person should be an editor, someone who understands the rules of the language.

4. **Check your links**—Have you ever heard of link rot? Link rot occurs when someone puts up a list of links and never checks the links. With the natural, high-speed rate of change of the Internet, more and more of the links become inaccurate over time, and the list becomes less and less valuable. Clicking bad links leads to *404—Link Not Found* errors in your visitors' browsers. It's irritating, and gives the impression that your site is old and out of date. Check your links regularly—once a week is ideal, though once a month is okay. FrontPage allows you to do this within the program, and there are also standalone products that'll check your links for you.

Link Checker Problems—*Link checkers show you whether a link is broken, but not whether the page that the link points to still contains the information you think it contains. The page might now be nothing but a "This page has been removed" message, and a link checker would not see a problem with that. Periodically you should probably use an offline browser to transfer all the pages referenced by links at your Web site and then take a quick look at each page. (You can find more information about offline browsers in Chapter 2, What You Need Before You Start.)*

5. **Make sure your site can be navigated without graphics, Java, or JavaScript**—One of the problems with Internet time being so fast is that people are always adding doodads to their sites to make the site more interesting; they flash or buzz or click, but they don't add real, usable content. Doodads are mostly harmless, but they become a problem when they are essential to the navigation of the site. For example, Java is interesting and can be used to create fabulous programs that do neat things, but you should not use Java as the only navigation tool. Some sites have nice little Java buttons that change color when the user places the mouse pointer over them, but in some cases those buttons won't work in browsers

that don't use Java or don't have it activated. The result is that people who don't have Java capability can't navigate around the site.

Sites that provide navigation links only via graphics are almost as bad. Such sites make things difficult for the visually impaired and those who surf without graphics (as many people do). At the very least, you should make sure that every important graphic has an ALT tag to tell what it is. The best solution is to provide a text menu as an alternative to your graphic navigation links. Please do not assume that everyone has the latest and greatest computer or the fastest Internet connection because lots of people don't. Show some consideration for them.

6. **Add an "about this site" page**—If you've put up a site that's a fan club for old 60's shows, you need one. If you're building an e-commerce solution for selling widgets, you need one. If you're setting up a site for the city transportation system, you need one. Somewhere on your site, you need a mention—at least a brief paragraph—of what your site is all about. If you're building a corporate site, you also want to have a section for press releases as well. Give people a place to go when they want to know how large your site is, how long it's been around, how they can get in touch, and a million other of those little questions that sometimes are hard to find an answer to on a Web site.

7. **Make sure your site is compatible with most browsers**—Don't rely on a single browser running in a single video mode on your computer to be sure that your Web site looks reasonable in all browsers. There are lots of different browsers out there, and lots of different screen sizes. Your visitor might be checking out your site on a 21-inch monitor, or the small screen of a Palm Pilot. Checking your site from as many different viewpoints and browsers as possible will ensure that it looks good to the majority of visitors. (You might find you can't look great to *all* visitors and screen sizes. That's okay; just go for *most*.) Checking your Web site from many different browser types and screen sizes will also teach you how long your Web site takes to load in different browsers.

ONLINE DIAGNOSTICS

Several online resources can help you ensure that your Web site is running as well as it can. One of the most popular is **Web Site Garage** at http://www.websitegarage.com/. Web Site Garage offers several free services for a one-page check: browser compatibility, load time, dead links, popularity, spelling, and HTML compatibility. Remember that the free service checks only one Web page at a time, so if you have a 50-page site and want to check each page, you'll be there awhile.

- **NetMechanic**, at http://www.netmechanic.com/, offers similar free services. NetMechanic can do a load-time check of your Web pages, a link check, and an HTML check. It even has a free image compressor to reduce your image sizes so your pages load more quickly. NetMechanic can check one page or twenty pages at a time, so it will check your site a little faster than the Web Site Garage can. It also offers services like site monitoring and search engine submissions.

- **LinkAlarm** (http://www.linkalarm.com/) is a pay service that provides extensive link reports; it summarizes the type and number of broken links and provides a detailed list of problems. The service costs 1 cent per page with a minimum charge of $10.00 and is calculated based on how often your pages are checked. For example, having your 100-page site checked every month will cost $12.00 a year.

- **Bobby**, at http://www.cast.org/bobby/, helps you determine whether your site is accessible by the disabled and whether your site conforms to different HTML standards (that browser-compatibility thing again). This site presents its results in rather technical terms, so try a different service first if you're not very HTML-savvy. Check out Figure 5.1 to see what problems Bobby had with the Netscape site.

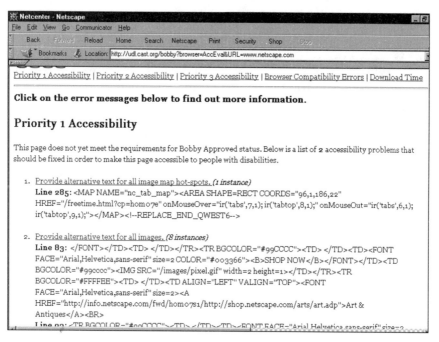

FIGURE 5.1: Oops, the Netscape site has some problems! Bobby found accessibility errors—links that can be used only through imagemaps.

- **Doctor HTML**, at http://www2.imagiware.com/RxHTML/, will perform a variety of tests on a single Web page: spelling, image analysis, document structure (making sure all HTML code is properly executed), image syntax (making sure each image has a height, width, and ALT tag), table structure (making sure HTML tables are set up properly), hyperlink verification, form structure, and command display (showing the HTML commands in a document). You can specify which tests to run. Doctor HTML is a good analysis to run if you've put together a page with very complex HTML, such as a page with lots of tables. This is an older resource, however, so it may not check to make sure that your code is compatible with the latest HTML.

- **Lynx** is a text-based browser that many UNIX machines run—no graphics, no doodads. You can see what your Web page looks like in a Lynx browser thanks to the **Salt Lake Community College Lynx** page at http://www.slcc.edu/webguide/lynxit.html.

With the help of all these resources and the seven steps, your Web site should now be ready. You've ensured that it's visitor-friendly and ready for real live visitors, but there's another step. Now you have to make it ready for another type of visitor—it has to be search-engine friendly.

Access Your Site with Different Devices—*If you have the chance, try using several different methods to access your site. Try a set-top box like WebTV, for example, or one of the Internet appliances. If you want your site to be accessible from wireless devices, see if you can access it from a cell phone or Palm Pilot. You can learn more about making your site compatible for wireless access devices at **WAPLINKS**, http://www.waplinks.com/.*

GETTING FRIENDLY WITH THE SEARCH ENGINES

Most search engines use programs called *spiders*, *'bots*, or *crawlers* to visit your site, index your content, and put it on the search engines. Of course they can't reason like humans do, so they make some assumptions about your content when indexing it. They don't always choose the most important words as the words that they index.

You can, however, point out to the spiders which words are most important on your page by using two elements: META tags and Title tags.

META Tags

META tags aren't viewed by your site's visitors, but instead are reviewed by the spiders and 'bots that index your site. They're strictly to tell the spiders which words on your site are most important, exactly what your site is all about, and so on. See Figure 5.2 for a shot of the META tags that Microsoft's site uses.

Without META tags, the spider can't make sense of the contents of your site; it views every word as a keyword. With META tags, you can supply a description and keywords that are given more weight when your site is indexed. That is not to say all search engines support META tags; they don't, but some do. Out of the several different types of META tags, the three that should concern you are the *description*, *keywords*, and *robots* tags.

Different META Tags

We don't have the space to go into all the different kinds of META tags, and you don't need to know about all of them anyway. We strongly recommend that you use the *description* and *keywords* META tags; the *robots* one is optional.

The META tags go within the HEAD part of your Web pages' HTML code, like this. (Notice the inclusion of the *title* tag; we'll talk more about that one in a minute):

```
<Head>
<Title>A Code Example</Title>
<META name="description" content="An example of how to
include descriptions in your Web pages and make them as
accessible as possible to spiders and other Web
crawlers.">
</Head>
```

Description

The *description* META tag is for describing your Web pages—see the previous paragraph for an example of how it's used. You want a 20- to 40-word description of your Web site to put in there. Try to avoid using dates, unless you feel that you really have to use them, as in the following example:

```
The model train Web is devoted to the collector of
1920-1950 model trains, with an emphasis on news,
pricing, and model train shows.
```

Spend some time coming up with a good description, because you can use the same description later when submitting your site to search engines (see Chapter Six, *Registering With the Search Sites*).

```
Source of: http://www.microsoft.com/ - Netscape
<HTML>
<HEAD>
<META HTTP-EQUIV="Content-Type" CONTENT="text/html; charset=iso8859-1" />
<TITLE>Welcome to Microsoft's Homepage</TITLE>
<META http-equiv="PICS-Label" content="(PICS-1.1 "http://www.rsac.org/ratings
<META NAME="KEYWORDS" CONTENT="products; headlines; downloads; news; Web site
<META NAME="DESCRIPTION" CONTENT="The entry page to Microsoft's Web site. Fir
<META NAME="MS.LOCALE" CONTENT="EN-US" />
<META NAME="CATEGORY" CONTENT="home page" />
<STYLE TYPE="text/css">
<!--
        A:link {color:"#003399";}
        A:visited {color:"#003399";}
        A:hover {color:"red";}
        -->
</STYLE>
</HEAD>
<BODY BGCOLOR="#FFFFFF" TOPMARGIN="0" LEFTMARGIN="0" MARGINWIDTH="0" MARGINHE
<script language="JavaScript" src="/library/toolbar/toolbar.js">

</script>
<script language="JavaScript" src="/library/toolbar/en-us/global.js">

</script>
<script language="JavaScript" src="/library/toolbar/en-us/local.js">

</script>
<SPAN ID="TBDownLevelDiv">
<TABLE WIDTH="100%" CELLPADDING="0" CELLSPACING="0" BORDER="0" BGCOLOR="#FFFF
```

FIGURE 5.2: Here are some of the META tags used by Microsoft's Web site.

Keywords

The *keywords* META tag gives you the opportunity to enter a list of appropriate keywords for your Web site, which is especially appropriate when your Web site contains words that might be somewhat misleading.

For example, say you have a site devoted to a new heartburn treatment. The treatment is designed for use by professional healthcare providers, and therefore you don't want consumers coming to your site looking to purchase this treatment.

```
<Head>
<Title>The Burn B Gone Anti-Heartburn Treatment
Solution</Title>
<META name="description" content="A revolutionary no-
pain, low-side effect heartburn treatment designed for
professional health care providers">
<META name="keywords" content="heartburn, healthcare,
doctor, nurse, heart, acid reflux, gastroesophageal
reflux disease, GERD">
</head>
```

We could go on, but you get the idea that professionally oriented keywords like *gastro esophageal reflux disease* and *acid reflux* are more likely to attract professional healthcare providers than consumer-oriented keywords like *chest pain* and *stomach acid*. (In retrospect, perhaps this is kind of a gross example. Sorry....)

Do you need to add META tags to every Web page you have? Probably not. However, you do want to add tags to every major page, such as index pages, introductions to sets of articles, and, of course, your home page.

The Content of the Page

Engineering the content of a Web page to look good to a search engine is almost an art form and a new one at that. The rules are changing constantly, so you may want to do some experiments to see what works for you. (This is not your high school algebra class; there isn't just one answer.)

Some search engines look at the first few lines of the page and collect them as a short abstract of the page. So make sure the headings at the top of the page and the first few lines of text are really descriptive of what you want the search engines to index. Try to use lots of words that your prospective clients are likely to be searching for in that first important paragraph.

Popularity Is Becoming Important—*The search engine, Google, sorts its pages at least partially by link popularity, so no matter how well you've set up the META tags, your listing will be determined, in part, by link popularity. What does that mean, besides the need to do promotion and marketing? Content, content, content!*

Even after the first paragraph, some search engines continue looking. AltaVista indexes everything, so the rest of the text on the page is important, too. Some people try to fool such search engines by including large lists of keywords at the bottom. This is sometimes known as *spamdexing*. You may run into pages in which the authors have tried to camouflage a list of hundreds of keywords by changing the color of the words to match the page background, for instance. (That's called *fontmatching*.) Other authors put hundreds of keywords in the Comment tags within the page, so they're not visible. Does this work? Almost always no. Most of the search engines in action these days are clever enough to figure out what's going on, and they ignore repetition, and many no longer index any text within HTML comment tags. Some will actually punish obvious spamdexing. They won't simply ignore the spamdexing; they'll actually dump the site from the directory and perhaps even blacklist the owners from the site so they can't get back in.

Some page designers feel that you should have pages that are focused on one topic and one topic only and therefore have many small pages whose fewer words will count for more in the search engines. Tara disagrees with this, feeling that administering many small pages makes your site more likely to have update problems and linkage errors. On the other hand, if you do have distinct areas in your Web site, it's a good idea to register each area. For instance, if you have a site related to model rocketry, you might have a newsletter archive, a directory of model-rocket resources on the Web, and an article about the history of rocketry. It's a good idea to register all these areas individually.

ALT Text in Images

Some search engines are now indexing the IMG tags so that people can search for graphics. Infoseek does this, for example, and even sites that are not creating image indexes may still read and index the text to get an idea of what the page is about. So it's a good idea to include a description of the images on your pages in the ALT attribute (not to mention the fact that it makes your Web site much more usable to people using text-only browsers and to the disabled).

If You're Using Frames

If you are using frames at your site, search engines may have trouble figuring out how to index pages. When the spiders or crawlers arrive at the site, all they get is the frame-definition document, a document that tells a browser how to set up the frames—how many frames, their sizes, their positions, and which document is displayed within each frame. However most search engines don't bother examining the documents referenced by the frame-definition document—the documents that will actually appear in the browser window.

If your site has frames, you can provide information for the search engines in two ways. You can add META tags to the top of the frame-definition document, and you can use the NOFRAMES tags (*<NOFRAMES>* and *</NOFRAMES>*), which enclose information that is not displayed inside the browser window unless the document is loaded by a browser that can't work with frames. It's a good idea to copy the information from the main frame into the NOFRAMES area of the frame-definition document. Then not only will nonframes browsers be able to see something, but so will the search engines.

Robots

As was said earlier, many search engines create a searchable database by sending out programs, called spiders and crawlers, to index your Web sit; but what if you don't want your page indexed? You might have a page that you'd like to keep out of the search engines because it changes constantly, because it doesn't provide meaningful information, because you want someone to visit the site to get to the information, or for whatever reason. The *robots* META tag tells the spider and crawler how to treat your Web page.

The *robots* META tag has six variables, as you'll see in the following list. You can use these variables in combinations to specify certain actions by the robot. The following list will show you how that tag works.

```
<META name="robots" content="variable">
```

All—Tells the robot to crawl through your site, following all the links, and to index all the files in your Web site. (This value is the default for your average crawler, so it is probably not necessary to insert this command.)

None—Instructs the crawler not to crawl through any of the site. It will not index the site and will not follow any links away from the site. (Using this command is a great idea when you're still putting the site together and don't want the draft version accidentally inserted in a search engine.)

Index—Indicates that the page itself may be crawled through but that every other page should be checked for its own META tag.

Noindex—Indicates that the page itself may not be crawled through.

Follow—Allows the crawler to follow the links on the page to other Web sites; this command works well in combination with the Noindex command, as you'll see in a minute.

Nofollow—Instructs the crawler to *not* follow links to other sites.

Let's see how you could use this in certain situations. Say you have a Web site with content that changes every day—it's a "tip of the day" page or something. Therefore, you don't want the page to be indexed by the search engines because it's changing all the time. However, the links from the site are good, and you want them to be followed. You could use the following META tag:

```
<META name="robots" Content="Noindex, Follow">
```

On the other hand, perhaps you have a page that's stable, and you want it to be indexed. However, you don't want the links away from the page to be indexed—perhaps they have content that's meaningless without the context of other pages. You could use a tag that's the opposite of the previous tag:

```
<META name="robots" Content="Index, Nofollow">
```

Of course, if you want to tell the crawler to go away, you could use

```
<META name="robots" Content="Noindex, nofollow">.
```

If you'd like more information about working with robots, see the *Standard for Robot Exclusion* document at http://info.webcrawler.com/mak/projects/robots/norobots.html.

META-TAG TOOLS

If you're intimidated by the idea of generating your own META tags, look online.

There's the **META-Tag Generator** at http://www.websitepromote.com/resources/meta/. Enter the title of the page, a few keywords, and a description, and the META tag code will be e-mailed to you. From there you can cut and paste it into a Web page.

WebPromote's **META Tag Builder** at http://www.websitepromote.com/resources/meta/ also offers a META tag building service much like the one at WebPromote. It also offers several tips for META tag generation and site promotion. **Web Site Garage** also has a META tag generator at http://websitegarage.netscape.com/turbocharge/metatag/.

There's also **Meta Medic** (http://www.northernwebs.com/set/setsimjr.html), a Web site that will check your META tags and tell you if they're too large or if you are repeating words too many times. (A more advanced version called SET SIM PRO is available for purchase.)

Meta Medic—*Meta Medic is a handy tool, but make sure each META tag on your page is on one line and not split into two or more lines, or Meta Medic will be unable to do its job.*

If you don't like the idea of doing all your META tag generation online, you can download a freeware META tag generator, **SiteUp Networks Meta Tag Generator**, at http://www.siteup.com/meta.html. Registration is required. There's also **Tag Master**, a $20 Windows shareware program (http://deadlock.com/promote/software/tagmaster/). This program comes with a spell checker, a 100,000-word keyword library, and a template tool that allows you to add META tags to scores or hundreds of pages at the same time. **TagGen** offers free trial available at http://www.hisoftware.com/TagGen.htm, but the full version costs $99.99. It does have a variety of features, including a spell checker, thesaurus, auto-correct, and support for a variety of metadata types.

For more META Tag resources, visit the **Yahoo! META Tag** page at http://dir.yahoo.com/Computers_and_Internet/Information_and_Documentation/Data_Formats/HTML/META_Tag/.

TITLE TAGS

The title tag is not a META tag; it's a regular old HTML tag; but you'd be amazed by how many folks don't use it, even though it's so helpful.

The title tag looks like this:

```
<Title>This is the title tag</Title>
```

Whatever appears within the title tag markers shows up as the page's title in the browser's title bar. For example, if you were using Netscape and you visited Yahoo!, the title of the page would be shown as *Yahoo!* in the title bar.

META Tag Training—*There are lots of different META tags used for various purposes. If you're interested in learning more and in finding more META-tag tools, see the WebDeveloper.com* **META Tag Resources** *page (*http://webdeveloper.com/categories/html/html_metatag_res.html*).*

Why use the title tag? Because many search engines weigh the words in the title tag more carefully than the other content of your Web page. As a matter of fact, some search engines can search only Web page titles. At **AltaVista,** for instance, you can tell the system to only search page titles (http://www.altavista.com/).

The text in your title tag may have a significant effect on where your page is placed in a search engine. In addition, the title loads almost immediately, so viewers on slower Web connections can get some idea of what your Web page is about without having to load the entire thing. Additionally, if you have a search engine for your site, you'll often get the results with the title of the page and a summary. Having a good title will make it easier to navigate through your search results.

Leaving the title tag off your Web page is like leaving the headline off a newspaper article, or a company name off business cards. Make sure all your Web pages have title tags—even the ones that you think aren't major enough to have META tags.

With all this discussion of META tags and title tags, you might be getting the idea that they're great inventions. You're right. You may also be getting the idea that they're open to a lot of abuse. You're right again. If you're not friendly to the search engines, as explained in the following section, you might be labeled a Search Engine Jerk (SEJ).

HOW TO BE A SEARCH-ENGINE JERK (SEJ)

You can set up your Web site to be friendlier to search engines—or you can set it up to manipulate search engines and try to get your Web page the highest listings and most hits possible. The second course isn't a good idea because these techniques can get you kicked out of search engines. We advise you to avoid the following courses of action unless you want to be known as a search-engine jerk, and, more importantly, risk losing your place in the search engines.

Add keywords that have nothing to do with your site—Some people add keywords to their META tags that have nothing to do with the content of their site. The theory is the more keywords they have, the more hits they'll get in the search engine and the more people will visit their site, but this is a silly idea. The extra people who visit their sites will be visiting because of keywords that have nothing to do with the content, so they're not likely to be interested in the content. Furthermore, they're unlikely to look kindly upon the Web-site owner for playing such a trick.

Add multiple instances of keywords to your META tags—Instead of adding a keyword one time in your META tags, you might add the same keyword ten or fifteen times. That's one way to try keyword stuffing, and most of the time, it won't work—spiders are too smart for that. (Note that putting *dogs, dogs, dogs, dogs* in your description META tag is not okay. However, putting *German Shepherds, Welsh Terriers, Boxers* is okay—as long as your page has something to do with each of these breeds.)

Use copyrighted or trademarked terms in your META tags—SEJ's might use copyrighted or trademarked terms to which they are not entitled as META tag descriptions. For example, if they've set up a site to promote one particular brown fizzy drink, they might use the names of other brown fizzy drinks to attract visitors to their site. At best they'll be deceiving visitors. At worst—and this is pretty bad—they'll be sued for misuse of a trademark.

Want a Lawsuit?—*Some people actually steal the entire META tag structure of a competing site that's at the top of the search engines. This is called metajacking and it's very naughty. In fact, it's a good way to get sued. Don't do it. Yes, there have been META tag lawsuits already, at least five of them (three of which involved Playboy magazine trying to stop Web sites from using the words Playboy and Playmate in their tags), one of which ended in a $3 million settlement. See the **Meta Tag Lawsuits** page at* http://searchenginewatch.internet.com/resources/metasuits.html *for more information. You can also check out* http://forums.law.arizona.edu/library/Chiorazzi/sknoell/metatag1.htm.

Add invisible words to the bottom of your pages—Sometimes to increase the incidence of keywords on a page, Webmasters resort to a sneaky form of keyword stuffing. They set up text the same color as the page background—so viewers can't ordinarily view it—and add lines and lines and lines of keywords. (In the search-engine business, this is sometimes called *fontmatching*.) This could get your page—and sometimes your entire Web site—kicked out of search engines. Some spiders also consider a preponderance of extremely small text as possible evidence of keyword stuffing, so be careful how much tiny text you're using on a page.

Set up multiple entrances to the same site—Other Web sites set up several copies of the same page so they'll show up in several places on a search-engine's results list. These pages are often known as *doorway pages*. There's a chance that using these will get you into trouble with the search engines, but we'll look at this subject in detail in a moment.

Title stacking—Title stacking (also called *title packing*) is when you use a perfectly legitimate way to enhance your search engine ranking—that is, using a title tag—in a nefarious manner. Specifically, you use several title tags at a time, like this:

```
<Title>The Best Example Title Tags Online</Title>
<Title>Thousands of Free Example Title Tags</Title>
<Title>Learn All About Example Title Tags</Title>
```

The theory is that search engines will add the information from all the title tags. It probably won't work anymore—if it ever did—and it might get you into trouble with the search engines, so don't do it.

All of these techniques may work in the short run; but they'll cost you a lot more in the long run by wrecking your credibility, attracting visitors you don't want to your site, and getting your site kicked out of a lot of search engines.

CREATING DOORWAY PAGES

Some people in the search-engine optimization business recommend the use of *doorway* pages, also known as *bridge* pages, *portal* pages, *jump* pages, *entry* pages, and so on.

The idea is that you create a number of pages—perhaps half a dozen or a dozen—and set them up with META tags and keywords. Then you register all these pages individually in the search engines. In theory you'll get more search engine hits, so you'll get more visits.

Does this work? Probably. Can it lead to problems with the search engines? Possibly. Among AltaVista's page-indexing no-nos are "duplication of content, either by excessive submission of the same page, submitting the same pages from multiple domains, or submitting the same content from multiple hosts…" and "pages whose primary intent is to redirect users to another page." Sounds like doorway pages to us.

Take that as a warning. The search engines don't like you playing these sorts of games. They're interested in providing a good service to the people searching at their sites, and these sorts of tricks make it harder for them to do so. All of the search-engine companies are looking for ways to make searching easier and more productive, and that means finding ways to filter out the effect of tricks. Google is now basing its search results partially on popularity, and this is just the beginning. In Tara's opinion, fewer of these manipulative tricks are going to work in the future.

So, it's up to you. You could try it...or not. We're not advising either way. If you'd like to learn more, though, see these articles:

What Is a Bridge Page or Entry Page?
http://searchenginewatch.com/webmasters/bridge.html

A Bridge Too Far
http://www.searchenginewatch.com/sereport/98/02-bridge.html

Promoters Call for Certification
http://www.searchenginewatch.com/sereport/9808-certification.html

MUCH MORE INFORMATION

You can spend a great deal of time fooling around with your Web pages, trying to get them just right. We're not convinced that all this time is necessarily time well spent, but if you'd like to investigate further, check these Web sites and newsgroups and their associated reports and newsletters:

comp.infosystems.search (A newsgroup related to search-engine issues)

META Tagging for Search Engines
http://www.stars.com/Search/Meta/Tag.html

PlanetOcean—Search Engine Secrets ($97 for a book)
http://www.hitmasters.com/

Search Engine Tips—Submit It!
http://www.submit-it.com/subopt.htm

Search Engine Watch (Free newsletter)
http://searchenginewatch.com/

Secrets to Achieving a Top 10 Ranking and the Marketposition Monthly Newsletter (Free with purchase of the WebPosition software)
http://www.webposition.com/

VirtualPromote (A discussion forum related to search engines, along with articles and services)
http://www.virtualpromote.com/

Web Ranking Tools
http://www.bruceclay.com/web_rank.htm

WebPromote (Free newsletter)
http://www.WebPromote.com/

Yahoo!—Site Announcement and Promotion Placement Improvement
http://dir.yahoo.com/Computers_and_Internet/Internet/World_Wide_Web/Site_An
nouncement_and_Promotion/

GET PROFESSIONAL HELP

If all this seems a bit much, there are many companies waiting to help you. These companies will play the search-engine tricks for you...for a price, of course. They may charge a set fee, or perhaps a per-click fee. We've seen rates between 12 cents and 25 cents per click. That is, for every new customer they bring in, they'll charge you that much. They set up pages on their Web sites, register those in the search engines, and then charge you each time someone reaches one of those pages and is redirected to your site.

For instance, one major search-engine optimization company, Did-It.Com, charges $399 to set up the system, and then 25 cents for each *clickthrough*. In other words, you pay Did-It.Com 25 cents for each person who visits your site as a result of the its listing. Now and then, the company runs promotions, and in addition it has a bulk rate available. We've seen the setup as low as $150, with a clickthrough rate of 12 cents.

The good news? That's not a bad price, compared to advertising (see Chapter 12, *Advertising Your Site*). The bad news? It could still be a significant cost. At those rates, 100 visitors would cost you from $12 to $29. That may be too much for some businesses, laughably cheap for others. Another problem, though, is that if you decide to drop its services, Did-It.Com has pages pointing to your site, carefully designed to catch searchers, but now they're directing searchers *away* from your site.

A number of the Web sites mentioned under *Much More Information* provide these services. You might also try these sites:

Beyond Interactive
http://www.gobeyond.com/

Web-Ignite
http://www.web-ignite.com/

Did-It.com
http://www.did-it.com/

PositionWeaver
http://www.searchpositioning.com/

Site-Promotion.com
http://www.site-promotion.com/

IS PROFESSIONAL HELP WORTH IT?

Is it worth it? We're not sure; but here's the way Peter looks at this sort of service: in effect, it's another form of advertising. These services send you people interested in your product or services, and you pay them for it, and 12 cents per clickthrough is actually a good price when compared to other Web advertising systems.

The search-engine optimization services say they can put your Web site in the major search engines near the top of the relevant category, boosting traffic to your site. Unfortunately a lot of the claims are hype. Here are a few of Peter's thoughts on the subject.

The first thing to consider is that these services cannot boost your rating in the most important search site of all, Yahoo!. More searches are done at this site than at any other. The submission services can't fool Yahoo! because search-engine optimization relies on tricking a computer program—some kind of search-engine 'bot that looks at your Web site—into giving you a high rating; but Yahoo! uses real live people to rate your site. If they like it, they'll add it; if they don't, they won't. In any case, you'll be added to a list in alphabetical order. (Although you can try using an *A* word in your page title to get near the top, the people at Yahoo! may not use your page title to enter you into the list. Remember also that the folks at Yahoo! list their most popular sites in a category first, and then list their favorites. Only then do they get into listing alphabetically, so it might not be as worth it as you think.)

Also, the search-engine optimization services may not really be as successful as they claim. An employee of Did-It.Com, one of the better-known services, told Peter that on average they were sending around 800 people a month to their customers, hardly a deluge. (On some days Peter's Web site gets that many or more.) The whole concept of promising large numbers of people that you'll push them to the top of their categories is a little strange; we can't all be at the top, can we? Even if you can find a way to trick a search engine into doing what you want it to do today, the search engine may change how it works tomorrow. The search-engine guys are constantly trying to keep ahead of the optimization people; it's a sort of battle of wits, with each side looking for the other's weaknesses.

You can spend an awful lot of time and energy—and money—trying to optimize for search engines, but you'll never be finished because you'll constantly have to keep up with what the search engines are doing. In fact, search-engine optimization can sometimes have the opposite effect. If you're too aggressive, it can get you banned from a search engine.

There are some simple things you can and should do to make your Web site attractive to search engine spiders and crawlers. Make sure you have a descriptive title tag in your Web pages, including the sort of keywords people are likely to use when searching for sites of your type. Use the META keywords and description tags. Make sure the main page at your site includes text that contains the keywords for which search engines are likely to look.

However, here's the most important secret for search-engine optimization, or at least for drawing people to your site, a secret you don't often hear when people discuss this subject. Make sure your site is worth visiting. Consider why somebody would want to visit your site, and ask yourself a simple question: if it wasn't my site, would I want to visit it? If you create a useful site and register with the major search engines, it will probably get listed and eventually the word will get around, and people *will* visit. The Google search engine has become incredibly popular with very little advertising and a lot of word-of-mouth.

A final thought. If you think getting your Web site listed in the search engines is all you need to do to bring people to your site, you have a problem. That may have been the case a couple of years ago, but today there's too much stuff out there. Unless you're really active in getting the word out about your site, people are not going to visit, regardless of how well search-optimized your site is.

This chapter has given you a good idea of what to do (and what not to do) when it comes to making your site friendly for search engines. We believe that it's worthwhile doing the basic things we've outlined in this chapter. However, we're not convinced that it's worth spending a great deal of time playing tricks on search engines; that time could probably be better spent concentrating on providing something really worthwhile at your Web site, and working on the other promotional techniques we'll discuss in this book. You can think of the search engines as being similar to the telephone Yellow Pages. Yes, you need to be listed, and yes, they can bring your Web site visitors; but most companies get only a small portion of their business from the Yellow Pages; they get most of their business from other promotional and advertising techniques. And so too, with search engines—you'll probably get most of your visitors elsewhere (and if not, you're probably not trying).

Now that you've got the site ready, you must submit it to the search engines. That's what we'll look at in the next chapter.

CHAPTER SIX

Registering with the Search Sites

G ot your page set up? Great. Filled to the brim with META tags? Fine. Got all your links checked, grammar confirmed, t's crossed, and i's dotted? Terrific. *Bring on the search sites!* In this chapter we'll explain how to go about registering with various types of search sites, places that people go to find the information they need. If people are searching for the sort of information you have at your site, they should be able to find your site when they search; but unless you do a good job of registering with the search sites...they won't.

A GREAT DESCRIPTION

No, wait a minute. You have to do one more thing. You have to write a description. Your description is what brings in your viewers. It's what attracts them to your site before they even get to your site. As you might imagine from this fact, a description is critically important. You might have the best site devoted to bass fishing in the world; but if the description reads "Really neat site on bass fishing. You have to come visit. Look at my bass fishing page," you're going to have trouble getting visitors.

***Use a Text Editor**—Don't write your description in a word processor, or you may end up with various typesetting characters (such as curly quotes and em dashes) that won't work properly when you fill in forms at the search sites. Use a text editor, such as Notepad (in Windows) or SimpleText (on the Mac). If you don't mind spending a little money, get **TextPad** (http://www.textpad.com/), which is a great text editor with word-processing features. **UltraEdit** (http://www.ultraedit.com/) is good, too.*

Write down a description of your Web site. Put down everything you can think of about your site. Now see if you can boil it down to 75 good words. Now see if you can reduce that number to 50. Now cut down to 25. Now take that all the way down to 10 good words.

Here's an example. Say you have a site dealing with origami. Start out with about a 75-word description:

```
Example Origami, the site devoted to paper folding.
Covers traditional paper folding as well as dollar bill
folding, toy-making, and other types of origami.
Information available for beginners to experts. Several
patterns on the site, with links to other origami
resources online and a gallery of classic origami. A
directory of worldwide origami organizations is also
here. Free monthly newsletter available on origami
folding. Origami paper, books, publications, and
tutorial videos for sale.
```

That about says it all, and in a way that makes an origami enthusiast want to come visit. (Note how we didn't make every sentence in the description grammatically perfect—sometimes you have enough space to get your information across but not enough space to impress your English teacher. On your Web page you have more room to pay attention to your grammar.)

Now, let's take that example and boil it down to 50 words:

```
Example Origami, the site devoted to paper folding. Covers
traditional paper folding as well as dollar bill folding,
toy-making, and other types of origami. Information
available for beginners up to experts. Several patterns
available, with links to other origami resources online.
Paper, books, and tutorial videos for sale.
```

You've pulled out some information and left in what you consider the critical stuff. Now, pare it down further to 25 words:

```
Example Origami, the site about paper folding. Also
dollar bill folding and paper toy-making. For beginners
to experts. Free patterns. Origami materials for sale.
```

Now you really start getting squeezed, and your ability to describe what your site offers suffers; but as you can see here, this description lets the viewer know that:

- A wide variety of things are available on your site (covering many types of origami folding).
- It's appropriate for a wide audience (beginners to experts).
- There's something there they might be interested in for free.

Finally, if they need some paper, they know that this site has origami materials for sale. Be as specific as you can! Every specific note (beginners to expert, materials for sale, dollar-bill folding) is a great keyword, helping your site stand out to visitors who want to find you.

Getting down to ten words can be a pain, especially if your site has a lot to offer; but it can be done:

```
Example Origami. All types of origami. Beginners-
experts. Free patterns.
```

Of course you don't have any room to be descriptive, but you can maintain the fact that the site covers all kinds of origami, that it's appropriate for beginners to experts, and that it offers free patterns. You have to tell what your site is about and give viewers a reason to come (thus we left in the phrase *free patterns*—not critical to the description of the site but a good incentive to visit for the casual browser).

You may be wondering: if you have only ten words to work with, why not make them all keywords? There are a few reasons you don't want to do that:

- Keywords all strung together are hard to read.
- You might choose a keyword combination that's confusing to your readers. Better to state what you're all about in plain English, even if it's grammatically fractured English.
- If you use straight keywords, it's harder to make statement/phrases like *free patterns*. The viewer will see every individual word as an independent keyword.

You'll have opportunities to use descriptions of all these lengths, so once you've put your descriptions together, save each of them. If you're using a clipboard utility (see Chapter 2, *What You Need Before You Start*), stash them there, so you can cut and paste a description every time you have to use one.

You've seen an example of a good description set, but there are some other rules of thumb to follow when putting together a description.

Good Descriptions Are Not Dated

Putting dates in your description automatically makes them look really, really old. For example, say we put in the description "Tara's example descriptions. The best descriptions of 2000." That looks fine in 2000. Two years after 2000 it's going to look horrible. Far better to put "Tara's example descriptions. Fine selections of example descriptions including satirical, metaphorical, and traditionally boring."

The same rule applies to mentioning time. For example, don't put in a description that you've been in business for two years. If you absolutely must, you can put that you've been "in business since 1996" but we wouldn't recommend even that. The Internet and its culture are unfriendly to time. Time on the Internet means abandoned pages, outmoded technology, and ancient resources. (Thankfully, it means something much different in the offline world.)

Good Descriptions Are Catchy

Tara's got a thing for words like *pep* and *verve*; they're so unique and interesting. Your description needs to have pep, and lots of it. It needs to be *catchy*. Consider...

```
The Example Cartoon Page has a very extensive
collection of example cartoons, like several cartoons
devoted to certain industries.
```

Yawn. There's little that's specific in this description, and the addition of *very*—one of the most dreadful words in our language—makes it drag. Let's take another thwack at it:

```
The Example Cartoon Page contains a plethora of example
cartoons, including cartoons devoted to fire fighting,
pumpkin tossing, and creosote production.
```

Isn't that a much more interesting description? Not only is it more interesting, but you've also put more specific keywords in there to attract searchers who are looking for information about fire fighting, pumpkin tossing, and creosote production.

Good Descriptions Are Not Mere Puffery

Puffery is an advertising term that means a description that's so subjective, or so hyperbolic, that it can't be taken as an objective measure of the quality of a product or service. The problem is that people can see through puffery. (Perhaps that should be part of the description of this term; if it's quite clearly hyperbolic nonsense, it's puffery.)

We believe that puffery won't get you far. (Occasionally it'll get you into a lawsuit, though, as in the case in which bookseller Barnes & Noble sued Amazon.com for claiming to be the world's largest bookstore.)

Once you have your descriptions together, and are assured that they're undated, specific, and puffery-free, you're finally ready to approach the search sites and subject indexes.

SEARCH SITES: THE BIG 'UNS

In this section we'll list the URLs for submitting to certain search sites and hit the highlights as to what these search sites do and don't want. However, don't take our word for it—check the pages yourself! Unfortunately things change so quickly online that it's hard for a mere book to keep up. Oh, and don't run out and register quite yet—not until you've read about the submission services and programs later in this chapter.

Sites, Engines, and Indexes—*You'll hear various terms related to sites where people can find information about other Web sites. They're often called search engines. We prefer to call them search sites because the term search engine often means a highly automated system. For instance, AltaVista is a true search engine. It uses programs to go out and index Web sites, and it provides a search system for users to find things.*

Some of these places have much more human interaction—Yahoo! has a staff of people who assess each site and decide whether it should be in the directory. Yahoo! has a directory of categories and subcategories, but also works in a similar way to many search engines. You can simply enter keywords and search for them.

There are other differences, too. Some search engines index just about every word in every page. (Sometimes they're called full-text search engines for that very reason.) A site such as Yahoo!, though, indexes just the URL, page title, and description. You may hear sites such as Yahoo! and LookSmart called searchable subject indexes, in fact.

Then there are other types of sites—directories and listings. They are often smaller and more specialized; all these sites have one thing in common; they are used for finding information on the Web.

YAHOO!

Main Site: http://www.yahoo.com/
Site Submission Page: http://www.yahoo.com/info/suggest/

Yahoo! is the most popular search site around, which means you really want to get listed there. However, it doesn't automatically list everything, and we're not aware of anything that clearly explains what it lists and what it doesn't, and why. The process is subjective, because Yahoo! uses real people to check all the submissions; most systems use programs to check submissions. If the person looking at your site doesn't like it, you're out! (Try again.)

Yahoo!'s submission procedure—find your category first, and then submit it—is a lot like LookSmart's, which is discussed in a later section of this chapter entitled "LookSmart." First, you have to find the most appropriate place in *its* index for *your* page. (As you probably know, Yahoo! is broken into a series of categories and subcategories.)

Once you do that, you'll be asked if that's really the category you want to submit to. You'll also be asked for the site name, URL, and a description. Yahoo! has some guidelines for what it does and doesn't want in a description (see Figure 6.1). Next you'll have the chance to suggest a second category. Then you'll be asked for your name and e-mail, and the geographical location of the site (if applicable.) Finally, you'll be asked if your listing is time-sensitive and if you have any comments.

Use the time-sensitive feature if it's applicable. The time-sensitive feature will set your site to be removed from the Yahoo! database after a certain date. This is

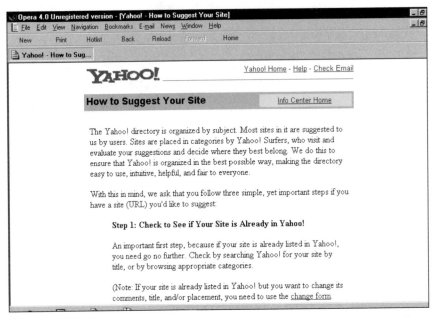

FIGURE 6.1: Yahoo! has very specific guidelines for suggesting Web sites. Be sure to follow them!

a great feature if you want to promote a convention, seminar, or some other date-related event. You'll be able to promote something and get some exposure, and you won't have to worry about it sitting in Yahoo!'s database, getting moldy.

If Yahoo! accepts you, you'll get an e-mail to let you know that your site will appear and when it will appear. Don't hold your breath, though. It can take literally months to get listed on Yahoo!. In fact, you probably *won't* get listed in Yahoo! the first time you try. On the other hand, the last time Tara submitted a site to Yahoo!, she received notification that she'd been accepted within about three days. She's also had her sites appear in Yahoo! *without* submitting them herself.

Yahoo! is the single most important search engine. At one point not so long ago, more searches were carried out at Yahoo! than at all the other search engines combined. Although that may not be the case today, it's certainly one of the busiest—if not the busiest—search site around, so it's essential that your Web site is listed there; but that's easier said than done. There's a good (if somewhat old) article on this subject at the **Search Engine Watch Web** site: http://searchenginewatch.internet.com/webmasters/yahoo/results.html. This article, based on a small, informal survey, indicates that most people who try to get listed at Yahoo! don't succeed (72 percent), and that in order to get listed the successful site owners had to try, on average, almost four times.

One important criterion noted by this report was that sites are far more likely to get listed if the submission is for a *root URL* (the domain name without subdirectories) than for a URL at a *members page* Web site (a site at America Online, CompuServe, and so on). We've said it before, and we'll say it again...you need your own domain name!

ALTAVISTA

Main Page: http://www.altavista.com/
Site Submission Page: http://jump.altavista.com/cs_au

AltaVista asks that you submit only one URL per site; its site crawler (named Scooter) will index the whole site eventually. While AltaVista supports META tags, it will kick out sites that abuse those tags (with practices like keyword stuffing and fontmatching). (It has a full list of unwanted practices on its URL submission page.) AltaVista also notes that it occasionally rebuilds its index from scratch, and some sites might get lost. If your URL vanishes from the site and you know you're not a Search Engine Jerk, resubmit the page. AltaVista's documentation pages include several discussions of how its search engine software works, what it considers inappropriate behavior for Web pages, and other behind-the-scenes information. It's worth a look if you're interested in what search engines want to index and why.

EXCITE

Main Page: http://www.excite.com/
Site Submission Page: http://www.excite.com/info/add_url/

Definitely read the "Getting Listed on Excite" section at http://www.excite.com/Info/listing.html. This section will inform you that Excite doesn't support META tags in an attempt to protect searchers from misleading information. However, it does use the description META tag to build site summary information if it's available. Excite also recommends that you improve your site's rankings by creating Web pages for very limited subjects, thus decreasing the number of keywords (and increasing the importance of each keyword) per page.

HOTBOT

Main Page: http://www.hotbot.com/
Site Submission Page: http://www.hotbot.com/addurl.asp

HotBot's site submission information page is at http://www.hotbot.com/help/. At this writing, the time for a site to get completely spidered into its index takes from 21 to 60 days, so put this one at the top of your list! HotBot does index META tags, but warns that META-tag abuse will lead to site rankings being "severely penalized." (No mention of kicking a page out of the index is made, but it does mention "severely downgrading" a site's ranking.) You can check to see whether your site has been indexed at http://www.hotbot.com/help/checkurl.asp.

LYCOS

Main Site: http://www.lycos.com/
Site Submission Page: http://www.lycos.com/addasite.html

Lycos is currently taking two to three weeks to add a site to their index. Lycos does not permit sites with certain characters in their URLs—ampersand (&), percent sign (%), equals sign (=), dollar sign ($), and question mark (?)—to be added to its index, as its spider (the program that runs around the Internet looking at the submitted Web pages) doesn't recognize them. Lycos will also delete from its "rolling catalog" any sites that cannot be indexed after four weeks. (If your site goes down, you move a page, or something else makes your Web page unavailable, you might be deleted from the rolling catalog. You can add the site back to Lycos again once it goes back up.) You can get more information on Lycos' policies at http://www.lycos.com/help/yoursite.html. Lycos is another of the search engines that does not index META tags.

Adult Sites Beware!—*You may notice that the proprietors of adult sites need to adhere to different standards from owners of sites viewable by a more general audience. That's because there's still a lot of controversy about what is and isn't appropriate content. We're not going to get into that in this book; however, we do suggest that if you have any content that's appropriate only to legal adults—pornography-related, drug- and alcohol-related, gambling-related, whatever—pay extra careful attention to the search-site submission rules because there may be exceptions that apply to you.*

NORTHERN LIGHT

Main Site: http://www.nlsearch.com/
Site Submission Page: http://www.northernlight.com/docs/register.htm

Northern Light is different from most of the other major search sites. It includes a special collection of material—news articles and the contents of press wires—in addition to indexed Web sites. Northern Light asks that you submit only one URL per day, and points out that it will only accept 120 submissions per user per day. (Any submissions over that will be discarded; Northern Light asks for your name and e-mail address when you submit a URL so it probably tracks your submissions that way.) At this writing, it takes about six weeks for a submitted site to make it into the index. Northern Light does not index or consider META tags; instead, it takes site descriptions from the title tag and the first 250 characters of a Web page (another good reason to have a great title tag).

GOOGLE

Main Site: http://www.google.com
Site Submission Page: http://www.google.com/addurl.html

Google's site submission page has a bare minimum of information. It does not guarantee when a site will be listed and there's no stated policy about META tags. Possibly this is because its results are ranked based on page popularity and there's little you could do, as a Webmaster, to influence that (except make your site more popular, of course).

ASK JEEVES

Main Site: http://www.askjeeves.com
Site Submission Page: http://www.ask.com/docs/help/#url

Ask Jeeves is a natural language search engine; therefore submitting a URL is not as simple as filling out a form. Instead, you're asked to send an e-mail with the URL of your site and a description. We'd recommend a brief description and then possibly a few questions that your site could answer since Ask Jeeves finds sites for users by answering questions. Be sure that you have plenty of content before submitting to this one.

LOOKSMART

Main Site: http://www.looksmart.com/
Site Submission Page: http://www.looksmart.com/h/info/subsite.html

You may not have heard of LookSmart; it's a searchable subject index a lot like Yahoo!. You can get a good idea of what LookSmart wants by checking its submission FAQ at http://www.looksmart.com/h/info/submitfaq.html. (Don't bother to submit pornographic sites, violent sites, or sites promoting illegal activity; LookSmart doesn't want 'em. LookSmart also warns against sites with too few pages. It's looking for meaty, meaningful pages.)

Surf the LookSmart categories and find a category that fits your site. (Don't submit to the "Best of the Web" categories because your submission will be discarded.) Click the Submit button. You'll be asked for a variety of information, including the title of the site, the URL, description, keywords (these are optional), date the site was launched (optional again), and contact information. LookSmart has rather exact guidelines for how long a description and keywords can be, so pay attention to those. It can take between six and eight weeks for your site to get listed, so don't expect your site to appear here overnight.

LookSmart's Express Listing—*LookSmart does have an express-listing option where you can have your site considered within 48 hours for a refundable fee of $199. Frankly, we don't think this is worth it unless you have $199 you won't miss and absolutely have to have the publicity quickly.*

FINDING SPECIALTY SEARCH SITES

As we noted, there are lots of other search sites out there—literally hundreds. They don't get as much traffic as the big ones we've mentioned here, but their visitors are often interested in specific subjects. If your subject and the search site's match, you have a unique opportunity to attract qualified traffic to your site. The following list includes sites that list both search sites and specialty subject indexes. These sites are a great way to find places to register your Web site, places that focus on the same subjects that you do.

BEAUCOUP

http://www.beaucoup.com/

Beaucoup is a great place to start—it has links to over 2,000 search sites, indexes, and meta-listings to help you submit your site to targeted sites. Sites are divided by category and subcategory.

ARGUS CLEARINGHOUSE

http://www.clearinghouse.net/

If you want more information about sites and directories before you start submitting to them, check out the Argus Clearinghouse. Argus has policies for accepting new listings into its directory (it says it accepts only about 5–10 percent of the guides submitted), and it reviews each resource and gives it a rating, so you can check that before visiting a search site or specialty index. Look here for high-quality, scholarly stuff.

THE BIGHUB

http://www.thebighub.com/

The BigHub links to thousands of searchable databases (Figure 6.2). You'll see that the name of the resource is a clickable link—that's how you get to the site itself. If you want to search it to see if your Web site is already there, use the search form. This is a fantastic resource, well worth visiting.

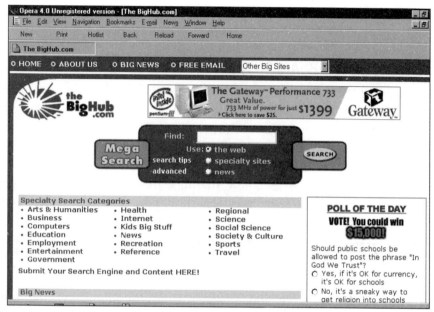

FIGURE 6.2: There are many different search engines in lots of different categories.

Meta Lists—*A meta-listing is an exhaustive listing of sites in one category. For example, if you had a site devoted to lighthouses and created a huge list of links devoted to lighthouses and nothing but, you'd have a meta-listing devoted to lighthouses. Meta-listings are sometimes better than general subject directories like Yahoo!, since site owners often invest a lot of energy in indexing sites of only one type.*

FINDERSEEKER

http://www.finderseeker.com

If you want to use a search site to find the search sites, check out FinderSeeker. This is especially good for those of you who might be looking for rather obscure categories because you can search by keyword. You can also narrow your search by category or geographical location. (Sometimes when searching you'll find things besides search sites; FinderSeeker also lists software archives, site-rating services, and so on.) There are several places where you can find lists of specialty search engines and indexes. Try these on for size:

InvisibleWeb
http://www.invisibleweb.com

direct search
http://gwis2.circ.gwu.edu/~gprice/direct.htm

SearchIQ
http://www.zdnet.com/searchiq/subjects/

AUTOMATED SUBMISSIONS

After reading all these listings, you may have tossed this book across the room a couple of times and decided this was all too much trouble. You don't have to do each site manually—though we recommend it if you want to be absolutely sure of how your site was submitted and when. If you want to save time, you can try third-party software and submission services. It's probably a good idea to submit Yahoo! by hand, and perhaps a few major search sites such as Google, and AltaVista. Some search sites require that you provide quite a bit of information—descriptions, keywords, and so on.

Goodbye Automated Submissions?—*The major search sites don't much like the idea of automated submissions because they're the cause of so much abuse. If the search sites really wanted to, they could easily stop almost all automated submissions by continually changing the way in which the submission programs work, making it virtually impossible for the submission services to keep up with the changes.*

The submission services are worried about this and have been lobbying the search sites for some kind of certification for submission services.

There's a wide variety of software and third-party services that will help you get your sites submitted to the search sites. These software packages and services ask you for a lot of information initially—your site name, URL, description, keywords, and other information that search sites and specialty indexes want. Then they take that information and send it to the search sites in the form in which they need it. This saves you from typing the same information over and over again, and saves you time by submitting to search sites automatically. The downside is that some search sites don't seem too keen on submissions from automated packages. We recommend that you use software and third-party services only for search sites and subject indexes that aren't top priorities for you.

Some services advocate things like keyword stuffing and multiple doorways to get better search-site ratings. Check out what's being offered before you get too much into it.

SUBMISSION SERVICES

Submission services are Web-based systems that you can use to submit to hundreds of search sites at a time. You enter your information into a Web form, include your credit-card number, and that's it—the service does the rest.

SUBMIT IT!

http://www.submitit.com/

Submit It! is one of the oldest submission sites on the Web. Currently it offers automated submission to over 400 search sites and directories. It also offers free verification of pages and the ability to re-announce changed pages. At the time of writing the price of a 12-month license was $59 for two URLs. (Since many of the search sites automatically index your entire site if you submit one URL, that's not as skimpy as it sounds.) You can get more expensive licenses for more URLs. In addition, you also have the use of Site Analyzer, which analyzes browser compatibility, link rot, load times, popularity, and spelling, among other things.

!REGISTER-IT!

http://www.register-it.com/

Now a part of Netscape, !Register-It! offers you the ability to submit to up to 400 sites on the Web and lets you get an idea of how it works by offering a free version that allows you to submit to a dozen or so search sites. !Register-It! offers a 30-day money-back guarantee and the ability to use a visitor-tracking service, and a service (*Hitometer*) that allows you to track how many visitors have been to your Web site and at what pages they were looking. (We'll discuss this subject in Chapter 14, *Tracking Results and Responding*.)

There are many other services on the Web; check out the following to get an idea of what's available:

@Submit! (Register with 20+ sites free)
http://www.uswebsites.com/submit/

A1 WebSite Promotions (Three months' submission for $89, six months' for $159, with other services available.)
http://www.a1co.com/

AAA Internet Promotions (50 sites for $99, 100 for $199. Also options to submit once a month for a year. No adult sites.)
http://www.websitepromote.com/dls/

JimTool Free Site Submitter (Several different submission options)
http://www.jimtools.com/

SiteLaunch
http://www.sitelaunch.net/

SmartAge Submit
http://www.smartage.com/submit/

TrafficBoost.Com (530 sites for $49, or 530 sites submitted four times for $99)
http://www.contactdata.net/

WebStep
http://www.mmgco.com/top100.html

Yahoo!'s List of Services
http://dir.yahoo.com/Computers_and_Internet/Internet/World_Wide_Web/Site_
Announcement_and_Promotion/

SOFTWARE

The other submission option is to use software programs that run on your own computer. Literally dozens of software programs can help you promote your Web site. The following few are noted as being at the top of their class at **Tucows**. (Tucows is one of the best repositories of Internet software. When you need some Internet software and don't know where to turn, start there first: http://www.tucows.com/.)

Why would you use a software package instead of the third-party services we mentioned previously? A few reasons. With a software package, you can submit to search sites as many times as you want. You can submit multiple URLs without having to pay individually for each, and, if you're the suspicious type, you'll know the submission work is being done if you do it yourself.

ADDSOFT

Publisher's URL: http://www.cyberspacehq.com/
Product URL: http://www.cyberspacehq.com/addsoft/

If you're trying to promote a piece of software, this is the program for you. AddSoft enables you to automate submitting your software to several shareware sites and software directories. The software is presented in a series of tabbed windows; you submit information about your company and software, and then click the Sites tab. The tab will give you a list of directories to which you can submit. (In the demonstration version, you can submit your software to only a limited number of sites.) Since software tends to go through many permutations, this is an excellent tool for you to use when your site undergoes an update, and you know that not every shareware directory will pick up on it. AddSoft is currently $89.

ADDWEB

Publisher's URL: http://www.cyberspacehq.com/
Product URL: http://www.cyberspacehq.com/addweb/

By the same publishers that put together AddSoft, AddWeb is for promoting Web sites. It's a collection of screens (see Figure 6.3). You enter all the vital information about your Web site (and your company) in one; choose the search sites to which you want to submit in another. (AddWeb currently works with about 5,000 search engines and sites); then begin the submission process that AddWeb will update for you in a kind of digital control panel. AddWeb has a search-site–analysis feature that checks several search sites to see where your Web site shows up

Many sites require a reciprocal link—they'll link to you if you link to them. AddWeb takes care of this by keeping track of those sites. It then spits out a Web page with all the reciprocal links on it, which you can go ahead and put on your Web site.

AddWeb has three versions. The standard version costs $69. The Gold version costs $119 and offers you the ability to submit more Web sites at one time to the search engines and directories, and allows you to create advanced submission reports. (These are both good options if you're doing a lot of URL submissions, or you're doing URL submissions on behalf of a lot of different people and you want

FIGURE 6.3: This is AddWeb, a submission program that gives you plenty of control over the process.

to send them reports.) The Pro version costs $169 and has everything the AddWeb Gold version has plus the ability to add new search sites to the database, submit even more URLs at a time, and more.

SUBMITWOLF

Publisher's Site: http://www.msw.com.au/wolfhq.htm

Product Site: http://www.msw.com.au/swolf/

SubmitWolf currently has information for over 1,500 search sites. These sites are divided into several different categories: Engines (search engines and sites), Links (Lists of links available), Manual (sites that have complicated submission arrangements or are fairly minor listings), Custom (a subset of engines and lists that are of particular interest to you and your Web site), and RIP (sites that aren't at this moment responding to SubmitWolf). You can try to submit to them but there's no guarantee that you'll get through.

Clicking one of the buttons next to a listing will give you a wealth of information, including the name of the search site, the URL, the submission URL, and the various rules for submission. (It's a violation of SubmitWolf's terms of usage to break these rules.) This program requires a little more work than AddWeb, but in return it gives you a lot more search-site information. SubmitWolf costs $95.

For more submission software, check out the following Web sites:

GlobalSpider
http://www.globalspider.net/

Hurricane WebPromo
http://www.theoffice.net/webpromo/

HyperHits
http://webmastertools.com/

Net Submitter Pro
http://softwaresolutions.net/

Register Pro
http://www.registerpro.com/

SoftSpider
http://www.designmaker.com/

Submission Wizard (Windows 95; 500 search sites—the program will run for one month for $30, six months for $85)
http://www.exploit.com/Submit Blaster

WebPosition
http://www.webposition.com/

www.SitePromoter (Windows and the Mac)
http://www.sitepromoter.com/

Check Your Search Site Position

Want to know how you're showing up in those search sites once you've been added? Some of the services we mentioned previously will give you an idea of your position with search sites—they have built-in utilities for providing feedback; but there are also independent services that focus solely on showing you how you're doing with the search sites. Check the following Web sites for more information.

MetaMedic (Online meta-tag checker for free, with a pro version available for pay)
http://www.northernwebs.com/set/setsimjr.html

MyRank (Free search-site rankings delivered by e-mail)
http://www.myrank.com/

Position Agent (Free trial for a commercial rank-checking service)
http://www.positionagent.com/

ScoreCheck (A free trial of a commercial rank-checking service)
http://www.scorecheck.com/

SmartAge SiteRank (A free trial of a commercial rank-checking service)
http://www.smartage.com/rank/

WebPosition (Rank-checking software; download version available)
http://www.webposition.com/

Yahoo!'s Listings
http://dir.yahoo.com/Computers_and_Internet/Internet/World_Wide_Web/Site_
Announcement_and_Promotion/Search_Engine_Placement_Improvement/

Search-site submission isn't something you can do in five minutes, so plan to spend a lot of time with it. A good rule of thumb is to start with the major search-site listings first, go to the searchable subject indexes second (concentrating on the groups you think are most important to your product or service), and then work on the specialty directories.

Even after you've registered your site, you're not finished. The next step is to try to get certified, recognized, notified, and awardified. Some of these will just make you feel good, while others will help build your visitors' confidence in your site. Check out the next chapter for more information on awards and certifications. Then visit Chapter 8, *Other Places to Register Your Site*, where we'll tell you about yet more places to register your Web site.

CHAPTER SEVEN

Getting Certified: Assurances, Awards, and Alliances

If you're fairly new to the Internet, you may remember how you felt when you first logged on. You had questions about the safety of your information. You didn't know how Web sites could accept your credit card without anyone else getting the number; you didn't know how to confirm the trustworthiness of the businesses with whom you shopped, and so on. Over time you got the answers to those questions and your Internet experience became more comfortable.

Your Web site visitors are all in various states of Internet enlightenment. Some of them know exactly how the Internet works—possibly better than you do. Some of them have a good idea of what's going on, and are comfortable visiting your site and buying online. Still others are nervous about giving out personal information online and need lots of assurance.

It's easy for you to post huge assurances about how great you are, how trustworthy you are, how wonderful your Web site is, and so on, but you are not going to be immediately credible. While reading all those accolades about your company, viewers will keep constantly in mind that the accolades are coming from...your company. (When you're reading a newspaper, which do you attach more credence to: an advertisement or a positive product review?)

There are companies out there that will vouch for your Web site in several areas—how you handle privacy, how suitable your content is for children, whether your Web site is accessible by any browser, and so on. By getting in touch with these sites and participating in their programs, you can assure your visitors you're complying with certain Internet standards.

Some companies award sites with special recognition for having great content, being especially appropriate for kids, and so on. By nominating your site for these kinds of awards, you can build your credibility to target audiences and increase overall traffic to your Web site.

Finally, you can make a statement about your beliefs and the causes you support by joining many of the alliance programs online. (Your jaw will drop when you see how many "wear a ribbon for a cause" campaigns are available online. Only you don't wear these ribbons on your clothes, you put them on your Web site.) With these programs you can establish a bond with your visitors by letting them know you believe in something in which they also believe. Of course, this has the potential to backfire if you show that you believe in something with which they disagree, but we'll get to that later in the chapter.

ASSURANCES

We've had friends who asked if the Internet could steal their credit card numbers from their computer. They had never made a transaction online, didn't intend to, and in fact had never entered their credit card numbers into their computer; but they were still worried.

Their fear might sound a little irrational, but perhaps they have the right to be irrational. It seems like every week brings a new privacy problem or security bug in the major browsers, some way that the always-on broadband connections can be exploited, and so on. Further, parents have concerns about the content their children can see, and may question whether your site is suitable for youngsters. Other visitors, who might have special needs, have other questions. It's hard to know everything—the Internet changes so quickly—and easy to feel overwhelmed.

You should not dismiss concerns like these out of hand. At the least you need to take some time to educate your visitors and help them understand why these kinds of things aren't a problem with your site.

This is where the third-party assurances come in. The third parties provide complete explanations of the issues and standards they support. By joining a program, you're connecting your visitors to its explanations and getting a little of the credibility of those third parties. The assurances can be simple (that your Web site conforms to an open HTML standard) or more controversial (that your Web site has a clear and easily accessible privacy policy, or that your Web content is suitable for children).

You can get involved in a variety of programs. A few are listed here in alphabetical order. Don't feel you *have* to work with any of these programs, but in some circumstances, you may find them useful or beneficial.

***Walk the Talk**—At this writing, the big watchword on the Internet is privacy, and a lot of companies are giving themselves black eyes by not living up to their promises. Doing this is a sure-fire way to kill your credibility, and you don't want to do that. Do everything you can to keep the promises you make to your customers.*

ANYBROWSER

http://www.anybrowser.org/campaign/

Not long after the World Wide Web got started, there was Mosaic. Then there were Netscape and Mosaic. Then there were Internet Explorer and Netscape. (These are the popular graphical browsers—programs that can display pictures. Lynx, a text-based browser, has also been around the whole time.)

These days, things are more complicated in the browser market. There's AOL, Internet Explorer, Netscape, WebTV, Opera, browsers on WindowsCE, and Palm computing devices, and Lynx, of course. You can hardly guess who's going to be looking at your site or what Web browser they're going to be using to look at it, and of course some things work on one browser that don't work on another browser.

The AnyBrowser program advocates that Web designers use HTML code that's accessible by any browser. If your Web site is standard text and graphics, you'll have no trouble adhering to this. If you're getting fancy with ActiveX, Java, or other bells and whistles, you'll have to check your code carefully.

This site has several small icons you can put on your Web page showing that you adhere to an AnyBrowser standard, design guides to make sure you're using compatible HTML, and links to like-minded assurance programs and resources.

BOBBY

http://www.cast.org/bobby/

That's Bobby as in British policeman. Bobby checks out your Web pages to make sure they're HTML-compliant and easily accessible to the handicapped. It checks for accessibility errors—like making sure all your images have ALT tags attached to them—and accessibility recommendations; that is, what you can do to make your Web site more accessible to people with disabilities. Bobby will also ask you accessibility questions related to your page to help identify problems that Bobby can't diagnose on its own and give you its own accessibility hints. (These hints will open your eyes to possible accessibility problems we bet you haven't even considered.) It'll also give you a summary of how long it took your Web page to load and how long each of the images took to load.

If you don't have any accessibility errors, Bobby will give you a banner to put on your site. (Incidentally, Bobby doesn't like the way ad banners that use server-side image maps work, so if you belong to an ad network that uses those banners, you will not be Bobby-approved—see Chapter 12, *Advertising Your Site* for information about banner networks.) The banner assures your visitors that your site is accessible to viewers with disabilities and that you've taken steps to be compatible with the HTML standard.

BBBONLINE PRIVACY PROGRAM

http://www.bbbonline.org/businesses/privacy/index.html

BBB stands for Better Business Bureau, an organization dedicated to protecting consumers against fraud. An offline mainstay for decades, in the last few years the Council of Better Business Bureaus has moved online and created Web sites to educate consumers about online frauds, hoaxes, and other things that online buyers need to be wary about.

Recently the Better Business Bureau has started accepting applications for a new BBBOnLine Privacy Seal Program. This program is designed to assure site visitors that any information they submit will not be misused. It's a lot like the TRUSTe program discussed in the next section of this chapter, except that there's an offline component to it.

Applicants to the program must have a U.S.-based Web site and have a satisfactory rating with the BBB. Other requirements include the following:

- The adoption of a clear privacy statement (what sites are doing with information they collect from visitors)
- An agreement to participate in the BBBOnLine Privacy Policy Dispute Resolution Program, a program through which the BBB helps consumers resolve issues when they have disagreements with a particular company
- Adherence to a compliance program set by the BBB

Applicants must also agree to participate in consumer-education activity, helping visitors understand what online privacy means

If you have a site that caters to kids, you might want to check out the privacy seal that's designed specifically for sites aimed at those 13 years old and younger; requirements for that seal are slightly different.

This program is not cheap (depending on what you regard as cheap, of course). Annual registration prices range from $150 (for sites with annual sales of less than $1 million) to $5,000 (for sites with over $2 billion in sales). At this writing, the BBB site is warning that its rates will go up as of September 2000. If you're selling products online, consider it an investment in consumer trust.

You might also wish to investigate the **BBBOnLine Reliability Program** at http://www.bbbonline.org/businesses/reliability/index.html. This is more similar to the traditional work of the Better Business Bureaus. The Reliability Program is a neat idea; the participating site agrees to adhere to the BBBOnline's standards of honest advertising and customer service. (This includes, of course, having a satisfactory record with the offline counterpart of the BBB.) The participating site puts up a BBB seal, and the BBB hosts the company's profile on the BBB server. When visitors clicks the BBB seal, they're taken to the profile page, which lists essential information with the company (how long it's been registered with the BBB, and so on). It's an easy way to create a credible repository for important company information.

TRUSTE

http://www.etrust.com/

Privacy is a huge buzzword online. People wonder whether their information is kept private, what Web sites are doing with registration information, and whether their e-mail addresses are going to end up on spam mailing lists. This is becoming a bigger and bigger issue every day.

In response to this, many Web sites are developing privacy policies. These policies make clear what information a Web site is gathering about visitors, how that information is being protected, what the site will and won't do with it, and so on. Sites that don't adhere to their posted privacy policy are asking for a huge PR problem.

That's where TRUSTe comes in. TRUSTe is "an independent, non-profit privacy initiative dedicated to building users' trust and confidence on the Internet and accelerating growth of the Internet industry." Its organizers spent a lot of time putting together an organization that educates users about online privacy and teaches Web publishers how to develop fair and sensible privacy policies.

With that in mind, TRUSTe has developed a *trustmark* that participating sites can put on their sites. The trustmark certifies that the site has an easily available privacy statement that makes it clear what's being done with visitors' personal information, and gives users a choice about how their information is used and shared. (There are other requirements as well. You can read the entire list of requirements at http://www.etrust.com/webpublishers/pub_join.html.)

The TRUSTe program is one of the best known on the entire Web, and many major businesses subscribe to it. That's the good news. (We would guess it is better known online than the Better Business Bureau's assurance services, though of course not nearly as well known offline.) The bad news is that it's going to cost you. The annual license fee depends on your company revenue, ranging from $299 to $6,999. However, the fee may be a good investment since it carries so much credibility and it does help you build a comprehensive privacy statement for your site.

We recommend you seriously investigate the TRUSTe programs if one or more of the following conditions apply to you:

- You require a lot of personal information from your visitors. A privacy statement backed by TRUSTe can help alleviate visitors' fears that the information will be used inappropriately.
- You are participating in e-commerce, which also requires the online use of sensitive personal information.

If you view this as a good idea but prohibitively expensive, take a look at the credibility TRUSTe has built up, and take a look at how much trust you're asking from your users in the way of personal information. It may turn out that for building customer relationships and making them comfortable in dealing with you, it isn't that expensive at all.

Incidentally, certifications such as this may become increasingly important over the next few years, partly due to government pressure from the European Economic Community (EEC). The EEC is creating strict privacy laws and mandating that data gathered in Europe not be transferred to countries with less stringent privacy laws. This is putting pressure on U.S. companies that want to do online business in both Europe and North America—and even on the U.S. government—to follow suit.

***Children's Sites Should Be Extra Careful**—If you run a site that was designed for an audience of kids, you need to be aware of legislation that limits what personal information you can ask of kids. The Children's Online Privacy Protection Act (COPPA), passed by the United States Congress in June 1998, prohibits a site from gathering personally identifiable information from pre-teens without getting their parent's permission first. Make sure that the information you're collecting is within the bounds of the law.*

RSACI

http://www.rsac.org/

Parents thought keeping track of what their kids are watching on cable TV was hard! The World Wide Web has many more than 50 channels, and there are all kinds of, um, interesting things on display. If you're trying to attract kids or families to your Web site, you need to make sure they know your content is safe to view by all ages, or if it's not, that the pages about which they should be cautious are clearly delineated.

RSACi stands for Recreational Software Advisory Council on the Internet. The council members have taken it upon themselves to help parents control their children's access to objectionable material. RSACi's ratings are integrated into Internet Explorer (IE); an IE user can use this content-advisor feature to avoid sites that have certain RSACi ratings, or to actually avoid every site that isn't rated with RSACi. In Figure 7.1 you can see a site that has registered with both RSACi for content and Bobby for accessibility.

Web-site owners are invited to register their site with RSACi and get both an RSACi banner and a special PICS-Label META tag to include in their HTML code. The registration process is fairly simple. First, you'll be asked to specify for what amount of a site you're generating a tag; you can rate an entire site, a section of a site, or a single page. Next, you'll be asked to complete a one-page questionnaire and to give contact information—address, phone number, and so on.

After that, you'll get into content rating. You'll be asked to give your site's level of nudity, sexual activity, language (from slang all the way up to making horses blush), and violence. Definitions are clearly provided for everything, so there shouldn't be any ambiguity as you create your ratings. You'll then be asked to agree with RSACi's terms and conditions. Finally, you'll be given your rating. Along with the rating you'll be given a META tag and an RSACi logo to use with your site. Registration is free.

If your site attracts any younger viewers at all, we urge you to consider this tag. If your site contains content that could be considered unsuitable for kids, you really should get this certification. Because it's supported by Internet

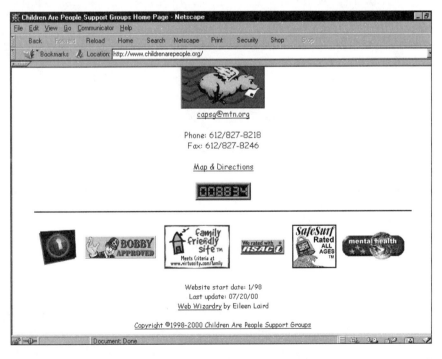

FIGURE 7.1: This page has registered with RSACi, so browsers can determine whether it's for children and with Bobby, to show that the site can be browsed by the disabled.

Explorer, it will become more widely used as time goes by and shows that you've made a good-faith effort to warn people about potentially offensive/harmful content on your site. This is a good message to get across.

SAFESURF RATING SYSTEM

http://www.safesurf.com/

The SafeSurf rating system, like RSACi, is intended to protect children from inappropriate material online. We don't know of any law that says you can't rate your site with both RSACi and SafeSurf, so we recommend you take the time to do both if your site is designed for families and young viewers, or if it contains material inappropriate for children.

Like RSACi, SafeSurf has a self-rating form. Initially you'll be asked whether you want to rate a single page or an entire directory. After that, you will be asked to provide the site's URL, the title, and your full name and e-mail, along with the recommended age range for site visitors (from "all ages" to "explicitly for adults.")

Banner Placement—*You might be thinking, "These are an awful lot of little banners to put on the front page!" You don't have to put them all there. Put ones that offer reassurance or guarantees on the front page, like the BBB banner or the TRUSTe seal; but other ones that are concerned more with operability questions than consumer concerns, might belong on your "about this site" or awards page. As you add more of these types of banners to a page, pay attention to the page's load time.*

In the content arena, you will be asked to identify the presence of any one of nine themes, including profanity, glorifying drug use, and different sexual themes. SafeSurf's definitions are not as extensive as RSACi's; you may find yourself confused at certain points. (Be sure to check the ratings FAQ for more information.)

When you've completed your self-assessment of all the themes, a Web page will be returned to you with your rating along with an explanation of how to use it. The same information will also be e-mailed to you. This service is free.

WEB INTEROPERABILITY PLEDGE

http://www.zdnet.com/anchordesk/wip/pledge.html

One browser company develops one standard; another company develops another standard, and those who employ second-tier Web access devices, such as palmtop computers, are forced to try to navigate some happy medium. There are many different ways for browsers to look at Web sites. It's frustrating for Web masters to try to second-guess which standard will end up being prevalent, and it's frustrating for viewers to figure out which standard they want to use.

ZDNet, a division of publisher Ziff-Davis, is trying to end all that with the Web Interoperability Pledge. The pledge for Webmasters is pretty simple: "I pledge to use only recommended HTML tags as defined by W3C." **W3C (The World Wide Web Consortium** at http://www.w3.org/) is the body that sets and creates new HTML standards. Taking this pledge will show a good-faith effort towards creating a usable Web site.

You can get assurances from the BBB and other online agencies that you're a square company and it's okay to do business with you. You can get assurances from other sites that you're doing your bit to create one Web standard and make your site as accessible to as many people as possible; but how do you get assurance that you're cool, admired, and beloved in all corners of the Web? You need awards, of course!

AWARDS

Awards started off slowly. There was a *Cool Site of the Day, The Top 5% of All the Sites on the Web,* and so forth; but Web site awards have exploded. There's a *Cool Site of the Second,* for crying out loud, a site devoted to cataloguing the best "page not found" errors online, awards for Best Dog Sites—there are all kinds of awards available. (Peter's favorites are *The Absolutely Meaningless Site Award* and *The Bottom 95% of All Web Sites Award.*)

As you might guess from the fact that there are so many awards, they're not quite as meaningful as they used to be. Reams of meaningless awards can be bought for the price of a few e-mails. Some sites will give you awards simply if you link to them. You probably want to avoid these; they don't do you or your site a lot of good.

On the other hand, there are some great awards that can have a big effect on traffic. We'll point you to some good ones, and, if you really want to learn about every available award, we'll give you some links to those too.

Submitting Your Site

The most popular awards get lots of nominations. You want your nomination to stand out even before an editor looks at your site. Keep these rules in mind when nominating your site for an award:

- Abide by the guidelines for submitting your nomination. If they want a 50-word essay in purple text, give them a 50-word essay in purple text. And don't nominate your site for an inappropriate award—your consumer-protection cat-litter site will not be served by winning a "Cool Dog Site" award, and you'll waste everyone's time by nominating it.

- Create a precise description of the site that you can send with your nomination. Make sure it's free of spelling and grammar errors.
- Double-check, triple-check, quadruple-check the URL you submit! You don't want it to be incorrect.
- If your site requires anything for optimum usage (like RealPlayer, Shockwave, and so on) make sure the editors know about it. (You don't want them to visit and then leave because they don't have the right software to make the most of it.)

Really Good Awards

Might as well start at the beginning. Let's look at some particularly useful awards.

PROJECT COOL

http://www.projectcool.com/sightings/

The first big award, where it all started, was *The Cool Site of the Day*. The guy who created this award in mid-1994 has developed Project Cool Sightings, which dishes up a new Web site every day. This is a great award, but it's not for sissies. Make sure you're good, and darn good, before you submit here (and if you have a pornographic site, a site glorifying crime, or a site that's just a link list—don't bother). Project Cool judges sites on the basis of content, use of the Web as a medium, and well-thought-out navigation.

To Win or Not to Win—*It's Tara's opinion that having no award is better than having an almost worthless award. Peter's not quite so sure, having had a lot of fun collecting awards through multiple-submission engines; but he'd certainly agree that you should be choosy when looking through available awards. Ask yourself, "Do I want to display this banner on my Web site?" Don't go for quantity; go for quality. Fifty awards that no one has ever heard of will be beaten hollow by one USA Today Hot Site Award.*

Once you've submitted your Web site, explore the rest of the Project Cool site. You'll find some great resources for site developers and a community for people who build Web sites.

USA TODAY HOT SITES

http://www.usatoday.com/life/cyber/ch.htm

Every weekday except Friday, USA Today dishes up five hot sites that you should take a look at. (On Friday there's a "Weekend Edition" with an extended list.)

Tara's won two of the awards and noticed a serious pop in her site visits after she won them. Peter won one for his Poor Richard site, and had 2,500 extra visitors in two days.

USA Today's hot site awards are won by a wide variety of sites—new search engines, educational resources, media, or whatever; but they all have a lot of great content, and more than occasionally a good sense of humor. The USA Today technology editor chooses the sites on the basis of content and appearance, sites that "push the envelope," and etc. If you do win a USA Today Hot Site award, your site has a chance to be listed in the offline, print version of USA Today—another great perk, probably more valuable than the Hot Site award itself. In fact one of Tara's sites (her Louisa May Alcott Web site) *did* make it into the printed paper.

Regularly reading the USA Today Hot Site Awards gives you a good feel for what's out there and can point you to some sites that are making great use of online technologies.

Design Counts Less Than You Might Think—*Having great content is just as important as design when it comes to winning most of these awards, so don't fret if your site's layout is plain. Tara, as mentioned in the main text, has won two USA Today Hot Site awards, and she couldn't Web-design her way out of a wet paper sack.*

YAHOO! PICKS OF THE WEEK

http://www.yahoo.com/picks/

When Yahoo! really likes a site, it puts a pair of sunglasses next to it in the directory. It also lists its favorite sites in the "Pick of the Day." There is an e-mail address at the bottom of that page, so you can suggest your site as a Yahoo! pick. Get mentioned in Yahoo! What's New, and the number of visitors to your site could skyrocket.

NETGUIDE'S INTERNET SITES OF THE DAY

http://www.netguide.com/

Each of NetGuide's various subject guides has a Site of the Day. Go into each guide and look for an e-mail link to submit your site. These are the guide subjects: Computing, Entertainment, Health, Internet, Living, Money, News, Shopping, Sports, Travel, Women, and so on. If you're really lucky, eventually you may end up in the overall Net Guide.

Lesser-Known Awards

There are literally hundreds of Web-site awards, and it would take another couple of books to list them all. Unfortunately, a lot of them aren't worth the electrons on which they're printed. Anybody can make a little banner for an award, but that doesn't make it useful! Furthermore, an award that's impressive to your target audience—that Yak Stalking Site of the Day award, perhaps—is meaningless to a different group of users.

You're going to have to judge a lot of awards for yourself. Some are not going to do you any good, yet some specialized awards may turn out to be well worth having. There are a couple of enormous directories you can use to check out what's available:

AWARDS EMPORIUM

http://www.momsnetwork.com/aemporium.shtml

The Emporium allows you to fill out one form and submit your site for consideration to all the Awards Emporium members. We could not find a listing of the members on the site, but a backwards link check in Google found that 25 pages were linked back to the page to which the AE requests its members link. The AE asks that its members be family friendly, and have an awards program in place for at least one month.

Nomination Fees—*The vast majority of awards are free. Sometimes, however, a site award may ask you to pay a nomination fee. There are enough site awards going around that we don't recommend doing this. If it's an award you really want or that you personally consider prestigious, explore the award extra-thoroughly before handing over any money.*

AWARDS SITES!

http://www.awardsites.com/

When we mentioned this site in the first edition, it covered over 900 awards. Now it covers over 1900. The awards are rated—from 1 star to 5 stars. Awards that are rated from 3 to 5 stars are given a description and a graphical link (usually their award badge). Awards that get 1 or 2 stars get a text description and link to the home page. This site also breaks down the site listings by higher ratings versus lower ratings. Check out its specialty ratings to see if there are any awards especially suited for your type of site.

WEBSITE AWARDS

http://websiteawards.xe.net/

This site offers a worksheet of over 800 awards site. You can download the site to your computer and then follow the links and use the worksheet to record when you applied for awards and what happened. This site also offers links to award indexes, pointers to winning awards, and Webmaster resources. This site is nicely done—tons of stuff here.

As you've seen, there are many, many awards. For a list of around 20 award-related sites—including directories that will point you to hundreds of awards—read the special report **Getting Awards for Your Web Site** at http://www.poorrichard.com/freeinfo/special_reports.htm.

GIVING AWARDS

Before we move on from awards, consider another way to promote your site, something that many award sites are doing. You might want to give awards to other sites. Each time an award is placed, the recipient has to put a link from the image back to your site. This may be a good way to bring people to you.

Giving awards can turn into a major operation if you're not careful and can take up a great deal of time; but you may be able to get something out of it without too much effort if you play your cards right. For instance, perhaps you can tightly target the awards. If you're in the model-rocket business, give awards for model-rocket sites; if you're selling homeopathic medicines, give awards for alternative-medicine sites; and so on. Begin by seeking out sites, and picking the ones you like, the ones that are really useful. Later, if your award becomes well known in your business, sites will seek you out pleading for awards, but here are some things to consider:

- Make sure your award image contains your domain name, so even if people don't click the link back to you (and they probably won't often), they may remember your site. Few awards contain the URL, but it's a good way to make the most of what is really a promotion for you.

- Don't give in to the temptation to award undeserving sites! Yes, every award is a link back to you; but if you present awards to sites that are of no use to anyone, you'll dilute the value of the award, and people won't pay any attention to it. Maintain your award's credibility by having it really mean something.

***

Fake Awards—*If you have kind of a wild and crazy Web site, and you don't find awards to your liking, you might want to check out some fake certifications, awards, and banners—awards such as This Site is Made in the USA by Illegal Immigrants certification and the Titanic Navigation Award. These are only for those who have a sense of humor and want to show it off. They're not appropriate for most corporate Web sites (unless you manufacture whoopee cushions or something). Since they tend to mock things in which people believe strongly, you may find something in these sites offensive.* **Visit The Boodle Box**: http://www.jwp. bc.ca/saulm/html/award.htm, or **The Corporation's Icon Gallery** http://www.thecorporation.com/icon/icon.html.

- Make sure you have an attractive award logo. A well-designed image lends credibility to the award. Besides, nobody wants to display an ugly award. If it looks good, more people will display it.
- Consider linking awards to other promotions. For instance, if you present a site with an award, ask if the site would like to hold a drawing for one of your products.
- Make the name of the award descriptive—the Estes Web Rocketry Award rather than The Estes Award, for example. It'll be more memorable, and you'll get fewer inappropriate submissions. If it's clear what your award is all about, people are more likely to exclude it if the award isn't appropriate for their site.

ALLIANCES

Once you've set up your assurances to your visitors, and shown off the awards you've won for your site, you might want to tell a little more about yourself. What you believe in, what you support—in short, your alliances.

There's a lot of politics on the Internet. It's not political-party type of politics, but rather controversies over what's good for the Internet and what isn't. People have different and strong beliefs about free speech, filtering, spam, and other Internet activities. Remember that the Internet is still being formed. There are still policies being created. Speaking up about what you believe in can change the shape of the Internet.

People speak up about what they believe in through ribbons. We can't say for sure, but we think the whole ribbon thing on the Web was started through the EFF (Electronic Frontier Foundation) Blue Ribbon free-speech campaign that started several years ago. (More about that in a minute.) Since then there have been dozens of ribbon campaigns—from black ribbons to invisible ribbons to tie-dyed ribbons to plaid ribbons. (Look at Figure 7.2 for the merest sample!)

Why should you join an alliance when joining has the potential to alienate people as well as cause them to feel they have something in common with you? Sometimes it's appropriate to your Web site. If you're an online publisher, you might feel that supporting free speech is important to your Web site. If you've put up a site that provides computer support services, you might want to join the lime-ribbon campaign, which supports the notion that all computer users aren't geeks. Since that notion is appropriate to a Web page offering support services, and says a little bit about the people who run the site ("Hey, we don't want to be considered nerds. We just happen to be good with computers."), it's a good fit. You could also find yourself attracting links from other like-minded—and lime-ribbon–wearing—Web sites.

Maybe you don't want to wear your opinions as ribbons on your Web page. That's okay; but at least check out the campaigns described in the following sections.

EFF BLUE RIBBON CAMPAIGN

http://www.eff.org/blueribbon.html

The Electronic Frontier Foundation's Blue Ribbon campaign was started as a reaction to the United States government's attempts to legislate what kind of information could and could not be transmitted on the Internet. The campaign also opposes mandatory filtering of Internet content. This was the first big ribbon campaign on the Internet, and a casual check with AltaVista shows over 77,000 pages linking to the EFF Blue Ribbon campaign page.

GOLDEN KEY CAMPAIGN

http://www.privacy.org/ipc/index.html#Key

This isn't a ribbon but the idea is the same. The Golden Key Campaign supports privacy for Internet users. It supports the users' rights to send information privately and to have access to technology, like encryption, that protects their privacy. The campaign founders specifically want users to have the right to these

FIGURE 7.2: We told you there are a lot of ribbon campaigns!

technologies without government restraint. (In several countries around the world, there is a limit to encryption access, for instance.)

These are a couple of serious campaigns, but don't get the idea that every campaign is this heavy. (These are just examples we chose because they're fairly well known; we're not endorsing them or advocating that you join these or any other ribbon campaigns.) For a list of almost 200 ribbons, check out **The Ribbon Campaigns Web** site at http://www.gargaro.com/ribbons.html.

Among other things, you'll find the Rage Against Chain Letters campaign, the Be Nice to Newbies Campaign, the Leave Gary Coleman Alone campaign, and of course the No More Ribbons campaign.

Why all these campaigns? Because the Internet is full of varied and eclectic people. They've all got different agendas, different ideas, and, as you'll see, different senses of humor. Signing up for such campaigns can help you convey your beliefs to your audience. People don't have years to get to know you through your Web site. So one of the ways you can let them know about you is by using ribbon campaigns like these. You can make a stand, let people know what your concerns are, give some insight as to your beliefs, or show the world you've got a sense of humor, by your choice of campaigns. Don't go crazy with these ribbons, though. A few will make a lot more impact than a dozen and still serve to give your visitors some idea of what you're all about.

Every page addition we've talked about in this chapter has its own purpose. An assurance lets visitors know you're serious about your business and want to establish yourself as a credible merchant, organization, or information resource. An award (at least a good award) shows that you've established an excellent Web site in your field—and will attract a lot of visitors to your site. An alliance is a short-hand way to let visitors to your site know what you're all about and what's important to you, and perhaps attract links from other sites that feel the same way.

In summary, you want to make a good impression on your visitors and make them feel comfortable. (We're not advocating that you lie and put up a banner you don't believe in. You can make someone feel comfortable without compromising your own beliefs.)

Over the last few chapters we've covered a lot of information about preparing your Web site for indexing, registering with the search engines, and attracting visitors and confidence with assurances, awards, and alliances.

But there's still a little ground left to cover, some things that haven't yet been mentioned. In the next chapter, we'll cover miscellaneous and unique places where you can promote your site.

CHAPTER EIGHT

Other Places to Register Your Site

If you've followed our advice in earlier chapters, you've spent a lot of time getting your Web site ready and registered. At this point your site should be optimized for search engines, and you should have submitted your site to all the major ones. By now you've set up whatever alliances or affiliations you find necessary, and you might have even picked up a couple of awards. But you're not finished. Before you start looking beyond the Web for your promotional efforts, you can go a little further and make the most of the Web. In this chapter, we'll be looking at more places to register your Web site.

There are three major ways to promote your Web site besides the traditional Web services:

Announcement services. These are part mailing list, part newsletter, and part town crier. The Web grows so quickly that the announcement services are essential to anyone who wants to keep up.

Free-For-All link pages (FFAs). The FFAs allow anyone to add a link to a list without editing or reviewing the link. In limited situations these might be useful, but they do have serious drawbacks.

Web rings. Web rings are sites that are gathered together by subject. Web-ringed pages have HTML code at the bottom of their pages, allowing interested visitors to move from one site to another. In effect the sites are joined together in a ring.

Like-Minded links. This is Tara's term for sites that link to your site for some reason. They're not necessarily set up as search sites or directories, but their proprietors may like your site enough to link to it.

You can use any or all of these methods to help promote your site—we'll show you how in the "Announcement Services" section. Announcement services can be *very* effective, but probably the most powerful of all these techniques is finding sites that have interests similar to yours and asking them to link to you. Doesn't seem like a big deal, does it? But each of those links is a doorway, as we'll explain later. First, let's talk announcement services, Free-For-All link lists, and Web rings.

ANNOUNCEMENT SERVICES

In the summer of 2000, one company predicted that the Web had over two billion Web pages. Wrap your mind around that—two billion Web pages. Furthermore, it was estimated that the Web is growing at the rate of seven million pages a day. Yikes! Most mere mortals despair of ever keeping up with the changes.

Paper and online publications, like *NetGuide* and *USA Today*, review Web sites, but there's usually a lag time between the announcement of the sites and their coverage. They also have limited editorial resources, so they can't take a look at and review every site. Traditional news outlets like television and radio shows can review and announce new sites, but they usually stick to announcing major sites and don't provide much of an outlet for small players.

With all that being the case, it's not a surprise that editorial services have evolved that are limited to solely announcing Web sites. They don't review them, and they don't package them into well-rounded stories—they just announce them.

The most famous of these services is probably **Net-Happenings** at http://listserv.classroom.com/archives/net-happenings.html. Net-Happenings is moderated by Gleason Sackmann, who's going to get a medal for it one day. Every day he skims several mailing lists and reviews lots of submissions. He picks the best 40–60 entries and sends them on to his mailing list. Since his list is distributed both via mailing list and on USENET, he reaches a lot of people. (Officially at this writing he has around 6,500 subscribers but that doesn't take into consideration the people who read his postings on USENET or who forward his postings to other people.)

Gleason does a lot of work for one guy. Because Net-Happenings is a small operation, you have to be very careful about how you submit. For example, you can't submit on the weekends because weekend submissions are automatically deleted (so he doesn't have a backlog when he comes back Monday morning). When he goes out of town he announces it in advance, and you can't submit during that time because, again, submissions are deleted. When you do have an item to submit, you must go to the submission page. (There's a link from the URL we gave you previously.) You'll be asked to give your name, resource title, category, URL, and description.

Tara's been on Gleason's announcement list for about 3,000 years now, and based on the many announcements she's read, she has a few suggestions to make when you use Net-Happenings.

- Remember that you're announcing to a global audience. Tara's seen dozens of announcements talking about "Scenic Hedgefield" and "Beautiful Spring County" when the announcements don't bother to mention the city, state, or even country to which the resource is referring. Similarly, local business announcements and conference announcements that apply to a limited geographical area should be considered twice before being submitted to this list.

- Make sure your description is clear. You don't have to write War and Peace, but make sure that the description of your Web site is quite clear. In Chapter 6, *Registering with the Search Sites*, we asked you to write several different descriptions, of varying lengths, of your Web site. Take the longest one, add a few more words if you like, and use this as your description. Some people use press releases as their descriptions, but Tara isn't too keen on that. She thinks that's too much for busy surfers to read. If they want the whole release, they can get it at your Web site.

- Announcements that are riddled with spelling and grammar errors reflect poorly on the Web site, as do announcements IN ALL CAPS, overloaded with punctuation!!!!, and so on.

- Limit the number of times you use this service. Unless you're doing major content updates every week, we wouldn't recommend that you announce to Net-Happenings more than once a quarter. We wouldn't want to wear out our welcome.

Net-Happenings is a real biggie, but there are several other announcement services you can use. Here's a sample:

BUBL Link Updates (Updates to the Catalogue of Internet Resources)
http://www.bubl.ac.uk/link/updates/current.html

LinkMaster
http://linkmaster.com/

Nerd World: What's New
http://www.nerdworld.com/users/dstein/whatsnew.html

Netscape What's New
http://home.netscape.com/netcenter/new.html

Netsurfer Digest
http://www.netsurf.com/nsd/

The NewPageList
http://web-star.com/newpage/newpage.html

The Scout Report (Mostly academically-oriented resources)
http://wwwscout.cs.wisc.edu/scout/report/

What's New (A search engine and weekly bulletin of what's new on the Web)
http://www.whatsnu.com/

What's New in Canada
http://whatsnew.canadasearch.com/

What's New in the UK Index
http://www.ukindex.co.uk/whatsnew.html

What's New Too!
http://nu2.com/

Yahoo!'s What's New list
http://dir.yahoo.com/Computers_and_Internet/Internet/World_Wide_Web/Searchi
ng_the_Web/Indices_to_Web_Documents/What_s_New/

FREE-FOR-ALL LINK PAGES

Free-For-All (FFA) link pages are just that: link lists that anyone can add to without paying a fee. Sometimes they're so quick that your link appears immediately. That's good for quick exposure on the Web that slower-adding search engines can't provide.

Free-For-All link pages really *can* drive traffic to your Web site. That doesn't mean you should necessarily use them, however; the disadvantages may outweigh the advantages. So what's the problem with them? Well, one problem is that anyone can add to a link list. Unfortunately, a lot of Web pages that aren't accepted by standard search engines resort to link lists to get exposure on the Web. This includes questionable business sites, poorly written sites, adults-only sites, and so on.

Prepare for Possible Spam!—*Sometimes you have to submit your e-mail address to get an FFA-link and if you're not careful, you'll be giving your permission to receive spam! Be careful and read the privacy policies of FFA lists carefully. Sometimes it's recommended that you get a throwaway mail box—a free e-mail account from a provider like Hotmail. That can be useful, but you could just avoid spam-generating link lists altogether.*

Does that mean every site on an FFA link list is going to fit into one of the those undesirable categories? Of course not. However, it does mean you don't know into what kind of company your listing is going. There are a number of other reasons not to work with these systems, which we'll discuss in a moment. First, though, let's have a look at where to find these things.

Finding Free-For-All Link Lists

There are thousands of FFA pages. How do you find them all? There are a variety of directories of FFA link pages. A few of them are listed in the sections that follow.

ACCUSUBMIT FREE LINKS SUBMIT STATION

http://accusubmit.com/ffa/

The AccuSubmit Free Links Submit Station allows you to auto-submit your URL to FFA link lists. The free service allows you to submit up to five URLs at a time, while the pay service will submit your URLs several times daily to AccuSubmit's entire database of FFA link lists. This is a good place to start submitting to FFAs if you're determined to work with FFAs but have absolutely no money. Figure 8.1 shows you how you can use AccuSubmit to submit your URL to lots of link lists.

STEALTH PROMOTIONS FREE-FOR-ALL LINKS (FFA) PAGE

http://www.stealthpromotions.com/ffa.htm

This site offers an instant submission and promotion to several FFA lists. There's a lot of other information on this site about site promotion and FFA lists—worth a browse.

FIGURE 8.1: AccuSubmit lets you fill out one form and submit your site to several different lists.

***Lots and Lots of Errors**—You'll learn something else about FFA links when you start using these link indexes—many FFA link lists have about the same life span as a fruit fly. Expect lots of "page not found" errors when you're checking out these sites.*

JILL STUDHOLME'S FREE-FOR-ALL LINKS PAGES DIRECTORY

http://www.users.zetnet.co.uk/studholme/freelink.html

This site lists only about 40 FFA lists, but they seem to be of high quality—lists that are long lasting and concentrate on having good content.

LINK-O-MATIC

http://www.linkomatic.com/

This is one of the better FFA sites. You can submit to over 470 FFA pages in one fell swoop. For $100 you can buy 16,000 credits—16,000 individual submissions. That's currently 34 submissions to the entire list. It has a free trial, too, so you can see how it works.

***Are FFAs Really Free for All?**—They're called Free-For-All link pages, but sometimes they're not really for all. Some link sites restrict the type of links that can be posted, refusing adults-only sites or multilevel-marketing sites. Still other sites are restricted to links pertaining to a certain topic—check out a **Reiki** FFA list at http://www.reikilinks.com/. There are sites devoted to all sorts of other things. Be sure that you know of any restrictions before posting to FFA lists.*

If you want to find more of these sites, check **Yahoo!'s Free-For-All Pages** page: http://dir.yahoo.com/Computers_and_Internet/Internet/World_Wide_Web/Searching_the_Web/Indices_to_Web_Documents/Free_for_All_Pages/.

To give you an idea of what FFA pages are all about, let's look at one of them. **Leave-A-Link** at http://www.toocool.com/guest/cool.htm requires that its links be listed by category, and Leave-A-Link's search box is at the top of the page, more like a traditional subject directory. Only 20 of the most recent submissions are included on the front page. Leave-A-Link also doesn't add the links instantaneously; it takes 1 to 3 days to add a link, according to the site's FAQ. (Spammers submitting the same site multiple times will be banned.) This site's strengths lie in its ease of design and searchability.

There are hundreds—perhaps thousands—of FFA sites. You could easily spend many hours finding them, evaluating them, and then submitting to them (or not). We recommend that you don't bother with FFA sites at all unless you're really desperate for visitors; your time is probably better spent some other way. In any case, don't make them a high-priority activity, and definitely don't choose them as a promotion vehicle over the other methods described in this book. FFAs can give you a good quick burst of promotion, but you pay for that in the time it takes to find them and the company in which you might find your site.

Here's a real-life account of an FFA campaign. This comes from Peter's newsletter, *Poor Richard's Web Site News*. (This is a free newsletter—visit http://PoorRichard.com/newsltr/.)

Beginner's Column: Announce Your Site Here

[This article contained information about the What's Nu service, mentioned earlier in this chapter. Then Peter talked about FFA sites ...]

You can also get a few free links at this site:
http://www.linkomatic.com/

It only takes a few seconds, and you'll get links placed at 10 "Free-For-All" Web pages. (These are long lists of links.) Of course, the question is: Is it worth the time it takes to place the links?

If you sign up for the Link-O-Matic service (it costs $100, but don't do it yet...I'll explain why in a moment), you'll be able to automatically submit your link to a list of 445 Free-For-All pages. You'll get 16,000 credits—that is, 16,000 individual submissions—so you can submit to this list around 40 times. In theory that's 6.25 cents per link. In practice, however, some of the submissions fail for various reasons. (You'll get a report telling you which ones succeeded and which didn't.) The actual cost per link is probably more like 7 or 8 cents.

However, I suggest that you don't use this service, at least not for the moment. I've wondered about these Free-For-All Link pages for a long time. I've always thought they probably don't work particularly well, but after reading Link-O-Matic's sales blurbs and testimonials from users talking about how much traffic they'd got by using the program, I just couldn't help plunking down 100 tax-deductible dollars.

Peter did try Link-O-Matic, and he did report back to his readers. Here's an excerpt:

A few weeks ago I wrote about Link-O-Matic, a service that automatically submits your URL to hundreds of free link pages (sometimes known as Links-For-All or Free-For-All pages). At the time I was a little skeptical, but said that having paid my $100 I'd run the course, submit all 16,000 times, and report back.

I haven't yet submitted 16,000 times, but I think I've got enough information to update you. It really can push some traffic to a site. But it may not be worth the hassle. I just looked at my logs and found that about 200 people have visited my site over the past few weeks. I still have 13,088 submissions left, so once I've finished with them all I may have brought 1,000 to 1,100 people to my site. At a cost of $100, that's around 10 cents per visitor, which is reasonably cheap as far as advertising costs go.

At this point you've probably got two questions. First, why aren't I more enthusiastic?, and second, why haven't I used all 16,000 submissions?

Well, there are a few problems. Right now there are 500 link pages in the Link-O-Matic system. (There were around 450 when I started, a month ago.) Most of the sites don't accept duplicate URLs, so you can't use all 16,000 submissions at once; either you have to submit around 32 times, with about a week between submissions—if you submit too soon, the link pages will simply reject your submissions—or you have to set up a number of different URLs, and then submit links for those different URLs. I could create 32 different URLs, then create 32 different submission sets, to 500 pages each, on the same day, I guess, but I decided that spreading them out, doing one set of 500 every week, would be less hassle and probably more effective—the links would be seen by far more people if spread out. So although this free-link scheme may be effective to some degree, it's a bit of a nuisance to use; there have to be easier ways to bring people to a site than this!

WEB RINGS

Web rings are a completely different animal from FFA lists. FFAs can have all kinds of different content, while Web rings are generally devoted to one topic at a time. Web rings can bring a lot of interested visitors to your site, but they might leave just as quickly as they came. Figure 8.2 shows you a very specific Web ring—one that's devoted to a single author.

A Rose by Any Other Name—You'll hear Web rings referred to in other ways, such as loops or railways, but a ring is a ring; for instance, see **LoopLink** at http://www.looplink.com/.

Web rings are pretty simple. Sites participating in a ring use special HTML code that creates several Web-ring navigation links. These links allow visitors to move to the previous or next site in the ring, to go to another page in the ring that is selected randomly, and perhaps to visit the ring's main page, where they can see a list of all the sites within the ring. In theory all the sites are strung

FIGURE 8.2: As you can see, this site belongs to a highly specific Web ring (Louisa May Alcott) and a more general one (American Authoresses).

together in a big circle, so by clicking the Next link repeatedly, it should be possible to travel all the way around and come back to your starting point.

The largest coordinator of Web rings on the Net is **WebRing** at http://www.webring.org/. At this writing, WebRing sponsors over 80,000 rings, with over 1,300,000 sites participating.

When you visit WebRing, you can start a new ring, join an existing ring, or just check out what rings are available.

When you visit the site, you'll see that there are all kinds of rings—rings dealing with religion, romance, science, news, and lots more. There are rings for people who are clumsy and rings for people who consider themselves unenthusiastic. You get the idea. Rings range from five participating sites to hundreds and hundreds of sites!

The advantage to being a part of a ring is obvious. You'll have visitors coming to your site who are interested in your topic. The disadvantage is more subtle; if your site isn't immediately useful and compelling, the visitor can keep going on the ring and pass right by your site. Furthermore, very general rings might serve less of a purpose. The more specific the ring, the better. If you have a ring dealing with unusual museums or the visual arts in Russia, you've developed a ring of content that won't be available many other places on the Web. On the other hand, if you have a Web ring devoted to Texas, or football, or nothing in particular, your ring won't be that unusual in terms of content.

You have to consider the company you're keeping, too. Do you want to live in the same neighborhood as the other sites in your ring? Some rings are very exclusive about what they accept, while others aren't exclusive at all. Guess which rings we prefer?

Go over the available rings carefully and see if there are any that fit your site. If there aren't, you can start your own.

Another Potential Problem—*If you have a commercial site, you might want to avoid a ring. Besides sending viewers away from your site, you might end up in a ring with your competitors or with sites you wouldn't want people to think that you endorse.*

Create Your Own Web Ring

To start your own ring, go to **Webring.org** at http://www.webring.org/wrnewring1.html. The site warns you that starting a ring is not for HTML beginners and can be time-consuming, and that as a free service Webring.org can't make guarantees as to reliability.

If you're not scared away, creating a ring takes a series of steps. First you choose an identifier for your ring (just a brief series of letters and numbers—*new-ring, ring-123,* and so on). Next, you need to name the ring, provide the home URL of the ring, provide contact information (your real name and e-mail address), and choose a password for administering your ring. After that, you need to categorize your ring, describe what audience rating your ring has (from G to XXX), and describe your ring in 100 words or less. Finally, you must provide 20 keywords that visitors can use to find your ring when searching the WebRing directory. Once you've done that, WebRing will set you up with your own ring.

There are a few things to keep in mind if you decide to go the ring route:

- Please, one ring at a time. Some Web sites join four or five rings. Besides giving up a lot of real estate to the ring's HTML code, it's awfully confusing for the viewer.
- Make your entrance page—the one on which you put your site's entry point to the ring—as engaging and interesting as possible. You don't want the visitor to look at your site for two seconds, get bored, and move on.
- Check out your neighbors. Learn who the other sites in the ring are. You want to know with whom you're sharing the ring.

Tempted by the Web ring thing? Here are a couple of places to look for more info:

Sadiq's Webring Directory
http://www.users.dircon.co.uk/~majaffer/webrings/

Yahoo!—Web Rings Page
http://dir.yahoo.com/Computers_and_Internet/Internet/World_Wide_Web/Searchi
ng_the_Web/Indices_to_Web_Documents/Rings/

FINDING LIKE-MINDED LINKS

Between announcement services, Free-For-Alls, and Web rings, you might think you have all the bases covered; but the most important item is the last. You need to find yourself some like-minded links.

You should think of every link to your site as a doorway. If you want traffic, it naturally follows that the more doorways you have the better.

But some doorways are better than others. Doorways that lead from similar sites to yours are the best of all, since the visitors to those sites are already interested in what your site talks about. The process of getting those kinds of doorways is what Tara calls hunting like-minded links. In the process of building and researching your site, you may have already developed a list of sites that cover ground similar to yours. That's great. Put those aside for a moment and we'll show you several more ways to find like-minded sites—awards and *backlink* checking.

Awards

In the last chapter we told you how awards might be good for your site. If you focus on specialty awards, they're awfully useful for finding similar sites.

If you've spent some time submitting your site for awards that were appropriate to your site type, go back and look at the awards list now. Look at the specialty stuff. Then go check those awards' archives. (Most awards sites have an archive list.) If you do this with specialty awards, you'll be able to assemble a list of sites with interests that at least overlap with yours—and that must be marginally good or they wouldn't have won an award (assuming you've chosen decent awards).

Backlink Checking

Sometimes if you want to find something, you have to go backwards. Sites like **Google** (http://www.google.com/) and **AltaVista** (http://www.altavista.com/) allow you to search for Web pages that link to another Web page for which you specify the URL. By backlink checking someone else's URL, you can see who is linking to it. If you have a site related to sheep herding, you might want to find other sheep herding sites, do backlink checks on them, and see who is linking to them.

(Why? We'll get to that…you're going to ask for links, or, as we'll explain in Chapter 10, *Grass Roots Marketing*, perhaps propose some kind of promotion at those sites.) Here's how you do it:

- Find one Web site that covers the same topic you do. This site can be a Web site you found with the awards trick we mentioned previously, a site that you found when you created your site, or a competitor's site. Choose a site that's reasonably popular, so it's likely to have a good number of links to it. (On the other hand, don't choose something that's so popular you get an overwhelming number of links, like CNN or Yahoo!.)
- Find a search site that supports backlink checking, such as AltaVista or Google.
- Search for that site's URL—you'll be given a list of the sites that are linking to it.

Here are a couple of examples of how to backlink search—at AltaVista and Google:

Google—Use the link special syntax, like this: *link:http://www.poorrichard.com*.

AltaVista—Use the *link:* keyword (we talked about AltaVista's keywords in Chapter 2, *What You Need Before You Start*), like this: *link:poorrichard.com*. (Don't include the *http://* bit. Don't even include the *www.* bit; you may reduce the number of hits if you do.) Of course you'll want to omit links to the page from the same Web site. You can do that by using *-host:*, like this: *-host: poorrichard.com*. So the complete search string would be link:*poorrichard.com -host:poorrichard.com*.

You'll find that you get some good results, a few *great* results, and a few results that aren't any good at all; but you will get enough that you'll find some places that would look good with your site linked to them.

Here's a really neat little service you can use to automate this backlink process: **LinkPopularity.com** (at, you guessed it, http://www.linkpopularity.com/). This site has a form into which you enter your URL—or the URL of some other site you'd like to check up on. The system does a backlink search at AltaVista, HotBot, and InfoSeek at the same time (see Figure 8.3).

Gather a list of appropriate sites together using the tools we talked about in Chapter 2, *What You Need Before You Start*. Once you have a list together, start cruising these sites. Don't spend more than a few minutes at each site, but keep the following questions in mind:

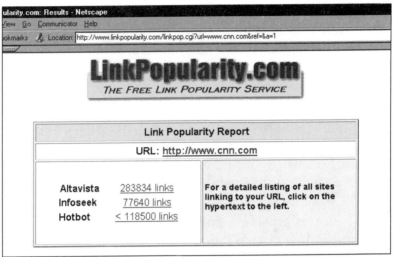

FIGURE 8.3: LinkPopularity.com lets you search for links to a URL at three search sites at a time. (One day, if you're really lucky, maybe you'll get a result like this for your Web site!)

- How's the overall composition of the site? Is it a professional presentation?
- What are the other links like? Are they links you'd want to be associated with?
- Is there a site counter available? If so, does the site seem to get a lot of traffic? Does it seem to be updated often?
- Does the Webmaster seem receptive to adding links?

The reason we ask you to keep these things in mind is because you visit a Web site for the first time only once. And in that one time, you get impressions that a lot of other visitors to the same site get. You need to analyze those impressions and ask yourself, "Is this the kind of company with which I want to be associated?"

Contacting the Webmaster

Suppose that you've found a great site, and you want to get a link from it to your site. Here's how to do it:

1. Find the Webmaster's address, and e-mail him or her. Address the Webmaster by name if possible. If not, address the message to Webmaster, or Site Owner, or whatever seems appropriate. Don't address the message "To Whom It May Concern"; that looks like a form letter or, worse, spam.

2. Tell the Webmaster you like the Web site and *name the Web site*! Tara gets e-mails from people saying things like, "I like your Web site. Please link to my Web site." The problem is that Webmasters often administer multiple

Web sites that cover completely different subjects, so they may have no idea which site you're talking about. If you're asking for a link from a popular Web site, be aware that the site administrator probably gets tons of e-mail. Make things as easy as possible.

3. Don't say "I love your site" unless you mean it. And if you *do* mean it, give an example ("I thought your bibliography page was great; I can't believe you've found over 200 references.") so you don't sound like you're just trying to get a link.

4. Ask if the Webmaster would consider linking to your site; give the Webmaster a reason. Why would your site be of interest to the Webmaster's visitors?

5. It's a good idea to provide a brief description of your site in addition to asking for the link. It gives Webmasters something to use so they can put the link up quickly. The description no-no's we talked about in Chapter 6, *Registering with the Search Sites*, apply doubly here—no puffery, etc.

6. Thank the site administrators for their time, no matter what they decide.

To Reciprocate or Not to Reciprocate?

Sometimes when you contact people and ask them to link to your site, they ask that you link to their site in return. Trading a link for a link is known as a *reciprocal link*.

Do you have to offer reciprocal links every time you ask for a link? No, you're not obligated to give a reciprocal link to anybody. And sometimes it's not appropriate. Let's take a look at an example. Say you administer a Web site that sells Toyota truck parts. You have lots of information on Toyota repair, parts lists, and so on. In short, your site is useful to a group whether they buy from you or not.

Perhaps you're already linking to lots of Toyota sites—racing trucks, repair information, and so on—so if you ask for a link to a new site about Toyota racing you've just found and the Webmaster has asked for a reciprocal link, you might as well give it. It fits in with your existing list, anyway.

However say you ask for a link from a broader site—like a specialty index that covers Japanese vehicles. That's probably too broad for you to link to, but your site is appropriate for *them* to link to. In that case a reciprocal link isn't necessary.

***Let's Be Honest**—It's in your interest to get as many links as possible, and, perhaps, to give as few as possible. Don't take inappropriate links in return for links to your site.*

Also remember that when you link to a site, for whatever reason, you may want to contact that site and ask for a reciprocal link. Actually, when Tara is in this situation, she links to the site and simply informs the site of what she's done. She doesn't ask for a reciprocal link because she considers it a little pushy. Nonetheless, she has discovered that around half of those sites give her a reciprocal link anyway.

Finding like-minded sites and asking the Webmasters for links should be an ongoing part of your promotional efforts. Keep an eye out for appropriate sites. Try to contact five or ten of them each week. You'll find as you do this that your efforts will snowball. Other sites will link to yours without your asking them to. You'll get pointers to other resources. This should be a high priority in your promotional efforts, but it doesn't need to take a lot of your time.

Part II of this book has been the meat-and-potatoes part if you have a Web site. If you don't have a Web site, these chapters have probably given you a few new reasons to have one, and some design tips you can use before you even crack any HTML. If you follow all the directions in this part, covering all your bases, you will get traffic.

However as anyone who used the Internet before 1994 knows, the Internet is not simply the Web, and the Web doesn't come near to encompassing all the Internet. You can go beyond the Web when it comes to your promoting and marketing; you can go to newsgroups, newsletters, and even other Web sites. Part III will help you learn more about how to get the word out.

PART III
GETTING THE
WORD OUT

CHAPTER NINE

Promoting in the Newsgroups and Mailing Lists

This is a sensitive subject. We're going to talk about promoting your products and services in the Internet's discussion groups—newsgroups, mailing lists, Web forums, and the online services private discussion areas (MSN BBSs, CompuServe forums, and so on).

It's a sensitive subject for a couple of reasons. First, many people feel that these discussion groups should not be used as promotional tools. Second, so many people have used these groups as promotional tools in such a grotesque and clumsy manner that it's easy to see why people think that discussion groups should not be promotional tools. Sending unsolicited commercial e-mails to newsgroups is called *spamming*—see the accompanying note for a little more information on that term and how spamming has affected newsgroup culture.

In fact, commercialism seems to be killing many newsgroups. It's so easy to push promotional messages into the newsgroups, thousands at a time, that many newsgroups are little more than junk repositories.

The History of Spam—*The term spam, although today applied mainly to e-mail, originated with newsgroups. Spam messages were newsgroup messages sent to hundreds, perhaps thousands, of newsgroups at once. This shouldn't be such a strange concept to you by now. We've discussed earlier how Internet marketing and promotion often seems to rely on giving something away; some of the most successful Web sites are those that provide something for free, something valuable for free. The freebies are used, in effect, to draw people in.*

However, that doesn't mean it's not possible to promote yourself or your products in discussion groups with out upsetting people. It most certainly is possible. Many of the most active participants in discussion groups have an ulterior motive for participating; but the people who are most successful at discussion-group promotions realize something important. In order to get something, you have to *give* something.

Well, it's the same with discussion groups. Many people successfully use discussion groups to promote themselves, by giving away information and advice. They turn themselves into discussion-group experts on a particular subject; they become known and respected within the group, and in turn people come to trust them and, perhaps, buy from them.

Before we go on, we have to make one important point. Discussion groups can be a huge drain on your time, especially if you're not quite disciplined enough to stop yourself from being drawn in too deeply. It's easy to get off track by jumping into every conversation and answering every question…and the next thing you know you've spent far more time than you really have available; but the next time you look at your discussion-group messages you'll see that someone has responded to you, or asked another question, so you jump back in.

The Road to Hell (Or at Least a Flame War)—*People nowadays have hair-triggers when it comes to spam. You may have the most innocuous post in the world, but if it has the faintest whiff of commercialism, it's going to bother some people and they might give you a hard time. Think long and hard about how much time you want to devote to posting in USENET newsgroups because it can cause you a lot of trouble. A better idea would be to concentrate on mailing lists, as you can get clear permission to post from the mailing-list owner before contributing anything to the group.*

Some discussion groups, including most of the really good ones, are based on the e-mail system. These are called *mailing-list discussion groups*, or just *mailing lists*. That means lack of discipline is even more of a problem because the messages arrive in your mail program's Inbox every time you get your mail. You just can't escape. If you have a hard time keeping out of every discussion, keep this in mind. Your credibility in a discussion group is directly proportional to the amount of useful information you dispense. So if you pick your responses carefully, and try to provide useful information to a large group instead of fielding every last little request, you'll build up a lot of credibility on that newsgroup.

Despite the dangers, discussion groups can be an important part of a marketing and promotion campaign—for some people even the primary part of the campaign. So let's see how to use them.

FINDING DISCUSSION GROUPS

The first step is to find the discussion groups that are useful to you. There are several hundred thousand mailing-list discussion groups and tens of thousands of newsgroups. Then there are thousands more discussion groups in the online services, private groups that you can get into only if you are a member of that service. There are probably more than 30,000 other discussion groups on

CompuServe, AOL, and the other major online services. (Okay, so that's a pure guess, but a slightly educated one.)

Newsgroup Programs—*We don't want to get into an explanation of basic Internet knowledge, but if you're wondering where to find a newsgroup program... you probably already have one. Netscape Messenger not only works with e-mail, it also works with newsgroup messages. Microsoft Outlook Express can work with newsgroup messages, too, and some online services have built-in newsreaders.*

In short, there are hundreds of thousands of discussion groups to which you could have access...if only you knew where they were. That's the hard part, of course, tracking them all down. On the other hand, you don't need to find every single group that's related to your market. You want the most important ones, and that's a much easier thing to find.

Finding Newsgroups

The first thing to do to find newsgroups is simply to use your newsgroup program. Your newsgroup program has a command that takes it to your service provider's news server and grabs a list of all the groups—not all the groups in the world, but all the groups your service provider has available. Some service providers may just subscribe to five or ten thousand newsgroups. Others may subscribe to thirty or forty thousand. Groups are arranged into hierarchies, as you can see in Figure 9.1.

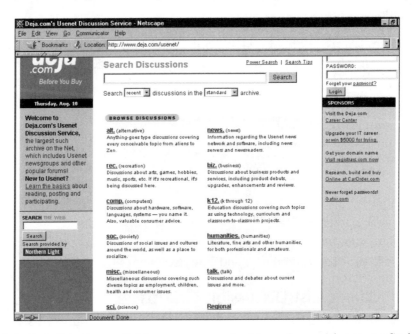

FIGURE 9.1: Deja lists the available newsgroups by hierarchy, so it's easy to find what you need.

Your newsreader will have a command that allows you to search the list, so you can search for particular keywords. But what if the subject in which you're interested turns up missing? Or you're sure that there are more newsgroups on your subject, but your service provider doesn't subscribe to them? Well, you could ask your service provider to subscribe, if you know the name of the group in which you're interested. Or you can use a public news server, a service that allows you to read newsgroups that your service provider does not subscribe to:

DejaNews (Free service, with access to 80,000 discussion groups)
http://www.dejanews.com/

Randori (Over 30,000 newsgroups; prices start at $15 a month)
http://www.randori.com/

Newsguy (22,000 newsgroups for $10 a month)
http://extra.newsguy.com/

RemarQ (Free access to over 35,000 newsgroups through their Web site, or you can pay a subscription fee and use your own newsreader. Subscriptions start at $13.95)
http://www.remarq.com/

Yahoo!—Public Access Usenet Sites
http://dir.yahoo.com/Computers_and_Internet/Internet/Usenet/Public_Access_Use net_Sites/

Of course if you're not sure what's out there, you can't know if your service provider doesn't have one of the newsgroups you need. You can find lists of newsgroups at these places:

Liszt
ttp://www.liszt.com/news/

Tile.Net
http://www.tile.net/

Usenet Info Center
http://metalab.unc.edu/usenet-i/

Yahoo!—Newsgroup Listings
http://dir.yahoo.com/Computers_and_Internet/Internet/Usenet/Newsgroup_Listings/

Finding Mailing-List Discussion Groups

When we wrote the first edition of this book, finding mailing lists was a little more difficult than finding discussion lists because mailing lists were scattered all over the place. Since then, two major free mailing list services have been set up—eGroups (http://www.egroups.com/) and **Topica** (http://www.topica.com/). These services allow you to set up newsletters and discussion lists for free. (The catch? You have to put up with advertisements at the bottom of your messages.) Just by searching the directories of these two sites, you'll find tens of thousands of lists. Lists are available thorough other services, however, so refer to this list to find discussion groups:

Liszt (Over 90,000 discussion groups indexed, now owned by Topica)
http://www.liszt.com/

Publicly Accessible Mailing Lists
http://www.paml.net/

NEW-LIST@LISTSERV.NODAK.EDU (Archives of new-mailing-list announcements)
http://scout.cs.wisc.edu/caservices/new-list/

TILE.NET (Lyris, majordomo, and listproc lists)
http://tile.net/lists/

Also, try searching at Yahoo!—or whatever your favorite search engine happens to be—for the term *mailing list*. At Yahoo! you'll find entries such as *Entertainment: Music: Mailing Lists, Arts: Humanities: History: Genealogy: Mailing Lists, and Recreation: Sports: Football (American): Leagues: National Football League (NFL): Teams: San Diego Chargers:* and *Mailing Lists.* Figure 9.2 just scratches the surface of the number of such categories available.

FIGURE 9.2: Yahoo! lists tons of mailing list categories.

The Online Services

The online services have a combined membership of tens of millions of people. AOL alone was over 20 million last time we checked. So somewhere on those services are thousands of people discussing subjects related to your business…in private discussion groups that you cannot get into unless you join the service.

The discussion groups in these online services are similar in many ways to Internet discussion groups, though they're generally not as convenient. In the online services, you have to visit each group individually, changing to a completely different area of the service each time, whereas with Internet newsgroups, you can set up your newsreader so that only the groups with which you want to work are displayed in the program, and then click one to read its messages. With mailing lists, you can read all the messages in your e-mail program. Still, the online services are well worth checking into and can bring you into contact with many people you won't find on the Internet proper.

In some cases, for historical reasons, the online services have discussion groups that are extremely important within a particular industry or business. For instance, there used to be a very popular Mystery Writer's discussion group on GEnie, and many people in the Windows-help authoring business used to hang out in a CompuServe forum. If you discover that *the* place for you to be is in one of these online-service discussion groups, maybe you'd better join. On the other hand, if you find that out on the Internet proper you have more work than you can manage, perhaps you should save your money and forget about joining an online service.

WORKING IN DISCUSSION GROUPS

Here's how to make a lot of enemies when you join a discussion group. Just jump straight in and pitch your product. Tell everyone how wonderful your product is, how you've got a special offer going on, why they should all come to your Web site *right now* or they miss out—there's only five days left—how your product has won the top awards in your industry, and so on.

That's just blatant commercialism. You just posted an ad to the discussion group, and people don't like that too much. It's as if someone called you at home on the phone during supper trying to sell you something—how would that make you feel?

There are more subtle ways to go about things. We're not talking trickery; we're talking about what we mentioned earlier; you have to give something to get something in return. Here, then, are a few ideas for working in the discussion groups.

Get a Feel for What's Going On

Before you begin posting messages to newsgroups and mailings lists, you should visit for a while. Just *lurk*, to use a little discussion-group jargon. That is, read the messages but don't take part in the discussion. Unless you take a look, you don't know for sure the slant of the discussion group. You won't know what types of messages you can post without upsetting people, and for the moderated groups this is especially important because if you send an inappropriate message, the moderator won't post it to the group. Many newsgroups and mailing lists have FAQs (Frequently Asked Question documents) and charters that explain the purpose of the group and what sorts of messages are acceptable. In the case of newsgroups, you'll sometimes find an FAQ posted to the newsgroup once or twice a week so it's always available. In moderated groups, you may find that the moderator puts a signature at the bottom of every message, with information about where to find the FAQ or charter. In the case of mailing lists, when you subscribe you'll generally be sent a document describing the group and explaining what is acceptable.

Another reason to visit without posting is to make sure you're in the right place. Is the discussion group really suitable for your purposes? Are many people taking part? Is there anything you can contribute to help the other members?

Check the Archives—*Sometimes archives are available—especially archives for free services like Topica and eGroups. Read through the archives to get an idea of what people are talking about, what the tone of conversation is, and how commercial posters get. You'll save yourself a lot of trouble if you try to figure out the boundaries before posting a message.*

Creating a Signature

Before you start posting to newsgroups and mailing lists, design a good signature. A signature is a little block of text at the end of your e-mail or discussion-group message that says something about the person who sent the message—something the person wants other people to know. These are great forms of advertising, especially if your message is intelligent and useful to other people in the discussion group. If people read a message and find something useful or interesting, they may want to know about the person writing the message, and they may spend a few moments visiting the person's Web site to learn more. Signatures are often used to carry little promotional ads, too, and this seems to be more or less accepted these days, as long as the signature isn't too large.

So think about what you want to tell people and how you can fit it into a few lines at the bottom of every message you send. You'll want to design several signatures and use the most appropriate for each discussion group. How many lines? It used to be said that four or five were about the maximum, but these days people often use nine or ten without too many complaints. Don't be too pushy in the signature, though. Try to give the person a reason to visit your site. For

instance, which is likely to be the more appealing of the following two
signatures? This one...

```
Buy from us! The best prices and the best rocket
products on the Web! http://www.podunkrocket.com/
```

Or this...

```
Meet Buzz Aldrin in our discussion group next week!
(March 3-7, 2001) Also, free classified ads, great link
pages, fantastic selection of model rockets and
accessories. http://www.podunkrocket.com/
```

Think about what you can offer people to come to your site. Certainly the
first signature may bring some people in, but the second is likely to be stronger
because it's not selling, at least not until the last few words. Rather, it's talking
about how your site gives something to its visitors.

What sort of things should you remember to include in your signature? The
following:

- The URL to the particular page at your Web site that you want people
  from this group to arrive at—which may not be the same page for each
  group. You may want to present different information first depending on
  who's arriving at your site. (And, as we'll discuss in Chapter 14, *Tracking
  Results and Responding*, you can use this method to track how many
  people from the discussion group visit your site.)
- The e-mail address of an autoresponder—many people still have slow
  Internet connections or minimal Web access, so they may prefer to obtain
  more information from an autoresponder.
- The e-mail address of a real person to whom questions can be directed.
- Reasons for people to visit your site. Don't list reasons why you want
  them to visit, but give them reasons why *they should want* to visit; these
  are two very different things.

How to Write Messages

Now you're ready to post messages to the discussion groups. Let's say you want
to promote your model-rocket site to various newsgroups. You could, if you
were really reckless, write a message like this:

```
CHECK THIS OUT! THE BEST MODEL ROCKET SITE ON THE
WEB!!!!!! COOL STUFF, REAL CHEAP, SAVE $$$$$!!!COME
```

```
VISIT US AT HTTP://WWW.ROCKETFOOL.COM/!!!
```

This sort of message is obnoxious, and people generally hate them. You'll probably make more enemies than friends posting messages like this. It's clearly an ad, and it sounds like a poorly written ad, too; but it's similar to thousands of messages being posted to newsgroups every day, and people are getting sick of them.

Think of newsgroup messages in a different way. Don't think of them as advertisements but as informational messages. Don't *scream* your message at people—talk to them. Try a message like this:

```
Hi, I've just started checking out the model rocket
discussion groups on the Internet. This one seems like
quite an active group. I run a mail-order model-rocket
business in Podunk, Texas, so I wanted to find out a
little about how other model-rocketeers are using the
Internet. We just set up a Web site (come visit us
sometime: http://www. podunkrocket.com/). We figured
we'd try to provide some services to other people who
love rockets, so we've got links to all the rocket
sites we can find (not just model rockets, but the real
things, too—lots of cool NASA links). We've got a
discussion group running, too—we're starting celebrity
discussions, soon, as well, so you'll be able to post
messages to the rocket designers at Estes, some top
prizewinners and so on. Let us know if you've got any
suggestions for people you'd like to talk with. And my
partner says I'm crazy to do this—why risk losing
business? he says—but we set up a free classified area.
If you have any rockets or accessories you want to
sell, you can post a classified ad (that's right, no
charge!).
If anyone else has any ideas for services we could
provide at our Web site, please let us know. Oh, and if
we're missing a link you know about that we really
should have, you can fill in a form at our site to add
it to the list.
```

Which message is more annoying? Which is more of an ad? They're really both ads, but the first is nothing but an ad, while the second has some character. You can *hear* a person's voice in that message—there's a real person there, not just a bulk-mail program. Notice also that this message isn't directly selling something; it's actually giving something away—three things, really: free classifieds, a rocket discussion group, and a useful link page. It's also asking questions: Have you any ideas for people we could invite to answer questions in our discussion group? Are there any services you'd like to see us provide? Any links we've missed? Nowhere in the message do we ask people to spend money; we just suggest that they might like to visit our site, and give good reasons why.

Now, it's quite possible that a message like this one could get complaints. (It probably will, actually. We don't know if anyone else said it originally, but we heard it from Julia Butterfly Hill first: "Every action has an equal and opposite criticism.") But because it's clearly from a real person and because it's chatty, any complaints are more likely to be similar to this: "Fred, we try to avoid ads in this group; could you be more careful in the future?" Not so much a flame as a gentle rebuke. So remember these basic principles about advertising in discussion groups:

- Pure ads (Buy, Buy, Buy!) irritate people.
- Ads in which you give people something are usually acceptable.
- Merchandise specials are not something you give. The chance to preorder something is not something that you give. Make sure you have something worthy of offering.

Look at your message carefully. Are you providing something useful to the members of that list? Is your message something that a significant proportion of the list of members is likely to find useful or interesting? Or is it purely an ad?

Not Sure about a Group?

What about groups that probably attract people who are interested in your products, but which are not directly related? Groups about rockets, though not specifically about model rockets, perhaps? We'd be very careful about what we posted in these groups, and we advise you to keep it short and to try to think about the services that your Web site provides that are more directly related to this newsgroup. For instance, you might try something like this:

```
Anyone out there want to swap or sell rocket-related
products—books, videos, magazines, NASA souvenirs? I
run a Web site with loads of links to rocket sites, and
we've got a free classified ad section too. You can
post messages to sell your stuff, for no charge. And
we're going to be having question-and-answer sessions
in our rocket discussion group soon; we're trying to
track down an astronaut or two to take part. If anyone
```

```
knows someone knowledgeable who might be interested,
please let us know.
```

In this message, we mentioned the things that might be useful to people on this list. It's a rocket discussion group, though not a model-rocket group, so we mentioned the rocket-links page and the discussion group. We've mentioned the free classified ads, as well; after all, it's likely that there's a lot of overlap—that many people who are interested in rockets are also interested in model rockets, and so may be interested in the classifieds. We also kept it low key and chatty again; it's not a Buy, Buy, Buy! posting.

If in doubt, see if you can determine who the owner of the mailing list is. (This is fairly easy to do on the free provider newsgroups like eGroups and Topica.) E-mail the owner and ask for permission to post the message, and include a sample of the message. If you're given permission, post it, and get flamed, you have a backup. You can point out that you asked permission of the list owner and got it before posting to the list. The philosophy of "forgiveness before permission" is really a bad idea when it comes to posting commercial messages online.

But That's Not an Effective Ad

Now, we know that some people, particularly people who are used to the world of direct mail, feel that this sort of discreet advertising in discussion groups is not real advertising—it's not direct enough. And indeed, you'll see many ads in discussion groups, in particular in newsgroups because it's so easy to post messages in newsgroups, that look something like this:

```
* * * * * * * * * * * * * * * * * * * * * * * * * * * * * * * * * * *
MAKE MONEY WITHOUT PRINTING MONEY
* * * * * * * * * * * * * * * * * * * * * * * * * * * * * * * * * *
SIXTY THOUSAND DOLLARS IN ONE YEAR
* * * * * * * * * * * * * * * * * * * * * * * * * * * * * * * * * *
```

and this:

```
Register for a free Internet downline and receive,
absolutely free, your own Internet Web site. Sign up now
and get a massive Internet downline and a Web page
absolutely free. It's FREE! It's easy and it can be your
answer to financial security. Visit my web site at ...
```

(What's downline? It's a bit of multilevel marketing—MLM—jargon, referring to income from people who you recruit; unfortunately, MLM discovered the Internet some time ago.)

Are we saying that ads like this can't work? No, they probably can. There's no doubt that spam can work—you need only a tiny response to make it pay. There are programs that will send your message to 20,000 newsgroups at once quickly and cheaply. Of course you may not like the reaction you get—everything from insulting e-mail to eventually, perhaps, prosecution, and there are systems out there designed to look for this sort of cross-posting and destroy cross-posted messages.

However, even if this type of advertising can pay, you should instead have a long-term interest in building a good reputation for your products and services, rather than in a get-in-get-the-money-and-get-out type of scheme. This book is about building a presence in the Internet, not hiding in cyberspace, which you'll have to do if you do too much of this sort of thing. (You may have noticed that a lot of ads are anonymous, in the sense that they don't provide a legitimate Reply To e-mail address or a URL; rather, they use phone numbers and mailing addresses, so the perpetrator cannot be "attacked" in cyberspace.) You're trying to build a visible presence, and that will be difficult to do if you make a habit of this kind of advertising.

How Often Can You Post?

Don't post the same message over and over to the same places. If you do so, your chatty announcement turns into a blatant ad, the very thing you're trying to avoid. That doesn't mean you can't remind people about your Web site, of course. You can announce new services now and again. In fact you may not want to mention everything in your first post; keep something back for later.

If you have an active chat or discussion group, you can announce activities such as celebrity chats or extended question-and-answer sessions in your discussion group, and, as we'll discuss next, you can provide information and become an advisor as another way to keep a regular presence in the discussion groups. Your signature will still act as a reminder and an ad, and if you've set up a truly useful Web site, you'll find that other people will start to talk about your site; you'll often see group members recommending another member's site.

Provide Information at Your Web Site

Another technique many people use is to provide information and post it at their Web sites. Then they can post messages in newsgroups and mailing lists that are directly related to the subject of that information. For instance, a lawyer who works in employment law might write an article about a particular issue related to that area of law and then post messages to the discussion groups related to employment law mentioning that the article is available. (Tara knows of a lawyer who does that on a couple of nonlaw-related lists. His profile is incredibly high on those lists, yet the group members don't complain because he's providing important information that most of them would not have easy access to otherwise.)

Also, if you see someone asking for information—something that requires more than just a few lines in reply—and if you have the answer, why not post it at your Web site and send a message saying where the information is available? This is commonly done, and isn't regarded as a teaser. It's not a matter of: "I've got the information, you can have it, but only if you come to my site." It's more a case of: "I have an entire article on this subject, but it's way too big to post to the mailing list because most members probably aren't interested, so if you *are* interested why not view it at my Web site?" You're not only providing a service, but doing it in such a way that you don't annoy people by posting a huge message to the discussion group.

Note, by the way, that you need to remember to set up your Web site so that people coming to your site for the information will see other things at your site. Some people doing this provide the main URL of their Web site, so the visitor must look for the information—don't make it too difficult to find, though—and at the same time is bound to notice other things at your site. Alternatively, you can give a URL to take people directly to the information while ensuring that there are obvious links to other information at your site.

Become an Advisor

Most discussion groups have a small core of regulars and a large number of lurkers—people who read the messages but never post responses or new messages. A group may have 600 or 1,000 members, for instance, but if you watch the group for a while you'll notice that it only has around 30 or 40 regulars who seem to post messages frequently.

Among the regulars there's often a smaller group—maybe only five or ten—who are what might be termed *advisors*. When people send messages posing questions, members of this group are the first to answer, and they provide the best and most useful answers.

Get involved in a few of the active groups. Become known to the members as someone who understands the subject being discussed and can answer questions and provide leads to useful information.

The problem with this level of involvement, though, is the time it can take. You'll need a lot of discipline, and you'd better learn to use the Delete key.

Immediately delete messages that are of little importance—the very chatty messages or messages about subjects that don't particularly interest you, and pick and choose what you get involved with carefully. You can't be expected to answer every question; just answer a few now and again with helpful information. Occasionally point people to your Web site, and make sure you have a good signature on all your messages.

Don't Answer Every Possible Question—*Don't try to answer every single question posted to the list. For one thing, it can make you look pushy and obnoxious. For another thing, it defuses your efforts. It's better to answer a couple of advanced questions thoroughly and helpfully than to answer five basic questions with quick, incomplete answers.*

Get to Know the Advisors

The advisors and moderators in newsgroups and mailing lists can be very useful to you. Get to know these people; send them free goods, in the same way you would with people who run Web sites associated with your area of business. (We'll discuss this a little in Chapter 10, *Grass Roots Marketing*.) Send them e-mail and chat with them a little. They'll remember you and may well check out your Web site. If you have something of value, they'll remember that and mention it to other people, and their status as advisors gives their comments and opinions great weight with many group members.

These people are often useful product reviewers, too. Sometimes they write in real-world magazines, and sometimes they have Web sites that review products. So keep a watch for people who can leverage your marketing campaign by talking about your products for you. Remember, the very best advertising you can get is product endorsements from people who are not directly affiliated with or paid by you or your company.

Here's an example. Peter wrote a book called *The Technical Writer's Freelancing Guide* in the early 1990s; this book was reviewed in four periodicals. In 1997 he revised the book, and it was republished as **Making Money in Technical Writing** (http://www.mcp.com/mgr/arco/techwr/). This time Peter actively recruited reviewers. Many came to him after he announced the book in mailing lists and newsgroups and asked for reviewers. Others read other messages he'd written, visited his Web site, saw the invitation to reviewers, and contacted him. By the time *Making Money in Technical Writing* was published, he had 90 reviewers lined up, some claiming to be planning multiple reviews.

Bear in mind, however, that the easier you make it to get a review copy, the more likely you are to be ripped off. Some of these 90 people perhaps asked for a free book without any intention of ever publishing a review; but even if only half of them publish reviews, it's still well worth the cost, and the rip-off rate is almost certainly much lower than 50 percent—probably less than 5 percent. If you ask for some kind of proof of purpose—for instance, ask reviewers to provide you with the names of the publications for which they're writing the reviews, for the dates when the reviews will be published, and the editors' contact information—the rip-off rate is likely to be pretty low. The Internet provides a really easy and convenient way to contact reviewers—a way to leverage your promotional efforts tremendously.

By being willing to make this and other books readily available to everyone who wants to review them, Peter gets a lot more coverage than if he vigorously screened every potential reviewer. (He doesn't have to spend time screening potential reviewers, either.) For every hoop you make a prospective reviewer jump through—whether it's asking for their credentials or for clips of other reviews—you'll lose some reviews. Concentrate on getting your products to reviewers, rather than on keeping them away from scammers. As small-publishing guru Dan Poynter puts it, "If in doubt, send it out."

Announcement Newsgroups

There are a number of newsgroups designed specifically for announcements, where you can post ads and nobody cares. Some of these are general; comp.infosystems.www.announce, for instance, accepts announcements about new noncommercial Web sites. Others are more specific; comp.security.pgp. announce, for instance, contains announcements related to the PGP encryption program.

In your newsreader, search for these words: *announce, forsale, market.* Or better still, search one of the newsgroup directories we talked about in the "Finding Discussion Groups" section earlier in this chapter. If you search in your newsreader, the program will find only those groups in which the word you are searching for is within the group name; at some of the directories, a group description is also searched. You'll find groups like the following:

- alt.fandom.cons—Announcements of conventions (SciFi and others)
- chi.places—Announcements of Chicago-area events
- alt.aquaria.marketplace—Fish and aquariums
- alt.art.marketplace—Art for sale
- biz.marketplace.computers—Computers and computer equipment
- ithaca.marketplace—Stuff for sale in Ithaca, New York

- alt.autographs.transactions—Ads related to autographs for sale
- edm.forsale—Stuff for sale in Edmonton, Canada

There's a flip side, too. There are also groups that take "Wanted to Buy" ads, and though you're not supposed to post messages selling things, you can look in these groups for people who may be searching for the products or services you provide. If you search for the word *wanted* in the directories, you'll often find groups that accept both for-sale and wanted ads, such as the following:

- alt.auto.parts.wanted—Described by its members as alt.american.automobile.breakdown.breakdown.breakdown
- aus.ads.wanted—Goods for sale or wanted in Australia
- comp.binaries.ibm.pc.wanted—People seeking software
- nj.market.autos—Vehicles wanted and for sale in New Jersey

Note, by the way, that some groups are really intended for classified-ad–type ads rather than for businesses. Also, many of the *announce* and *announcement* groups are for announcements that are not necessarily goods for sale—announcements about upcoming events, for instance. Another category of newsgroup that takes announcements of various kinds is the net-happenings groups, such as comp.internet.net-happenings. There are also a few newprod groups for announcements of new products, such as the following:

- biz.next.newprod—New product announcements for the NeXT computer
- can.newprod—New products/services of interest to Canadian readers
- comp.newprod—Announcements of new products of interest
- eunet.newprod—New products of interest to Europeans

Also take a look at the biz newsgroups, many of which contain announcements about commercial products, and there are also the Clarinet releases newsgroups, though you can't post messages directly to these groups. Rather, you must send a press release through one of several press-release services, which we'll discuss in Chapter 17, *Electronic Press Releases*.

Finally, there are scores of mailing lists and newsgroups that review products—books, software, music, theater, restaurants, bicycles, cigars, and so on. Search for the word *review*, and you'll find these groups. Then visit the appropriate ones and see if you can find someone to review your product. With luck, you may be able to contact a review writer who also sells reviews to magazines and newspapers. Some of these review groups—such as alt.books.reviews—allow redistribution of reviews, so a review of your product may end up going further than just the newsgroups—into newsletters and on Web sites for instance.

The Internet's discussion groups provide a tremendous resource for the promoter. Many people have used them successfully, in particular to promote themselves as experts and consultants. This is real grass-roots promoting, a low-cost technique for reaching people, though it does require a large investment of time and patience. In the next chapter, we'll look at other grass-roots promotional techniques, such as giving away products at other people's sites.

CHAPTER TEN

Grass Roots Marketing

You've probably heard the term *guerrilla marketing*. It was coined long ago, many years pre-Internet, by Jay Conrad Levinson, who has written a series of books about the subject. Guerilla marketing is all about how small businesses can market their products using low-cost techniques. Like a guerrilla army fighting with whatever weapons it can scrape together to take on a much more powerful military force, small businesses can use guerrilla-marketing techniques to win their battles in the marketplace.

The Internet provides a multitude of guerrilla-marketing opportunities. Of course many of the techniques we speak about elsewhere in this book could be regarded as guerrilla marketing—using large databases of journalist contact information, listing your Web site in appropriate places, and so on. All these things are low-cost, yet effective techniques for getting the word out about your products and services.

TOTAL PERSONAL MARKETING

In a sense, the Internet is all about grass-roots promotions. It's about you scratch my back and I'll scratch yours; it's about friends helping friends to get the word out. **Christopher Locke** (http://www.rageboy.com/), Internet commentator extraordinaire, calls this the era of *Total Personal Marketing*.

This is the era in which a kid with a cheap computer and an Internet connection can sign up a hundred thousand subscribers and have his words read by those hundred thousand people—and by thousands more people to whom they forward his words—every week or so. This is the sort of power that just a few years ago was unimaginable. To reach that sort or audience you had to own a magazine, or have a low-paying job at a magazine, or be willing to spend $50,000 each time you wanted to reach 100,000 people.

"The net is not a passive medium," Christopher Locke e-mailed us recently. "Which means (to me) you gotta *work* the thing! Everyone now has a say, even 11-year-olds (and by the way, I know some sharp 11-year-olds). Being an anarchist at heart, I think this state of affairs is just terrific. You just need to call in a few favors and get your pals to the barricades."

Now look at what Peter just did. Some time ago Peter mentioned Christopher's publication, *Entropy Gradient Reversal*, in his newsletter, *Poor Richard's Web Site News*. It's not huge, but 15,000 subscribers is still worthwhile (it has many more subscribers than that now). Later, when a few bad reviews turned up at **Amazon.com** related to Peter's ***Making Money in Technical Writing*** book (http://www.amazon.com/exec/obidos/ASIN/\0028618831/), Christopher jumped in and boosted the ratings a little, and then encouraged another reader of this book to do the same. Now Peter's mentioning Christopher's site in a book….Christopher, as you may know, is one of the authors of the fiery business book *Cluetrain*. If you're looking for something to open up your skull and scrub out your brainpan, this book will do it.

In fact, the Amazon.com *Making Money in Technical Writing* page is an interesting illustration of this principle in action. It's not a very widely read book, which is not surprising considering the subject matter; but it does get a lot of good reviews and testimonials from people in the technical-writing business. It also gets a number of complaints, from people who simply don't believe it's possible to make much money as a freelance technical writer. When the book first appeared at Amazon.com, it wasn't long before someone posted a review—a glowing, five-star review. Then no more reviews appeared for a long time, until almost exactly ten months later in fact, when two reviews appeared, both negative. All of a sudden the book's five-star rating dropped to a one and one half-star rating.

Christopher jumped in with a few comments of his own—not saying that he'd read the book (he hadn't), but praising Peter's writing and pointing out fallacies in the other reviewers' comments. Then another friend reviewed the book, giving it a five-star review, and Peter posted a number of comments, both replying to the criticisms in the earlier reviews and posting readers' testimonials. Then another five-star review turned up, pushing the total up to four stars.

Around this time, the book's Amazon.com ranking started to rise. (Amazon.com assigns every book a sales rank—the higher the number, the more copies are being sold.) The book's rank rose from somewhere around 40,000 to about 17,000. It remains at that rank at this writing—quite respectable for a three-year-old, nonfiction book. Was this caused by these little comments and reviews? Hard to say…in fact probably not, at least not directly. Something else may have happened—a press review, for instance—but at least when people visited the Amazon.com page to take a look at the book, perhaps after reading about it in a magazine, they saw a four-star book rather than a one-star book, and they read plenty of glowing praise. Does this help sell books? Yes, absolutely.

Christopher mentioned two other authors "who have benefited hugely from hot debate about their work on Amazon.com: David Siegel (*Killer Web Sites*) and Michael Wolff (*Burn Rate*)." Take a look at the *Killer Web Site* reviews (currently over 275 of them), and you'll find comments ranging from "pathetic" and "hype," to "excellent" and "a must read." Take a look at Figure 10.1 and you'll see just a few of the wide variety of opinions.

So this is what Christopher Locke refers to as "getting your pals to the barricades." It's a new way of looking at the manner in which your products and services are represented to the world. You can react to criticism—or praise, for that manner—immediately, if you're paying attention to what's going on, and you can recruit friends and well wishers to help you man the barricades.

GIVEAWAYS

Now let's look at a specific grass-roots technique: giving products away in high-traffic regions of the Internet. Let's say, for instance, that you are Mr. Estes Rocket. Having read this far into the book, you probably have a good idea of which Web sites are of interest to you: model-rocket related sites. You may have

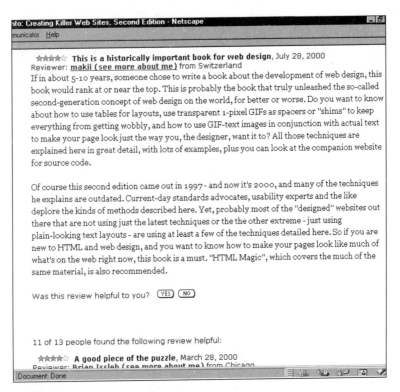

FUIGURE 10.1: There are a world of opinions about Killer Web sites.

also found several discussion groups related to model rocketry, and perhaps some e-mailed newsletters or discussion groups.

Now, the next step is to review your list of sites, discussion groups, and newsletters, and determine which of those are receiving the most traffic. That's not always easy—you have to take an educated guess. Is this a site (newsgroup, newsletter) that people talk about a lot, and to which they refer other people? Is it a Web site that is obviously well designed, with useful resources? The sort of site that requires a lot of time and energy, and perhaps even money? It's generally not hard to figure out which site is the busiest sites.

Next, contact the site owners, the discussion-group moderators, the newsletter editors, and suggest a giveaway. The principle is simple. You offer to give away a number of your products—for example, a few of your mid-level rocket kits, and perhaps one of your top-of-the-line products as a grand prize. You might hold a contest for one particular Web site, discussion group, or newsletter, if it's big enough to warrant that, or perhaps combine a few together into one contest.

You'll set up a form at your Web site, in which entrants can provide their information: at a minimum their e-mail addresses, perhaps also their names and some sort of survey information that you may find useful. (Don't overdo things; if you make it too difficult to enter, you won't get many entrants.) The Web sites, discussion groups, and newsletters can now publicize the giveaway. Why would they care? It adds value to them, of course. You'll find that many people are quite happy to be involved in such an arrangement; they like to be able to tell their visitors or subscribers about such offers, especially if it's an exclusive.

What's in it for you? First, you get mentioned in these places; it's low-cost advertising. Not only will you be mentioned in the places publicizing the giveaway, but you may even find that Web-site owners go to *other* places and say "come to my site—we're giving away stuff."

Secondly, you persuade people to visit your site. You need to set up the entry form so that visitors can also see links enticing them further into your Web site. That shouldn't be hard. If they're interested enough to be at the other site, in the discussion group, or reading the newsletter, and if they're interested enough to enter your contest, they're well qualified, to use a sales term. That is, these are people you can be fairly sure are interested in your products.

Finally, here's another benefit. On your entry form, you can place Yes and No option buttons to respond to a label such as, "Would you like to receive the Internet's best Estes Rocket newsletter free every couple of weeks?" You should set the option buttons so that the Yes button is already selected. The entrants can change the button to No if they wish, and some will, but probably not many.

Peter's found that only around five percent of entrants declined to receive his newsletter.

Have a Visible Privacy Policy—*Any time—and we mean any time—you collect information from your readers—you need to have a visible link to your privacy policy. Make it clear how you're going to use the information you collect. You'll get a lot more respondents that way, as long as you use the information in a responsible manner.*

Essay Contests Don't Work

We recommend that if you carry out this kind of promotion, you do a simple drawing. Use a form to save all the entries in a text file, and then, at the end of the contest, pick the winners. You might do so using a random-number generator (you can find these at the shareware sites listed in Chapter 2, *What You Need Before You Start*), or even print them out and throw darts at the pages.

There's one form of contest that we don't recommend: the essay contest. In the past magazines offered essay contests that, for example, asked readers to submit a 20 word essay such as "Why I feel I should be running this country." More recently, the use of essay contest as a marketing tool has fallen into disfavor. (We've only seen a few recently, but they offered really big prizes—one we saw last year offered an established business.) Peter has had bad luck with essay contests in the past. The first one he did was for *Entrepreneur Magazine*, which has a busy Web site. It wasn't his idea—he simply suggested a drawing, but the staff of the magazine wanted to try an essay.

There were fewer entries than in the drawings Peter had held at Web sites with a tiny fraction of *Entrepreneur's* traffic. He tried another such contest recently at another busy site. Again, almost no response. It seems that few people are willing to spend time on this sort of thing any more. So Peter's conclusion is that drawings really do work. Essay contests don't.

Is It Legal?

Are these contests legal? That's difficult to answer because it depends on where you happen to be. It seems that within the United States at least, they are. Now, we're not lawyers, so you can take whatever we say here with a pinch of salt if you wish. (In other words, don't come complaining to us if your state government doesn't like what you're doing; it's up to you to make sure it's okay.) However, it seems that if you are running a simple drawing, with no money changing hands—the entrants are not paying an entrance fee—then you're okay. There's a little confusion about this. Some people assume that a drawing is a *sweepstakes*, but it's not. In a sweepstakes, money is being exchanged—the entrants pay to enter, and the winnings come from the combined entry fees, for instance.

Contest laws are really aimed at contests in which the organizer charges money. If you're just giving away products, without any entry fee, you should be okay; but don't take our word for it. Call your local city or state government officials and ask whether there are any regulations in your area covering these sorts of things. Make sure they understand what you're doing, that you're not selling lottery tickets, for instance. (And yes, we know that the Internet raises all sorts of questions about legal jurisdiction, but that's getting way out of our legal league.) You might also look at the **Sweepstakes and Contests** page (http://www.arentfox.com/quickGuide/businessLines/sweeps/contestsSweepstakes/contestssweepstakes.html) published by Arent Fox, a law firm in Washington.

WATCH FOR NEWSLETTER OPPORTUNITIES

While most of the media seem to be focusing on the World Wide Web, they're missing an incredibly important development in communications: the e-mail newsletter. The media spends so much time fussing about glitz—pretty Web sites with cute little graphic-design tricks—that it's really missed the point about the Internet. People are not going online looking for eye candy. They get enough of that watching TV, videos, and movies—the Web can't compete with those media forms. (One important exception—a very big exception, admittedly—is online pornography.) People really are interested in *content*; and content means information—preferably well-written, well-presented information.

It's possible to present information effectively through the use of an old technique—typed words, just plain text, in an e-mail message. As we discuss in Chapter 11, *Creating Newsletters and Discussion Groups*, there are now many influential newsletters, with subscriber lists in the hundreds of thousands. They're written by a wide range of people, with many different writing styles. They're often a love 'em or hate 'em sort of thing, with some people unsubscribing after the first issue and others hanging on every word.

These newsletters can be *very* influential. When Chris Pirillo featured *Poor Richard's Web Site* in his newsletter, Peter got thousands of visitors to his site and over a thousand new subscribers to his newsletter. (By the way, Chris is the author of *Poor Richard's Email Publishing*.) When Dan Butler's **Naked PC** (http://www.thenakedpc.com/) was mentioned in Fred Langa's **LangaList** (http://www.langa.com/), *The Naked PC* received 1,000 new subscribers in just one morning.

There's only one thing better than getting mentioned in one of these newsletters—it's getting mentioned in them more than once. Cultivating newsletter editors can be a very worthwhile endeavor (See Chapter 9, *Promoting in the Newsgroups and Mailing Lists*, for hints on finding these editors.) Try to get mentioned; try to give things away. Whatever you do, don't miss out on this very powerful way to reach people. To paraphrase a popular *Placebo* song, "A friend in need's a friend indeed, a friend with a 100,000-subscriber newsletter is better."

LOOK FOR OPENINGS

Keep your eyes open and your wits about you; this is a guerrilla operation. Make friends with people in the same business as you; get to know newsletter editors; spend time finding out who's running the discussion groups that are important to you, and so on. You'll see opportunities turn up out of the blue, and you can go searching for them. Also read some of Conrad Jay Levinson's *Guerrilla Marketing* books. Most of these are about marketing in the real world (though he also has a book about marketing on the Internet). But you'll find that many of the principles and ideas he discusses in his books can be applied in cyberspace. What it all comes down to is keeping a lookout for opportunities in which you can, at a low cost, reach people with a message about your products and services.

CHAPTER ELEVEN

Creating Newsletters and Discussion Groups

The Web has a lot going for it. It's huge, it's accessible practically worldwide, perhaps two billion Web pages are available online—figures vary widely and the number is constantly growing—and millions of people surf them every day. The Web also has a lot of disadvantages, though. For example, it's huge, it's accessible practically worldwide, perhaps two billion Web pages are available online, and millions of people surf them every day.

When you put your Web site online, you are competing with millions of other sites. That's quite a daunting thought. You have to get visitors' attention, keep it long enough to make a pitch, and then make enough of an impression on the visitors for them to keep coming back.

Fortunately, you do not have to end your promotional efforts with the Web, as we've discussed in earlier chapters. Not only can you mention your site in subtle, appropriate postings to newsgroups and mailing lists (discussed in Chapter 9, *Promoting in the Newsgroups and Mailing Lists*), but you can also push content beyond your Web site through your own newsletters and discussion groups. You can even put a discussion group on your site and leave it to your visitors to create site content! You can do both these things—creating discussion lists and newsletters—without paying a dime beyond the value of your time.

When you put together a mailing list and deliver it via e-mail, you're not asking people to remember to come to you; you come to them. This is an easy way to stay in front of your visitors, keep them thinking of you, and give them something to pass on to other people. Similarly, creating an e-mailed discussion group gives you a forum through which you can help solve problems and share your expertise.

Creating this kind of content can have a big payoff, as it can increase your credibility and visibility. On the other hand, it takes a lot of work to create good content.

NEWSLETTERS

You've probably seen newsletters put together by offline businesses. They show up in your mailbox every month or every quarter, and hold your attention for at least a few minutes, causing you to think about that company and helping bring its name to mind when you need something from its industry. Offline newsletters are a big investment in time and money, because printing and postage have to be paid for. Online newsletters are just as big of an investment in time.

To get a newsletter together, you need three things: content, a good format, and an audience. Let's take a look at how to create your content, your formatting options (HTML or plain text?), and how you can distribute your materials to an interested audience. Do you want to use a free service to distribute your newsletter, or do you want to pay for it—or maybe even do it yourself? This part of the chapter will show you your choices and help you make an informed decision.

Newsletter Content

You might think that doing a weekly newsletter is no big deal. Believe us, do it for a few issues and you'll realize that it is a big deal. Putting together all that information can turn into much more work than you might at first realize.

How do you think of what to write? It's best if you start from the perspective that you're writing for an audience that needs a problem solved, wants to learn more about your industry, or uses products similar to yours and wants to know how to use them better. You're not writing for an audience that loves hearing product pitches, wants to hear your slogan four billion times, or just can't wait for your next clever marketing idea. Your audience members don't give a fig for your company or product; they just want you to help them fix their problems.

If you look at things from that perspective, you'll find you have plenty of content. How did you solve that last customer request for a software feature? How did you handle that last rush job for your client? (Don't present it as bragging; instead, make it a point to go over what you did with enough detail that the reader could use it, too.) What are some things you've learned in working with your industry? All of these things can make a great series of articles.

Be Subtle—*Don't make every third word in your newsletter the name of your company. You're trying to increase visibility and mindshare, not ram your product down somebody's throat. Make it a soft sell.*

Tara calls developing content this way industrial editorship. Nobody knows as much as you do about your product or service. Therefore, it stands to reason that you're always learning lots of little things about your industry—how this thing works, where to go to find that thing, how to make the most of this service, or invest most effectively in that product. You can use those bits and pieces of information to establish your expertise and share your knowledge with prospects and customers alike.

If you're from the old school of entrepreneurship, the idea of sharing the fruits of your work might strike you as a bad idea. Why should you give away all your secrets? Well, naturally, if you've built an economic empire on a secret crispy chicken formula, we don't want you to give it away. It's the heart of your organization; but we bet you know a lot about how to drain fried chicken so it doesn't get too greasy, how to reheat it so it doesn't taste rubbery, and how to make a great chicken salad out of leftovers. You can share that information without mentioning one ingredient of your secret formula. You can use every scrap of information and knowledge this way to your benefit, by sharing with your customers and prospects and establishing yourself as a center of expertise.

What's the Frequency?—*How often are you going to put your newsletter out? Weekly? Monthly? Daily's probably too often unless you're a real net-head or several people are sharing publishing duties. Tara finds once a week comfortable. More than that and she feels too pressured; less than that and she finds herself forgetting about it; it's hard to put it into a routine. Less than once a month is a hard schedule to maintain; it's too easy to forget about it or make it a low priority that somehow never gets done. Peter's newsletter goes out every two weeks.*

The mantra on the Internet is "give it away, give it away, give it away." Only by giving away some of what you know can you establish credibility and expertise. Only by giving away can you make a name for yourself. So keep in mind that you want to protect the essential secrets of your organization, but consider also what you can give away.

If this is still a little fuzzy to you, let's use Tara's work as an example. A lot of her work involves Internet research. She's written a book about it and does a lot of research in her consulting business. For that reason, she has to keep up with the latest research resources and changes to the major search engines. Instead of hoarding that information, she shares it via her Web site and a free newsletter. When she figures something out about how a search engine works or how searches can be performed better, she shares that, too. She wants everyone to learn how to search better, while realizing that not everyone will have the patience to perform the kind of detailed, exhaustive research that she does in the course of her work. You got content? Great. Let's talk about laying it out.

Laying out the Newsletter

A newsletter doesn't have to be 10 or 12 pages—a couple of medium-sized articles (400 or 500 words), a few newsbits of a couple dozen words each, and a

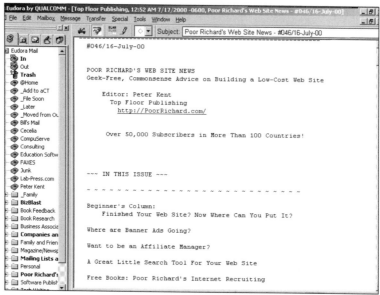

FIGURE 11.1: Peter's newsletter, Poor Richard's Web Site News.

little editorial comment on the state of the world, and you have a newsletter. More is not always better—you don't want to intimidate your readers with something that's several pages long. Tara's of the opinion that you should create something just large enough that the viewer can go through it without investing a lot of time. If you create a really long newsletter, it may sit around in readers' e-mail boxes until they get around to reading it. They never do get around to reading it and eventually it's deleted unread. On the other hand…it depends. Peter's biweekly newsletter is quite long, but he also has a loyal readership that doesn't seem to have a problem with it; a number have said that they print the newsletter and put it in a binder.

You may want to develop departments and regular features, though perhaps it's better to let these evolve over time and as a reaction to feedback from your readers. If you start with a rigid structure, it's more difficult to adapt to feedback and the ideas of your readers.

Regardless of what you decide about your newsletter content, be sure to follow these rules for putting together a readable newsletter:

- Unless you're absolutely sure your entire readership can handle it, no HTML. Make everything plain text. (If you put your archives up on the Web later, you can add HTML then.)

- Be sure to write out URLs with the *http://* included—some e-mail readers can interpret this kind of text as a clickable link. You should probably write URLs in such a manner that they stand alone—no other character touches the beginning or end of the URL. For instance, don't put the URL in-between <> characters (for a discussion of this subject, see Peter's newsletter at (http://www.poorrichard.com/newsltr/019.htm#begin).

- Put a line of space between paragraphs. Don't just run paragraphs together; it turns your text into a giant block that's hard to read. Also try to keep paragraphs short. Keep one line between paragraphs in the same story, and two lines between different stories and different sections.

- Keep your columns 60–65 characters wide or less. That'll keep the lines from breaking up strangely on most e-mail readers.

- Don't try to create justified text, in which each line is the same length. Let the text be ragged, where each line is a different length. (The text in this list is justified.) Long stretches of ragged text are easier to read.

- You can use text characters to break up sections in your newsletter—like this: ——-, or =====, but don't overdo it.

- Don't try to center things and line up columns; many mail programs these days display messages with nonproportional text, so centering and lining up things doesn't work well. Try to make your newsletter look good using a font such as Times New Roman, rather than a monospace font such as Courier. (Monospace means a font in which every character—including spaces—takes up the same amount of space.) If you do use a monospace font—because you want to display information in tables or something like that—put a disclaimer at the top of the newsletter. If it says something like "this newsletter best read in 12 point Courier font," the readers will know how to adjust the fonts they're using to read the newsletter properly.

HTML Mail—*Refers to e-mail messages that are formatted using HTML coding—the tags used to create Web pages. HTML mail messages are much more attractive than plain text; you can use color, tables, images, and so on. But there are two problems with HTML mail. First, many users are working with e-mail programs that cannot display these messages; they'll probably display a jumble of codes making the text unreadable. Secondly, even if the recipient is working with an e-mail program that, in theory, can display HTML mail, it may not do so well. All the HTML-compatible programs work slightly differently, so what works well in one doesn't work well in another. For this reason most newsletters are still plain text. That's not to say HTML mail should never be used. There are a number of extremely successful HTML-mail newsletters, like* **Lockergnome** *(http://www.lockergnome.com), shown in Figure 11.2.*

FIGURE 11.2: *Lockergnome* is an HTML newsletter.

- Before you send out your newsletter, send it to yourself—make sure that it looks okay when it comes back. Look in the header of the newsletter for this line:

```
Content-Type: text/plain; charset="iso-8859-1"
```

- If you see something else, you have a problem. You may have some kind of typesetting character—curly quotes, an em dash (—), or an ellipsis (…), for instance. That's a problem for many mail programs, which may display all sorts of strange characters within the newsletter. It's a good idea to write newsletters in a text editor, such as Windows Notepad or SimpleText. (A really good text editor for Windows, with many word-processing features, is **TextPad**—http://www.textpad.com/.) Tara really likes **UltraEdit** (http://www.ultraedit.com/).

Resources for Creating a Great Newsletter

For more information on creating a great newsletter, check out the sites on the Web discussed in the following sections.

INKSPOT

http://www.inkspot.com/

Inkspot is both a wildly successful newsletter and a great clearinghouse for writing resources on the Web. As a newsletter, it reaches over 30,000 subscribers with each issue and contains regular market information and columns from a variety of writers and other professionals with writing-related information. As a Web site, you'll find links to all kinds of writing and writing-related resources. Especially check out the article *How to Start an Online Newsletter* at http://www.inkspot.com/craft/newsletterinfo.html.

THE NEWSLETTER EDITORS' RESOURCE LIST

http://www.tedgoff.com/erlist.html

The Newsletter Editors' Resource List is a lengthy, and we mean *lengthy*, list of Web sites found useful by newsletter editors. You'll find media links. You'll find links of use to editors. You'll find reference links, and you'll find a great section covering online publishing.

INFOBOT.NET

http://www.infobot.net/

InfoBot.Net has a great list of articles on e-mail publishing and a database of free content for use in e-mailed newsletters. There's a lot of great stuff here. InfoBot.Net used to have a directory of resources for newsletter publishers, but it has moved to **List-Resources.com** (http://list-resources.com/), which maintains a Yahoo!-type directory of resources for newsletter publishers.

E-ZINEZ

http://www.e-zinez.com/

E-ZineZ claims to have "everything you need to know about starting an E-Zine." Plenty of stuff is offered here—including a template sample for a plain-text e-zine, elements of essential e-zines, and a huge resource list. If you like fill-in-the-blank applications, use this site's template to build your e-zine online. Put this site on your surfing list!

ZINEBOOK

http://www.zinebook.com/

Zinebook is focused more on 'zines—small magazines with a limited circulation, often on paper instead of in cyberspace. There's a large resource listing on this site and plenty of attitude. If you're an independent publisher or are promoting a cultural item (like a band or a TV show) this is a must-see for you.

ALL REAL GOOD INTERNET: E-MAIL PUBLISHING

http://www.allrealgood.com/email_publishing/index.shtml

All Real Good provides information in a variety of categories for e-mail publishers; there's information on design and writing, distribution, distribution, and samples of "real good" newsletters. One gets the impression that the site founders really want to do your newsletter for you, but there's still a lot of good stuff here.

Distributing the Newsletter

Once you have your content together and used the sites mentioned previously and your own resources to put the first issue together, you need to figure out how to distribute it. You have three choices: do it yourself, go for a freebie, or pay for it.

Newsletters don't distribute themselves, and once you have more than a couple hundred readers, you're talking about a serious administrative task. If you decide to do it yourself, you're in for a lot of work. If you decide to get a freebie, you'll get a lot of administrative chores taken off your hands but it comes at a price. Nothing's really for free, after all. If you pay for it, you'll get premium service but it'll hit you in the wallet. The way you should distribute really depends on how large a subscriber base you expect to have and how often you're planning to distribute your newsletter.

DOING IT YOURSELF

Tara doesn't recommend this. Tara administered her own weekly newsletter on Internet advertising issues for a little over a year. She had a couple hundred subscribers and administered the list by hand—adding and removing subscribers, dealing with bounced messages, and so on. She did all this in Eudora Pro, an e-mail program. While Eudora could handle the newsletter, Tara had a hard time keeping up with the bounced messages, manually handling the subscribes and unsubscribes, and basically doing things besides producing content, which is what she wanted to do most.

On the other hand, Peter thinks it's okay to do it yourself, if you set things up carefully. His list was up to almost 2,000 subscribers, and he handled it through his own e-mail program before he switched to a for-pay system. It may take a little fooling around to get everything set up correctly—you may have to install a particular e-mail program, too—but it can be done.

There are two things you need to be able to do to administer a newsletter mailing list yourself. You need a program that can filter e-mail addresses into and out of the address book, and you need a program that allows you to import lists of addresses from text files into the address book.

Unfortunately only a few programs can do both of these things. We only know of two: **AK-Mail** (http://www.akmail.com/), and **Pegasus** (http://www.pegasus.usa.com). Worse, the first, though available, is no longer in development. The major e-mail programs—Eudora Pro 4and Outlook, for instance—cannot do these things.

Your options are therefore limited. If you want to run a list from your own system, we advise you to use AK-Mail or Pegasus. You can use the filters in these programs to grab an e-mail address from an incoming message, and then drop it into an address book (or *distribution list*, as it's called in Pegasus). For instance, take a look at Figure 11.3. This is the box in which filters are set up in Pegasus Mail for Windows, and it's fairly straightforward.

What these sorts of filters allow you to do is publish subscription information for your newsletter, and then set up the e-mail program so that whenever you receive a message using the particular address or code word in the Subject line, the address of the sender is placed into the address book. You can do the same for unsubscription information, too; whenever you receive a message to a particular address or using a particular word in the Subject line, the address is *removed* from the address book. (Be careful of spam being sent to the trigger address! A spammer may get the e-mail address of your subscription address, and send it e-mail. If you have an automatic filter in place, you'll add the spammer's e-mail address to your subscription list. This will cause you a couple of problems. First of all the address is probably fake, so every time you send a newsletter to this address it'll bounce back to you. Secondly, your subscriber count will be wrong.)

FIGURE 11.3: Setting up a filter in Pegasus Mail for Windows.

Sending Out Your Messages

Once you have a subscriber list of e-mail addresses, what do you do with it? How do you mail to all these people? It's important to get this right, or you'll upset a lot of recipients.

Most mail programs allow you to mail to an address book, a

distribution list, or an alias or nickname that contains multiple addresses; but if you simply enter the address-book or distribution-list name into the To: text box and send the message, you've just committed a faux pas. Everyone who receives the message will see everyone else's e-mail address in the To: line. (And it's no longer a To: line so much as a To: page if you have a big list.) I've received e-mail messages containing literally hundreds of addresses in the To: line.

Instead, you must use the Bcc: line, which stands for blind carbon copy. It means that everyone on the list gets a copy of the message, but nobody can see who else got a message. Although you place the address-book or distribution-list name on the Bcc: line, when a recipient views the message, only that person's address appears on the To: line. We'll discuss using e-mail headers properly in Chapter 16, *Reaching Journalists Online*.

Some e-mail programs won't let you mail just to the Bcc: line; you must have an address in the To: line as well. So you can put your own address on the To: line, and the address book or distribution list name on the Bcc: line.

Bcc Lines Work Differently—*Unfortunately different programs handle the Bcc: line differently. Some will place the address from the Bcc: line onto the recipient's To: line. Others display the Bcc: address on a Bcc: line, and display the original To: line as well. Experiment to see how your program works; mail to a few friends and to yourself.*

Using a Freebie

If you're a noncommercial or nonprofit enterprise, if you want to send out issues once a day or more often, or if you have a small list, freebies are probably the way to go. Free services host your mailing list—they use their programs to handle your subscription list and send out the messages. That's the up side. The down side is that there are usually some restrictions with how you can handle your mailing list, and the services keep the sites free by selling advertising on the mailing lists they host. (Of course, many of these services also offer ways for you to pay to get rid of the advertising, which means they're not just freebies.) Several Web sites offer such free services.

Be Careful!—*It's a good idea to set up your mail program so that the Cc: field does not normally appear on your message composition screen. Turn on the Bcc: line so it's always there. Not all programs will let you do this, but many will. If you leave the Cc: line visible, one day you will send a couple of hundred messages on the Cc: line. If you're lucky, people won't be too mad at you.*

EGROUPS

http://www.egroups.com/

eGroups offers free discussion-type mailing lists (and moderated ones that can be set up as newsletters). eGroups' service can also poll newsletter readers and will archive your newsletter on its Web site if you like. eGroups protects Internet users from bogus subscriptions by sending confirmation messages to eGroups users before adding them to a mailing list. eGroups does sell advertising within the mailing lists it hosts, and it used to offer to remove the ads for $4.95 a month, but we can no longer find mention of that on its Web site, so either it doesn't or it tucked that information away in a corner somewhere. It has a limit on the size of messages, but does not have a limit on the number of subscribers a newsletter may have.

Not Just Lists, but Communities—*The free mailing lists discussed in this chapter have integrated a lot more services than just mailing lists now. For example, eGroups offer polls, chat rooms, and file storage for mailing lists. When you're investigating these distribution options, be sure to check out these extras and see if they're applicable to your list.*

LISTBOT

http://www.listbot.com/

ListBot is affiliated with LinkExchange, one of the first and certainly the most famous banner-exchange program on the Internet (see Chapter 13, *Affiliate Programs*). Like eGroups, ListBot does not have a limit to how many members you can have or how many messages you can send to your list, and like eGroups, ListBot doesn't sell or give away the e-mail addresses of subscribing members. ListBot is advertiser supported, but it does have an option called ListBot Gold.

Newsletters vs. E-Mail Discussion Groups—*In the "Distribution" section of this chapter, we'll be talking about distribution options for your newsletter, and you'll notice that a lot of the services that can distribute a newsletter can also maintain an e-mail discussion list. What's the big difference between a newsletter and an e-mail discussion list? Technically speaking, not much. Newsletters go from one entity to many readers; whereas an e-mail discussion list goes from many writers to many readers. In the case of a newsletter, it's one person's editorial content being distributed to many readers, like a newspaper. In the case of a discussion list, it's many people inserting their own content—like a telephone "party line" or a discussion group.*

ListBot Gold has a 250K per message size restriction versus 100K for free list members, does not contain advertisements, and allows you to import existing mailing-list subscribers into the new list. In addition, you can set up a series of customized demographic questions by which you can track what type of person is reading your newsletter. ListBot Gold costs $99 a year, which provides you with

5,000 message credits a month. One message to one person equals one credit. Therefore, if you sent out a monthly newsletter to 5,000 people, you'd use 5,000 credits. If you sent four weekly newsletters to 1,250 people, you'd use 5,000 credits. If you sent ten issues of a newsletter to 500 people, you'd use 5,000 credits. You get the idea. You can buy additional credits in bulk if you're going to use more than 5,000 credits a month.

Registration Before Subscription—*Some free services require that participants register at the Web site before they can sign up for a newsletter or discussion group. The services do this so that they can get enough demographic information to sell advertising on the mailing lists they're sponsoring. The problem is, it's one more hoop that a potential subscriber has to jump through. For every hoop you make potential subscribers jump through, you lose a certain number of the subscribers. Keep the hoops to a minimum.*

TOPICA

http://www.topica.com/

Unlike some mailing list services that try hard to be community oriented and offer lots of features, Topica sticks with just offering mailing list services. Its directory is nice—you can search for both messages and mailing lists—so browse around in there a while to get an idea of what other Topica users are offering. If you decide to start a list with Topica, you can also join its network, which will allow you to swap ads with other list owners and actually earn revenue on the ads being displayed in your mailing list.

What Happens When You Leave—*Make sure there's an easy way to get your subscription list out of the system before you sign up. Consider what will happen when you want to move to another service.*

If you don't know whether you want to pay for a mailing list, using a freebie is a good way to get your feet wet. You can run a mailing list for a while, see if you can keep up with the content responsibilities, and get reaction to your writing. The problem is, if you decide to move to a different mailing list provider, you have to do several things. You have to move what could be a substantial mailing list to a new provider, alert everyone who knew about your old service to your new service, and make sure that there are no places on the Internet or your own Web site that mention your old newsletter. To get around that, you might use a free service for six issues or so without promoting your newsletter to make sure you can handle the schedule of doing a newsletter and then move to a pay service and seriously promote. If you decide you don't want to direct your energies into the newsletter, you can simply shut it down without having paid any money.

Really Temporary Lists—*Did you ever want to discuss something on your own in a private group, but didn't want to go to all the hassle of setting up a mailing list? QuickTopic, at* http://www.quicktopic.com/ *gives you a quick way to start a brief discussion without any permanence. This is a great way to finish up a tangential conversation you start on a mailing list or newsgroup.*

Pay Service Newsletters

If you want to control the advertising in your newsletter, or you want lots of administrative control—or if your newsletter is getting big—you can't beat a pay service. If your newsletter is small, though, and you're not sure if you want to spend a lot of money, investigate one of the freebies that offers a pay option to remove advertisements.

LYRIS

http://www.lyris.net/

Tara uses Lyris for her newsletter, and she's fairly happy with it. (Though she doesn't know if she'd use it again if she hadn't signed on before the rates went up.) In fact Lyris may well be the best program available; many major newsletter publishers are working with this system.

Lyris gives you extensive control over the different messages your list sends out (the welcome message, goodbye message, and so on) and gives you very precise information about your list. You can view a list showing the number of subscribers who joined per day, for example. You can also merge each reader's name into each message (if you feel like using that much personalization). Lyris uses a simple subscribe/unsubscribe function that makes it easy for people to unsubscribe even if they didn't bother to save the directions for doing so. The tech support is quick and is good at unraveling problems. Lyris is stacked full of features, such as these:

- Schedules messages to be sent at particular times.
- Customizes headers and footers that are automatically added to the message; place ads, announcements, subscription information, etc.
- Customizes welcome and good-bye messages so you can include information about your newsletter and your Web site, for instance.
- Archives all the messages at the Lyris Web site, so visitors can search and view old messages or newsletters.

- Produces detailed delivery reports, showing how many messages were sent out and when, and how many bounced back.
- Carries out sophisticated bounce management. Tells the program how long it should accept bounce messages before putting an undeliverable e-mail address into a held list (a list of what messages to send to held addresses and how often; when to purge held addresses if the address remains undeliverable; and so on).
- Carries out mail merge operations. You can incorporate the recipient's name into the message body. Peter could, if he wished, start each of these newsletters with Dear John (or whatever a reader's name is).
- Provides sophisticated management tools. You can send messages to the server to carry out various commands, or use a Web form.

If you'd like to see exactly what Lyris can do, read the **Lyris User's Guide** at http://www.lyris.com/help/. It looks a bit daunting, but remember that most features are optional so you don't have to learn it all! If you want to buy software and run it on your own server, see http://www.lyris.com/. (You'll need somewhere between $500 and $10,000, depending on the size of your list and how many messages you want to distribute.)

On the other hand, you can pay monthly for the service (you can find information about using the **Lyris service** at http://www.lyris.net/). Lyris ain't cheap, though. It charges $5 per thousand messages, with a minimum of $100 in charges a month. (1,000 messages is 1 message to 1,000 people, or 10 messages to 100 people, or 500 messages to 2 people, and so on.) Furthermore, those prices are based on an average message size of 10K—messages over 10K are priced on a sliding scale based on the size of the message. If you have a small mailing list of a couple hundred people, the cost minimum will be unattractive to you. However, if you have a large list, or even a small list that's daily instead of weekly or monthly, Lyris is more cost effective than the premium versions of the free lists.

Confirmation Required—*Lyris.net now requires that all its lists obtain confirmation from new subscribers. If you don't like that, look elsewhere for list-hosting services.*

There is another way to get the Lyris service, though; find a company that has bought the Lyris server and is selling the service. For instance, **Dundee Internet Services** (http://www.dundee.net/) sells Lyris at a much lower rate.

SPARKLIST

http://www.sparklist.com/

SparkLIST also offers mailing list hosting services—both for discussion lists and newsletters—and a Web-based interface for managing the newsletter. SparkLIST's price is $1 per 1000 messages, with a set-up fee based on the number of existing members. If you would like a server to process large mailing lists, it offers several different levels of server options, as well as different levels of Lyris servers. There does not seem to be a limit on the number of messages that may be sent to a member list. SparkLIST also offers several different promotional packages to help get the word out about your newsletter.

L-SOFT EASE

http://www.lsoft.com/

L-Soft EASE is produced by the same folks that brought the Internet Listserv, at one time the most popular mailing-list management software on the Internet. L-Soft offers several different kinds of services, but EASE is probably the one you want to look at. EASE offers several different kinds of services—EASE Business, EASE Bulk, or EASE Home.

Your Hosting Company—*Before you take advantage of one of these services, you may want to check with your own Web-hosting company. Some companies offer free mailing lists if you use their Web-hosting service. However, these services are generally not as easy to use or as powerful as the services we're looking at in this section.*

EASE Business—This is for smaller lists, those that have between 150 and 500 subscribers. Costs vary depending on how much technical support and L-Soft involvement you require—it ranges from $500 a year to over $1,000 a year. These lists can support 150 postings a day, so they're really more for discussion lists rather than newsletters.

EASE Bulk—EASE Bulk is for newsletters and other one-way services. EASE Bulk charges as if for a minimum of 1,000 users, so unless you plan to build up to that many readers quickly, you won't want to start with this service. EASE Bulk offers a wide variety of pricing options, depending on how many readers you have, how regularly you send out your newsletter, what time of day you want to send it out, and so forth.

EASE Home—If you're a noncommercial entity, you definitely want to check this service out. EASE Home supports very small lists—for 25 to 100 users—at really cheap prices. Twenty-five subscribers will run you $8 a month; 100 subscribers will run you $15 a month. (EASE Home lists will support up to 1,000 readers, but you'll need to contact L-Soft for a price quote.) Note that EASE Home lists cannot be used for commercial endeavors and no more than 100 messages a day may be posted.

If you want to get information about L-Soft's software, **Listserv**, check out the software's Web site at http://www.lsoft.com/.

If you're a noncommercial or nonprofit organization, or you plan to run a really small newsletter, free services (or premium free services) are probably the best idea for you economically. There's no point in footing a minimum pay charge for a list that only has 50 subscribers. (In fact, a list with only 50 subscribers is probably small enough for you to manage yourself.) If you want to make money off advertising or send out high volumes of e-mails, check out a paid service.

What do you want once you have content and a distribution mechanism? You want readers, of course! And to get readers you need to promote your newsletter. We'll look at that next.

Publicizing Your Newsletter

There are lots of places you can go to publicize your newsletter:

ETEXT Archives (A huge repository of zine and newsletter information; if you need a place to archive your newsletter, check this out)
http://www.etext.org/Zines/

E-Zine Ad Source (If you plan to sell advertising make sure you're listed here. Your e-zine must be delivered by e-mail, have at least 1,000 subscribers, and accept advertising to apply)
http://www.ezineadsource.com/

Ezine-Universe (Over 3,000 ezines listed)
http://Ezine-Universe.com/

E-ZineZ (A search engine and searchable subject index just for e-zines)
http://www.e-zinez.com/

EZineSeek (A zine subject index)
http://www.ezineseek.com/

Liszt (Lists over 90,000 discussion groups and newsletters)
http://www.liszt.com/

Low Bandwidth
http://www.disobey.com/low/

NewJour (An e-mail publication carrying announcements about online publications)
http://gort.ucsd.edu/newjour/

NEW-LIST (Another publication dedicated to announcing new newsletters; it's got some of the same restrictions as Net-Happenings—see Chapter 8—so pay attention)
http://listserv.classroom.com/archives/new-list.html

Newsletter Access (Paper and electronic newsletters; you can add a little information for free or a full listing for $19.95 a year)
http://www.newsletteraccess.com/

Newsletter Library (Currently lists over 11,000 newsletters; free samples of any are available. Cost to be listed in this resource is $50)
http://pub.savvy.com/

There are more, many more. Peter has a special report called *Places to Register Your E-mail Newsletter*, which you can find at http://www.poorrichard.com/freeinfo/special_reports.htm. The report currently lists over 48 useful sites.

Search Engines—*If you have a Web site associated with your newsletter, don't forget to register it with the search engines; see Chapter 6, Registering with the Search Sites.*

Finding Readers

Though you can do a lot to simply promote your newsletter—make sure it's in all the newsletter search engines and subject indexes, run an announcement in Net-Announce (which we mentioned in Chapter 8, *Other Places to Register Your Site*), and so on—you can also do a lot to court readers themselves. Perhaps the single most important thing you can do is to put a form at your Web site in which people can subscribe to the newsletter. If you're working with one of the for-pay or freebie services we talked about, you'll be given a form that you can incorporate into your Web site. Otherwise you'll have to create a form using a CGI script or perhaps the form tools in MS FrontPage, if you're using that tool.

Make it as easy as possible for someone to subscribe to the newsletter. Most of the services we've described above will give you some HTML code to put on your Web page. The code usually creates a small form in which readers can enter their e-mail addresses and click a button, which will sign them up for the newsletter. Some mailing list services use an authentication process, which means that new subscribers will get a validation letter that they'll have to return before they're signed up for the newsletter. (The authentication process is so people can't be signed up for newsletters or mailing lists without their consent.)

However, there's a problem with this. If you set up your mailing list so that the person has to confirm receipt, you'll lose 15–20 percent of all your subscribers—that is, somewhere between one in seven and one in five will not confirm the subscription. Some publishers set up the system so that a confirmation letter is sent, but no reply is required to complete the process. This way you won't lose so many subscribers, yet the subscribers have received a notification, so that if they have been subscribed by someone else (which is actually relatively rare) they can quickly remove themselves from the list. (The ability to play games like this, configuring your system in different ways, is one of the big advantages of working with a system such as Lyris.) A confirmation policy that requires a reply protects you from accusations of spamming.

Where Will You Put the Form?—*Newsletter publishers often put introductory information about their newsletter at the front of the site and lead people to a subscription page. You may find you get more subscriptions if you put the subscription page up front. Randy Cassingham, publisher of the* **This Is True** *humor newsletter (*http://www.ThisIsTrue. com/*), told us that his subscription rate tripled after moving the subscription form up front. So make the form obvious and easy to get to.(Check out Figure 11.4 for Randy's new subscription form placement.) In fact, consider putting it on several pages at your Web site. Tara puts hers on every page of her Web site in the same place, along with a quick link to her privacy policy.*

Make your policies clear. When Tara moved her newsletter to Lyris and began promoting it, she didn't make it clear on her sign-up page that she would never rent or sell the list of subscribers to her newsletter. To her, it was a no-brainer—of course she wouldn't do anything like that; but enough people e-mailed her and asked if she was going to rent or sell her mailing list that she appended a privacy disclaimer to her Web page. Then she started getting e-mail asking if her newsletter was free. That was another no-brainer to her; but she added the word *free* to her Web page.

Are you making any assumptions about your newsletter policy? Have you made it crystal clear how much it costs, what its frequency is, what its copyright statement is, and how you will treat the aggregated list of e-mail addresses? Don't get blindsided by a no-brainer.

Make it easy to spread the word. Your newsletter should always have a copyright statement, though under current copyright law, copyright does not have to be explicitly stated. Copyright is secured automatically as soon as the work is created. (For more information on this, visit the **US Copyright Office** and check out the copyright primer: http://www.loc.gov/copyright/ circs/circ1.html.) However, stating an explicit copyright allows you to grant

FIGURE 11.4: Randy puts his subscription form right out front.

certain rights. For example, you might want people to feel free to pass your newsletter along via e-mail, but you don't want them to use it as part of a book or include it in a CD-ROM. You could issue a copyright disclaimer like this:

The example newsletter is copyright 2000 by so-and-so. All rights reserved. Feel free to forward this newsletter to others as long as you forward it in its entirety and leave this notice. This newsletter may not be included in any compilation, electronic or printed, or as part of any commercial endeavor without written permission from the copyright holder.

Give Them Plenty of Opportunities—*Give visitors to your Web site plenty of opportunities to subscribe to your newsletter. For instance, if you sell a product at your Web site, include option buttons on the order form that allow people to sign up for your newsletter. Peter does this on all his forms, and sets the option buttons to Yes. People filling out the forms can change the setting to No, of course, but only five percent do. If people are interested enough to place an order or fill in some kind of response form, chances are they're interested enough to get your newsletter, too.*

That's all you have to say. If you want to attach specific details—like granting reprint permission for single articles, or excerpt information, create a Web page for your details and include the page's URL in the copyright disclaimer.

This copyright disclaimer does a couple of things. First, the disclaimer makes it clear to your readers what they can and cannot do with the newsletter (and perhaps helps them feel free to pass it on to other interested potential subscribers). Second, if people do perhaps do something inappropriate with your material, they can't claim ignorance of your wishes.

Spread the word yourself. When you mention another mailing list, Web site, or other Internet resource in your newsletter, be sure to let it know what you're doing and send a copy of your newsletter. The owners may find it interesting enough that they subscribe. Better, they might find it interesting enough that they mention your newsletter or link to it from their Web sites.

Keeping the Momentum Going

When you first start your newsletter, you probably won't lack ideas. After all, you wouldn't have started the newsletter unless you had a good idea of what you wanted to write about. But as time goes by, you might find that the well's running a little dry and you're finding it hard to fill a newsletter. Don't wait until you're completely out of ideas; anticipate the problem and answer it before it threatens the existence of your newsletter.

Recruit your readers. From your first issue, ask your readers for feedback. Ask them for ideas. Ask them what they want to learn from your newsletter. You can't keep up with the resources on the Internet about your subject all by yourself, but if you get a couple thousand readers who know what you're interested in, you're well on your way to making the most of those resources available.

Pay attention to your company communications. Pay attention to what's going on with your corporate structure. What are callers to technical support asking about? What features are sales prospects after? You might also want to pay attention to what's being said about your products and services on the Web and USENET, and build articles around exploring strengths and answering criticisms of your product.

Get other people to contribute to your newsletter. Sometimes you can do so by offering to trade writing for promotions ("Check out this great new writer and her home page!"). You could even trade writing for text ads. Once the circulation of your newsletter is high enough, you could approach writers like this with the idea that they provide you with a certain amount of material—like a column a month or a certain statistic every week—in exchange for a certain amount of promotional consideration. The only potential problem with something like this is that you have to coordinate with your writers on a regular basis and make sure they make your deadlines. Try to get a lot of material in advance if possible.

Selling Advertising

One way to offset the cost of your newsletter is to sell advertising. In fact one way to make a living is to sell advertising; a number of newsletter publishers make a good living from their newsletters. Some e-mail newsletters can bring in hundreds of thousands of dollars a year. These levels are rare…but partly because this is such a new game that few people know how to play it right.

How many subscribers you need to sell advertising depends a lot on how specific your newsletter is. If you have a rare-book restoration service and your newsletter is read by 500 rare-book sellers, you have a highly targeted audience and something you can easily sell to potential advertisers. On the other hand, if your newsletter has 5,000 subscribers and it's about cool stuff on the Internet, you probably have a vague demographic that would be less valuable to potential advertisers.

CPM—*Means cost per thousand (the m coming from the Roman numeral for 1,000). Newsletter publishers who know what they're doing sell advertising according to a CPM of some kind. (Publishers who don't know what they're doing often publish flat rates without even explaining how many subscribers they have, so that you don't know what you're getting for your money.) For instance, a CPM of $30 means for every one thousand e-mail messages in which an ad appears, it'll cost $30. Thus if the list has 10,000 subscribers, the ad costs $300 ($30 x 10).*

If you have enough subscribers to take a mailing list, check out the competition. How much are they charging? (If you have a targeted demographic, you can charge more than if your newsletter is general interest.) We've seen advertising rates vary from a CPM of 45 cents to a CPM of $40.

When you have an idea of how much you can charge, consider whether it's worth your time. You might be someone who can keep track of ads, work with prospects and sell advertising spots, keep track of who's paid what, and pester those folks who have problems with their payment. If so, then it might be worth your time. But if merely thinking about all those chores makes you itch, you might want to bypass advertising entirely or take on an agreement like Topica's (see the "Using Freebies," section of this chapter for more information about Topica)—or find an advertising broker of some kind. Tara sells her own advertising and allows **Advertising.com** (http://www.advertising.com) to sell ads on her list. She's better at selling ads on her list than they are, though.

Another option, if you don't want to formally sell advertising, is to swap ads with Web sites and other newsletter publishers. This helps publicize your Web site and your newsletter without you having to spend money on advertising and keep up with a lot of accounting. **List City**, at http://list-city.com/, maintains a list of e-zine publishers who are interested in exchanging advertising.

DISCUSSION GROUPS

Newsletters can be difficult to create because you have to come up with all that content—the stuff that goes into the newsletter. It takes one person, or a team of people, to produce a set amount of content on a regular schedule. It's hard enough to do that in itself; but when you're doing it as a sideline, or to promote the thing in which you're truly interested, it becomes even more difficult.

Newsletters are one-to-many. You create the content and send it to everyone on your list; but there's a way to cheat. Why not let someone else create the content for you? You can do that by setting up a discussion group based on the e-mail system; all the newsletter distribution services we looked at earlier can be used to do this. With a discussion group the people involved in the discussion are, in effect, providing the content. (Though you could also publish small, occasional articles as part of a discussion list.) But in some ways discussion lists can take as much time as creating a newsletter, and the content is sometimes not as good.

E-mail discussion groups—or discussion lists, as they're often known—can be free-for-all conversations. Everybody can talk to everybody. Discussion lists come in a couple of flavors.

Discussion lists that are *unmoderated* have no restrictions on how posts can be made to the list. If a member posts something, it goes to all the members of the list immediately. There are also *moderated* mailing lists. Postings to a moderated mailing list go to the list moderator (there may be more than one) who must approve the messages before the messages go to the rest of the list. Messages that aren't approved are deleted so that most list members never see them.

Moderation—*Some people view moderated lists as too controlling and restrictive of free speech. Some others view moderated lists as a reasonable way to control excessive amounts of traffic and keep a list of traffic. If you choose to moderate a mailing list, you have to be careful of how you moderate and how objectively you evaluate contributions to your mailing list. You want your moderation to be considered fair and evenhanded. Moderating is about the worst job in the world. If you do it well, no one will know you exist. If you do it badly, a lot of people will dislike you. It's not a bad idea to cultivate a few people on your mailing list who can help you evaluate if you're acting appropriately in your moderating.*

Between these two extremes there are several different degrees of list control—for example, a mailing list may not be formally moderated but the list owner may exert a high degree of control over the kind of topics might be discussed on a list. (If you're concerned about your moderation skills, information moderation is the best way to go; all users see the posts and can see for themselves how off-topic they are.) Another option is to moderate the first few messages of list members so you're sure they understand the rules and requirements of the list.

The smaller the discussion group, the less difficult it is to control. Smaller groups seem to be cozier, and peer pressure seems to make people behave. Once you get more than a hundred people, however, you have to watch out for fighting, harsh words, straying way off the topic, and so on. (On the other hand, it's also possible for a list to be too small; there's a point at which there are not enough people on the list to keep the list going; if it's too small, it may just die.)

You don't need to keep the list in an iron grip. Tara actually thinks it's healthy to stray a little off-topic; it helps keep the list fresh. Without going off-topic a little, mailing lists can fall into a rut and cover the same topics over and over again. But sometimes discussions can get quite ugly—fighting and wars of words are not healthy and not something you want to happen under the aegis of your discussion group.

Who's Responsible?—*Remember, if you sponsor a discussion group or mailing list, everything that happens on that mailing list may appear to reflect on your company, for better or for worse. You'll want to make it clear that you are providing the forum, but are not responsible for everything that is said. Also, there's a danger to moderating a group. If you are clearly moderating the group, you may become legally liable for things that are said in the group. By taking up the position of moderator you are, in effect, screening out the bad stuff. So if people don't like what's being said, they can claim that you are partly responsible.*

Whether you choose to formally moderate a list or not (and if you're creating a list for support of your product or service, we recommend that you impose some sort of moderation, formal or informal), you will have to keep up with reading your own list. It's like an ongoing editorial process—there's all this content coming and you need to make sure it stays appropriate, focused, and on topic. The more you work to maintain the quality of that content, the better and more valuable the list will be. If you do not have that kind of time to invest, an out-of-control discussion group can reflect poorly on you and your company. In fact, Tara would say that if you don't have the resources to keep an eye on a list, just don't do it. Forget it. Do a newsletter.

Discussion groups can, properly administered, be a powerful promotional tool. David Rogelberg, founder of Studio B (a company providing services to the computer-book business), says that the single most important promotional technique he used to build his business was the **Studio B discussion group** (http://www.studiob.com/).

You can set up discussion groups via e-mail with many of the lists we covered earlier in this chapter—the ones that also handle newsletter lists. (See the Distribution section of this chapter for more information on creating mailing lists.)

WEB FORUMS

You can also set up discussion lists on the Web, using what are often known as *Web forums* (see Figure 11.5). A Web-based discussion list means that most of the conversation takes place right at your Web site, instead of via e-mail or on USENET. A Web-based discussion list may be useful if you do a lot of updating, expect your board to be busy, or have periodic events or product releases that would lead to a lot of activity at one time. (For example, suppose you have a mailing list that covers Christmas ornaments and is only really busy three months of the year. It's hard to promote it, and it's hard to justify paying a mailing list pay service a minimum usage fee that your mailing list won't even use one quarter of the time.) However, there's a big problem with Web forums: you have to rely on people visiting your site to take part in the discussion. This greatly reduces the number of people who are likely to be involved over the long term; it's just way too easy to slip out of the group. With mailing-list groups, however, the information goes to each subscriber—the subscriber doesn't have to take time out to go get the information.

Everything we said about maintaining a good flow of content on a mailing list goes double for a Web forum. In addition to maintaining order on the forum, you also have to maintain a steady list of postings. Nothing is more disheartening than going to a Web forum and seeing there have been no postings on it for two or three months. You'll need to fight off spammers who plaster your list with XXX advertisements and get-rich-quick schemes, too.

There are several places where you can get a free online Web forum, which we discuss in the sections that follow.

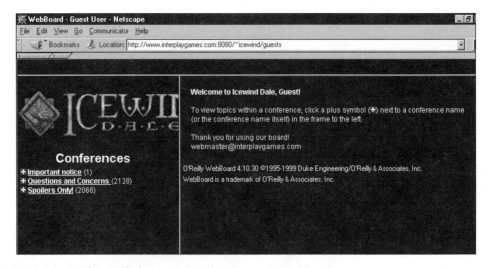

FIGURE 11. 5: This Web forum is used to promote a computer game.

INSIDE THE WEB

http://www.insidetheweb.com/

Inside the Web hosts your web forum on its Web site for free. It offers options for moderated and unmoderated message sites. Moderated sites have messages that stay on until you delete them; whereas unmoderated sites have message expiration times that you can set between 0 and 999 days. (We recommend you don't let messages stay on the board for more than a couple of months, unless you're comfortable that the information on the discussion forum won't get stale.) Inside the Web notes that spammers are getting clever in invading online Web forums and states that they're trying to figure out how to stop it. If your forum is inactive for 45 days it will automatically be deleted. Note also that Inside the Web has restrictions about the kind of content that can be discussed on its Web forums and will delete any forums that violate that content policy.

NETWORK54

http:// ://network54.com/

Network54 is another free forum service that offers both free forums and chat rooms (where visitors to your site can chat in real-time). The service makes money from the forums by putting an advertising banner at the top of the site. Network54 requires you to register to use its service. Once you've registered (which requires only your e-mail address), you're asked to give a name and description to your new forum. Network45 will automatically create your forum and give you a URL to link to for access to your forum. Once you've created the forum, you have a lot of control over it. You can block users based on IP (Internet Protocol) address, turn moderation on and off, customize the look of your board, and so on. There's a lot of power here, but it looks easy enough that even a beginner could use it.

YOURBBS.COM

http://www.yourbbs.com/

YourBBS is another advertiser-supported free Web forum service. It's got lots of options, including spell check for users, file attachments in mail, image attachments to subject lines, bans certain IP addresses, password-protecting your BBS (so that users have to enter a password before they can post), and different templates that you can set up.

By using mailing lists and discussion groups, you're taking content beyond the Web and into mailboxes (or onto dynamic Web pages, if you're hosting discussion groups on a Web page). While discussion groups allow users to generate lots of content, you have to stay vigilant; making sure content stays on topic and is useful to the readership of a discussion group, ensures that your discussion group or newsletter is valuable. Similarly, giving away plenty of information and helping your readers solve problems makes your newsletter a valuable property. Trumpeting about your great sales and bragging about yourself does not.

You Need This Book!—*Publishing using e-mail is quite a new thing; the vast majority of all e-mail publications, over 99 percent, are less than three years old. (Peter made up that statistic; feel free to use it if you wish.) There's a lot to learn, much more than we can cover in one chapter. For further information, see Poor Richard's E-mail Publishing: Newsletters, Bulletins, Discussion Groups and Other Powerful Communications Tools (ISBN: 0-9661032-5-4), by Chris Pirillo.*

CHAPTER TWELVE

Advertising Your Site

H ere's another of those good-news-bad-news things that we seem to run into so often. We'll start with the bad news. The bad news is that much of what you may have heard about advertising on the Internet is completely wrong. Advertising, contrary to the claims of many pundits (and, of course, of the companies selling advertising), is not a sure-fire affordable way to bring people to your site. Yes, you'll bring people to your site, but can you afford what it's going to cost per visit? In many cases the answer is no. We'll come to that in a minute.

The good news, though, is that advertising *can* work, if you don't pay too much attention to people pushing banner ads. The real advertising bargains are often elsewhere. We're not saying that banner ads never work, or that you should stay away from banner ads completely. We're just saying that if you decide to try banner advertising you should enter into the process with your eyes wide open—and with just a little skepticism to guide you along the way. And if you're not using banner ads? You have another other option; e-mail advertising. It's not as flashy or glamorous as banner advertising, but it can get a lot of results.

WHAT'S CPM?

Let's clarify a little terminology. Advertising prices are generally stated according to a CPM—cost per thousand. (Why M for thousand? M is the Roman numeral for 1,000.) This isn't an Internet thing; it's an advertising thing.

A *cost per thousand* what? Generally a cost per thousand impressions. An *impression* may be one of several things. If we're talking about banner ads, 1,000 impressions means that the banner ad is loaded into Web pages 1,000 times. That doesn't mean that the ad was seen 1,000 times, though. Visitors to that page may not look at that particular ad; and in fact the ad may even be at the bottom of the page, "below the fold," as it's known—invisible to viewers unless they choose to scroll down the page. (For this reason banner ad placement is important, and above-the-fold ads generally sell at a higher price. Some banner exchange programs, which we'll look at in the Banner Swaps section of this chapter, require that they be the only ad above the fold on a Web page.)

If we're talking about e-mail advertising, 1,000 impressions means that the ad is placed into 1,000 e-mail messages. Again, that doesn't mean that 1,000 people read the ad. Many recipients simply delete the message without opening it. On the other hand, newsletters are often forwarded to the recipients' friends and colleagues. That's why a really good newsletter, one with a loyal readership, is more valuable than some piece of badly written garbage thrown together to act as an advertising vehicle.

Here are a few more terms you should understand before you begin investigating ad buying:

- **Click through or clickthru:** When someone clicks a banner ad or a link in an e-mail ad to visit your Web site, that's a click through, also known as a clickthru. Note that a click through is not always the same as a visit to your Web site; while people clicking through may intend to visit, a proportion will change their minds and cancel before or soon after your first page loads.

- **Click-through rate:** The click-through rate is the percentage of people viewing your ad who click through.

- **Targeted and untargeted:** A targeted ad is one that is displayed to people who are probably interested in your product. An untargeted ad is one that is shown to a group of people whom you have no reason to believe want your product. These terms are relative, of course, and the targeting of ads is often imprecise.

By the way, there's a myth that targeted ads are always more effective than untargeted ads. All things being equal, this would be true. Show the same ad, at the same CPM, to a targeted list, and you'll do better than showing it to an untargeted list. (If you don't, it simply means that the list you thought was targeted actually wasn't.) But things are never equal; you'll pay more for a targeted list. In fact, you may pay so much more that even though you'll pull more sales, you won't cover your costs. So when you're talking with advertising salespeople, take what they say with a pinch of salt. Buying a targeted list may be a good idea...if it's the right price. Also, remember that it's difficult to compare an untargeted ad in one medium with a targeted ad in another. In other words, an untargeted ad in one medium may actually be far more effective than a targeted ad in another.

BANNER SWAPS

Getting into advertising can cost a pile of money, or it can cost nothing at all. In this section we'll talk about swapping ads, which you can start doing with practically nothing (except something to swap). We'll also get into paid advertising opportunities, and why you might want to avoid banner ads if you're selling certain kinds of products.

The easiest way to get into the advertising business is by swapping ads. Don't worry—this won't take a lot of time. It's remarkably easy to do using a number of automated swap systems. Here's how it works. You go to one of the banner-swap sites and sign up for the service. You then take a little bit of HTML and insert it into one or more of your Web pages. This HTML uses the `<IMG>` tag to insert an image—the banner—into your Web page, and pulls the image from the banner-exchange site. The banner-exchange site sends a different banner each time and has a program that keeps track of how many times your site pulls in a banner. This record is used to keep track of your credits and to assign your banner to other sites according to how many credits you accrue. Some services provide free credits when you sign up, so your ad starts displaying on other sites right away.

Don't Overdo the Banner Swaps*—When it comes to banner-swapping networks, show a little restraint. Nothing is more annoying—and adds more to a page's load time—than three or four banner-swap network ads piled on top of each other. Yuck.*

In order to participate in a banner swap you need a banner, of course. This is generally a standard size; it's usually 468 pixels wide by 60 pixels high, though a few other formats are used now and then. They have to be a particular file size, too, generally 10 Kb or less.

Wee Ads*—There's an 88x30 ad size, sometimes called a bug or a stamp. Such ads are usually on the side of a page. They're advantageous in that they stick out a little, but they can also get buried in a graphics-heavy site, leading many viewers to ignore or just not see them.*

Some of these banner-swap systems sell advertising; that's how they make their money. In other words, you get your ad shown for free, but you don't get equal time. Generally, your ad will be shown once for every two times that someone visiting your site sees an ad from the banner exchange. The banner displays that aren't given away are used by the exchange itself to advertise its services, or are sold.

Some of the services allow you to specify, to a limited degree, where your banner will be shown, so you can target your advertising. Others accept only certain types of banner ads to make sure you don't get inappropriate advertising at your site. Some even allow you to pick with whom you will swap; they provide a way for people wanting to swap to meet and arrange to swap.

Creating Banners—*A banner's file size is in part determined by color depth—the number of colors in the art's palette. There are many services that will create low-cost, or even free, banners for you. Search for the phrase "banner generator" or "banner design" at a full-text search engine like Google.*

Another service provided by these banner-swap sites—and an important one—is statistical reports. You'll be able to find out how often you displayed an ad and how often your ad was displayed. This information is important because it can help you decide how effective the service is. Check out these sites for more information about banner exchanges:

1-2-Free Banner Exchange
http://www.1-2-free.com/

BannerAd
http://www.banneradnetwork.com/

BannerSwap
http://www.bannerswap.com/

Cyber Link Exchange 2000
http://cyberlinkexchange.usww.com/

Do the Wave
http://DoTheWave.com/

Exchange-It
http://www.exchange-it.com/

Internet BannerExchange
http://www.bannerexchange.com/

Link Exchange
http://www.linkexchange.com/

LookSmart Clicks
http://www.looksmartclicks.com/

NarrowCast Media
http://www.narrowcastmedia.com/

PostMaster Banner Network
http://www.PostMasterBannerNet.com/

Web Site Banner Advertising (A large list of banner-swap programs, including a number of European programs; this is a really good site)
http://www.adbility.com/

Yahoo!—Banner Exchanges
http://dir.yahoo.com/Computers_and_Internet/Internet/World_Wide_Web/Annou
ncement_Services/Banner_Exchanges/

Make Your Own Network*—Is your site a little too esoteric or niche-oriented for the traditional banner exchanges? Check out* ***MyBannerSwap*** *at http://mybannerswap.com/; this site allows you to set up your own banner exchanges and makes money from this by retaining 25 percent of your banner impressions to fill with its own advertising.*

What's the advantage of using a banner-swap system? You get your banner posted on other sites for free. The disadvantages? There are two main disadvantages. First, you'll probably have a limited choice about where and when your ad appears. Second, if your site is not busy, your ad is not going to be placed on many sites. You're swapping placements, remember, so if you don't display many ads from the banner exchange, you won't get much in return.

Ugly Banner Syndrome*—Another possible disadvantage to banner swaps—and we just don't know any way to say this nicely—is that you might end up with some really ugly banners on your site. Do you really want your wonderfully designed site to host a flashing, bright purple-with-mauve-lettering ad for a thumbtack collector?*

PAYING FOR YOUR BANNER ADS

The other way to place banner ads is by paying for them. Plenty of companies will take your money and place your ads for you. In fact once you have a banner ready to place and you're signed up with a banner-advertising network, you can be running ads in minutes.

But is buying ads a good idea? There's a general principle in the PR business that money spent on PR is more effective than money spent on advertising. So you may want to forget about advertising and think a little more about the public-relations methods that you can use to promote your site, such as contacting journalists and acting as an expert (which we'll discuss in Chapter 16, *Reaching Journalists Online*).

Obviously public-relations people are biased towards PR, but they're probably correct; remember, the most effective promotional claims are those that appear to come from people not directly affiliated with your company. Everyone knows advertising is biased toward the person paying for the advertising, whereas reviews and feature stories in the press are generally trusted. By using the techniques discussed in Chapter 16 and Chapter 17, *Electronic Press Releases*, you can get your products and services mentioned, for little cost, in media spots that would cost hundreds of thousands of dollars if you had to buy the equivalent advertising. Additionally people are getting used to tuning out ads, especially banner ads, which can be counted on to be in generally the same area on a Web page. Check yourself—go Web surfing. See how easy it is to ignore banner ads?

Still, if your company budget can bear the burden, you might want to experiment with a little banner advertising. One of the best ways to experiment is using **Flycast** (http://www.flycast.com/). This company provides you with a program, which you run on your computer, to select where your ad will run. You pick the banner you want to use, select the actual Web sites on which the ads will run—or select a low-cost *run of the network* option, which means Flycast places your ad wherever it has space unsold—enter the amount of money you want to spend, click a button, and away it all goes. It's easy to get started, and also easy to see results. It's really fun, almost like a form of gambling. You can begin watching the results as soon as the first banner is placed; you'll see how much you've spent so far, how many click throughs the banner is getting, and even the cost per click through.

Banned Banner?—*Tara carried advertising from Flycast on one of her sites for a while. She had the option of rejecting many types of banners, including those featuring alcohol, gambling, and "false alerts" (things like "Warning, your connection is too slow!") messages. You may want to keep in mind that that kind of content can be rejected when you create your own banner.*

Banner ads vary greatly in price, from a CPM of around $5 to $60 and up. You may occasionally hear of rates as high as $150 per thousand, though that's probably quite rare. Yahoo!, for example, might charge $1,000 for a one-week placement on its Web Launch page. (We don't know how much they actually do charge; this is hypothetical.) This page contains just six ads; each ad also appears in a banner that appears on the various Yahoo! category pages. Yahoo! guarantees that each ad will be seen by at least 120,000 people during the week, so that's a CPM of just $8.33, perhaps less. However, the Web Launch banners are not targeted—they appear in all areas of Yahoo!—and each ad gets one third of a banner, hence the low CPM.

If you want to put a banner ad of your own at Yahoo! and have it appear even in targeted categories, you'll be charged for each impression (that is, each time someone sees the page). Rates might vary from 1.5 cents per impression ($15 CPM) to 6 cents per impression ($60 CPM) depending on the type of service. You can provide keywords for some of the service levels so that when someone searches for a particular word, your ad will appear. Most of the other major search engines have similar features except for Google, which shows only text ads that are linked to particular keyword searches. To see if there are already banners linked to the keywords in which you're interested, try **BannerStake** at http://www.bannerstake.com/.

These keyword banners may be a good deal and can have fairly high click-through rates. If users enter a keyword, and then almost immediately see your banner, there's a good chance they'll click it. Jim Daniels, writing in an article that ran in Peter's *Poor Richard's Web Site News* newsletter, says that he got an 8 percent click-through rate using the keywords *home business, business opportunities,* and *online marketing.*

If you want to look into banner advertising, try some of these places:

24/7 Media
http://www.247media.com/

Ad.Up
http://www.ad-up.com/

AdCentral
http://www.adcentral.com/

BURST! Media
http://www.burstmedia.com/

DoubleClick
http://www.doubleclick.net/

Public-Service Announcement Banner Ads for Nonprofits
http://www.adbility.com/

ValueClick
http://www.valueclick.com/

Yahoo!-Advertising on the Web
http://dir.yahoo.com/Computers_and_Internet/Internet/Business_and_Economics/
Advertising_on_Web_and_Internet/

Banner Advertising May Not Work

Be careful about some of the advice you hear on the Internet; a number of Internet publications have suggested, over the last year or so, that banner advertising is good, easy, and effective, and that every business should be involved. This is simply untrue, and generally the conclusion of journalists who have investigated banner advertising but never actually paid for a banner-advertising campaign.

The truth is, there's a good chance that banner advertising won't work for you. We've heard that banner ads are often quite effective for Web-hosting companies. If you're charging, say, a $50 initial setup fee and $30 a month, and you expect someone who signs up for an account to stay with you for perhaps 18 months, each sale is worth $590. If you sell ancillary products and services, too—design services, upgrade hosting services, and so on—your income per sale may be much more. In such cases banner advertising may be highly effective.

What if you're selling a $20 or $30 product, though? Ah, well, it depends what game you're playing. A number of large businesses, companies such as Amazon.com and CDnow, played a "grab as much cyberspace real-estate as quickly as possible" game. Advertising doesn't have to lead to profits right away for them—as long as it leads to regular customers who, perhaps, will be profitable over the long term. You can play this game only if you have a lot of money and are prepared to lose money for several years. But what about the average small business? A business that has to turn a profit, and can't afford to lose money this month, let alone for several years? In that case, banner advertising is probably not a good way to sell a low-cost item.

Before you jump into an expensive banner-ad program, run all the numbers—see what sort of click through you'll need to break even, and if possible do a small test. Don't believe a salesperson who tells you that to test properly you need to spend a minimum of $5,000, as one told Peter. This ignores basic rules of statistics; you can get a good idea of your possibility of success with a much smaller sample than 100,000 impressions!

Here's a quick rule of thumb. Assume that one in five or ten thousand impressions leads to a sale, and then figure out how much those impressions will cost you. One in five to ten thousand is a pretty common range for this sort of thing. Yahoo! has in the past claimed an average click-through rate of two percent, while ZDNet has claimed click-through rates as high as five percent at its site. We have seen average industry click-through rates at everywhere from .5 to 3 percent. Tara would tend to dismiss as too high anything over 1 percent, and even that may be too high.

It's simple; there are lots of banner ads and they're generally in the same place every time, and people tune them out. There's also a lot of concern over privacy. There's at least one software firewall that blocks banner ads, and countless software programs that do the same thing. The public response to ads is getting poorer and poorer as they're squeezed on everything from elevators to cars to pharmacy bags.

So let's say one or two people in 100 who see your ad will click it to visit your site, and one in 100 visiting your site will buy something; that's one impression in five or ten thousand leading to a sale. (Your numbers may be better; but then, they may be worse.) Can't make money with one in five or ten thousand at the CPM you've just been quoted for a banner ad? Then there's a good chance the banner-ad campaign won't work for you, unless you have good reason to believe you can get significantly more people clicking the banner, and convert more of them to sales.

E-MAIL ADVERTISING

There's another important form of advertising beyond banner ads, one that is too often ignored and one that presents the shoe-string marketer with a way to buy effective advertising at a low cost. That's e-mail advertising.

We're not talking about spam. We're talking about advertising to people who have signed up to receive e-mail for some reason. There are essentially two types of e-mail advertising: opt-in lists and e-mail newsletters.

Opt-in lists are lists of people who have signed up to receive advertising. Some people sign up for "I'll scratch your back, you scratch mine" plans. In other words, they agree to receive e-mail in return for something else. For instance, a company may hold regular drawings, giving away computers to the winners. To be included in the drawing, participants must be on the company's mailing list. Of course, the problem with this sort of list is that the people who sign up may have no interest at all in receiving the e-mail, and may delete it without reading it. All they want is the chance to win a prize.

The other reason people sign up for opt-in e-mail is because they have a genuine interest in getting information. For instance, hundreds of thousands of people who are trying to learn how to do business on the Internet have signed up to receive e-mail about doing business on the Internet, in the hope that some of the mail will lead them to information and services that will help them.

Create a Doorway Page—*When you advertise in e-mail, you should create a doorway page so you can measure the amount of traffic coming to your site in response to the ad. See Chapter 14, Tracking Results and Responding, for more information.*

The other form of advertising is in e-mail newsletters (which we discussed in Chapter 11, *Creating Newsletters and Discussion Groups*). In this case people subscribe to a newsletter and, if it's a good one, continue to receive it because they find it useful or entertaining. The newsletter has ads embedded into it. If it's a plain-text newsletter, the ads are plain-text ads—generally six or seven lines, about 65 characters wide. If the newsletter is an HTML-mail newsletter, the ads may be banner ads or some other kind of graphic.

Check the Reputation Carefully—*Check the reputation of any opt-in list carefully; all it takes is one mailing to a spam list to ruin your credibility.*

There are a number of companies selling opt-in lists; you'll find lists targeted at about any group you can imagine, from antique collectors to writers. Here are a few places you'll find opt-in lists. To find other ones, search Yahoo! for opt-in e-mail.

BulletMail
http://www.bulletmail.com/

Direct E-Mail List Source (A list of companies with opt-in e-mail lists, electronic newsletters carrying ads, sponsorable discussion groups, and so on; a very useful site)
http://www.copywriter.com/lists/

Direct Marketing Online
http://www.directmarketing-online.com/services/opt-in.htm

Intellipost
http://www.intellipost.com/

PostMaster Direct (One of the largest and best-known opt-in companies)
http://www.postmasterdirect.com/

Yahoo!—Direct E-mail
http://dir.yahoo.com/Business_and_Economy/Business_to_Business/Marketing_and_Advertising/Direct_Marketing/Direct_Email/

Some of the companies in the previous list charge by response rather than by recipient. In other words, instead of charging you, say, 15 cents for everyone who receives your message, they'll charge you perhaps 50 cents for everyone who visits your Web site as a result of your e-mail message. Negotiate with these people, and see if you can get a lower rate.

To find newsletters to advertise in, see these directories:

Advertising.com
http://www.advertising.com/

Direct E-mail List Source
http://www.copywriter.com/lists/

E-Zine Ad Source Directory
http://www.ezineadsource.com/

Lifestyles
http://www.lifestylespub.com/

MeMail
http://www.memail.com/

Places to Register Your Email Newsletter special report
http://www.poorrichard.com/freeinfo/special_reports.htm

What Works, What Doesn't

Peter has tried a number of e-mail advertising systems, some of which worked and some of which didn't. The following two sections compare an opt-in list and a newsletter:

POSTMASTER DIRECT

http://postmasterdirect.com/

PostMaster Direct is a company that sells many thousands of names, in hundreds of different lists, from lists for animal lovers to woodworkers and writers. Peter mailed to around 2,000 people for $300—15 cents per person. He sold a grand total of one book, and received not many more than 200 visitors to his site. PostMaster Direct later offered him a per-order campaign; that is, the company would provide him with orders, and he'd pay a fee per order; but it turned out that they thought he was going to sell the book on a billing basis. The book would be sent to customers free and then they'd receive a series of bills later, so they could make three payments or so. (PostMaster Direct works with Rodale Press, which sells books in this manner.)

PostMaster Direct also told him that it's difficult to get people to buy something outright using e-mail, and when its representatives discovered that was just what he wanted to do, they declined to carry out a per-order campaign.

JOKE OF THE DAY

The Joke of the Day mailing list is, not surprisingly, a list that transmits a joke to its readership—all 205,000 of them, reportedly—every day. Each joke is sponsored by a single advertiser; the ad comprises a few lines of text above the joke.

Now, the nice thing about Joke e-mail is that this is mail that people actually read. Jokes...well, isn't that why the Internet was invented? To save fax paper? People really do read joke e-mail. They subscribe to joke mailing lists because they want that humor fix. They open and read the e-mail because they want a laugh. Additionally—this is really important from our point of view—if they think the joke is funny, they send it on to their friends. Often to many of their friends. With luck they simply click the Forward button, and away it goes...

with the ad still in place. So although a joke list may be sent out to 205,000 people, who knows how much further it travels? To 225,000 people? 250,000? Many more? At this writing Joke of the Day claims that 82 percent of its readers say they frequently pass the jokes to their friends.

Peter's ad in Joke of the Day cost $75. (At the time the list had only 110,000 subscribers, and rates have increased significantly since then.) It didn't bring in enough business to buy a new car or send him to Hawaii, but it did bring in around 930 visitors to his Web site, and sold about seven or eight books (around $220 to $260, not including shipping fees), more than enough to pay for the ad.

Notice, by the way, that he paid around eight cents per visitor. That's cheap in the world of Internet advertising, far cheaper than most Web banners, which are measured in dollars per visitor.

Not All E-mail Advertising Works

E-mail advertising really can work. E-mail advertising is getting a good reputation these days, as people realize that it can be affordable and effective, but not all e-mail advertising is such a great idea. There are three main problems to watch out for: classified ads, very expensive ads, and the lack of "real numbers."

CLASSIFIED ADS

Some newsletters sell classified ads. You buy a few lines and your ad runs along with scores of others. These ads almost never work. Few people read these ads—in fact many of these newsletters probably aren't read at all, having been subscribed to in order to enter a drawing. Even if they are read, people tend to quickly scroll past the classifieds.

If you can find a newsletter with cheap classified ads, go ahead and try it. Create a doorway page to track incoming visits and see how many people hit that page. Probably very few. Remember, the best way to place an ad in a newsletter is in the editorial content, separated from any other ads the newsletter may be carrying. The better the content and the fewer ads in the newsletter, the better your ad is likely to work. Tara, for example, runs just one ad in her newsletter, between the editorial comment and the week's news. She doesn't want to clutter her newsletter and she wants the ad space to remain valuable to potential subscribers.

What's a Classified Ad—*Some people use the term classified ad to mean any text ad placed in an e-mail newsletter. By classified ad, we mean a small ad that is placed together with other similar ads. So some of the directories of classified ads that you may find can still be useful to you because they're listing newsletters that accept all types of newsletter ads, not just true classifieds.*

EXORBITANTLY EXPENSIVE ADS

Some opt-in lists are way too expensive. We looked at a number of opt-in lists recently and found that prices seem to be from as little as eight cents up to as much as thirty cents a name. Eight cents per name is a CPM of $80, which is toward the high end for banner advertising. Thirty cents a name represents a CPM of $300!

Can you make money at those rates? In many cases the answer is clearly no! It may be possible if you're selling a high-cost item. For instance, if you are selling Web-hosting services and expect each customer to bring you $300 in the first year, you may find it effective. If you're selling a book that costs $19.95, however, the chance of you making money with this sort of advertising is slim to none. It's quite possible to find advertising in newsletters at much lower rates. The CPM for targeted newsletters is often around $35, but rates can be much lower, around a dollar or two.

THE "REAL NUMBERS" ISSUE

The numbers problem is tricky, and right now, there's no easy answer. If you buy advertising in a newsletter, how do you know you're getting what you paid for? If you pay for 50,000 subscribers, how do you really know that you're getting 50,000, and not 40,000—or 10,000? We can tell you that some newsletter editors are inflating their numbers…at least, that's the rumor among newsletter editors, and after all, it makes sense that some would be doing so. It's too easy to get away with.

Right now most newsletter-advertising money is being spent on faith; people are simply taking the seller's word. In a lot of cases numbers are inflated. Many list owners probably don't clean their lists often, for instance, and a large list can quickly build up thousands of bad addresses.

A Few Things to Remember about E-Mail Advertising

Here are four points to remember when looking into e-mail advertising:

- Classified ad e-mails probably don't work. The message may be a newsletter with classified ads at the end, or may carry nothing but ads, but either way, why would people read these ads? Some will, but most won't.
- E-mail message ads sent by themselves to opt-in lists probably won't work well. If the message carries nothing but an ad, people will read the subject line, and unless it's a *really* good subject line, just delete the message. Remember, people are flooded with e-mail, so they're using the Delete key a lot.

- The most effective e-mail ads are probably those that are inserted into something that you know will be read, a newsletter or bulletin that people have asked to receive. If the information held in the message is entertaining or interesting, people will open the message and read at least part of your ad.
- Advertising rates are all over the place. We have seen CPMs vary from 42 cents to $300. Peter's had ads running at a CPM of 42 cents that far outpulled ads running at a CPM of $150. Look hard and you can find good deals.

OTHER FORMS OF ADVERTISING

Keep your eyes open for other forms of advertising that are not Web-based and that may be more direct and effective than Web advertising. For instance, a number of discussion groups sell sponsorships. Either they put a small text ad at the bottom of every message distributed to subscribers, or perhaps they have a special advertising bulletin that's sent out periodically. With the free mailing list services available, like Topica and eGroups, it's easy to get targeted advertising like this. (You can get more information about Topica and eGroups in Chapter 11, *Creating Newsletters and Discussion Groups*).

For example, Tara puts together the Studio B Buzz, the thrice-weekly newsletter for **Studio B Productions** (http://www.studiob.com), a literary agency focusing on computer book authors. Advertisers can buy an ad in the newsletter, but the ad is actually on a Web page and the teaser headline runs in the newsletter with a direct link back to the ad. This allows the advertisers to create larger ads than they would if they were hampered by space constrictions in the newsletter and it makes the ads easy to skip if the reader isn't interested. (Since the ads are unusual and highly targeted to the readership, Tara expects that most readers at least glance at the ad headlines.) The ads are included with news and announcements about Studio B clients, making for an interesting newsletter with a variety of information.

Another form of advertising is available through companies that build products designed to distribute information automatically. The user of one of these products doesn't go to a Web site to retrieve information; instead, the information comes to the user's desktop automatically through *push technology*. (The products that receive and display the pushed information are variously described as Web scrubbers, personalized broadcast products, micro-browsers, and push programs. Not so long ago they were hyped as the Next Big Thing, something that would be as big or bigger than the Web, but somehow that never happened.) Some of these companies sell advertising space, and will push your ad to thousands of desktops each day.

Then there are services such as **GoTo.com** (http://www.goto.com/), a search engine for which you have to *pay* to get a high listing. Companies that pay are listed first; after the companies that pay come the regular search results. You actually place a bid for placements on search pages. For instance, if you are selling CDs, you might offer to pay, say, 13 cents for every time your site is displayed in a response to a search for various keywords: *music, rock, van halen,* and so on. Ray Owens, owner of **Joke of the Day** (http://jokeaday.lyris.com/), reported that he spent $250 on placements at GoTo.com; he bid 13 cents per placement, and because that was higher than anyone else bidding for those keywords he came up first on the lists and received almost 2,000 new visitors to his site. That's not bad, considering that with banner ads you can easily spend many times that sum.

WHERE TO FIND MORE ADVERTISING ADVICE

A number of sites can help you in your search for the right advertising. Try a few of the choices discussed in the following sections.

AD-GUIDE.COM

http://www.ad-guide.com/

Ad-Guide is actually a searchable subject index of all things dealing with Internet advertising—banner advertising programs, service providers, e-commerce, etc. At the time of writing it had 99 resources dealing with banner advertising. There are dozens and dozens of banner exchanges and other banner programs online; you can get a great idea of their scope here.

CLICKZ NETWORK

http://www.clickz.com/

Another advertising and e-commerce search engine, ClickZ will give you both listings of advertising programs and articles about the way they work. You'll find searchable directories of different types of advertising services, too, from banner design and banner networks to e-mail copywriting services and opt-in e-mail lists.

INTERNET ADVERTISING RESOURCE GUIDE: MANAGEMENT

http://www.admedia.org/internet/management.html

This site lists Internet-banner advertising networks, ad-management software, and links to pricing guides and campaign-management services. Browsing through these listings will give you an idea of what other people are doing and what you could do.

MARK WELCH'S WEB SITE BANNER ADVERTISING

http://www.adbility.com

This site is an exhaustive overview of all forms of Web site banner advertising, from advertising networks to ad registries to lists of available ad-creation resources and even banner-ad creation programs. You'll also get Mark Welch's down-to-earth commentary about the business and particular companies.

As you can see, you have a lot of options for advertising your site. Unless you're selling really high-ticket items, we urge you to try e-mail advertising and banner ad swaps. It's just too easy to spend a lot of money on banner advertising for little return.

Banner advertising is straightforward—you pay your money and you get a certain number of banner ad impressions. But what if you could pay commissions based on items sold? What if you could provide Webmasters with specially coded links that would pay a percentage of sales they sent to your site? You can. It's called *affiliate marketing* and you'll learn about it in the next chapter.

CHAPTER THIRTEEN

Affiliate Programs

The Internet has been the impetus for many new businesses. Tens of thousands of entrepreneurs have seen the Internet as a completely new opportunity, and now they're struggling alone trying to build their new enterprises. If this describes your situation, wouldn't it be helpful if you could recruit a sales force? Better still, wouldn't it be helpful if you could recruit a sales force and pay members of it only if and when they actually sold something?

Of course this would be beneficial to many businesses, and in fact many large businesses have already tried this, by setting up what are known as affiliate or associate programs (or revenue sharing programs, and other similar terms). Amazon, for example, in the summer of 2000 claimed its 500,000th affiliate.

Here's how an affiliate program works. The first step is to find Web-site owners who might want to sell your products on their site. If you sell camping equipment, perhaps you can find Web sites related to camping and other outdoor sports. If you sell CDs, you can find music- and band-related sites. And if you sell books...well, you can recruit sites related to just about any subject, because for just about any subject there's a book.

The next step is to set up special links from your affiliate sites to your site. You need some way to code links so that when someone clicks a link at an affiliate's site and reaches your site, it's clear from where the person came.

Finally, you need some way to track sales and pay commissions. When someone clicks on a link at an affiliate's site, reaches your site, and buys something, you have to record that sale, calculate the commission (typically between 5 and 20 percent), and pay the commission to the affiliate.

In this chapter we're going to take a look at what affiliate programs can do for you, some of the dangers and pitfalls, how you can set up your own affiliate programs, and how you can integrate those programs into your online shopping carts.

GOOD NEWS AND BAD

Affiliate programs can do wonders for a business, if run properly. Jason Olim, co-founder of CDnow, told Peter that CDnow's affiliate program was essential to its success, that it was as important to them as any of the expensive partnerships they'd bought into with companies such as Yahoo! and Rolling Stone. Yet it cost a fraction of the price of those partnerships.

The good news, then, is that affiliate programs really do work. The bad news is that they can be difficult to set up and a lot of work to run. Ideally an affiliate program should be completely automated, so that people can sign up as affiliates without any human interaction on your part beyond an initial review to make sure that the potential affiliate is appropriate for your site. (We're sure that everyone can think of some kind of site they'd rather not have as an affiliate.) A program should take all the details, provide the necessary coded link, and record all visits from people passing through the affiliate's site.

Affiliate programs can work well for the companies running them, and, sometimes, for the people signing up for them. Peter makes $100 to $150 a month from a couple of programs. He sells books at his Web site himself, but also points people to these books stores. He figures that some people would rather buy from a bookstore than from his site, so he signed up as an affiliate at those stores. Most affiliates probably make little money, though. But many site owners are happy to put up an affiliate link to a site selling a product they like, even if they only get enough to buy a beer or two each month.

AFFILIATE DIRECTORIES

There are a number of affiliate directories you may want to look at. These sites can be useful in a number of ways. First, you can see how other companies are running their affiliate programs; you'll find links to sites with programs, and articles about the different programs. You may find advice on running your program, including information about affiliate software, and discussion groups where you can ask questions. (**AssociatePrograms.com**, http://www.AssociatePrograms.com/, has a Web forum, for instance.) These sites also list what they regard as the top affiliate programs, too, so you can get an idea of what it takes to make it work. If you do decide to set up your own program, you'll probably want to register with these sites as another way for people to find you and sign up. Take a look at these sites:

AffiliateHelp
http://www.affiliatehelp.com/

Affiliate Trade Links Network
http://www.atlnetwork.com/

AssociateCash
http://www.associatecash.com/

Associate-It
http://www.associatecash.com/

AssociatePrograms.com (Free newsletter available, lots of materials here)
http://www.AssociatePrograms.com/

CashPile
http://www.cashpile.com/

ClickQuick
http://www.clickquick.com/

ClicksLink
http://www.clickslink.com/

LinkShare
http://linkshare.com/

Mark Welch's Web Site Banner Advertising
http://www.adbility.com

NetAffiliate
http://www.netaffiliate.com/

SiteCash.com
http://www.sitecash.com/

Note that these sites are generally slanted toward site owners wanting to sign up for affiliate programs to make money, rather than to site owners wanting to set up their own programs. Nonetheless, you'll find them useful; who knows, perhaps you could sign up for a program to increase your own site's income?

THE TYPES OF PROGRAMS

There are several forms of affiliate programs, each with their own benefits and drawbacks. If you know anything about the world of advertising, you may recognize that these plans have real-world parallels. The whole concept of the affiliate plan, in fact, is simply another version of the per-sale advertising programs, in which advertisers pay the media for each sale that is made, rather than pay for the advertising itself. There are several types of programs, which we'll cover in more detail:

Per Sale—Gives a payment for every sale made on the site.

> **Per Inquiry**—Gives a payment for every information request (like a request for a free sample, request to be put on a mailing list, etc.).
>
> **Pay-Per-Click Programs**—Gives a payment every time an affiliate link is clicked.

Per Sale

This is the most common form of program; if an affiliate sends you a visitor who ends up buying a product from you, you pay the affiliate something. It may be a flat fee. On the other hand, the payment may be a percentage commission. Percentage commissions seem to be more common than flat fees, partly because they seem to make more sense if your company sells a lot of different products.

The advantage of a per-sale payment is that it's performance based. Ultimately what you're trying to do is make a sale, so you're paying for the final result. And it's hard, impossible one might say, for an affiliate to cheat with this kind of program. A sale's a sale, whereas, as we'll see in a moment, an inquiry or a click may not be the real thing.

Per Inquiry

Some companies with affiliate programs are using a per-inquiry program; when someone visits their Web site and requests information, the affiliate gets a commission. For instance, **Web Card** (http://www.wbcards.com/) will pay affiliates $1 each time a visitor provides address information so that it can send a few sample postcards. (It also pays a 10 percent commission on sales.) The disadvantage with this type of program is that you're not paying for an end result; you're just paying for the first step in the process, so you'd better be *really sure* you know how many inquiries you can convert into sales! Another disadvantage is that there's some potential for fraud. If an affiliate encourages all his friends and relatives to make an inquiry, you're paying for inquiries that have no value.

Pay-Per-Click Programs

With one of these programs, you pay people to send clicks to you; you're paying, in effect, for referrals rather than actual sales or even inquiries. Each time someone visits your site thanks to the actions of an affiliate, you owe some money. Note, by the way, that a per-click program is really a form of advertising program; banner advertisers generally pay each time their banner is seen, but sometimes they pay for each time someone clicks a banner—so per-click programs are often set up by mainstream banner-advertising companies. **NameBoy** (http://www.nameboy.com/) pays a nickel per click, for example.

You may already have figured out the major problem with this sort of plan: misconduct that can cost you a lot of money. All the affiliate has to do is to register a click, and many ways to do that won't benefit you. Affiliates can trick people into visiting your site, perhaps using spam to reach tens of thousands of people and overselling your site in some way; you may get lots of visits, but visitors may not stay for more than a few seconds. It's even possible for an affiliate to set up a *program* to click through to your Web site so the visitors you see aren't even real visitors.

CREATING YOUR OWN AFFILIATE PROGRAM

Now we come to the tricky part. How do you set up an affiliate program? It's okay for big companies, who can hire programmers to build the necessary programs for them; but if you run a small business, how do you set up such a program?

It's not necessarily easy. Ideally you need a program that automates every step of affiliate sign-up, visitor tracking, and commission tracking. Better programs will allow affiliates to visit your site at any time and view their stats—see how many people have visited your store after going through their sites, see how many sales were made and how much commission was earned, and so on. The affiliate software you use has to be compatible with your shopping-cart software, too, or built into the software itself. In fact you may find that unless you have the shopping-cart system running on your server, the affiliate system will be unable to work with it. You might find that if you're using one of the shopping-cart services that run on someone else's server (see Chapter 2 *What You Need Before You Start*), you will be unable to use a separate affiliate program. (On the other hand you may be able to find a shopping-cart service with a built-in affiliate-program utility, as you'll see in the next section.)

Affiliate Software

At the time of this writing, there are relatively few low-cost affiliate systems to choose from. The following sections provide a few places to look, and at the end of the section, we'll give you a few more possibilities.

AFFILIATE SHOP

http://www.affiliateshop.com/

Affiliate Shop was launched early in 1999. It charges just $24.95 a month to host an affiliate system on its server plus a $199 setup fee. It provides the first two months of hosting free, giving you a chance to try it out. Affiliate Shop recently announced the acquisition of its 100th customer for its service.

AFFILIATEZONE.COM

http://www.affiliatezone.com/

AffiliateZone.com will install an affiliate program on your server for $350. If you visit the site you'll find a list of the shopping-cart systems it has worked with in the past, and an evaluation-request form to have the site check out your system and see if it can work with it. If you don't want the program installed on your server, or it's incompatible in some way, you can have Affiliate.Zone.com host the affiliate program for you on its own servers. That costs $29.95 a month plus a setup fee and is available at http://www.affiliatetracking.net/title.html.

COMMISSION JUNCTION

http://www.cj.com/

The guys at Commission Junction will actually run your affiliate program for you. A year of network access costs $795. You put $250 on deposit (money used to pay your affiliates), and then they run the program for you, maintaining the system and paying affiliates. You'll have to pay a 20 percent fee to Commission Junction for the service—for every dollar you pay an affiliate, you'll pay them 20 cents. After your first year, renewal is $595 a year. As you can see in Figure 13.1, Commission Junction has many different types of commerce sites using it.

FIGURE 13.1: Commission Junction is used by many different types of sites.

LINKSHARE

http://linkshare.com/

LinkShare not only has the software you need to set up an affiliate program, but it also has a network of thousands of Web sites that are signing up as affiliates with LinkShare clients. It provides a simple form that affiliates can use to join multiple affiliate programs at the same time.

CLICKTRADE

http://www.clicktrade.com/

This company has no sign-up fee, but charges a commission of 30 percent on everything you pay to your affiliates; if the payout to the affiliate is $100, you pay ClickTrade $30. (You will have to deposit $500 for payouts, though.) ClickTrade supports both pay-per-click and percentage-pay affiliate programs.

BE FREE!

http://www.befree.com/

Be Free! the real thing, the affiliate system used by barnesandnoble.com, Staples, IBM, and a number of other large Internet retailers. barnesandnoble.com representatives picked it, they say, because they believe it's the best system available. As you can imagine, this is not a cheap system. (Here's a hint: when a software publisher doesn't publish its prices on its Web site, you know it's going to cost a lot of money.) If you don't want to spend several thousand dollars for software installation, plus customization fees, plus a percentage of your gross sales, don't bother contacting Be Free! Inc.

Here are some other systems you may want to look at:

EComWorks (Creates and runs complete affiliate programs)
http://www.ecomworks.com/

WebGenie
http://www.webgenie.com/

Shopping-Cart Systems

It's perhaps a little simpler to work with a shopping-cart program that has built-in affiliate support than try to blend an existing shopping cart in with an affiliate program. We've found a couple, which we discuss in the following sections:

YAHOO! STORE

http://store.yahoo.com/

Yahoo! Store makes it simple to add affiliates to an affiliate program, although it's not fully automated; you have to physically add a site. You enter the URL of the affiliate site, and Yahoo! Store generates two more URLs for the affiliate. The first URL is for the affiliate to put into the link to your site to identify visits as being generated from its site. The other URL is for the affiliate to check out how much traffic has come through its site and how much it has earned. (As you can see in Figure 13.2, Yahoo! can track where all its store visitors are coming from.) You can also specify how much commission the affiliate earns—either a percentage of the sale or a flat fee for the number of visits sent to the site.

MERCHANDIZER

http://www.merchandizer.com/

The Merchandizer shopping-cart system is one of the best on the Internet, and it includes a built-in affiliate tracking system. This is a fully automated system; affiliates can visit the site and sign up to join your program. The software generates the URL and provides all the information the affiliate requires, tracks sales, figures out commissions, and so on. And this is all included in the

Figure 13.2: Yahoo! can track where its store visitors come from.

shopping-cart price of $79 a month ($149 setup), which is a pretty good deal. (That's the price for the standard service. Premium levels of service, of course, cost more.) This system was a *PC Magazine* Editors' Choice in November 1998; the only problem with this system is that it has so many features it will take you a little while to figure it all out!

A Cruder Method

There's a simple method for setting up affiliates, though it's not automated; you'll have to set up and track each affiliate manually. You simply provide each person with a Web page at your site. For instance, you might create a sales-pitch page—selling the visitor on the features and benefits of your product—and duplicate it, providing each page with a different number or name. You then give the URL of the appropriate page to each affiliate, such as http://www.topfloor.com/orders/0123.htm, or http://www.topfloor.com/orders/0124.htm.

Some shopping-cart systems can track where visitors come from when they enter the shopping-cart system. (See the information about the referrer report in Chapter 14, *Tracking Results and Responding*.) The shopping cart looks at the referrer information—the URL of the page containing the link the user has just clicked—and saves it with the order. You can then look at the order information to find the name or number of the Web page, and figure out which affiliate sent the visitor.

Sometimes You Won't Get the Referrals—*Some people have software installed that blocks transmission of the referrer URL to a Web server. So if you're relying on referrers to track affiliate activity, be aware that they won't always work.*

MAKING THE MOST OF YOUR AFFILIATE PROGRAM

Creating an affiliate plan is all very well, but how do you get it to actually make money? As with most other promotional programs, it works *only if you work at it*. It's unlikely that you can just set it up, let it run, and hope that it will be successful. In fact many small businesses have experimented with affiliate plans and given up, finding that the work involved wasn't worth the payoff. A few companies have so much traffic that an affiliate program is bound to work for them, but most of us need to really push a program.

The affiliate program should be integrated into your promotions, of course. If you have a newsletter, you should use it to encourage people to sign up as affiliates. It's also a good idea to have an affiliates' newsletter to encourage affiliates to actually send people to you. You'll want to register with the affiliate sites we've mentioned in this chapter, of course, and perhaps work with those affiliate sites to get attention for your program; do some kind of special promotion to get yourself mentioned on the first page.

Also be sure to offer lots of goodies. Make your affiliates feel loved, wanted, and needed. In short, treat them like customers because it's that feeling you want them to impart to the potential customers they're going to send your way!

What in the world do we mean? Well, say you have a site devoted to football memorabilia. You could give away tickets to football games, or maybe even a satellite system with a football game subscription page. You could give away an autographed football to the affiliate that sells the most autographed memorabilia. You could give away a limited edition player's jacket to the affiliate who sells the most football clothing. You could even do something as simple as sending little gifts with your commission checks—magnets or pens or drink holders with your logo on them, or some enthusiastic football motto.

The point is you're doing something to let your affiliates feel like they belong. You're giving them a reason to help you sell beyond just the lure of cash. You're giving them something to work toward by offering special incentives and prizes, and you're keeping their interest—you're giving them a reason to think about you.

Watch for Spammers—One danger that companies running affiliate programs have to watch out for is spammers. Some spammers sign up for affiliate programs, put their affiliate link into an e-mail message, and then send it to millions of people. This is a great way for you to get a lousy reputation! Many affiliate programs avoid this problem by instantly closing spammer accounts, refusing to pay their commissions, and by making it clear that spammers get no commissions.

Affiliate programs can really work well, if you are prepared to work hard. They're part of the new direction that Internet commerce is moving in, away from old concepts toward using the real power of networking to bring in business. They're not necessarily something to be entered into lightly because of the work involved in setting them up and running them, but they're certainly worth taking a look at.

CHAPTER FOURTEEN

Tracking Results and Responding

You're spending a lot of time and energy, and perhaps even money, to promote your products and services on the Internet. How do you know if it's all working? How do you know which bits are working and which are not? How can you measure the results of your efforts?

One of the nice things about operating on the Internet is that it's possible to track things much more closely than you could in the real world. There are tools you can use to see when people are talking about you, how people are arriving at your site, which sites are linking to you, and so on. This information can be useful if used properly, or a great distraction if not.

In this chapter, we're going to look at a variety of ways that you can measure results:

- Using your hit logs
- Looking at the referrer report
- Creating doorway pages to receive hits
- Backlink checking
- Searching at search sites
- Using automated search utilities
- Employing Web clipping services
- Monitoring discussion groups
- Checking offline publications
- Analyzing the *real* results

WHAT ARE HITS?

First, what's a hit, and why do we care? There's a lot of nonsense spoken about hits. You'll often see huge hit claims pertaining to particular sites: 10,000 hits a day, 50,000 hits a day, 1,000,000 hits a week, and so on. Some Web-site owners are clearly trying to imply by such claims that they are getting this number of *visitors* each day. But what is a hit really? It's a transfer from the server to a browser. So here's a quick way to double or triple the hits at your site: add more graphics. Each time a browser transfers a text page that has no graphics, that's one hit; but if the page has a graphic inside it, that's two hits—the page itself and the graphic. If it has five graphics, that's six hits. Each transfer is a single hit. Or simply add a lot of errors—links to nonexistent graphics. That's one way to increase your hit count because each error will be counted as a hit, yet you won't be transferring much data. This means, of course, that a site designed to carry lots of small graphics on every page, or a site with lots of broken links, can generate large hit rates.

A single visit to your Web site might generate a single hit—or ten hits, perhaps, or several hundred, as the visitor makes his or her way through a variety of graphic- and error-laden pages. Each page viewed, and each graphic on those pages, is a single hit. A while back Peter saw a Netscape press release that began with this statement:

2.9 Million Visitors Propel Netscape Internet Site to Over 100 Million Hits a Day.

It also included this:

Nielsen I/PRO undertook an independent audit of the Netscape site, which found that an average of more than 2.9 million visitors accessed the site daily, with an average visit length of 9 minutes. On the average business day, visitors to the site view a total of close to 10 million pages.

Let's consider this: 2.9 million visits, 10 million pages, 100 million hits. In other words, for every 100 hits, Netscape is getting only 2.9 visits and the average visitor is viewing only 3.5 pages, so an awful lot of those hits are being taken up with in-line images and other bits and pieces.

In addition to hits, you might hear other terms, though hit is the most popular. There's *page request* or *access*, defined by some as a page that is transferred; it doesn't include the in-line graphics or errors. A visit means that a single browser comes to your site and requests single or multiple pages. You'll also hear the term *unique visits* or *unique hosts*. As people are getting wise to the "lots of hits" nonsense, this unique visits statistic is becoming more commonplace. It means forget hits, forget pages, we get x visits to our Web site. Of course this is a far more useful statistic, although still open to some abuse, depending how it's measured. For instance, every time someone visits your site, the server can look at the IP (Internet Protocol) number that identifies the visitor's computer. Suppose that the statistics program regards a visit as pages transferred to a particular IP number over, say, a 30-minute period. A visitor comes to the site, and looks at a few pages. Thirty-one minutes later—after going for coffee—the same visitor looks at another page. That's counted as two visits. In contrast, if the program regarded a visit as activity from an IP number over a two-hour period, this would be only a single visitor.

As you can see, statistics can be made to work in many different ways—lies, damn lies, and statistics—but at least the unique visitors statistic is much more useful than some of the others. Using it, you can get a good idea of how many people are visiting your site each day, each week, or each month.

ACCESS OR HIT LOGS

An access log is a record of activity at your Web site. The Web server records information in the log each time someone requests something from your Web site. If your Web site is hosted by a Web-hosting company, you'll probably have access to some kind of log.

What sort of information is saved in the log? It varies, depending on the system being used to create the log, but typically it's information such as the following:

Weekly Report—the number of requests for data and amount of data transferred each week

Daily Report—the number of requests and amount of data transferred each day

Hourly Report and Hourly Summary—the number of requests and amount of data transferred each hour of each day, and the amount transferred each hour of an average day

Domain Report—the number of requests and amount of data transferred to different domains...that is, a report showing you the domains of your visitors

Host Report—a list showing the domain names of the top 100 host computers visiting your site (the people who spent the most time at your site)

Directory Report—the number of requests and amount of data transferred from each directory in your Web site

File-Type Report—the number of requests and amount of data transferred, broken down by file types (.htm, .gif, .zip, and so on)

Request Report—the number of requests and amount of data transferred, broken down by specific file names

Referrer Report—the number of requests that originated from the top 100 referrers; that is, it shows you who is linking to you

Browser Report—the number of requests broken down by the type of browser sending the request

Status Code Report—the status codes sent to the browser, such as error codes for missing pages

Not all systems provide all this information, and some provide more. The reports listed previously come from a program called Analog, from the University of Cambridge Statistical Laboratory.

You can use this information in a variety of ways. You can see, for instance, which areas of your site visitors find most interesting. Perhaps you should find out why they're so important to people, and perhaps even highlight these areas of your site in promotional efforts. You could apply the information to your site design. For example, are most visitors coming through the front door, or main page, of the site, or are they getting to various pages of your site via search engines? If they're coming through the front door, maybe you need to design the navigation of the site around the front door. If they're coming to many different pages of the site, however, you need to be sure that the site is easily navigable no matter how users entered.

You can correlate visits with your promotional and advertising efforts and use the correlation to figure out how well you are turning visitors into customers. If visits increase after a magazine article appears, for instance, the article has probably helped send visitors to you; but if you notice only a small rise in sales of your products, you're not doing a good job of turning those visits into sales.

You can also get a good feel for the hit-to-visit ratio—that is, how many hits the average visit generates—which indicates how busy each visitor is at your site. Do visitors mostly come, look around for a moment, and leave? Or do they give your site a thorough viewing? You can also experiment with your content and see how changes cause people to move through your site in different directions. You can see in which areas people are interested in; if you've created an area of your site that nobody spends any time+, for instance, perhaps you should dump it and focus on the more popular areas.

GETTING TO YOUR ACCESS LOGS

Most Web-hosting companies provide logs. Some companies even e-mail you a log regularly; with others, you have to go to a specific Web page to view your logs. You can see an example of a log page in Figure 14.1. This particular log shows information about the browsers that requested data from a Web site; each line represents requests from Web browsers in a particular domain. In the right column, you can see the host name. In other words, this information won't point back to an actual browser, but rather to the domain in which that browser is operating. You may in some cases find that visitors are coming from a particular small domain—one of your competitors' domains, for instance, or a customer's

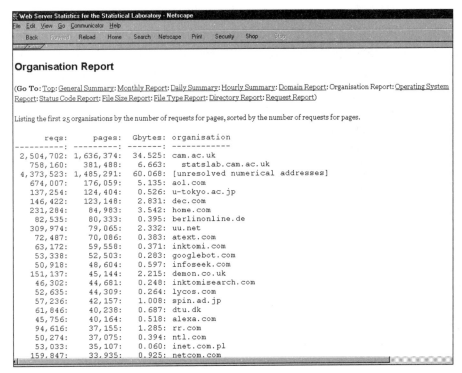

FIGURE 14.1: A log file from Analog, a very popular log program.

domain—but more often it will be a domain owned by an ISP or online service. For instance, if you found, say, *ad19-039.compuserve.com* in the report, this would be a domain owned by the online service CompuServe.

However, in some cases, you may be able to follow a visitor through your site using this domain name; it will remain the same throughout the session. For instance, look at this information extracted from a report provided by a different log program:

```
dialup-06-38.netcomuk.co.uk "GET /ipn/techwr/
dialup-06-38.netcomuk.co.uk "GET
/ipn/techwr/guideline.htm HTTP/
dialup-06-38.netcomuk.co.uk "GET /ipn/images/redarrw.gif
HTTP/
dialup-06-38.netcomuk.co.uk "GET
/ipn/techwr/testimon.htm HTTP/
dialup-06-38.netcomuk.co.uk "GET
/ipn/techwr/$100k_frm.htm HTTP/
```

This program provides specific information about particular data transfers. In this case, a single visitor started by requesting *lipn/techwrl;* in other words, the server sent the default file (index.html) from this directory. But then the user clicked a link to the *guideline.htm* file. You can also see that the *redarrw.gif* file was transferred, but this doesn't mean much, as that's probably an embedded file inside *guideline.htm*. We can see that the visitor then went to *testimon.htm*, and finally to *$100k_frm.htm*.

Making a Path—*The way a user goes through your site is sometimes called a path. Identifying and analyzing these paths can help you create a better user experience. If 30 percent of your users always visit your front page, and then immediately visit your news page, and from there go all over your site, maybe you should put your news on the front page. Pay attention to how people navigate your site and you can make it easier to use.*

Some Web-hosting companies also provide simple log summaries showing the hosts that accessed your site, the files that were requested, when all this took place, the total amount of traffic, and so on. These may be daily, weekly, or monthly reports, so you can get a quick overview of what's happening at your site. You can see a sample in Figure 14.2.

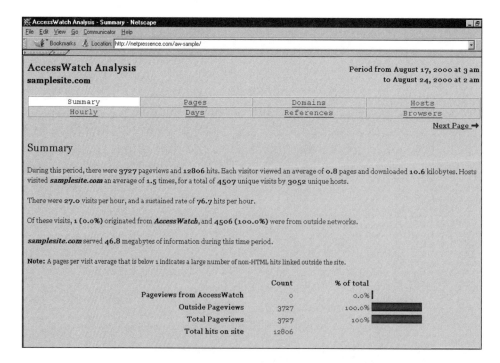

FIGURE 14.2: A summary report from a program called AccessWatch.

MANIPULATING ACCESS REPORTS

If you want more statistics than your Web-hosting company provides, you can add your own log programs, from simple single-page counters to sophisticated $10,000 programs. You can also use services provided by other companies, which may be necessary if you want to sell advertising; the third party keeps track of your traffic and provides the report to you and any advertisers you authorize.

What sort of statistics might you expect if you use a good service or logging program? The following list is an example taken from the NetIntellect Web page:

- General Summary
- Visitor Profile by Origin
- Visitors by Continent
- Top Visitor Organizations
- Top Visitor Countries/Zones
- Top Requested Files
- Top Referring URLs/Sites
- Top Requested File Types
- Top Referred Files
- Activity by Hour of the Day
- Top Visitor Browsers
- Activity by Day of the Week

- Technical Summary
- Peak Day of the Week
- Server Errors
- Client Errors
- Daily Statistics
- Weekly Statistics
- Monthly Statistics
- Executive Summary Report
- Complete Summary Report
- Marketing Summary Report
- Technical Summary Report
- BPA Standard Report

Some of these programs don't run on the server at all. Rather, they take the log files created by the server and manipulate them to put the information into a useful form. So while the server may be a UNIX server, the analysis program may be running in Windows NT. Following are some programs to check out:

AccessWatch
http://accesswatch.com/

net.Analysis
http://www.netgen.com/

NetIntellect and NetIntellect Express ($49 and up)
http://www.webmanage.com/

Web Page Access Counters and Trackers (A very good list of programs and services)
http://www.adbility.com/ba_counter.htm

WebTrends ($299 and up; Tara's favorite)
http://www.webtrends.com/

Yahoo!-Log Analysis Tools
http://dir.yahoo.com/Business_and_Economy/Business_to_Business/Computers/So
ftware/Internet/World_Wide_Web/Log_Analysis_Tools/

Also, a number of services provide free site statistics for small sites, sometimes in exchange for your carrying a banner at your site. Most provide only simple statistics, though. The following are low-cost and not-quite-so-low-cost services:

Accrue Insight ($15,000 and up)
http://www.acrue.com/

Audit Bureau of Circulations (Charges big bucks!)
http://www.accessabc.com/

HitWatchers
http://www.hitwatchers.com/

PageCount
http://www.pagecount.com/

Site Meter
http://www.sitemeter.com/

StatTrax ($5 per month to 100,000 hits)
http://www.stattrax.com/

The Counter
http://www.TheCounter.com/

WebSideStory's HitBox (Free)
http://www.websidestory.com/wc/world.html

We're not suggesting that you run out and find a program or service, by the way. Most small businesses have more important things to do than track this sort of stuff, as we'll discuss in a moment (see the "*Not Just Hits*" section that follows).

YOU WANT E-MAIL ADDRESSES, RIGHT?

Many new Web-site owners want to be able to grab the e-mail addresses of their visitors from the log files. After all, they've heard people talk about these wonderful log files and heard that you can track *who* visits your site. Unfortunately—or fortunately from the visitor's point of view—the term *who* has been used loosely in the Web-tracking business. You cannot grab an e-mail address from a browser unless the user chooses to give it to you.

We know many people won't believe this. After all, they've read in the press that it's possible for Web sites to grab e-mail addresses that have been entered into the browser's mail program settings. This is completely incorrect. While there is a system called identd that works on UNIX servers that can do such a thing, this is rarely used. For identd to work, the Web server and the computer the browser is working on must both be running UNIX and both must be using identd, a rare situation these days.

There's another trick, in which the Web page includes an *<IMG>* tag that uses FTP to grab the embedded image. If the browser is one that can send the user's e-mail address as a login name to FTP sites, and if the user has told the browser to do so, that address is sent to the FTP site and included in the log. In Netscape Navigator, this option is turned off by default; that is, the browser won't use the e-mail address unless told to. Apparently some older browsers may launch an FTP program, but then the user can see what's going on. All in all, this method is, to quote one Web administrator who's tried it, "pretty useless."

There is currently no reliable way to grab e-mail addresses from Web browsers visiting your site; the only way to grab addresses is by using one of these unusual exceptions or by exploiting a software bug in some browsers. No browser company with the slightest bit of sense would knowingly create a browser from which a Web site could take an e-mail address without the user realizing it. In any case, it would be a trifle rude to steal e-mail addresses even if there were a reliable way to do it.

NOT JUST HITS

People have gotten a little too obsessed with hits. Hits don't often mean much. Don't get carried away with simple hit statistics. You have to know what a hit really means. So what does a hit to your site really mean? It means that something was transferred from the Web server to a Web browser. It doesn't mean that the data actually arrived or that the person receiving it wanted it or paid any attention to it. It doesn't prove that the person receiving it took action as a result, or plans to return, or will act in any manner that is beneficial to you or your company.

Surely, there has to be a better way! Of course there is. Far more important than a measure of hits is genuine activity at, or related to, your site, such as the following:

- How many people are filling in a form to give you their e-mail address, so you can tell them when the Web site is modified or when you release your next product?

- How many people are signing up for your electronic newsletter?
- How much activity is there in your discussion group or chat group?
- How many hits to your autoresponder are you getting—that is, how many people are looking for more information?
- How many people are adding links to your link pages (if you have an automatic link-adding CGI), or sending you links via e-mail?
- How often is your Web site mentioned in the newsgroups and mailing lists, or in the press?
- How many sites have links to your site?
- How many people are e-mailing you directly with questions?
- How many orders are you taking?

These are all strong indications of how your Web site is doing, of how useful it is to other Internet users—and to you. So hits can be useful, but don't concentrate on them to the exclusion of more important measures. You can spend an awful lot of time analyzing hits, requests and visits, time that, in many cases, can be better spent in some other way—by setting up some kind of promotion to bring people to your site, for instance.

That's not to say that you should simply ignore these reports. There are a couple of ways in particular that the reports can be useful: looking at your referrers and creating doorway pages.

The Referrer Report

Most logs will contain a referrer report or something similar. Take a look at it; it can be a great way to find out from where people are coming. For instance, you might see something like this:

```
Referrer Report
Printing the first 100 referring URLs, sorted by number
of requests.
#reqs: URL
---   --
172: http://webdesign.miningco.com/blnew.htm
93:
http://dir.yahoo.com/Business_and_Economy/Companies/Book
s/Shopping_and_
Services/Booksellers/Computers/Internet/Titles/World_Wid
e_Web/Web_Page_Design/
56: http://www.topfloor.com/cgi-bin/hazel/hazel.cgi
```

```
53: http://www.score.org/resourceindex/resource.html
42: http://www.webjump.com/jumppoint/
36: http://www.hostfind.com/info/help/host.feature. html
29: http://search.yahoo.com/bin/search?p=free+web+site
[etc....]
```

When a browser sends a message asking for a Web page, the message includes information saying where it found the link; it sends the URL of the page containing the link the visitor clicked. (Of course if the visitor typed the URL into the browser's location box, no referrer information is sent.) This information is saved in the log. As in the previous report, only the top referrers may be saved, so if you have a busy site, some of the referrers that brought you few visitors will drop off the bottom.

Your Referrer Report Won't Be Complete—*Because privacy issues are becoming more important these days, not every visitor to your site will have a referrer. Some firewalls, for example, block referrer information from being sent to a site. Accept the information in your logs as helpful but not complete.*

You can often find interesting stuff in these logs. You may find sites linking to you that you hadn't found any other way, and even if you use some of the other methods in this chapter for finding out who's linking to you, the referrer report shows you something more important. A link is nice, but much more important is a link that is actually sending visitors to you.

Creating a Doorway Page

If you've ever paid attention to a TV infomercial, or read mail order ads in papers and magazines, you've probably noticed that they often include a department number. Infomercials often ask you to request a particular extension number, and sometimes order forms contain suite or box numbers. They are generally unnecessary for you to get your order to the right person. They are codes to track responses. Dept. EM05 may mean an ad in the May edition of *Entrepreneur Magazine*, extension 1299 may mean an infomercial running in December of 1999, and so on. Why bother? So you can see from where orders are coming. If Dept. EM05 gets a huge number of orders, you know your *Entrepreneur Magazine* ad is worthwhile; if it doesn't, there's probably no point running it again.

Well, you can play the same little coding game on the Web, too. You can use a special link for particular ads and promotions, so that you can measure how many people use that link. You have many ways to do this. Affiliate programs (as discussed in Chapter 13, *Affiliate Programs*) often use a special program. For instance, if you use the following link, the Web server at CDnow will track your movements around the **CDnow** site, and if you actually buy something, Peter will earn a commission: http://www.cdnow.com/from=sr-919191.

***Don't Always Use the Doorway Page**—While you may want to use the doorway page for all links—in ads and special promotions carried out on the Web—you may not want to use this technique for all your print promotions. It's nice to be able to measure responses to print ads, but it's also nice to be able to give people reading the ads a nice, simple URL, rather than a URL with some kind of coding built in.*

But you have a much easier way to do this sort of thing. You've already seen how to look at your logs for information. Now you need to know how to create a special page—often known as a doorway page—so that you can use this page as the equivalent of a department or extension. For instance, you put an ad in *The Yak Herder's Info Newsburst* e-mail newsletter. In the ad you include a URL something like this: http://heyneat.com/visit/yak. htm. You create a page called *yak.htm* in the *visit* directory. The ad runs, and you can then look at your hit logs to see how many times the *yak.htm* file has been viewed.

Got it? Simple. But there's one catch. You don't necessarily want people to really visit this *yak.htm* page. You want them to visit your main page. Of course you could create lots of copies of your first page, but then you have to maintain all those pages—if you change one, you'll have to change them all.

An easier system is to forward people from the yak.htm page to your main page. Here's how it's done. You need to add a META tag right below the *<HEAD>* tag at the top of the Web page. If you use an HTML authoring program and never see the HTML tags, look for the command that allows you to view the source of a page, the underlying HTML codes. At the top of the page you'll see this tag: *<HEAD>*.

Put the cursor right after this tag, press Enter, and type this:

```
<meta http-equiv="REFRESH" content="xxxx; url=yyy">
```

Replace the *xxx* with a number, the number of seconds delay before the visitor is forwarded to the next page. You may want the page to wait a few seconds, to tell the visitor what's going on; that's useful if you're using a redirection page to tell people that you've moved your site, for instance. However in this case, when you're using the page to measure results from an ad, you'll probably want them to move as quickly as possible, so you can put a 0 there, which means, "go to the next page right away."

Next, replace *yyy* with the full URL of the page to which you are forwarding the visitor—probably your site's main page. You want to end up with something like this:

```
<html>
<head>
<meta http-equiv="REFRESH" content="10;
url=http://www.poorrichard.com/">
```

By the way, you should also include a normal link from this page to the new one. Not all browsers will forward (most will, but a few older ones won't), so you can create a link telling the visitor to click it to go to the site's main page.

If you want to see a forwarding page in action, use this link: http://www.poorrichard.com/examples/autofwd2.htm.

This page is set to forward after ten seconds, so you'll have plenty of time to see it. If you'd like to see this page's source code, click your browser's Stop button as soon as you enter the page; that ensures that the page won't forward. Then you can use the View|Source command in your browser.

Now you have the redirection page—the doorway page—set up. Each time someone uses the URL pointing to this page, the Web server will keep track of it. Periodically you can look in your hit logs and search for that filename (in our Yak example, *yak.htm*) and see how many times it's been used. There's one catch, though. If it hasn't been used often, it may not turn up in the logs; your logs may only show you the 100 busiest pages, for instance; so if you have a large site and a poorly performing ad, you may not see the page in the logs.

Your logs can show you a lot about what's making your page popular and where your visitors are coming from; but you can also get that information from another place—the Web.

BACKLINK CHECKING

Another way to check your results is to find out how many people are linking to you. The referrer report discussed in the preceding section shows one method—or rather, it shows you the 100 or so links that are sending the most people to you; but backlink checking gives you the same kind of information. We've already covered this technique in some detail—see Chapter 8, *Other Places to Register Your Site*.

You can use backlink checking to see who's linking to your site and what they're saying about your site. Maybe they're saying, "This is a great site!" If they are, drop them a note and thank them. If your site is just part of a list, don't worry about it. Just check to make sure everything's spelled correctly and send a note to the site owner if it's not.

While backlink checking, look for other promotional opportunities. Perhaps a site reviewed one of your products...ask if it'd like to review another. If you have an affiliate program (see Chapter 13, *Affiliate Programs*), ask if the site would like to sign up. Maybe you can find sites to do drawings (see Chapter 10, *Grass Roots Marketing*). There are many ways you can work with sites that have linked to you, so keep an open mind.

WHAT ARE THEY SAYING ABOUT YOU?

You can use the Internet to find out if your company is being talked about in newsgroups and mailing lists or on the Web. You can also check to see if your site is being talked about offline, in newspapers, and other publications.

The Internet is a free speech forum of major proportions. Lots of people talk about lots of stuff, and one of the things they're talking about might be your company. In many cases, that's harmless. They might mention that they bought something at your store, sent a donation to your organization, or used your company to do some work at their office. It's when someone starts posting negative information about your company that you should be concerned.

Every negative statement about your company is an opportunity for you. If you catch it, maybe it's something you can act on. Maybe customers misunderstood the guarantee policy or are posting something that's factually incorrect. In either case you can correct them (nicely) and make an impression on the other people on the newsgroup or mailing list. In the case of a Web site, you have to convince the site owner to put up your side of the story, though sometimes you won't be able to do that.

And in the case when your business did do something bad and is in the wrong? In that case, you apologize, you make good if you can, and then you shut up.

You can use several different tools to find out what people are saying about you, your company, and your products—from basic work with search engines to paying thousands of dollars for professional online monitoring. We'll take a look at all the levels of your options in the sections that follow.

Trademarks and Copyrights*—If you have trademarks and copyrights, you might want to monitor the Web to protect them. In this case, be careful; you can set yourself up for some bad PR. If your trademarks are being blatantly misused or your copyrighted material is being posted online without your permission, you have a lot of legal leverage to get those problems corrected. But use some common sense. What, for instance, if a 12-year-old is using a trademarked name of yours as a domain name? Heavy-handed legal posturing could backfire, as it did when the Prema Toy Company, owner of the Gumby and Pokey trademarks, discovered a child using pokey.org as a domain name. The negative publicity was so extreme the company eventually had to back down. When you come across what looks like a trademark or copyright violation, first get all the facts you can. Second, try to settle the issue in a positive manner, without threatening letters from lawyers. Turn to legal leverage only as a last resort. Your public relations department will thank you!*

Using Search Engines

Tracking the occurrence of your name on the Web is easy. Throughout this book we've been giving you hints about using search engines. So to search for *your* products and company name, simply enter those words into the search engines. But perhaps your company or product name is generic. Say the name of your company is ACME and it sells electrical supplies. If you enter ACME in AltaVista, you're going to get over 60,000 results. Enter additional keywords appropriate to your company—like *electric*—and you'll trim down the results considerably.

Beware of Case-Sensitive Search Engines—*It's popular today to do strange things with the capitalization of product and company names, capitalizing letters within the name for instance, or using a lowercase letter at the beginning: GEnie, CompuServe, eMerge, and so on. Your customers may or may not remember how to capitalize your company name, so when searching for your company's name on case-sensitive search engines, such as AltaVista, use all lowercase letters. In other words, if you are searching for GoodExampleCo using AltaVista, enter it in the search box as goodexampleco. Searching for goodexampleco will find goodexampleco, GOODEXAMPLECO, GoodexampleCo, GoOdExAmPlEcO, and so on. Searching for GoodExampleCo will find only GoodExampleCo, and will miss all the other results noted here.*

You'll get even better results once you've been tracking your company's name for a while and you get a sense of what keywords the people who talk about you use.

Obviously you don't want to spend every day going over search engines and finding examples of your own company name. There are resources—some online, some software—that will help you automate your search for your company name.

Free Automated Search Utilities

If you're looking for ways to track changes to search engines and Web sites, the Web has a few great resources for you.

TRACERLOCK

http://www.peacefire.org/tracerlock/

TracerLock is a free service, sponsored by Peacefire, which allows you to monitor AltaVista for the occurrence of up to five sets of keywords. For example, you could monitor for all of the following:

```
acme AND electric
acme AND electrician
```

```
"acme electric"
"electrical supply"
acme AND electric AND purchased
```

Each day TracerLock will search AltaVista for pages that matched your search term and were indexed exactly three days previously. If there are results, the first ten will be sent to you in an e-mail. TracerLock only searches AltaVista, but AltaVista has a big database. If you want to track your company, this is an excellent addition to your toolbox.

Check the Page Source—*Did you get a match for a Web page that mentions your company, but you can't find a mention of your company anywhere on the page? View the source code of the page using your browser. You might find that your trademark is being used as a Meta-Tag keyword.*

THE INFORMANT

http://informant.dartmouth.edu/

The Informant works a little like TracerLock, but covers a lot more ground. Here's what happens. First you have to register (the service is free) and specify how often you'd like to receive search engine updates—once every 3, 7, 14, 30, or 60 days. Next, you specify three queries—sets of words where you'd like to find all the words in the set (an AND query) or any word in the set (an OR query). We don't recommend using OR queries unless the keywords are unusual. For each query, you'll have the choice of searching Excite, AltaVista, Lycos, or Infoseek. After that you'll be given the option of monitoring five specific URLs for changes—that is, The Informant will take a look at these pages to see if any of them have changed, and inform you if so.

Now, at the interval you specified, The Informant will find the top 10 Web pages that are most relevant to your keywords. If there is a new page in the top 10, or if any of the pages in the top 10 have changed, you'll get an e-mail. It'll also look at the five pages you specified to see if there are any changes.

Since The Informant checks out only the top 10 pages at each search engine, you won't get the comprehensive results that you'll get with TracerLock, but you have more search engine choices and you can monitor specific URLs. (Hey, they're both free, so there's no reason you can't use both services.)

SPYONIT

http://www.spyonit.com/

SpyOnIt doesn't specifically query search engines; instead, it tracks changes to particular pages. You can use this resource to check on competitor's pages, check on pages important to your industry, and so on. You give it your e-mail address and tell it the URLs to watch. SpyOnIt can alert you to page changes in several different ways, including by pager or instant messenger.

Of course you can also use this system to track changes in the search engines for you. In a different browser window, enter a query on a search engine—like AltaVista—and click the Search button. After you get the results, you'll see a strange-looking URL in the URL location box at the top of your browser.

Let's do an example. Say you search for *acme electric* on *.com* domains. The search query would look like this:

```
+"acme electric" +domain:com
```

The URL in your browser's URL location box would look like this:

```
http://www.altavista.com/cgi-
bin/query?pg=q&kl=XX&q=%2B%22acme+electric%22+%2Bdomain%
3Acom
```

All you have to do is cut that URL from the location box and paste it into SpyOnIt's Spy On This Page box. You can do this as many times as you like with as many different search queries as you like. SpyOnIt supports an unlimited number of URLs to update. Once you've gotten used to the "mind this spy," explore the site a little bit to discover the other types of spies available. For example, SpyOnIt can periodically query AltaVista to see if any sites are linking to yours. Or you can monitor pages to look for particular words. SpyOnIt's a powerful system! You can even set up spies that your site visitors can use to keep up when your own site changes.

Web-Clipping Services

As you see, each of the online tools discussed in the preceding sections have some drawbacks and limitations. However, if you use all of them and spend a little time searching the search engines occasionally, you'll cover a lot of ground; but perhaps you have more money than time. In that case, you should check out the for-pay Web-clipping services, such as those discussed next.

CYBERALERT

http://www.cyberalert.com/

CyberAlert uses a combination of software and human review to conduct a daily search for *topics* (keyword sets) on *feeder sites* (any searchable Web entity—general search engines, online databases, specialty search engines, and so on). The clippings generated by this service are gathered, sorted, and the duplicates eliminated. They're saved in an in-box accessible to you when you log in to the Web site.

As you might imagine, CyberAlert offers comprehensive coverage of the Web, and even of USENET newsgroups if you include DejaNews as one of your feeder sites. On the other hand, this service is expensive, starting at $395 a month per search string. There are no *per-clip* (per item found) fees.

CYBERSCAN INTERNET CLIPPING SERVICE

http://www.clippingservice.com/

CyberScan has a per-clip fee of $1, but its base rates are much lower than CyberAlert (and you can limit the number of clips per report that you receive). This service searches the Internet for the keywords you specify and returns clips to you every business day, weekly, or monthly via e-mail, fax, Federal Express, or postal mail. CyberScan's costs start at around $200 depending on the services you want and the frequency with which you want to be sent clippings.

A variety of other services offer online monitoring. Check here:

EgoSurf
http://www.egosurf.com/

eWatch
http://www.ewatch.com/

URL Minder
http://www.netmind.com/

Webclipping
http://www.webclipping.com/

Yahoo!—Clipping and Monitoring Services
http://dir.yahoo.com/Business_and_Economy/Business_to_Business/Corporate_Ser vices/Public_Relations/Clipping_and_Monitoring_Services/

The services and sites described in the previous list can search mostly the Web, but can also search Usenet in certain cases as well. Many search engines, including AltaVista offer searches of USENET, but there are tools that are specifically designed to search mailing lists and USENET newsgroups. See the next section for more information about mailing lists and newsgroups.

NEWSGROUPS AND MAILING LISTS

USENET newsgroups are like particularly crowded, noisy, and opinionated public forums. Everybody on the Internet can drop by, sound off, start fights, and occasionally quietly and intelligently express an opinion. USENET newsgroups have a lot of spam, too, which greatly cuts down on their effectiveness as a public forum. That's one of the reasons that mailing-list discussion groups are becoming much more popular than newsgroups—they're easier to control than newsgroups.

Searching Newsgroups

DejaNews is probably the most famous newsgroup-searching tool. A number of Web search sites also provide the ability to search newsgroup messages, too. Yahoo!, for instance, allows you to search newsgroup messages…but in fact it simply links to DejaNews to actually carry out the search.

DEJANEWS

http://www.dejanews.com/usenet/

DejaNews offers access to over 80,000 newsgroups, with simple searching and advanced searching that allows you to search archives all the way back to 1995 (though at this writing archives before May 1999 are not available). You can even specify a particular newsgroup to search, and search for messages from a particular e-mail address or with a specified subject line. You can register on DejaNews to get free Web-based access to newsgroups, and a free DejaNews e-mail account.

Searching Mailing Lists

It's difficult to find out what's being said about your products in mailing-list discussion groups. If you had the time, you could check with individual groups. (See Chapter 9, *Promoting in the Newsgroups and Mailing Lists*, for more information about finding these groups.) Many groups have archives, often stored at a member's Web site. If there are one or two important mailing-list discussion groups that you track, you can search those archives now and then. To search many mailing lists at once, check the free mailing-list services we discussed in Chapter 11, *Creating Newsgroups and Discussion Lists*. **Topica** in particular (http://www.topica.com/) is a must-see for searching mailing lists.

CHECKING OFFLINE PUBLICATIONS

The tools discussed in earlier sections of this chapter give you plenty of ways to search discussions throughout the Internet; but some Internet tools are useful for tracking what's being said in offline publications, too. Plenty of free and pay resources are available, and even the pay resources are reasonably priced. The free ones usually track only a few weeks' worth of news. The pay services, not surprisingly, track much larger collections of news.

Free Tools

Several search engines offer tools for tracking news in offline media. Excite and Northern Light are two of the biggies.

EXCITE'S NEWSTRACKER

http://nt.excite.com/

Excite's NewsTracker tracks the news from around 300 online newspapers and magazines. You can do a search from the NewsTracker site or you can set up a clipping service that allows you to track up to 50 different topics (your company name, the name of your industry, competitor names, etc.). Every time you log in to NewsTracker, you'll be able to access your customized clipping file.

NewsTracker has a couple of drawbacks. From Tara's experience searching it, she doesn't think the stories in its database are more than a couple of weeks old. Furthermore, 300 publications isn't that much. (At your local library, yes. At your favorite newsstand, absolutely; but 300 publications only scratches the surface when it comes to Internet-based repositories of information.) The service is free, however, and the clipping service is handy.

NORTHERN LIGHT CURRENT NEWS

http://www.northernlight.com/news.html

Northern Light has a premium search service that allows you to search through publication articles for a fee (we'll discuss that in the next section), but its "Current News" service is free. The Current News service searches through a two-week archive of news from over 50 sources, including newswires and press release wires.

The drawbacks to this service are obvious: only two weeks' worth of information and a low number of sources. However, where Northern Light shines is that you can specify just how recent the stories should be (within the last two hours, within the last day, or within the last two weeks) and you can search by category. Eleven categories are available, including Business, Sports Articles, and

Weather Conditions. You can also sign up for *Northern Light News Alert*, which will send you e-mail when new news items meet the criteria you specify.

There are several other free places online where you can search through news archives:

InfoJump
http://www.infojump.com/

HotBot: News Channel
http://www.newsbot.com/

MagPortal
http://www.magportal.com/

Moreover
http://www.moreover.com

Newshub
http://www.newshub.com/

TotalNEWS
http://www.totalnews.com/

News Hunt (A collection of links to newspaper and other publication archives)
http://www.newshunt.com/

Pay Services

The drawback of the free services is that they're limited. Unless you've been tracking your company's appearances in the media since the beginning of your promotional program, the limits to these archives are going to frustrate you. You might also find yourself annoyed by the limited number of publications the free services cover, especially if your product or service is highly technical or otherwise oriented towards a niche. There are some pay services available, however, and some aren't particularly expensive.

THE DOW JONES PUBLICATIONS LIBRARY

http://www.wsj.com/Publib/

Free search access to the Dow Jones Publications Library comes with a subscription to the online Wall Street Journal, which costs $59 a year. Accessing news stories from the DJPL costs about $2.95 each—less if you want only a citation.

The DJPL has, in Tara's opinion, the most complete archive of publications this side of a super-expensive resource like online research business **LEXIS-NEXIS** (http://www.LEXIS-NEXIS.com/). You'll find hundreds of resources here, gathered from all over the world. They run the gamut from mainstream periodicals like *USA Today* to highly specialized business and technical publications. Some of the available archives go back decades; most go back at least a few years.

You can get really lost searching here, and you can spend a lot of money, too. Tara's a cheapskate, so she'll use this resource to find media occurrences of a company name and then try to find the article somewhere else. If you anticipate retrieving a lot of articles here, you'll want to check out subscription options that allow you to pay a certain amount each month and get a certain number of articles free.

ELECTRIC LIBRARY

http://www.elibrary.com/

The Electric Library has a smaller publications database than the Dow Jones Publications Library, but you get unlimited searching and retrieving for $9.95 a month. (There's no per-article cost like with the Dow Jones Publications Library.) Electric Library indexes the archives of over 150 publications, including a few newswires and press-release wires. The basic search is a little hard to get used to. (Sometimes the queries you enter don't react like you'd expect.) However, the power search gives you a way to narrow down your search easily, including by date and publication type. (You can search pictures, television transcripts, and other types of media in addition to publication archives.) If you have searches you want to do regularly, you can use Electric Library's search tracker service, which will send you notification of new stories by e-mail.

If your company is a mainstream company and wouldn't appear in the more esoteric and specialized media covered by the Dow Jones Publications Library, you could do a lot of your searching via Electric Library. Keep in mind, however, that the Electric Library doesn't carry nearly as many local newspapers as the Dow Jones Publications Library, so if you're getting a lot of mentions in smaller papers, you'll miss them.

NORTHERN LIGHT

http://www.nlsearch.com/

Northern Light is an interesting Web-search hybrid. When you search Northern Light, you search both a database of Web sites and what it calls a special collection. The *special collection* consists of over 6,900 books, journals, reviews, magazines, and news wires. Searching the special collection is free, but when you find something, you have to pay to read it. Accessing content in the special collection will cost you per item. (Prices range from $1 to $4, depending on the article.) The Northern Light special collection has especially strong collections of publications covering science and health.

Northern Light's collection is far smaller than the Dow Jones Publications Library. However, since it's a pay-as-you-go plan, those who access small numbers of articles will find this a much less expensive research option. Furthermore, Northern Light's special collection content offers abstracts that can be reviewed before paying for the content. The abstracts give you a good idea whether the information you're looking at is relevant to the subjects in which you're interested.

Point and Clip—*Once you've gotten your past press mentions squared away, you might want to try media clipping services. Clipping services offer you the chance to track mentions of your company name or news related to your company's industry.* **NewsPage** *at* http://www.newspage.com/*is a great way to track information and news related to particular industries. Every business day, NewsPage will send you a summary of information related to your industry. If you're interested in tracking news by keyword, like your company name, name of your competitor, etc., check out* **Intellisearch** *at* http://www.intellisearchnow.com/. *Intellisearch filters publications by keyword and sends you an update of new keyword matches every business day. You can have an unlimited number of these search terms for only $29.95 a month. This is a great, but little-known service.*

LUCE ONLINE

http://www.luceonline.com/

Luce Online is part of **Luce Press Clippings** (http://www.lucepress.com/), a company that's been in business over 110 years. This is a serious press-clipping service. The employees read 15,000 U.S. newspapers and magazines and work with affiliates in other countries if you want to go further afield. This service can be expensive, but if you need a top-of-the-line service, it's hard to beat a clipping service such as Luce.

THE REAL RESULTS

Ultimately there's only one way to figure out how your promotional campaign is going: by looking at what you are trying to achieve and seeing to what degree you have achieved it. Trying to sell books? Well, the real feedback you want is book sales. Trying to get donations for your nonprofit organization? The real result, then, is whether you are getting donations.

However, these other techniques we've discussed—for measuring visits to your sites and how often and where you are mentioned on the Web and in the media—are still very important. Think of a marketing and promotions campaign as a *flow* of people. You want people to talk about you, your products, and services, so that people will visit your site, so that some of them will do whatever it is you want them to do—buy something, be convinced by your ideas, donate money....

These techniques help you measure that flow. You can see whether people are talking about you; if they're not, there's your problem. You can see whether people are visiting your site; if they're not, then maybe you have to get far more people talking about you than you realized! Finally, you can see whether people are doing what you want them to do once they reach your site. If they're not, perhaps your sales message simply isn't very good; but there's another thing to consider. You can't evaluate whether your site is working well until you understand a critical fact about Internet visits.

We've discussed hits and we've discussed visits. You've learned that a lot of hits could mean lots and lots of visits...or perhaps not quite so many. But what does it mean if your site is getting a lot of visits? Have you succeeded? And what does "a lot" or "many" mean on the Internet? There's something you need to understand about Internet enterprise. It's not like the real world.

Imagine, for instance, that you own a small store on a small-town main street, or maybe in a mall. Each day you get, oh, let's say, 1,000 people visiting your store. Happy? Probably. Different businesses vary; but in most real-world businesses 1,000 visitors probably translates into significant sales. Perhaps 80 percent of the visitors buy, perhaps just 50 percent; but in most cases 1,000 visits means a lot of sales.

It's different on the Internet. While 1,000 visitors a day may be exciting, it's much less so when you realize that the numbers work differently on the Internet. An Internet visitor is not worth as much as a real-world visitor because a visitor on the Internet is far less likely to buy. If you're selling a product at your site, what proportion of your 1,000 visitors are likely to buy? Eighty percent? Very, very unlikely. Fifty percent—not much chance. No, bring the numbers way down. Start thinking in terms of one or two percent.

Of course there are many variables involved—your sales will depend on the type of product you're selling, how well you pitch the product, on the guarantee you offer and your shipping terms, and so on. In some cases it may be possible to *convert*—to get sales from a visitor—for a much higher proportion of the time; but in general Internet commerce, conversion rates are in the single digits. For instance, Jason Olim, writing in *The CDnow Story* (Top Floor Publishing, co-authored with Peter, by the way), says that, "Conversion rates vary tremendously, depending on where the visitor comes from, for instance, and even from which page they come from at a particular site. Some pages send us visitors that 'convert' at the rate of as low as 0.1 percent...others may send visitors that convert at a rate of 10 percent."

So if you use the techniques in this chapter and find that you have lots and lots of visitors, yet you're not selling much, reappraise the numbers. Are you converting 10 percent of your visitors? You're way ahead of the pack! Converting just one percent? Well, it's still normal for this type of commerce.

This may come as a disappointment to many, but knowledge is power. We want you to understand the reality and then work from there. If you have lots of visitors and convert only one or two percent, there are two things you can do. First, you can work hard to bring *more* people to your site. Sorry, but it's constant work. (There's been enough hype about how the Internet is paved with gold; the reality is that it's not…it takes a lot of effort to succeed on the Internet, just as it does in the real world.)

Second, you can realize that this problem of numbers is a double-edged sword. If you are converting a small percentage of visitors, you should realize that if you can convince just one person in one or two hundred to buy from you, you've just increased your business tremendously.

We hear a lot about Web stores. Companies set up shops or stores online, as if these sites are cyberspace versions of the real thing; but a better parallel with the real world may be catalogs. In two important ways, Web sites that sell things are similar to real-world, mail-order catalogs. Changing the way you think about your Web site may help you refocus and find new ways to sell products.

The first parallel with catalog companies is that a Web site, as we've seen, needs to reach a large number of people to make a sale. It may take 40, 50, 100, perhaps 200 or more visitors to a Web site for every sale. Real-world stores are not like this. You can bet that out of every 100 people that walk into The Gap or Sears, far more than just one will buy. Catalog sales *are* like this. Catalog companies know they need to send out a huge number of catalogs to keep the sales coming in. The other major parallel between Web sites and catalogs is that catalog companies spend a lot of time, money, and energy tweaking and testing things. This is a natural outcome of the conversion ratio. Low conversion rates mean you have to find a lot of people to get one to buy, but they also mean that small changes can make a big difference. For instance, if you only get one person in a 100 to buy, that means if you can tweak things slightly and convince one *more* person out of every 100 to buy, you've just increased your sales by 50 percent. The catalog business is a mature business; it's been around a long time, and long ago it learned that it had to tweak things, that small changes could produce large increases in sales. Eventually, Peter believes, people running commercial Web sites will have to learn direct-mail skills and will gradually come to realize that they're not really running stores at all.

PART IV
E-MAIL PR

CHAPTER FIFTEEN

E-Mail Basics

The Web is just one of several important software systems running on the Internet, yet it's the one that gets the most press and attention; but e-mail is in many ways more important than the Web. We know plenty of people who don't spend much time on the Web, but spend plenty of time rummaging through an e-mail box. E-mail provides a direct communication channel rather than a broadcast channel. The Web is a great place to let visitors and prospects know all about your products and services. It's an excellent place to have press releases, product shots, and technical information available for journalists. When it comes down to building relationships and staying in touch, you just can't beat e-mail.

This chapter is all about getting the most you can out of e-mail, whether you're sending out press releases or newsletters. We'll look at programs that you can use, and deadly sins of e-mail (like spam), and how to personalize the e-mail you send to your customers.

Let's start with applications. What program are you using to send out your e-mail?

E-MAIL APPLICATIONS

You may be using the e-mail application that came with your Internet setup package. That application might be Eudora Light, or the e-mail programs that come with Netscape Communicator or Microsoft's Internet Explorer.

Those applications might be good enough for what you've been doing; but if you want to take your e-mail to another level, you should investigate other possibilities. Several great packages out there can help your online marketing and promotional efforts.

Eudora Pro

http://www.eudora.com/

Eudora Pro is one of the oldest personal-computer e-mail packages on the Internet, and until the last couple of years, it was indisputably the most popular. There's a free version called Eudora Light, and that might be the one you're using. (Many ISPs bundle it with their introductory software.) There's also an adware version, which is just like the pay version except while you're using it you have to look at advertisements. Upgrading to the pay or adware version has a lot of payoffs:

- Eudora Pro allows you to make filters for your e-mail. (More on that in the "Filtering" section of this chapter.)
- Eudora Pro has a built-in spell checker (always important for making a good impression).
- Eudora Pro offers stationery, great for sending personalized versions of messages you have to send often. (*Stationery* is a boilerplate e-mail message—you create a message in the normal way, specifying the subject line and body of the message. Then instead of actually sending the e-mail, you save it as stationery. When you want to reply to a message with a form letter that you've created as stationery, you can select the Reply With command and select the stationery you want to use.)

These are just a few of Eudora Pro's features compared to Eudora Light. As you see, Eudora Pro offers many more options for organization, which you'll need as you accumulate thousands and thousands of e-mail messages. Eudora Pro is available for Windows and the Macintosh.

Keep Up To Date—*It's a good idea to keep up to date with your e-mail software. They all have bugs and serious design flaws, and now and then there are potential security problems discovered related to e-mail programs. To make sure you have the most recent and secure version; check the publisher's Web page every couple of months or sign up with the company's mailing list so you're alerted every time a new version of the program comes out. (Upgrades, even for commercial programs, are often free.)*

Pegasus

http://www.pegasus.usa.com/faqs.asp

You won't see full-page ads for Pegasus in your favorite computer magazine, and you won't get direct mail encouraging you to try the new version of Pegasus. That's because Pegasus is completely free. That's right, free; the only thing you have to pay for is a paper version of the documentation if you want one.

Don't assume that Pegasus, just because it's free, is a weak program. It isn't. It has a powerful filtering system, for example, and is quite capable of mailing to several thousand people at a time; it's one of the few personal e-mail programs that is suitable for use as mailing-list discussion group programs or for newsletter publishing. (Many of the popular commercial programs are not capable of being used for this purpose.)

It also has a great address book and works with networked computers. The downside of Pegasus is that because it does so much, it can take awhile to learn. Nontechnical users who want to just read and send e-mail would be better served to stick with a program like Eudora. If you're a real geek, though, and want all the control you can get, Pegasus is worth playing with. Pegasus is available for Windows, DOS, and Macintosh.

Converting Address Books and Mailboxes—*If you're converting from one e-mail program to another, be sure to check whether there are programs that convert e-mail boxes and address books from your old program to the new program. If such programs are available, the Web site for the e-mail program you choose should mention them. You can learn more about converting Eudora mailboxes at* http://mango.human.cornell.edu/kens/MoreFAQ.html#Convert. *There's an online service for converting address books at* http://www.interguru.com/mailconv.htm.

Microsoft Outlook

http://www.microsoft.com/outlook/

Of course Microsoft has an e-mail client. What, did you think they would leave it up to everybody else? The core advantage of Microsoft Outlook is that it integrates well with other Microsoft Office applications, including Microsoft Word and Internet Explorer. If you've acquired a Windows-based computer in the last year or so, you probably already have Outlook Express, a simpler version of Outlook that contains the e-mail portion, on your computer. (In earlier incarnations of Outlook, there were two separate programs: Internet Mail and Internet News.)

The core disadvantage of Microsoft Outlook is that it integrates well with other Microsoft Office applications and Windows. At this writing there have been several well-documented security issues with Microsoft Outlook, and we unfortunately can no longer say that just receiving an e-mail won't hurt your computer. With Outlook, it can. It's a powerful program, but you'll need to keep up with patching it and upgrading it religiously.

Outlook combines contact management with sending e-mail, allowing you to do scheduling and follow-up via e-mail. Outlook also offers several pre-created forms that allow you to save and forward information in different formats (library card catalogs, "While you were out" messages, and so on). On the other hand, in many ways Outlook is not as powerful as Eudora or Pegasus.

If you already have a contact manager, Outlook may be overkill for you. On the other hand, if most of your contact-management needs are e-mail based, you might find Outlook is suitable both for sending e-mail and keeping in touch.

Test, Test, Test—*Most of the programs mentioned here have light and evaluation versions available. Do as much software testing and evaluation as you can stand. You're going to be using your e-mail an awful lot, so be sure that you're comfortable with what you're using!*

Netscape Messenger

http://www.netscape.com/messenger/start/

Netscape Messenger comes bundled with Netscape Communicator, so it's free. Unfortunately it's not as full-featured as the other e-mail applications we've mentioned. On the plus side, because it's integrated into Netscape Communicator, you can view HTML mail (that is, e-mail messages formatted using HTML) with no problems and without opening a separate browser program. It also allows you to read newsgroup messages, so if you work in newsgroups often you'll find it convenient to be able to use the same program to read them. On the other hand, Messenger's filtering is not as good as the other programs, so keeping your messages organized might be more of a challenge. Messenger is available for Windows and Macintosh.

Other E-mail Programs

There are dozens of e-mail applications available. Here are just a few of the other ones you might want to check out.

Calypso (Windows and Windows NT)
http://www.mcsdallas.com/

DTS Mail (Windows and Windows NT)
http://dtsoftware.simplenet.com/

MailSmith (Macintosh)
http://web.barebones.com/products/msmith/msmith.html

PowerMail (Macintosh)
http://www.ctmdev.com/

Choosing an e-mail program isn't something you can do in five minutes. You'll need to work with the different products available and get a feel for the features you like and use the most. E-mail will be a lifeline of contact between you and your customers, so make sure you're using a program with which you're comfortable.

THE BASICS OF GOOD E-MAIL

We can't give you instructions on how to use every possible e-mail program. So instead of giving you click here/click there kind of instructions, we're going to give you an overview of how to best use e-mail. For the purposes of this chapter, we're dividing e-mail into three sections: address lines, subject line, and body.

Address Lines

The address lines in an e-mail message are the instructions that you provide to tell the e-mail system where the message should go. Putting someone's e-mail address in the To: line means you want the e-mail to go to that person. Your name and address in the From: line shows that the e-mail came from you. This isn't rocket science (see Figure 15.1 for a layout of a Eudora e-mail message and how the headers work); but there are a couple of lines that you might not know about, or might not understand how to use properly—namely, the Cc: and Bcc: lines.

> To:—You think you know how to use the To: line; but did you know that you can put multiple e-mail addresses on that line? Quite likely; but did you know you probably shouldn't in most cases? It's *very* rude to put dozens of e-mail addresses in the To: line, particularly if the people don't know each other and have no reason to—because each address on the To: line will be visible to every recipient. For instance, don't put the addresses of 1,000 of your closest friends on the To: line when forwarding a joke a colleague just sent you. (You should use Bcc: for that.)

> Cc:—The Cc: line means *carbon copy.* Putting e-mail addresses in the Cc: line means that a copy of the e-mail will be sent to those e-mail addresses, in addition to the address on the To: line. In some programs you can use the Cc: line as the sole address line—you don't need to put anything on the To: line. In others, you can only use the Cc: line if you use the To: line as well. In general, you can list as many e-mail addresses in the Cc: line as you like. Again, you probably shouldn't. The Cc: line is visible to everyone getting the message, so don't use it if the people receiving the message don't need to know that others received the message.

Bcc:—Pay attention: the proper use of a Bcc: line is one of the secret weapons of good e-mail. Bcc: stands for *blind carbon copy*. The Bcc: header works like the Cc: line: it sends copies of an e-mail to the e-mail addresses you specify. The difference is that the Bcc: recipients' identities are protected from other recipients. People receiving Bcc: copies can see all the addresses on the To: and Cc: lines, but the To: and Cc: recipients cannot see the Bcc: addresses. In addition, if you have multiple Bcc: recipients, they cannot see the addresses of one another either.

When would you want to use Bcc? When you're sending e-mail to dozens, perhaps hundreds, of people at a time. Say you wanted to send a product update to 100 e-mail addresses—or perhaps you're running a small newsletter using your e-mail program, mailing out to 1,000 subscribers. If you put the e-mail addresses in the To: header or the Cc: header, the recipients of the message would have to scroll through 100 (or 1,000) e-mail addresses to get to the update. That's inconvenient, but it's also going to get you complaints. People don't want you to give their e-mail addresses to hundreds of other people like that. If you put the addresses in the Bcc: header, however, nobody will see anyone else's address.

If your e-mail program allows you to send a message to just the Bcc: recipients—as, for instance, Eudora Pro 4.0 does—you can leave the To: line empty. If your program forces you to use the To: line, then put *your* address on the To: line, so you'll get a copy back.

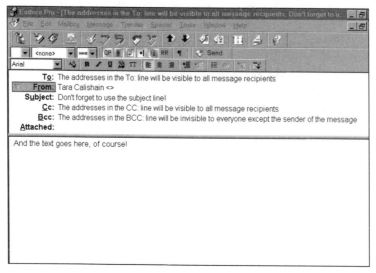

FIGURE 15.1: Be careful how you use your header lines.

Subject Line

Using the address lines appropriately is important, but so is using the subject line effectively. The better your subject line, the better the chance that your e-mail message will be read. The subject line is like the cover of a book. The impression your readers get from the subject line plays an important role in whether your message is read. With that in mind, we have some Dos and Don'ts for you:

- *Do* make your subject line as specific as possible. If you're replying to someone's e-mail, use that person's subject line with whatever clarification is necessary.
- *Don't* use generic subject lines like "Your phone call," "The information you requested," or "What we were talking about." Those subject lines used to be okay, but more and more spammers are using them.
- *Don't* make subject lines to long—generally no longer than about 10 words.
- *Don't* USE ALL CAPITAL LETTERS OR EXTRA AMOUNTS OF PUNCTUATION IN YOUR SUBJECT LINE!!!!!????????
- *Don't* use a misleading subject line. If you're sending out a press release, don't use the subject line of "Your phone call." This will damage your credibility and possibly get your e-mail address tossed into receivers' e-mail filters so they never see any more of your e-mail messages.
- *Don't* leave the subject line blank. That's like having a book with a blank cover. Make sure your subject line says something, even if it's just a basic "My feelings on xyz."
- *Do* learn how to use informal subject lines for business. The real trick to many business relationships is to change them from formal to informal. There are so many stodgy, formal, boring business communications that one that reads smoothly and easily can stand out—but this only works if you can write well.
- *Do* make sure your spelling and grammar are correct.
- *Do* make sure your subject line is compelling, interesting, and screams out, "Open this e-mail!"

Once you have a subject line that works—one that makes the recipient want to open the message—you want to write an e-mail body—the actual message—that lives up to it.

The Body of Your E-mail

The body of the e-mail is, of course, where you get your message across. For that reason you want to have a lean-and-mean e-mail body, as concise as possible. Do we have some Dos and Don'ts for you? Of course we do.

- *Do* quote. Quoting is when you include a portion of a previous e-mail message when you reply to it or forward it to someone else, to add context to your current e-mail message. Many people get huge amounts of e-mail, and it's easy to forget what you said in an earlier message, or what a particular correspondence relates to; quoting earlier text makes it easy for recipients to quickly figure out what's going on.
- *Don't* over-quote. You'll often see messages in which someone quotes an entire 40- or 50-line e-mail message, and then adds two or three words at the end, making it hard to find the response and cluttering up the message. Just quote the piece of the message to which you are replying, or just a snippet to remind the recipient what you were discussing. Be sure to cut out the headers, or technical information the computer network uses to send you your message.
- *Do* make sure your e-mail is spell-checked and uses good grammar. Many e-mail programs have spelling checkers, and you can always run important messages through a word processor's grammar checker, or have someone edit it for you.
- *Do* keep your e-mails to about 60–70 columns wide. That way you're assured that most e-mail readers will be able to read them all right. If you make them more than 80 columns wide, then your

    message might be broken up

  into raggedy, short,

  and uneven lines like this.
- *Do* make sure that you're sending an e-mail message to the right address. It's really embarrassing to send a private e-mail message to an entire mailing list (and you'll probably do it at least once in your Internet life, so get ready for it).
- *Do* keep the emoticons to a minimum. Emoticons are little symbols that are a substitute for voice tone and facial expressions. This, for example— :-> —is an emoticon of a smiling face. Emoticons are sometimes useful to make the point that you're kidding or that a reader shouldn't take you seriously, but a lot of people find them annoying. Keep the emoticons and other emotional notations—<grin> or <smile>—to a minimum.

- *Don't* write a message in your word processor and then paste it into the e-mail program. Word processors often add special typesetting characters, such as curly quote symbols, em dashes, ellipses, and so on. If you place these symbols into an e-mail message, the message *may* go through okay. But many e-mail systems don't like these symbols, and will scramble the message in some way—for instance, the recipient may see each line break in the message preceded by =20.

- *Do* make sure that your e-mail messages are text-only. Some e-mail readers cannot display HTML mail well, and others can't display it at all. Also, be sure that you don't put attachments to your e-mail. What you think is so cute and something you want to pass on can turn out to be a computer-crashing headache for someone else. (Some programs have plain-text and HTML settings that you can choose.)

As you look over these Dos and Don'ts, you'll see that a lot of them are common sense. There's a reason for that; e-mail is a lot like business communication. As long as you keep that in mind, you'll be fine. As we've stated over and over in this chapter, e-mail is an exceptionally powerful tool; but it's also subject to a lot of abuse.

Attachments—*E-mail messages are just plain text; but you can send computer files of various kinds by attaching them to e-mail messages. Theoretically you could send anything as an attachment, but we don't recommend it unless the person you send the attachment to knows about it in advance and agrees to it. People don't like receiving attachments for various reasons. They can't be sure that the attachments don't contain viruses; executable files, and programs, can carry viruses, and programs such as Word and Excel can carry viruses embedded in macros. If you send attachments, you're telling the recipient, in effect, to spend time opening it to see what's in it, which is a little rude. And in some cases large attached files can crash e-mail programs.*

E-MAIL PROBLEMS

Every time you send regular mail, whether it's with a 33-cent stamp or a bulk-mail indicia, it costs something to send mail. On the Internet, however, many people don't have to pay anything beyond their connection costs, removing one of the barriers to communication. This gives rise to a lot of silliness. The two biggest examples of this silliness are spamming and chain mail.

Spamming

Free direct business mail to potential customers all over the world! Send thousand and thousands of pieces of mail without spending a dime! Sounds great, doesn't it? That's the whole problem!

What is Spam?—*Tara defines spam as unsolicited bulk e-mail. Peter prefers to be a bit more specific, calling it unsolicited and indiscriminate bulk e-mail. Unfortunately some people have taken to defining spam as unsolicited commercial e-mail (sometimes written as UCE). This definition is a real problem, as we explain in "The Spam Overreaction" in this chapter.*

Since discovering the Internet and the ease by which they could contact millions of people, a wide variety of people have started taking advantage of spamming, otherwise known as unsolicited bulk e-mail. Their unsolicited advertisements may be promoting good products, but all too often they're promoting scams, pornography sites, inaccurate information about stocks, and so on. In any case, whether the products being promoted are legitimate or not, the flood of unwanted e-mail into your inbox is a real nuisance.

Does that mean all spam is for illegitimate companies and causes? Of course not; but much of it is. If a legitimate company relies on spam to get its message across, it's immediately putting itself in the same class with porn companies and get-rich-quick schemes. Is that a place you want to be?

Some people react to the condemnation of spam with the response, "What's the big deal? Just hit the Delete key." Let's look at that argument for a minute, and examine the possibility of just legitimate companies using e-mail. There are about 4,500,000 companies in the United States. Since the Internet doesn't have distance restrictions, let's say all of these companies want to send you unsolicited e-mail once a year. Just once.

Just one e-mail a year from each of these companies means you'd be getting over 12,300 messages a day in your mailbox. And that doesn't count companies that send more than one e-mail a year and companies outside the U.S. Right now you might think that unsolicited e-mail isn't that big a deal because these companies are not on the Net. However the Internet population, of citizens and businesses, is only going to get larger, and the problem of unsolicited e-mail, as more and more businesses decide that there isn't any harm in sending one unsolicited e-mail, is going to grow exponentially.

Furthermore, in many cases—particularly outside the United States—phone costs are calculated by the minute. Having to stay connected to download spam means that these unfortunate users have to pay to download e-mail they don't want.

Please don't let your business add to this problem. Help support responsible use of e-mail by using only opt-in e-mail lists (where the addressee has requested to be added to the list), and by protecting the e-mail addresses of your customers and prospects by refusing to rent or sell your lists of e-mail addresses.

We haven't mentioned the negative repercussions of sending unsolicited bulk e-mail. Things like, oh, lawsuits, criminal prosecutions, threats from ticked-off hackers, mailbombs (attacks by huge numbers of e-mail messages that will overload your mailbox), and the complete loss of respect in the online community. Stuff like that. Think twice.

For more information on spamming and what you can do to prevent it—and what can happen to you if you indulge—check out the following Web sites:

Stop Spam FAQ
http://just4u.com/webconsultants/spamfaq.htm

Junkbusters (Covers telemarketing and junk mail in addition to spam)
http://www.junkbusters.com/

O'Reilly Stop Spam Center
http://stopspam.oreilly.com/

The Coalition Against Unsolicited Commercial E-mail
http://www.cauce.org/

Junk Email Resource Page
http://www.junkemail.org/

Fight Spam on the Internet!
http://spam.abuse.net/

The Spam-L FAQ
http://oasis.ot.com/~dmuth/spam-l/

The Spam Overreaction

Many people and anti-spam organizations have taken to defining spam as UCE—*unsolicited commercial e-mail*. Originally the definition was different, but some anti-spam groups have forced it to evolve toward this definition. If you're doing business on the Internet, especially if you're publishing an e-mail newsletter, you should be careful about endorsing such a vague and sloppy definition.

For instance, Peter once received an e-mail that was completely unsolicited—he'd never heard of the person before, let alone given her his e-mail address or asked her to contact him. It was definitely commercial; she contacted him in relation to her job, and asked him to give her something of economic value. It was, according to this absurd definition, spam.

However she was a writer for *PC World*, asking for a review copy of his book, *Poor Richard's Web Site*. He was happy to hear from her, of course, so he didn't regard it as spam. But according to the UCE definition, he could, if he decided he didn't want to hear from her, justly consider it to be spam. According to many anti-spam groups, he should then be allowed to sue her or force her ISP to close down her account. With a definition as vague as this, if you don't like what you hear, it's spam; if you do, it's not.

Consider the opposite of this case. If you contact a journalist who you've never spoken with before, that journalist could, under the UCE definition, regard your message as spam. In most cases journalists won't, but now and then you will run into people who will be rude, accuse you of spamming, and even contact your ISP to complain. Note that Peter has used the methods in Chapter 16, *Reaching Journalists Online*, to contact thousands of journalists quickly. He's had overwhelmingly good reactions—journalists thanking him for the offer of a review book, for instance, and asking for a copy; journalists thanking him for thinking of them but turning down the offer; journalists turning him down, but suggesting he contact a colleague. He's received a handful of messages asking, quite politely, to be removed from his list, and he's received just one or two rude messages accusing him of being a spammer.

In fact Peter's been accused of spamming far more often in the case of *solicited* e-mail! Thanks to this anti-spam hysteria, newsletter publishers are routinely accused of spamming by people who have subscribed to the newsletter! They forget they've subscribed, or perhaps share an account with someone who subscribed. For instance, Peter once received a rather rude e-mail message telling him to stop sending his garbage. He wrote an article in his newsletter (http://PoorRichard.com/newsltr/) about spam, quoting this message. A day or two later someone sent Peter a message apologizing for the behavior of his wife! This gentleman had subscribed to *Poor Richard's Web Site News*, but when his wife found the message in their inbox she just assumed it was spam.

Peter prefers to define spam as unsolicited and indiscriminate bulk e-mail. It's unsolicited because the recipient has had no contact with the sender and did not request anything. It's indiscriminate in the sense that the sender has no real reason to think you have any interest in his product or service; all you are to him is an anonymous e-mail address. And it's a bulk mailing; it's sent to a large number of people at one time. The bulk mailing is what really wastes the time and resources of the Internet.

There's a real difference between buying millions of e-mail addresses on a CD and sending everyone a message asking them to visit your foot-fetish Web site, and carefully selecting a number of Web-site owners who might want to review your product and mailing them all a polite message suggesting this.

Chain Letters

Just as irritating as spam, but usually done for better intentions, are chain letters. Once you've been on the Internet long enough, you'll get one: a plea to help a child who's dying of cancer, or an ominous warning about a new virus.

Chain letters are usually sent from one person to dozens or hundreds of people. (If they don't use the Bcc: header, you can see exactly how many people it went to.) They're often sent because someone wanted to warn everyone that the government is about to tax Internet access, or some similar altruistic reason. The problem is that most of these legends, warnings, whatever, are fake. You can help stem the flow of urban legend chain letters by ignoring them, or perhaps e-mailing the sender and letting him know that the messages are false. If in doubt, please don't send it out.

For more information about these false messages, see the following Web sites:

CIAC Internet Chain Letters
http://ciac.llnl.gov/ciac/CIACChainLetters.html

CIAC Internet Hoaxes
http://ciac.llnl.gov/ciac/CIACHoaxes.html

Computer Virus Myths Home Page
http://www.kumite.com/myths/

Don't Spread that Hoax!
http://www.nonprofit.net/hoax/hoax.html

The Email Folklore Homepage
http://www.people.virginia.edu/~ymb5v/

The Urban Legend Combat Kit
http://www.tourbus.com/archive/tb102998.htm

Urban Legends at About.com
http://urbanlegends.about.com/

HANDLING E-MAIL—FILTERS, BOILERPLATE, AND AUTORESPONDERS

Once you've been on the Net for a while and you've done a lot to promote your business, you'll find yourself getting a lot of e-mail. Tara gets over 200 e-mail messages a day and she doesn't even want to think about how many messages Peter gets. Eventually you have to do something that organizes the messages a little bit even before you look at them. That's where filtering comes in. You can also use programs to actually respond to messages, and build the basic text of responding to messages. That's what autoresponders and boilerplates are for.

Filtering

All good e-mail programs allow filtering. (Some light versions of e-mail packages don't, however; you may have to pay to get good filtering…or, paradoxically, get a free program such as Pegasus.) A filtering system takes a look at the information in the incoming mail—what the subject line says, for example, or who the e-mail is from—and acts on the information that's filtered. For example, you could set up a filter in your e-mail to play a sound when you get e-mail from certain people. More importantly, you can create filters to automatically sort all your incoming and outgoing messages into separate folders and boxes. You could set up filters to perform any of the following actions:

- Automatically delete e-mail from certain people. (Sometimes that's called a killfile.)
- Play an alert when you get e-mail with a certain subject.
- Put e-mail directed to certain e-mail addresses (if you use more than one) in certain folders in your e-mail box.
- Mark a message from a particular person in some way—with a particular color, for instance.
- Automatically forward a message with a particular word in the subject line, or from a particular person, to someone else.
- Add or remove an e-mail address from an address book. If you're running a newsletter mailing list using a mail program, having a filter automatically unsubscribe an e-mail address is a good way to set up an automatic unsubscription feature.

Filters can be invaluable in your business communications, especially if you're a single-person operation with several different e-mail addresses. You could filter different addresses—support@, marketing@, or owner@, for instance—into different folders, assign them different priorities, or even send automatic responses to them.

Pegasus has the strongest filtering system of any e-mail program we know of that is in current development. You can even build a mailing list with it. If you want to set up several elaborate filters, check out Pegasus as a potential program, or look at Eudora Pro because its relative simplicity will make it more likely that you will create filters. Check out Figure 15.2 for an example of a created filter. If you don't plan to do much filtering and don't need more than basic filters, a program such as Netscape Messenger, or MS Outlook will probably do.

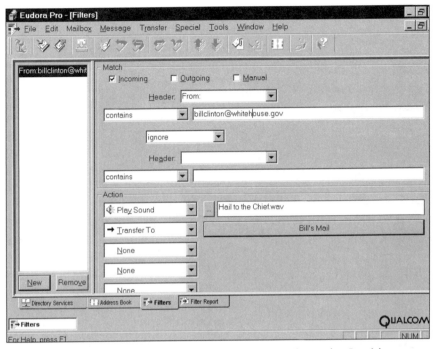

FIGURE 15.2: This filter moves all the mail Peter receives from the President—a considerable quantity, of course—into a particular folder, and plays Hail to the Chief when it arrives.

Whatever program you're using, learn to work with the filters. You *cannot* effectively work online if you simply dump all your incoming e-mail messages into one box and all the outgoing ones into another. You *must* find some way to organize them.

Filters Must Be Easy—*Unfortunately the e-mail software publishers don't seem to understand that powerful filtering features are no good unless they're easy to use. If it takes you five minutes to create a filter, you won't do it often. So if you get scores of e-mail messages each day, you won't be able to keep it all well organized. Currently the program that creates filters the quickest is Eudora Pro. You can create filters with as few as four mouse clicks—still too many, but better than most other programs.*

Using Stationery or Boilerplate

Some e-mail packages offer some kind of boilerplate feature—the ability to save boilerplate message text, and to insert that text into outgoing messages. Eudora, for instance, has *stationery*, which means that boilerplate can be turned into e-mail messages that you can customize with a few keystrokes. Pegasus even includes a mail-merge feature, which means that each e-mail can be customized with the recipient's name.

For instance, Peter has a number of messages he has to send repeatedly. When people inquire about advertising in his newsletter, he has to send out a message containing rates and subscription information; when someone's credit-card was declined, he has to inform them; and so on. He uses Eudora's stationery feature to create boilerplate messages, and then picks the appropriate response.

If your e-mail package doesn't offer these kinds of features, you can fake them. Create the text of your message in a text editor. (Make sure that it's in a text editor, and not a word processor. As we noted before, if you use a word processor you'll get weird characters that won't translate into plain-text e-mail.) When you're ready to send out several copies of an e-mail, you can paste the text of the message into a new e-mail and customize it in a few places. (You can mark them with ***, or @@@, or some other way to signify that those blanks need to be filled in.) The only problem with this approach is you have to remember to fill in the subject line. The most lovely e-mail in the world is going to get hurt badly by a blank subject line.

Autoresponders

Filters can be configured to act as autoresponders. *Autoresponders* immediately respond to an e-mail message by sending an e-mail message back. This message contains some kind of information—if someone e-mails to your adinfo@ address, for instance, you could send back information about advertising rates. If you prefer not to work with many different e-mail addresses, you could also set up filters to work on a particular subject line; you might tell people to e-mail you with the words *Newsletter Advertising* in the subject line, for instance.

If you use a lot of autoresponders, you might also create them through your hosting company's autoresponder feature. Any POP e-mail account should come with the ability to set up autoresponders (see Chapter 3, *Web Site Basics*). When you get a Web-hosting account for your domain, you'll get a POP account, too, and you should get a number of autoresponders. If you set up the autoresponders at the server, you can often tweak the settings so the mail will never even reach your e-mail program; rather, the POP server will automatically respond for you.

Autoresponders can be useful in many ways. Peter has used them in association with newspaper articles, for instance. In the articles he offers free reports to people who e-mail to the autoresponder address. You might also use them for free drawings—you could tell people to e-mail a particular autoresponder to join your newsletter and to be entered into a free drawing for one of your products.

However, there are two problems with autoresponders running on a server. First, they may not be very good. Some are too simple to be particularly useful. A good autoresponder should be able to do the following:

- Quote the incoming message in the autoresponse
- Save the incoming message
- Grab the e-mail address from the incoming message and put it in a text file
- Redirect the incoming message somewhere else (to a mailing list server, for instance)

The last two of these are particularly important, as they enable you to build mailing lists from messages sent to your autoresponders. You may have trouble finding an autoresponder with all these features, unfortunately; it may be easier to set up a complicated autoresponder using your e-mail program (which is okay unless the autoresponder is getting hit by vast amounts of e-mail and spam).

The other problem is that many hosting companies make setting up the autoresponders too complicated. Some companies expect you to understand the intricacies of writing e-mail scripts that tell the companies' e-mail servers how to run. The company you choose either should have a simple system that allows you to fill in a form to create your autoresponders, or should offer detailed, step-by-step instructions.

Autoresponders can be useful when all you want to do is send a piece of boilerplate back to someone. Sometimes, however, although you need to send back something that is 90 percent boilerplate, you may still need to customize a little bit. So you'll probably end up combining autoresponders with stationery features. This is where boilerplate and autoresponders work together.

Making Boilerplate and Autoresponders Work Together

Say, for example, that you're selling advertising for your newsletter. People could send an e-mail to an address you've set up—maybe your adinfo@ address—and immediately receive your ad rates and terms. Once they've decided to run an ad, they would send another e-mail to you personally with the text of the ad.

When you receive their ad, you will want to return a notice that you'll be running the ad, when it will be running, and how much it will cost. However, you can't use an autoresponder to convey that kind of information. That's where a boilerplate or stationery message comes in. You can use a boilerplate message to provide most of the details—the terms of your advertising, a notice of when your newsletter runs, and legalese. You can then fill in the blanks with custom information, such as the text of the ad, the cost of the ad, and any additional information.

Major Mail Merge—*There's another way to combine boilerplate and e-mail addresses—using a mail-merge program such as WorldMerge or Campaign. We'll look at that subject in Chapter 16, Reaching Journalists Online.*

The amount of personalization you can do with your e-mail program varies according to the program. Be sure to check for stationery and mail merge when you're looking for an e-mail application that uses a lot of personalization. (Unfortunately, few currently have mail merge.) Some programs, like Eudora, also offer different personalities or accounts—ways to insert different e-mail addresses and signatures into your e-mail. When you're handling many different kinds of e-mail—technical support, working with vendors, collaborating with different people in your company—it's time-saving to use different addresses for different purposes, and then filter the various outgoing messages and responses into different folders.

Now that you know how to create good e-mail, you need to parlay this skill into communicating with editors. E-mail can be your most powerful tool in building relationships with media and making the most of your PR, so check out the next chapter for the basics of online PR.

CHAPTER SIXTEEN

Reaching Journalists Online

The goals of Internet PR are almost the same as the goals of offline PR. You're trying to get coverage for your product or service—favorable coverage, hopefully. Alternatively, you're trying to tell your story or publicize a cause. Where online PR starts differing from offline PR is in the tools you have at your disposal. You have many more resources to find journalists, reach journalists, and keep up with journalists online, and doing so doesn't require the outlay of time or money that traditional methods require.

You also have the opportunity to make your job and the editor's job a lot easier. Further, you have the opportunity to personalize your content, and doing so is worthwhile. So few PR people do this that it'll make you really stand out. (Tara's been on both ends of the PR machine, and she knows whereof she speaks.)

The major focus on promotion can be divided into three parts:

1. Finding the journalist
2. Contacting the journalist
3. Staying in touch with the journalist (substitute editor, or columnist for journalist)

Initially in this chapter, we will be focusing on resources for print media only. A later section in the chapter, "Contacting Radio and TV Media," focuses on— you guessed it—radio and TV media. After that we'll explore staying in touch with journalists, and having journalists come to you by positioning yourself as an expert.

WHAT ARE YOUR GOALS?

We're going to be talking about how to contact journalists. But *why* are you contacting journalists? What do you want, ultimately, to happen because of this contact? There are a few things you could be going for. Which one you want is up to you.

Product story—Maybe you want a story written about your product or service, so that more people can learn about it. This is difficult coverage to get unless you have an unusual hook you can present to the journalist. A new coffee shop isn't going to attract a product story unless it serves unusual food, the waitresses wear roller skates, it's open between midnight and noon, etc.

Product review—Sometimes when you can't wrangle coverage, you can convince a journalist to review your product. The catch here is that your product has to be useful to a wide range of the journalist's readership. If you write a software program designed to help build pacemakers, your daily newspaper won't review this product. However, a medical-software journal might. You have better chances of getting your product reviewed if you stay aware of editorial calendars and what journalists are looking for at particular times, too. (See the accompanying tip "What's an Editorial Calendar?" for more information about editorial calendars.) What's the difference between a product review and a product story? The review tends to be more focused on what the product can do for the reader. The story has a wider appeal, and is related to the background of the product rather than the product itself.

What's an Editorial Calendar?—*Magazines plan issues months in advance. To plan their issues effectively and to help advertisers know when their advertising dollars are best spent, they publish editorial calendars. Editorial calendars are overviews of what each issue will contain. The editorial calendar might be as detailed as a list of articles and special features, or as vague as listing that the issue will cover home networking. Monthly magazines, since they're put together months in advance, have the most rigid editorial calendars; they usually don't change. Weekly magazines are more flexible since they don't need to be completed months in advance and can change their content in reaction to current events. Newspapers, of course, change constantly, though even they cover topics according to a calendar (like holidays, tax information, and summer vacations).*

A human-interest story—Sometimes you can create a human-interest story out of your situation; the journalist gets an interesting or fun story, while you get your product or company mentioned in the press. For instance, in the early days of **CDnow** (http://www.cdnow.com/) the company used to pitch the *twib* story to journalists; *twib* meant "twins in the basement," and referred to the founders, Jason and Matthew Olim, working in their parents' basement. Journalists wrote about how these two kids were building an online store on a shoestring, how Matthew brushed his teeth in front of the computer, how Jason spent his guitar fund on the business, and so on.

An interview—If you can get interviewed in the press you can position yourself as an expert in your area. Although the article will not directly focus on your products or services, you can mention them and the journalist may mention them in the introduction to the interview.

A mention in a story—Sometimes if journalists are doing a story on your industry or something related to your industry, they might want to interview you or someone else in your company as an expert. While this doesn't give your company or service a lot of exposure, you can get your company mentioned and sometimes establish yourself or your company as an expert. This often works well when you're a company of one person, an author, or in some other way running a solo operation.

A little mindshare—Occasionally you'll contact journalists who will immediately want to do a story on you. But more often the journalists will listen to your pitch and let you know that there's no coverage opportunity for you at the moment. In that case, you want to establish yourself in the journalists' minds as an expert, so that when they do plan to do a story that might involve you in some way—either through a quote, coverage, or review—you'll come to mind. That's why establishing a relationship with a journalist is so important.

You should have some idea of what you want before you contact the journalist. You may contact journalists hoping for a review, but find they need an interview instead. It's important that you can respond quickly to their needs, and if they don't need anything, you should be prepared to work on building a relationship with them if that's possible. (We'll talk more about building relationships later in the chapter.)

FINDING THE JOURNALIST

High-powered PR firms use really expensive means to find out which editors cover their products and services, the kind of stories they're running, and when they're being run. Products from places like MediaMap and Press Access can run hundreds, and sometimes thousands, of dollars. If you're reading this you probably can't immediately afford to do something like that—but there is a way to get information from these big companies for free. We'll explain how in a minute.

Track Media by Specialty

In the first few chapters we urged you to make a list of the several different kinds of groups that would be interested in your product or service. If you have that list of groups now, you're going to find looking for editors a much more organized process. Track media by specialty, using the resources in the earlier chapters to find editors. If you have a Web site for educational software, for example, you could divide media into resources for parents, teachers, grandparents, and possibly even kids.

Some of you are going to find this easier than others. The inventor of a new onion-cooking machine can look for the food editor, and the writer of a baseball trivia book can give the sports editor a try; but what if you're heading a nonprofit organization that encourages pet owners to walk their cats on leashes? What if you've started a Web page devoted to the many uses of the color mauve?

There are a few rules of thumb to find out who's who, and where. When checking out a publication's Web site, look through the Web site for links that say things like "About this site" or "Press Releases." You may also wish to keep an eye out for a "masthead" link, like you'll see in Figure 16.1.

If you're trying to get the attention of a particular columnist, check the column first. A lot of times columnists put contact e-mail addresses at the end of their columns. Try to contact the addresses on a columnists' page before trying to find the columnist in a staff list. Often, though, especially in large publications, these are not personal e-mail addresses but just addresses put there to make it look like they're responsive to their readers; the chance of actually getting to someone through such an e-mail address is slim. (The smaller the publication, and less well-known the writer, the more likely the address will actually go straight to the columnist.) You won't know until you try.

Some newspapers have only a small presence on the Web and a single e-mail address for the entire paper. If you can't find the information you're looking for, you can send e-mail to that address and ask for a direct e-mail address.

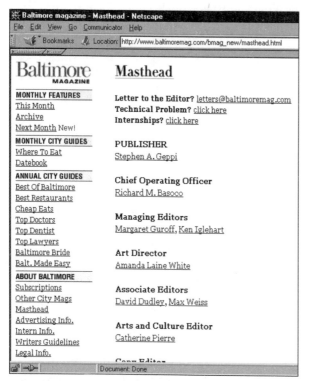

FIGURE 16.1: A masthead typically lists editors with or without contact information.

Other papers list several e-mail addresses. For small papers, try contacting the managing editor when you're unsure of which department you should be seeking out. For larger papers, look for an assistant or associate editor in the department you think is the most appropriate.

As you gather contact information, you can drop people into your contact-management program or database (see Chapter 2, *What You Need Before You Start*), or put them in a simple addressing program and spit them out on Rolodex cards. Whatever method you use to keep them organized, be sure to note the full name, title, publication name, address, phone and fax number, e-mail address, and Web site; and be sure to denote any keywords that'll make clearer how they might be interested in your product or service. That way, if you're looking for promotional opportunities later, you can search your contacts by keyword. For example, if you add a math homework helper to your line of educational software, you'd want to reach teachers and possibly parents. If you search by keyword for publications targeted to teachers, you'll find your promotional work a lot easier to do. This information will come in handy later as you track your contacts with editorial people.

You might be a little concerned about e-mailing these people out of nowhere and asking, bold as brass, who should get a press release and how they like receiving it. Most of the times when we've done this people have been pretty nice about it. It all comes across in your presentation. Consider this e-mail:

```
Dear Sir/Madam,
I am writing to find out who at your paper might be
interested in my new Web site, "The Tightwad's Guide to
Yak Stalking." I have a news release I want to send you
so please let me know where to send the news release.
```

You haven't given any indication that you've looked on the site, haven't even bothered to personalize the query letter at all, and basically have behaved as if the editor's time is worthless and that the editor has no more important things to do than wait on PR people hand and foot. Compare it with this letter:

```
Dear Ms. Smith,
I was reviewing The Bugle's Web site and was wondering
if you could help me. I've put together a new Web site,
"The Tightwad's Guide to Yak Stalking," and I'd like to
know where to send a press release. As you may know,
yak stalking is an extremely expensive hobby, and as my
Web site shows how to cut costs by over 40 percent, I
thought it might be appropriate for Mr. Jones in your
```

```
financial section. On the other hand, yak stalking is
an internationally recognized sport so I thought Ms.
Griffith in the sports section might also find it
interesting. If you could give me some guidance in this
matter (both who should receive the release and in what
form it should be sent), I would much appreciate it.
```

See how different these two letters are? In the second letter you've shown that you've looked at the paper, you've made an effort to find out where your press release belongs, and you've given a bit of additional information on exactly why you want to send a press release. Don't be worried about approaching these people. Most people are nice about it; and if they don't want to get a news release from you the worst they can say is no.

Actually, the worst they can say is something like, "Get away from me, you stupid PR jerk! How you could possibly get the idea in your pointed head that I would be even remotely interested in your pathetic little press release?" You're going to get that sort of response now and then; you're now doing for-real promotions. (You've heard of trial by fire? That was your trial by rudeness.)

THE MORE THE MERRIER

Contacting particular media outlets one by one is all very well, but it's a lot of work. There has to be a better, faster way. Luckily there is. A number of companies are in the business of creating lists of media contacts, and keeping the lists up to date. (Writers and editors move around between publications, so these companies track their movements.) Two of the best of these companies are PressAccess and MediaMap.

PRESSACCESS

http://www.pressaccess.com/

If you have a lot of money, consider one of PressAccess' guides to the media. These are not cheap: PressAccess' materials start in the high hundreds and work their way up. They offer printed materials and access to online databases of information. If you can't afford that, check out PressAccess' free Hot News feature, which gives you the latest moves in the online editorial community. (It's available at http://www.pressaccess.com/main.htm#HotNews.) While you're there, check out their other PR resources, like the PR case studies and links to publications.

MEDIAMAP

http://www.mediamap.com/

MediaMap's prices run much the same as PressAccess', but a lot of free materials are available at http://www.mediamap.com/pr_resources/default.asp, such as *Web PR*, a weekly column on using the Internet for better PR.

More Affordable Resources!

So you think several hundred to a few thousand is a little much, eh? (And after all, this is *Poor Richard's Internet Marketing and Promotions*.) Well, you have other options. A number of directories are available at a much lower cost (though, not surprisingly, the quality of the data is not going to be quite the same as these high-priced sources). There are various ways you can get media-contact lists without spending an absolute fortune. Let's explore how you can build your own contact lists.

PR Resources Available in Print and Online—*Until recently, the many resources offered by many large media and PR companies were available only in printed format. Now, however, many of them are available on CD-ROM and, of course, many of them are available on the Web. Check out all the different resources and take some time to think about what you'd be most comfortable with before you part with the big money. The Internet stuff is more up-to-date, of course, but you can't take it with you on an airplane and sometimes it's not easy to browse with a dialup connection.*

BUILD YOUR OWN CONTACT LIST

You can build your own media contact list if you have the time. This may be laborious, but if you work smart, you can cut the time it takes to build a list dramatically. For instance, there are directories of links to newspapers on the Internet.

Try a Search Engine—*This isn't a foolproof method, but sometimes you can get direct contacts by working with a search engine. For example, say you want food editors. Take that title and add a couple of newspaper editor titles, and plug that in a search-engine query. For example, you might use this as an Google query: "food editor" "sports editor" "news editor". By searching for three or more newspaper titles at once, you'll often find online newspaper contact pages. This won't work all the time, but it's worth trying if you're having a hard time finding contacts.*

If you use an offline browser (see Chapter 2, *What You Need Before You Start*), you can use the directories as a starting point to download pages at each newspaper and then find the newspaper's contact information. The following are some useful directories of media contacts:

Editor & Publisher's Newspaper List (Links to thousands of papers, magazines, radio shows, syndication services, and so on)
http://emedia1.mediainfo.com/emedia/

Electronic Newsstand
http://www.enews.com/

Gebbie Press (A great site; includes a free downloadable directory of almost 8,000 papers and TV stations)
http://www.gebbieinc.com/

John Hewitt's Trade Magazine List
http://www.poewar.com/links/trade.htms

MediaUK
http://www.mediauk.com/

NewsDirectory
http://www.newsdirectory.com/

Publist (Also includes pre-launch publication listings; see Figure 16.2)
http://www.publist.com/

Yahoo!—News & Media
http://www.yahoo.com/News/

Yahoo!—News and Media Directories
http://dir.yahoo.com/News_and_Media/Web_Directories/

Then there's the library. Yes, that's right, get off your backside—you've probably been staring at the screen too long, anyway—and walk/run/bike/drive to an actual library and look for the following guides:

- *Bacon's Newspaper-Magazine Directory*
- *Bacon's Radio-TV-Cable Directory*
- *Newsletters in Print*
- *Writer's Market*

If you're not in the U.S., you'll find that your country has similar directories; talk with your librarian. However, consider the law of diminishing returns. You can get a huge amount of media-contact information online. You can get contact information for most U.S. papers online, for instance, so trying to fill in the gaps by going to Bacon's directories may not be worthwhile. You'll spend a lot of time—that is, money—for just a few more contacts. On the other hand, you'll

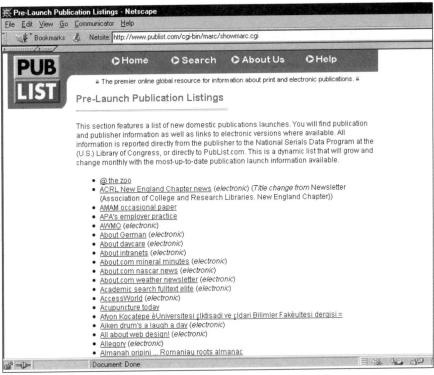

FIGURE 16.2: Publist not only helps you find existing publications, but shows you new ones.

be able to find much more detailed information, such as the names of individual editors and writers, and some directories may provide information that's difficult to find online, such as real-world—that is, paper—newsletter addresses.

BUY A LIST

You can also buy media lists. Two of the most affordable are the U.S. All Publicity Blitz from Bradley Communications, and the All-In-One Media Directory from Gebbie Press.

Bradley Communication's Publicity Blitz database is a huge contact list. It has a database with around 19,600 entries. You can also get a one-year subscription that provides four quarterly updates. You can buy this directly from Bradley Communications (we can't find a Web site for them, but you can call them at: 800-989-1400 or 610-259-1070), or from **Open Horizons**, a publisher of books and databases for the small-publishing business (http://www.bookmarket.com/, 515-472-6130, 800-796-6130).

Gebbie Press (http://www.gebbieinc.com/) publishes the All-In-One Media Directory. For $295 you can get its TV/Radio, Dailies/Weekly Newspapers, and

Magazines directories, with a total of over 23,000 entries. Gebbie Press told us that virtually all of the entries have e-mail addresses (in the electronic version of the database—not in the printed version).

Just a Few Problems—*Unfortunately a number of low-cost databases have some serious formatting problems. Peter has bought and worked with three low-cost media databases, including one of those we've mentioned here, and all three had problems with the way in which data was entered into the database or formatted, making importing the databases into a program difficult, and meaning that they had to be cleaned up before use. So be prepared for a little work before you can use them. If you're not technically capable, see if you can find a friendly database geek to help you.*

For a really massive list, see **MediaFinder** (http://www.mediafinder. com/), which sells several different directories, including *Samir Husni's Guide To New Consumer Magazines*, *The National Directory of Magazines*, and the *Oxbridge Directory of Newsletters*. Be sure to check out the publications directory, which offers plenty of free publication information (http://www.mediafinder.com/indexc.cfm).

CONTACTING THE JOURNALIST

After you find journalists, you must contact them. Here's rule number one: use the delivery method that each journalist specifies. If journalists ask you to e-mail your release, e-mail it. If they ask you to fax it, fax it. If they ask you to send it by carrier pigeon…well, at least explain that you can't and apologize. If you find out the delivery preferences and then ignore them, you have two strikes against you already.

Distributing Wide-Area Press Releases—*You can also send press releases across the wire services, reaching hundreds, perhaps thousands, of journalists at once; see Chapter 17, Electronic Press Releases.*

Before you start contacting journalists you'll need a couple of things:

Boilerplate—A boilerplate is basic promotional information that gives information about what you're promoting. It's different from a press release in that it's brief, usually just a couple of paragraphs, and is specific to the group you're targeting. For example, you wouldn't send a parent's magazine the same boilerplate you'd send a teacher's magazine, but you might send them the same press release.

The press release—The press release is the information about your product or service. If you don't know how to write a good one, we'll explain in Chapter 17, *Electronic Press Releases*. Press releases are a lot longer than boilerplates and contain a wider variety of information. You also don't always have to write different ones targeted to different groups. (If you are sending press releases to extremely different groups—to doctors and to lay people, for example, you might want to write two different press releases.)

Contacting Radio and TV Media

In this chapter we're focusing mostly on print journalists—editors of magazines and newspapers. However, there are lots of TV and radio opportunities out there, too.

For radio, you should concentrate on contacting particular radio shows instead of the station as a whole. Different shows have different producers, and different people looking for different types of talent. A morning show might want something light, something interesting but not controversial to talk about. A drive-time radio show, on the other hand, might want to talk politics, or religion, or something else that keeps the audience active and involved. You can get an idea of the various radio shows online at **Yahoo!'s Radio Programs** page: http://dir.yahoo.com/News_and_Media/Radio/Programs/. Check out the **Talk Radio Show Prep Site** at http://members.aol.com/cookeh/prep.html to get an idea of what talk radio DJs are looking for and what they need to get their shows done. (Remember, they need news as much as newspapers, and they have to fill an hour or two every day.) You can also take a look at **ShowIdeas** at http://www.showideas.com/.

If you have some money to spare, you can invest in a couple of items designed specifically to help you book radio shows. Bradley Communications offers, among other things, the Radio-TV Interview Report. This report goes out to producers and other people who book radio and TV talk shows; they turn to the Report when they're looking for show guests. Bradley Communications also offers promotional materials for general PR (like lists of media broken down by category) and materials for specific kinds of PR (like the Book Marketing Update). You can visit the site for the **Radio TV Interview Report** at http://www.rtir.com/default.asp.

You can also check out **RadioTour.Com** at http://www.radiotour.com/. For a fee, this company will make sure that radio talk shows know about you, and help you get booked on radio shows. There's also **GuestFinder.Com** (http://www.guestfinder.com/), a Web-based directory used by the media. Television shows, unlike radio and print publications, are more interested in visual things. Do you have a juggling act? Do you use common household items to illustrate principles of science? You might be better on TV than radio. For TV, in addition to the boilerplate we described in the preceding section, you should have a tape of previous television appearances and a picture of yourself. You'll need to contact the producer of a particular television show, and you'll need to get contact guidelines; producers have particular deadlines, want to receive materials in a certain way, and so on.

There are a lot of TV talk shows represented online. You can get a good listing at **Yahoo!'s Talk Shows** page: http://dir.yahoo.com/News_and_Media/Television/ Shows/Talk_Shows/. You can also get additional information at **TV Talk Shows** at http://www.tvtalkshows.com/, or **The National Talk Show Guest Registry** at http://members.aol.com/ntsgr/homepage.html. Radio-TV Interview Report and GuestFinder.Com are also read by TV reporters.

Once you have your information (boilerplate, tape, etc.) together, you're ready to write the journalist. Here are some tips to get you started:

- Write to only one journalist per publication. If a writer in one section turns you down, you can write to another one, but don't e-mail several at once. All you'll do is alienate all of them. Don't make it obvious, at least, that you're contacting several at once.

- If you must write to more than one publication's journalist at once, send each message separately, or use the Bcc: line of an e-mail address. (See Chapter 15, *E-mail Basics*, for more information about the Bcc: line.) *Don't* send the same e-mail message to two journalists with both names on the To: line or one on the To: line and the other on the Cc: line. If each knows that you've written to someone else, it's too easy for them both to let the other one handle it.

- Use a subject line that means something. Don't POST IN ALL CAPS, and don't use a misleading subject line (like Re: Returning your phone call). We'll talk more about the elements of good e-mail in the next chapter.

- Address the journalist by name if you know it. Tara prefers to address the journalist as "Dear Mr./Ms. So-and-so." She knows some people address editorial contacts by first name, but she finds that too informal. If you don't know the name of the journalist, address it to "Job Title of the Magazine Name"—like Business Editor of the Seattle Times, for example. Try to avoid "To Whom it May Concern;" it looks like mass mail.

- Structure your e-mail like this: personal comments ("I saw your column on such-and-such, and I wanted to suggest the following story idea"), the appropriate parts of your boilerplate, and then your press release if it's necessary. (A press release is useful if you're doing a straight review pitch—in which you want your product or service reviewed—or a coverage pitch—in which you just want coverage for your product or service. It's not so important if you're just letting the journalist know you exist and you're trying to make a connection.)

- Never, *never* send a press release that's anything other than plain text. Don't make it a Microsoft Word document, don't attach screenshots, and don't send the press release itself as an attachment! If journalists want that material, they can get it from you later. *Never assume that they want it.*

- Be sure to include an e-mail address or some other way they can contact you within the body of the e-mail. Don't assume they can simply reply to your e-mail. You don't know what's going to happen to that e-mail; it might get forwarded, printed, or any number of things.

- If a journalist e-mails you asking for something—a review copy of your product, a paper copy of the press release, a technical contact from which to get some answers—answer as quickly as you can. Even if you can't get what the requested material immediately, let the journalist know you've received the request. Don't leave journalists hanging; they're often working under tight deadlines and time is of the essence.

- If journalists reply to you asking to be taken off your list, *take them off* and apologize.

- Don't follow up with a phone call unless the journalist specifically asks for it. You can follow up a few weeks after you send e-mail, but follow up with e-mail. Don't call and ask, "Did you get my e-mail?" You're going to come across as pushy—overly pushy.

- If at first you don't hear from a journalist, try again—but don't send 50 e-mails in the course of a month. Once every couple of weeks will be fine.

Yes, Editors Can Be Rude—*Sometimes harried journalists might treat you in a way that you might consider a bit rude. Don't let it rile you; it probably has less to do with you than with a tight deadline or a really heavy workload. Keep your communications courteous, and don't get into a flame war.*

When Tara was working in PR for a living, her goal was to be the PR person that journalists were glad to hear from. She wanted to distribute such great stuff, in such an easy-to-use format, that journalists would always be glad to see her name in their inboxes. She facilitated this by trying to always answer requests for more information promptly and helping in any way she could.

Try to approach your journalist contacts the same way. A lot of books on publicity make the point over and over again that journalists need PR people; they need them for leads and for help in making the news. That's true; but it's also true that it's a symbiotic relationship. You don't inherently deserve coverage;

you earn it. One way you earn it is by distributing high-quality information about high-quality products and services.

One of the best ways to learn how to work with journalists is by listening to what they say about the whole PR process. Several places on the Web can give you Dos and Don'ts on contacting journalists via e-mail.

THE CARE & FEEDING OF THE PRESS

http://www.netpress.org/careandfeeding.html

This site was written for members of the PR profession by journalists who have a whole bunch of sad stories to tell. Thrill as you get several good ideas for press releases. Chill as you look at some truly bad examples of PR writing. Cringe as you recognize mistakes you might have made had you not known better.

TIPS AND TRICKS FOR THE PUBLIC RELATIONS CLUELESS

http://www.strom.com/awards/27.html

David Strom is a long-time computer journalist who puts together a nice package of PR tips and tricks on this page. Our favorite tip is number seven: "Learn the lost art of follow-through."

PRESS RELEASE TIPS FOR PR PEOPLE

http://marketing.tenagra.com/releases.html

Andrew Kantor (*not* Andy), senior editor of *Internet World*, gives you eight tips to make his and other editors' lives easier. Take heed.

HALLAHAN COURSE RESOURCES: PUBLICITY PRIMER

http://lamar.colostate.edu/~hallahan/hpubty.htm

If you need a lot of inspiration, or aren't clear on what makes good subject for news, you need to check out this site. It consists of several lists—four keys to success in publicity, a publicity materials checklist, etc.

INTERNET NEWS BUREAU: TIPS ON WRITING AND MEDIA RELATIONS

http://www.newsbureau.com/tips/

This site is a clearinghouse of links for PR hints and tips.

HOW TO GET THE PRESS ON YOUR SIDE

http://www.frugalfun.com/press.html

Shel Horowitz, author and marketing whiz, provides several ideas for getting publicity. Shel's ideas are oriented toward low-budget marketing and small-business marketers. He also has a free monthly newsletter of marketing tips available.

Your initial series of contacts will take a lot of time. You're going to have to send a lot of e-mail and write a lot of personal notes. There's going to be a lot of research involved. The key to getting it all done is breaking it down into doable chunks.

Your initial promotion, to get everything moving, will take a lot of time, but don't look at it like you're going to have to do that much researching and contacting forever. John Kremer, a renowned expert on book promotion, puts forth the idea of just doing five promotionally oriented things a day (he calls this the Rule of Five). Just five things a day will build into a strong, ongoing effort. You'll maintain a lot of momentum and get into the habit of looking for promotional opportunities.

Sooner or later you'll be all done. You'll have finished all your research, checked all your resources, and contacted all the editors you want. Does this mean that you just sit back on your laurels and wait for the reviews to go in? Heck no! Your real work—establishing relationships with the press and staying in touch—has just begun.

Track Your Contacts—*After you've developed a media contact list, you can do something as elaborate as working with a customized contact database (see Chapter 2, What You Need Before You Start), or something as simple as just keeping copies of all the e-mails you send to a journalist. Just make sure you do something to track when you've contacted a journalist, what you sent, and what the response was. It'll keep you from re-sending information, and help you learn more about what the journalist does and does not want to see.*

MASS MAILINGS

If you have a large list of journalists' e-mail addresses, you may want to consider a mass mailing. Rather than contacting journalists one by one, you can contact a thousand or two at the same time.

You can use this method in a number of ways. You could use it to distribute press releases (see Chapter 17, *Electronic Press Releases*), for instance. Peter uses it to ask journalists if they want review copies of his books. Now, we're not talking about spam. First, you shouldn't send e-mails to everyone on a list—you should only pick appropriate media contacts. If you're trying to distribute review copies of a book about the economics of yak herding, don't send e-mails to the music and sports magazines.

Be Careful with Mass Mailings—*Mass mailing lots of journalists makes Tara nervous. She'd rather e-mail one tenth as many and give them lots of attention because she feels that enhances her chance of coverage.*

Secondly, it's possible to use lists of media contacts made up of e-mail addresses of journalists who have asked to be included. Now, this means that many of these addresses will be e-mail addresses that get a lot of traffic—not so much personal addresses, but addresses set up to catch press releases and various other clutter. That doesn't mean that mailing to these addresses won't work, though. Peter generally gets a 10–20 percent favorable response when mailing to a targeted list looking for book reviewers.

How, then, do you mail to all these people? The simplest way is to copy the e-mail addresses and paste them into an e-mail message, but as we've mentioned before, you should *not* paste hundreds of e-mail addresses into the To: or Cc: line. Use the Bcc: line.

But even pasting addresses into the Bcc: line isn't the best way to handle a mass mailing, though. Some e-mail programs won't like you pasting hundreds, perhaps thousands, of addresses into the Bcc: line. Wouldn't it be nice if you could do a simple mail merge, putting the journalists' first names at the top of the messages?

A number of mail-merge programs can help you personalize mass e-mails, and some contact-management programs (see Chapter 2, *What You Need Before You Start*) have e-mail merge utilities built in.

Peter has worked with two mail-merge programs **Campaign** (http://www.arialsoftware.com/), and **WorldMerge** (http://www.coloradosoft.com). Campaign has significant bugs and user-interface problems. Campaign is unusual in that it can pull data out of a database. Most mail-merge programs require that you import the addresses you want to work with into the program's own database; but Campaign allows you to point to a database—for instance, to an Access database—and then tell it which fields to pull data from. It provides a quick way to create and run a mail-merge campaign, once you understand how to work it…but it may take a little while to learn. It even allows you to modify individually merged messages. For instance, you can generate 1,000 different mail-merged messages, each with the recipient's name at the top of the message. Then, before you send the messages, you can go in and modify some of them individually—add a personal note to a few of the messages, for instance. It's a great little program, despite the design problems and bugs.

You can try a demo version of Campaign, which you can use as long as you want for free. However, it appends an advertising message to the end of each message, so you probably won't want to use it for real. The full version of

Campaign costs $995 from Arial Software. WorldMerge is the easier of the programs that Peter's tried, and it will also pull data out of a database. Peter stores his data in an Access database, points to the database within WorldMerge, and then sets up a *query* (that is, tells WorldMerge how to choose which contacts to send to). It doesn't have some of Campaign's advanced features. On the other hand, it's much easier to use, and costs only $49. There is a free demo available from the WorldMerge site. There are other mail-merge programs available:

eMerge (For the Mac—$99)
http://www.galleon.com/

InfoPress Email-On-Demand ($995)
http://www.castelle.com/

WWMail ($39.95)
http://wizardware.com/

THE LONG-TERM VIEW: STAYING IN TOUCH

With some editors and journalists, you don't really click. You send them your information, and they might give you a review, and they might not, and the whole thing's pretty lukewarm.

On the other hand, there are some editors with whom you really hit it off. You have a good time talking product and they seem interested in your product. They may or may not agree with your views, and they may have some concerns about your product, but they give you good feedback. This sounds like the beginning of a beautiful friendship; but it's only a beginning. You're going to have to do some work to keep it up, as discussed in the following sections.

Read

It sounds like a no-brainer that you need to read if you want to keep up a relationship with journalists. You want them to be interested in you. Be interested in them! Read their stuff and drop them a note every now and again when you have a reaction to one of their stories. (Don't pepper them every week with "Hi! Great column!" Give them some feedback.) Let them know what you think about their stuff. You don't have to be a sycophant. If you disagree say so. Sometimes a well-thought-out, articulate disagreement is more engaging than the most ardent fan letter.

Help Them

If you see something you think a journalist would be interested in, send it their way. However, keep a balance—don't send ten resources a day, and don't send knuckleheaded information (like chain letters, scams, and obvious resources). Don't be too pushy when using a referral; don't focus on your own online resources and nothing else. Rather, try to be unbiased, and refer to your own resources only when they are really appropriate.

But Don't Fake It—*Don't think you're interested enough in a journalist to read their stuff? Then don't read it. We're not advocating that you read stories you don't care about. Your apathy will show in your communications, and we're not out to create a nation of phonies.*

Assume Nothing

When building a relationship with a journalist, some promoters think they only have to do so much helping, communicating, and relationship building, and then they will have earned coverage from the journalist. Hogwash.

This is not a game of basketball. You shouldn't be keeping score of how many resources you've referred to journalists, how many ideas you've given them, or how much feedback you've offered. Would you track how many movies you've recommended to your friends, or how many favors you've done them, and then demand that they do you a favor before you'd be friends anymore? Your focus should be on helping reporters do their jobs better. If your helping involves a reporter using you in a story or some other coverage, great. If it doesn't, you have still positioned yourself well in the mind of the journalist.

When those journalists need something in your field of expertise, they'll likely think of you. Besides, not everything is within a journalist's control. A journalist may interview you, get several quotes, and then everything in the story that referred to you and your company may get cut out. This happens all the time. It's happened to both of us now and then. For instance, Peter's e-mail newsletter was just about to be named by a major computer magazine as one of the most useful newsletters on the Internet…when the sidebar containing that piece of praise was cut from the article at the last moment.

Do you feel that building a relationship with a journalist doesn't provide enough immediate benefit to be worth your time? Fine; consider the fact that you will have participated in a dialogue with a journalist that will have taught you a lot about how to do your public relations better. You'll also get good karma and the Poor Richard's Seal of Approval. But don't decide that it's not fair, or unjust, if you don't get editorial coverage after you've been communicating with a journalist for six months and giving good resources.

Are there times when you should consider investing less time in your relationships with journalists? Sure. When they repeatedly ask for review copies of your product and never seem to review anything. When they take up huge amounts of your time—say, two or three hours at a stretch—getting help on a story, do this several times, and never attribute the information you provide or get a quote from you. There's a difference between a mutually beneficial relationship and getting run over.

You might notice a similarity here between the methods we're discussing for keeping in touch with customers and prospects, and those for keeping in touch with journalists. In both instances, you're trying to build credibility and help the person you're contacting. A customer or prospect wants to solve a particular problem. A journalist wants to get a story researched or written. Come at it from that perspective—from what they want and what they need.

Putting together your list of journalists will take the most time initially. Contacting them will also take a lot of time, but since you'll get some immediate feedback, you'll find it's a lot more fun; but where you can really get a lot from this chapter, both personally and professionally, is investing some time and effort in building relationships. We recommend you make this an ongoing priority. Take advantage of John Kremer's Rule of Five and build some momentum toward your promotion.

BONUS TIP: GETTING JOURNALISTS TO COME TO YOU

Ongoing promotion is important, but a lot of it is a game of chance. When you send a news release to journalists, you're hoping that your information will be so compelling and interesting that they'll want to do a story on it right away, or that they're getting ready to do a story on your field and that they can use your information.

Of course, if you're using an editorial-calendar service (a service you can purchase from Media Map, Press Access, or other companies that let you know a publication's schedule of coverage throughout the year) you'll know when the publication is going to cover a certain topic, which can help you decide when you should approach them for coverage. But the editorial calendars change, and daily publications, like newspapers, are much more flexible. One major event may cause the coverage to shift completely from a couple of days to a couple of weeks.

When something like this happens, journalists need to be able to find a source of expertise for the topics they're writing about. They can do that via search engines (and that's one reason to promote your Web page), but they also use their own sources of experts. If you're willing to invest a little money (from about a hundred dollars to several thousand dollars), you can be a part of these online resources.

Online Expert and Guest Resources

There are many places online where you can position yourself as an expert. While "ask an expert" sites are becoming more common these days, the sites following are aimed at journalists seeking resources.

THE EXPERTISE CENTER

http://www.expertcenter.net

The Expertise Center provides a listing of speakers, consultants, and trainers. This site will provide you with three levels of listings. A basic listing (all your contact information except for a Web page) is free. A link to a Web page costs $150 per year. A full business presence on the Web varies in price. This site is oriented more towards speakers and those who make public appearances.

EXPERTS DIRECTORY

http://www.experts.com/

This site positions itself as the Internet's Worldwide Directory of Experts. It lists several different types of experts and resources, including breaking them out by "New and Notable," "Political Resources," etc. It's also searchable. A basic listing on this site will cost you $249 for the first year and $195 for every year after that. There are several other options here—you can set up a guest book for your page, include a form on your Web page, get your entire Web site hosted with the Experts Directory, etc.

GUESTFINDER

http://www.guestfinder.com/

GuestFinder is extremely media-oriented. As you might guess from the name of the site, GuestFinder is oriented towards guests—of radio, television, newspaper, or magazine interviews. GuestFinder is searchable and also lists guests by category. Guests are also mentioned on the front page when current events come up that coincide with the guests' interests. GuestFinder does have certain requirements. Authors must have a book listed in *Books in Print*. Spokespeople must be the official listed contact for the organization listed on their page. Speakers must be experienced professional speakers, and experts must be recognized experts in their fields. These restrictions make for a high-quality guest list. However, if you're kind of unusual and off-beat, but still an expert, consider GuestFinder anyway (its guests include a man who eats bugs, for instance). GuestFinder contacts the media monthly to alert them to new site and guest information. A page listing for this site costs $199 a year.

NPC DIRECTORY OF NEWS SOURCES

http://npc.press.org/who/sources.htm

A service of the National Press Club, the NPC Directory of News Sources is a searchable directory of news sources. Obviously the clout of the NPC adds a lot of appeal to this site, and the sources seem to lean more toward news resources and less toward guest resources like GuestFinder. Check out the quotes on the site to get an idea of who's using this directory. With this directory, you can do two things: submit a listing or buy an ad. A 100-word listing costs $445. A 100-word listing with a logo is $460. Adding your listing to more than two directory topics costs extra. An ad is a bit more expensive; a full-page ad starts at $1,025, and a half-page ad starts at $695.

PROFNET

http://www.profnet.com/

ProfNet is designed to help reporters who are researching stories. Its expert database contains leads on over 4,200 different expert sources. ProfNet Search sends out media inquires to ProfNet members four times per day. (Queries are divided into categories, which you can choose, so you aren't get smothered with inappropriate queries.) ProfNet also has a searchable experts database, which at this writing is undergoing a transition. ProfNet expects to automate the addition of profiles, though, so if you're reading this after September 2000, check it out.

YEARBOOKNEWS.COM

http://www.yearbooknews.com/

YearbookNews.Com is the online version of the *Yearbook of Experts, Authorities & Spokespersons*, a large book you might have seen at your local library. The print version of this resource is entering its twentieth year, and currently lists almost 1,500 people. The cost to be included in the Web and print versions of the Yearbook is $695. While you might have to wait to be put in the print version of the yearbook (it's only published once a year), you'll be added to the Web site almost immediately.

Will it Work?—*The sites mentioned in nearby sections of this chapter are great if you really are an expert or noted person. However, if you're not an expert, don't try to fake your way into the experts-only resources. You could lose your credibility and the money you've invested if you're kicked out of a listing. Even if you are an expert, that doesn't mean you'll be flooded with media inquiries. Some people have done well from some of these listings, while others haven't benefited much at all.*

Other Sources for Experts and Guests

There are plenty of other places online that list guest and expert resources for the media. Check out the following and see if you or your Web site is a fit.

> **Pitsco's Ask an Expert** (Experts from all over the Web who have volunteered to answer questions)
> http://www.askanexpert.com/

> **ShowIdeas** (An online magazine for radio and TV producers; listings start at $125/year)
> http://www.showideas.com/

> **BusinessWire** (Offers an Expert Source service)
> http://www.businesswire.com/

> **ExpertFind**
> http://www.expertfind.com/

You remember the old saw, "You never get a second chance to make a first impression?" It's just as true when making media contacts as when meeting your next-door neighbors. It's important to spend some time researching media materials, polishing your materials, and creating a great contact e-mail so you can make the best impression possible.

Once you've made the initial contact, you can make the most out of your promotion campaign by staying in touch with journalists, helping them do their jobs, and positioning yourself in a few online guides so that, when necessary, journalists can find you.

One important tool of the promoter or publicist is the *press release* (or *news release*, as some say it should be called). There are many tools available for sending out press releases; you can use press-release services, or perhaps your own e-mail program. In the next chapter, we'll take a look at the anatomy of press releases and your options for sending them out.

CHAPTER SEVENTEEN

Electronic Press Releases

Press releases—boring waste of time or powerful PR weapon? From their typewritten beginnings, they've been the way to get the company line out on any number of things—new products, new personnel, events, ideas, and other information. And in many cases they're a colossal waste of paper...or, in cyberspace, an enormous waste of perfectly good electrons. It doesn't have to be that way, though. *You* don't have to produce boring, pointless press releases.

In fact press releases can be a critical part of your promotions. In this chapter, we'll take a look at the whys and hows of press releases, give you a crash course on writing great press releases, and let you know how to distribute them.

WHY A PRESS RELEASE?

Millions of pages are being added to the Web every day. How do you stand out above the crowd? You use a press release and get the information on your new site to news desks all over the world. Whether your press release gets coverage is another matter, but getting the information to the press is the first step.

A new Web site isn't the only reason for a press release. You might also want to write a press release for any of the following reasons (and you may be able to come up with lots more):

- Announce the release of a new product or service
- Kick off a new sales event
- Respond to a national event or announcement by a competitor
- Announce significant personnel changes
- Keep in contact with shareholders

The press release is a great package into which you can put information like this. It's an accepted format and is simple for journalists to read. It's also easy to archive on your Web site so visitors can get an idea of your history.

Are there topics that are inappropriate for a press release? Sure. Don't use a press release to nationally announce the fact that you've painted all your trucks. Don't use a press release to announce your Christmas party. Don't use a national press release to announce the fact that you now deliver to Elm Street in addition to Pine Street.

Remember the power of the Internet—you're reaching a global or national audience, depending on which distribution service (we'll cover those in the Press Release Distribution Services section) you use. You may have news that's appropriate to announce only in your town. In that case, call the business desk of your local newspaper and tell them what's up, or write a letter. Don't waste the money and effort of an Internet-distributed press release on local news. You've heard of the boy who cried wolf? You don't want to be the company who cried news; it's not only that you'll get a reputation for putting out bad press releases, but you'll also waste your time and money.

If you're not sure whether your local news deserves a national push, ask yourself whether you could see it on the AP wire as a unique or interesting happening. If in doubt, don't distribute.

What's AP? What's a Wire?—*AP is short for Associated Press. It sends news all over the world. Pick up your local newspaper and you'll see that a lot of stories come from AP. If you want to see stories from the AP, you can check out an AP wire feed— several of them, actually—at* http://wire.ap.org/.

When developing an idea for a news release, try to get a great hook. Focus on the benefit of what you're offering, not just the offering itself. For example, say you've created an online directory of chess clubs throughout the United States. (You're a company that sells chess strategy books, and you correctly figured it would be a good way to get people interested in chess to your site.) There are two ways you can angle this. The first is simply to announce that you've put up an online directory of chess clubs. Whoopdee do. The second is to promote your great new resource as devoted to bringing together chess aficionados all over the country and to promoting one of the oldest strategy games in the world.

See the difference? We've already said this a couple of times, but we want to repeat it until it's stamped on your brain in inch-high letters:

Nobody Cares Like You Do

Nobody cares about your product or service as much as you do. People care only about how it will benefit *them*. Make it easy for everybody by immediately letting them know the benefits through your marketing communications—and that includes your press releases. Press releases should focus on benefit-to-the-user. *Benefit, Benefit, Benefit.* Try this. Go to the **Yahoo! Press Releases** page (http://dir.yahoo.com/Business_and_Economy/Companies/News_and_Media/News_S ervices/Press_Releases/), and take a look at a few press releases. This page links to various press-release services, at which you can find many releases. Dig around and you'll find some that are good and some that are bad. And you'll probably discover that what characterizes a bad release is that it doesn't seem to be saying anything to you, or to anyone else probably. It's written by someone who doesn't understand that a press release has to be written from the standpoint of the reader—*what's in it for me?*—not the company issuing the release.

Could we make it any clearer? Probably not without getting even more annoying. Now that you know what's news and what's not, and now that you know how to slant your news so it's of interest to others besides yourself, you too, can put together a great press release. The next section explains how.

ANATOMY OF A GREAT PRESS RELEASE

Not all press releases are created equal. Putting a little extra time into making sure you have an excellent headline and compelling content will mean the difference between having your press release read and having it ignored. And this, of course, affects your chance of coverage. There are two things to focus on when writing the press release: the headline and the body. There are also a few other elements, like contact information, to consider as well. Let's begin with the headline.

Headlines

Let's look at an example to illustrate how important a good headline is. Figure 17.1 is a screen shot of BusinessWire's list of high-tech news releases.

As you can see, all this screen contains is a stack of news release headlines. They're all crammed together and they're kind of hard to read. Tara reads the BusinessWire press release summary every day, and that's a big document. Usually she just skims it, looking for headlines that jump out.

You need to write a headline that stands out from the pack on a list such as this. Let's take a look at some imaginary scenarios with good and bad headlines.

Scenario—You're announcing a new service to sell custom-designed letter openers to large corporations.

Bad Headline—Custom-Designed Letter Openers Now Available

Good Headline—New Service Creates Unique, Personalized Desk Tools for Businesses

The Big Idea—The first headline attracts only those who are interested in letter openers. The second headline, on the other hand, attracts anyone

FIGURE 17.1: BusinessWire's High-tech News Releases.

who's interested in desk tools (ambiguous enough to get people curious), personalized items for business, and so on. Even if they're not specifically interested in letter openers, by making your headline compelling you get them to read the body of the news release. You get two chances to get them interested in who you are and what you're doing.

Scenario—You've just hired a former high-level executive to run your company's marketing operations.

Bad Headline—Chris So-and-so named Marketing VP of BadExampleCo

Good Headline—Former Fortune 500 COO Named Marketing VP of GoodExampleCo

The Big Idea—Journalists read about hundreds, sometimes thousands, of people per day. You can't expect them to remember who Chris So-and-so is (unless his real name is Ted Turner or Michael Jordan). Instead of naming a name, name an accomplishment. Journalists might not know who Chris is, but they know that a former Fortune 500 COO could be serious news. If the company for which Chris So-and-so has high visibility, like Ford or Microsoft, use that instead.

Scenario—You're a computer company giving away uninterruptible power supplies in the wake of a recent series of lightning storms in your area.

Bad Headline—BadExampleCo Offers New Power Supplies to Storm Victims

Good Headline—GoodExampleCo Vows to Give Away 5,000 Power Supplies After Lighting Storms

The Big Idea—In the first headline, it isn't clear that your company is actually giving away power supplies. The extent of your generosity also isn't clear. Give away and 5,000 make a real splash.

Creating a great headline is a balancing act. You want to give a lot of detail without using too many words. You want to create interest without giving away the entire release's contents. And you want to create excitement without appearing to be nothing but hype. The headline should also flow easily into the body of the news release.

How Long Is a Good Headline?—*You can't judge the impact of a headline by its length. You can get a lot across in just seven or eight words. If you find your headline going beyond a dozen words, consider a subheadline, like this:* <u>Headline</u>: *BadExampleCo Vows to Give Away 5,000 Power Supplies* <u>Subheadline</u>: *Company to help community after devastating lightning storms.*

The Body of the Release

News releases have a structure that makes them most effective. They're not as elegant as haiku, of course, but by putting each element in its place, you can create an effective release. Tara's found that the following structure for a news release works well.

FIRST PARAGRAPH—OVERVIEW

This should be a one-paragraph summary of the entire news release, giving editors enough information that they can decide how valuable the release is to them without having to read the whole the whole thing.

> ***Example:*** *Following the lightning storms that took place in North Carolina last week, BadExampleCo pledged to give away 5,000 uninterruptible power supplies to small-business owners who lost data due to power outages.*

SECOND PARAGRAPH—A FEW DETAILS

Add a few details to the summary. The details shouldn't be critical, but should help flesh out the summary.

Example: GoodExampleCo's giveaway comes in the wake of a week's worth of lightning storms that caused over 100 power outages and destroyed an estimated $4 million worth of unsaved data.

THIRD PARAGRAPH—A QUOTE

A quote should support the press release. If you've read a lot of press releases, you know the quotes sound canned ("'This is a great day in the history of BadExampleCo,' said CEO John BadExample."). Make the quote relevant to the story, something that journalists can follow up on if they decide to pursue the story. You can add a little descriptive information (and a statistic works well) but try to make the quote the core of the paragraph.

Example: "We feel we should support the community," said GoodExampleCo CEO John GoodExample. "The data loss caused by this storm was devastating. Since we can do something to prevent this in the future, and help the economy of North Carolina, we will."

A Little Trick: Include Ticker Symbols—*Here's a little trick we learned from our newsletter-publishing friend,* **Randy Cassingham** *(http://ThisIs True.com/). When he writes press releases he tries to include the names and stock-market ticker symbols of major companies—Netscape (NSCP), Microsoft (MSFT), and so on. Many people search press-release archives for company names and their ticker symbols. Of course you should only mention companies that are relevant to the press release—BusinessWire, at least, discourages this use of stock symbols and warns its clients of inappropriate stock symbol use in press releases.*

THE REST—INFORMATION FROM MOST TO LEAST IMPORTANT

You may have read about an *inverted pyramid* form of news release, where the most important information should appear early in the news release, followed by less and less vital information. That seems to work well. Tara has had press releases run in a publication practically as-is, which is great when it happens because the publication runs exactly your point of view, with no details removed. That doesn't happen often, however. What does happen is that the editor might not have time to read all the way through your press release, so you should make sure all the important stuff is really early on.

Other Body Elements

Once you have the essential "who, what, where" in the release, there are a few more things you should address to round out the press release.

About the company—*About the company* information is vital when you're a publicly held company (since you may be required to disclose certain information by the Federal Exchange Commission), and helpful if you're a small company or unusual in your structure or product offerings. After the subject of the press release has been covered, a couple of paragraphs outlining your company, services, and products are helpful. Sometimes you'll see a press release with six paragraphs of body information and six paragraphs of "About the company" information. Every product the company has ever released is listed, every office they have around the world is listed, several top executives are mentioned by name, etc. That strikes us as overkill; we don't recommend it.

Press Release Length—*A question we sometimes hear is, "How long should a press release be?" The smart-aleck answer to that question is long enough to say what needs to be said. A more helpful answer is probably not more than 400–500 words. If your release requires more space, use it, but realize you'll pay distribution services more for sending out longer releases. Leave out enough information so that the editor has to follow-up, but don't leave out so much that it isn't clear what the release is announcing.*

Disclaimer—If you're a publicly held company and are making statements about your earnings or your future activities, you might have to insert a disclaimer about the contents of the news release being forward-looking statements or something like that. Be sure to put this disclaimer after the rest of text, before any trademark statements, and before your contact information.

Trademark statement—Sometimes, especially if you're announcing a partnership, you'll end up scattering a lot of registered trademarks throughout your press release. At the end of the press release copy—after the body of the information and any disclaimers—your trademark statement makes a good wrap-up paragraph. Some people put the trademark statement at the absolute end of the news release—after the body copy and contact information. We think that if it's at the absolute end like that, it won't get read. On the other hand, it'll be easy to refer to if an editor needs to check the status of a trademark mentioned in your news release.

Contact information—You're going to think this is pretty basic, but contact information is possibly the most vital part of your news release. You write a riveting headline. You write a mind-bending news release body. The editors who read it are absolutely falling all over themselves to run it in their publication; but what if they can't contact you to get additional information or clarify something in the news release? Make sure that you have thorough contact information: name, phone number, address, and *e-mail address!* You'd be amazed at how many press releases available online don't include e-mail addresses. (We have words—and they're not nice words—for Internet companies that don't bother to include e-mail addresses with their press releases.) Fax numbers are optional. Try to list two contact people, so if there's a problem with reaching one, an editor can try for another.

Basic Press Releases—*If you're using a press release to announce an event, or provide basic information, you don't have to create the sort of formal, fully fleshed-out press release that we've described in this chapter. Instead, you can merely list the 5 W's and fill in the blanks that way, like this:* **Who: What: Where: When: Why:** *Every W should have an explanation of no more than a paragraph. Bear in mind, though, that this release format doesn't work if you have a lot to say. If you try to use this to fill out a product launch news release and the Why: section takes up about four paragraphs, it's better just to write a regular press release.*

Different press-release distribution services include different levels of contact information in their press releases, but when you're distributing news releases yourself, make sure that you have as much contact information as possible. And while we're on the subject of press releases, we might as well mention one of Tara's pet peeves: corporate press release archives without PR contact information. When you add press releases to your corporate archives, make sure that PR contact information remains available in the archives, either from a separate page or on the press releases themselves.

Once you've written the news release, proofread it. Twice. Then have someone else proofread it (preferably a professional editor). And then check to make sure all the contact information works. (Would you be surprised if we told you we've tried to contact companies after reading press releases, only to discover the contact e-mail address provided in the release didn't work?) By the way, this is a good rule of thumb for *all* communications that include cyberspace addresses—e-mail addresses, URLs, FTP site names, and so on. Always check that what you wrote is correct. It doesn't matter too much if you slightly misspell your street address or city name; we may complain about the post office, but correspondence will probably still get through; but make a mistake with a single character in your e-mail address or URL, and it's as good as useless. Finally, find someone who isn't familiar with your company to read your press release. Ask whether everything's clear. Ask what your reader thought the press release was about. Sometimes if you know your company really well, you make assumptions about how much other people know. Make sure that someone outside your company can read your press release and get the gist of what you're trying to say. (The reader doesn't have to know anything about your new super-widget to know your press release is about an upgrade to version 2.0 of the widget.)

DISTRIBUTING PRESS RELEASES

It doesn't matter how good your press release is; it's no good to you unless you can get people to read it. You have to find some way to distribute it to the right people. You can either distribute a press release yourself, or you can hire a service to do it.

If you have a general press release that would be of interest to a lot of people, a press-release distribution service can help you get your message out to writers and editors you might not even know about. On the other hand, if your news release is of interest to only a narrow range of people, you might be able to reach all of them yourself without paying for a press-release service.

***Press Releases for Other Purposes**—You can use a press release for some of the announcement services like Net-Happenings (see Chapter 8, Other Places to Register Your Site), but you might want to cut it down to the most essential 200–300 words. Don't use a really long press release for announcement services; it won't get read.*

For example, let's say you represent an organization dedicated to the prevention of infant blindness. Your potential audience is anyone concerned about their kids' health. That's a pretty large audience. You should use a press-release distribution service. On the other hand, you might represent a medical company that makes a device that tests the sensitivity of infant corneas to light. Your potential audience includes health clinics and hospitals. That's a narrow audience. You could still use a press-release service, but you'd want to make sure that you could target medical journals and other relevant publications and editors.

Distributing press releases via e-mail is a lot like distributing newsletters. (If you've followed the instructions of the last couple of chapters, you should have a nice list of journalists and publications that are appropriate to your product or service.) Make sure the press release is in plain text, and send it in the body of the e-mail—and not as an e-mail attachment. Make sure there are blank lines between paragraphs so the text of the news release is easy to read. Make sure the lines of the press release are not more than about 60–65 characters.

Also, try to personalize the press releases. Include some kind of salutation and an informal introduction to the press release—a sentence or two about why the press release is relevant to them.

One more thing: put the headline of the news release in both the subject line and the body of the e-mail message. If the editor copies the body of the e-mail message, you want to make sure the copy includes the headline.

Even if you've gathered a great list of editors together from all your research, consider using a press-release distribution service if you have a general-interest or large audience. Even if you did thousands of hours of research, you probably didn't find every appropriate editor for your news release. Press-release distribution services can help you fill in the holes.

When it comes to press-release distribution services, there are the big two online services: BusinessWire and PR Newswire. There are the also other services that offer more customized help, specialized news-release distribution (news releases sent to specialized lists of editors), and the ability to put your news release on the Internet for free.

When Should You Distribute?—*When it comes to press releases, not all days are created equal. Mondays seem to have an inordinately high number of press releases, while Fridays are not as busy. Tara doesn't like sending out news releases on Mondays because she doesn't want to get lost in the shuffle of editors catching up on weekend news. She also doesn't like sending releases out on Fridays because who knows which editors have decided to take a three-day weekend? Unless you have an emergency, don't distribute press releases on the weekend; you'll miss a lot of editors who don't monitor the wire on the weekend. And please—if you're a public company and you have to give bad news, don't do it on Friday just after the closing bell. It's a cheap trick and it doesn't work anyway.*

The Big Services

These are the big distribution services: BusinessWire and PRNewswire. They can cost you some money, but on the other hand, they have a reach that smaller press wires may not be able to achieve for you.

BUSINESSWIRE

http://www.businesswire.com/

BusinessWire is one of the largest distribution services. BusinessWire offers press-release distribution services worldwide. It distributes to thousands of television stations, radio stations, newspapers, magazines, wire services, and other media. In addition to plain-text releases, it can also distribute photographs, streaming video, streaming audio, spreadsheets, and even PowerPoint presentations. Not only does this service offer national and global distribution of press releases, it can also distribute to particular states and special-interest markets (college newspapers, sports media, legal media, etc.). The cost for distributing a release through BusinessWire depends on what kind of release you send and to what markets you send it. BusinessWire charges for a certain number of words, with an additional charge for more words (yet another reason that you don't want to write an overly long news release). BusinessWire also has a membership that offers you the ability to distribute a corporate profile, a free newsletter, recaps of your news release on headline roundup services, and a certain amount of media monitoring for mention of your news.

BusinessWire offers other services in addition to just distributing news releases. For a fee, you can be added to BusinessWire's Expert Source service, which helps connect journalists to experts of the day. If you don't want to keep a press-release archive on the Web, you can keep one on BusinessWire with its Electronic Media Kit service. BusinessWire even helps you design a Web site.

PR NEWSWIRE

http://www.prnewswire.com/

PR Newswire also distributes news releases worldwide, and, like BusinessWire, it offers distribution to specialty media groups and can even create media sites. PR Newswire, like BusinessWire, also offers a variety of fax services, including fax-on-call services and fax distribution. PR Newswire's release headlines are a lot easier to read online, since they're not all stacked up together, as you can see in Figure 17.2.

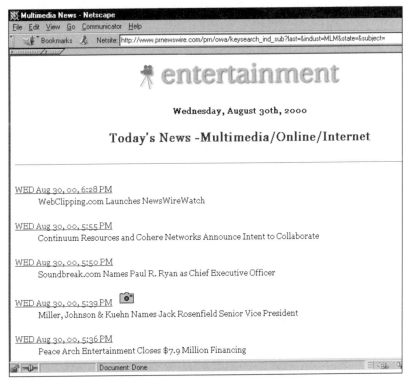

FIGURE 17.2: Reading PR Newswire press releases online.

PR Newswire charges by the number of words in the press release, and of course charges vary depending on how widely you distribute the press release.

BusinessWire and PR Newswire are the two biggest press-release distributors online, and because of this you'll find that you get a lot of bonus distribution. Your press release will show up in Northern Light's specialty publications search, Excite's NewsTracker, and the Dow Jones Publications Library. It'll end up on NewsPage and other online newsgathering services. You'll get a lot of extra reach if you use these extremely popular services.

Another Option

If you need lots of press releases distributed and you don't mind that they don't have as wide a reach as "the big two," consider M2 PressWIRE.

M2 PRESSWIRE

http://www.presswire.net/

M2 PressWIRE is also a large service, and is distributed on some Web news-gathering services like NewsAlert. However, the news releases it distributes do not appear to be archived on as many Web sites and databases as either BusinessWire or PR Newswire. Unlike PR Newswire and BusinessWire, however, M2 PressWIRE sells memberships to its newswire. Once you've paid for a membership (currently $160), you can send as many releases using its wire services as you like. You don't pay by the length of release or by to whom you're sending the release. However, the type of data that it will transmit is limited. It seems to be primarily text; M2 PressWIRE gives no indication that it transmits any nontext information like audio or video.

Many other press-release distribution services offer large-scale media distribution. The following list gives you an idea of just a few of them:

Bacon's Info (Bacon's offers a wide variety of publicity tools and services; press-release distribution is just one of them)
http://www.baconsinfo.com/

The Press Release Network (Dubai, United Arab Emirates; strengths include distribution to global, India, and Middle East media)
http://www.pressreleasenetwork.com/

Internet Wire (Distribution to over 6,300 media for $275; also offers multiple-release rates)
http://www.gina.com/

PRESSline Database for Press Releases
http://www.us.pressline.com/

Yahoo!'s Press Release page
http://dir.yahoo.com/Business_and_Economy/Companies/News_and_Media/News
_Services/Press_Releases/

"Handmade" Press-Release Distribution

Sometimes, especially with a large potential audience, sending out press releases en masse can be the best way of reaching the editors who might be interested in your product or service. However if your audience is smaller, or your product or service unusual, or you simply want distribution with a more human touch, you might want to check out handmade press-release distributors. These are distributors that specialize in custom delivery of press releases, *opt-in* lists for journalists (that is, e-mail lists that journalists can choose to join, or at least consent to be added to), and specific media targeting.

XPRESS PRESS

http://www.xpresspress.com/

Xpress Press offers an opt-in distribution service for journalists who are interested in receiving press releases. Journalists request to be added to the Xpress Press service and indicate what type of releases they're interested in. When a company wants to distribute a press release via Xpress Press, Xpress Press goes through its database and finds journalists who are appropriate for that news release. In other words, a custom list targeted toward the release is built every time the service is used.

Xpress Press targets pretty well, too. Tara receives its research-oriented releases and has been happy with the quality and appropriateness of the materials she has received. Every now and again Xpress Press gets one wrong, but much of the time its right.

Sending a release via Xpress Press is $225. (Xpress Press will write the release for you for an additional charge.) Since a custom distribution list is created for every release that goes out, there's no way to know in advance how many editors will get your release, but Xpress Press does generate a list of the media contacted when the job is done.

If you have an unusual news release or news that defies the typical categories that are available through other distribution services, Xpress Press would be a good resource to investigate.

URLWIRE

http://www.urlwire.com/

We spoke in the last chapter about building relationships with journalists. It appears that the whole idea behind URLWire is building relationships with journalists full-time. Eric Ward, the guy behind URLWire, will build a distribution list for you from his list of over 3,000 contacts around the world. Like Xpress Press, his is an opt-in list of journalists who have asked to hear about specific topics. As you might guess from the name, Eric only distributes news on Web-related topics. If you want to distribute your press release on new financing or the nifty delivery trucks you just bought, go somewhere else. If you really want to go all-out with your promotion, have a highly specialized resource, or have an unusual resource that defies categorization, investigate URLWire.

NETPOST

http://www.netpost.com/

Eric Ward also has a service called NetPOST, a similarly detailed and customized service. The difference is that NetPOST is for publicizing your Web site to search engines and subject listings, and isn't for distributing news releases.

TARGETED PRESS RELEASES

Maybe you want to target your releases but you don't need the customization levels of these services. There are some services that target releases without building customized lists. Check out these sites:

BookFlash (Promotes books)
http://www.bookflash.com/

Collegiate Presswire (Distributes to college newspapers)
http://www.cpwire.com/

eworldwire (Can customize by several factors, including category, state, and area code)
http://www.eworldwire.com/

News Bureau (Offers targeted releases in a variety of categories, including food and drink, travel, and sports)
http://www.newsbureau.com/

Press Flash
http://www.pressflash.com/

PRWeb (Free posting of news releases in dozens of different categories)
http://www.prweb.com/

TechWire (Promotes technology information)
http://www.ezwire.com/

Yahoo!—Press Releases
http://dir.yahoo.com/Business_and_Economy/Business_to_Business/News_and_
Media/News_Services/Press_Releases/

This chapter and the previous two give you a crash course in media contact: how to find editors, how to contact them, how to make the most of that great power tool e-mail, and finally how to write and distribute press releases. A lot of the skills you'll gain in the online world will carry over into the offline world, too, as you go about promoting your product and service. In fact, there's a lot of real-world promotion you can do to give your online concerns—Web sites, newsletters, or what have you—a push. In the next chapter, we'll take a look at offline promotion possibilities and why they shouldn't be neglected.

PART V
OUTSIDE
THE INTERNET

CHAPTER EIGHTEEN

Real-World Promotions

If you focus too closely on the Internet, you're missing the big picture. Of course everyone assumes that the Internet *is* the big picture. They think that from now on, everything can be done online, so there's no need to worry about the offline world. This attitude doesn't make a lot of sense. The Internet is new, so new that most people aren't using it as much as they're using other media like televisions and newspapers. (Actually, recent studies have shown that a lot of people like to watch TV and surf the Internet at the same time.)

The real world is full of ways to reach millions of people at once—radio, TV, magazines, and newspapers. How many places on the Internet can you reach millions of people at once? Few—and the ones where you can are expensive—yet there are many such opportunities in the real world.

Experienced Internet marketers know that one of the best ways to get people to visit their Web site is to leave the Internet for a while and go looking for people out in the real world. Surveys of users show that one of the primary ways in which people learn about new Web sites is through the *non*-Internet media. You've noticed the big Internet companies advertising on TV and in national magazines, haven't you? The Internet is merely a tool. It has a number of unusual and remarkable characteristics, but these characteristics are not such that the Internet can replace all other tools. So let's consider what you can do *off* the Internet to promote your business enterprise *on* the Internet. Let's start with the simple stuff—your print materials. Then we'll explore the possibilities of a real "cyberspace"—radio—and the possibilities of advertorials.

DON'T FORGET YOUR PRINT ADS

We've seen dozens of print materials—such as flyers and brochures—from companies that seem ashamed of their Web sites. For instance, one small publishing company, selling books and software, has a flyer that explains how to place orders; it provides the full street address, a telephone number, and even a toll-free phone number; but it includes neither an e-mail address nor a Web site

URL. Yet the company has both a Web site and an e-mail address. So why aren't they on the flyer?

One reason might be that the company has a lousy Web site. Perhaps it's a billboard-style Web site—it just sits there in cyberspace, a couple of pages of vague description about the company and its products. It gives no way to order online, and no way even to find much information online. Perhaps the Web site isn't mentioned because the company doesn't see how to get any value out of it, and the Web site is there only to catch people who pass by in cyberspace—which it will rarely do, unless people already know where it is. Why isn't the information in the flyer online?

This sort of thing is still common—companies have Web sites and e-mail addresses, but don't mention them in their print ads. It's a simple step to include your cyberspace addresses in everything you print—on business cards, in newspaper ads, Yellow Page ads, brochures, flyers, and everything else. If you put your phone number on these things, why not your e-mail address and URL? If your Web site provides value to your customers and prospective clients—if it provides information and customer support, a way to order online, and ancillary services that you've created as a complementary service—don't hide all this. Let people know about it.

Including Your E-Mail Address Isn't Always Good*—If you're bad at answering e-mail, or your customers often have stock questions that could be answered by visiting your Web site, don't include your e-mail address in your ads. Just use the URL.*

Don't just put your URL in your print ads, though—explain *why* people should visit your site. Mention the services you offer, and give people a reason to come to your site. If you plan to use your Web site as an extension of your business—as a way to reduce order-taking and customer-service costs, for instance—then send your customers in the right direction. Mention, for example, that your customers can get the latest product information at your site. (They can, can't they?) That's important to many people in this instant-gratification world. People want information right away, and your Web site is a way to provide it.

Here's an example of a simple, yet effective, use of print materials. *Mile High Comics*, a chain of comic stores in Denver, CO, distributes flyers at science-fiction conferences. All people need to do is fill in their e-mail addresses on a form and drop it in a box; Mile High Comics then adds these people to its mailing list. (Why doesn't Mile High Comics simply provide its e-mail address and tell people to e-mail them to subscribe? Because the more hoops people have to jump through, the less likely they are to do something. It's better to grab someone's e-mail address now on a paper form than hope they remember to subscribe when they get home.) This is an easy thing to do, and something that can be combined with other forms of print advertising, too. For instance, your ads can have a line at the bottom saying: "Sign up for our free e-mail newsletter! E-mail us at signup@yakherding.com."

WEB CARDS

Here's a nice way to promote your Web site in a visual way: use Web cards. At least two companies on the Internet are selling postcards with pictures of Web sites on them; you provide the URL of the page you want to put on the card and the text you want to go with it, and these companies create the cards and mail them to you. These postcards have a glossy picture of your site on one side, and text on the back—they can look really good, if your Web site is photogenic, that is. You can get free samples at these sites:

Web Card Press
http://www.webcardpress.com/

Web Cards
http://www.wbcards.com/

You can use Web cards in all sorts of ways. Mail them to people as postcards; insert them in information you are mailing to existing clients, so you can be absolutely sure they know about your Web site; pin them up on billboards; pass them out at tradeshows; and so on. Web Card Press, which you can see in Figure 18.1, offers their own list of uses. At Web Card Press you can actually design the card online. You get to pick the font, type a message, and specify how the card should be laid out. You'll see a picture of a card online, with your Web site on the card...at least you will if the system's working properly, though sometimes it's not.

One caveat: if you need a large number of cards printed, you may find it cheaper to work with a full-service printer; there are a number that specialize in creating full-color postcards, and can probably do your job more cheaply; but in smaller quantities you may not be able to beat Web Card Press or Web Cards.

PLAIN OLD BUSINESS CARDS

You don't have to spend a lot of money to promote with cards. You can even use plain old business cards. Our friend Randy Cassingham, publisher of **This is True** (http://www.ThisIsTrue.com/), has simple printed cards that he gives away in mass quantities. *This is True* is an e-mail newsletter with around 150,000 subscribers. It contains weird but true stories gleaned from the news wires.

Randy had a few simple business cards printed at a print shop. They are the thermographic (raised letter) cards, so they look good. At one point, he managed

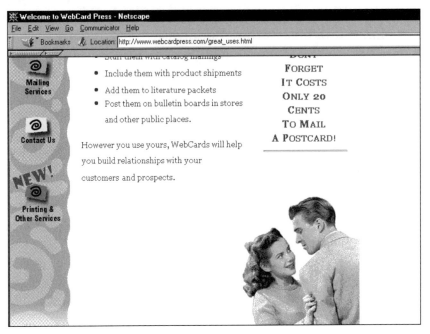

FIGURE 18.1: There are lots of uses for Web cards besides postcards.

to hand out 5,000 in 18 months or so. They cost $50 for 2,000, so that's still only $125 worth. Just *how* does one get rid of that many so quickly? Well, Randy sells books to his subscribers, compilations of the This Is True stories that many subscribers buy as Christmas and birthday presents. "The cards go out with all the books," he says. "I leave them around, I put them in with the check when I pay bills (They give me bill stuffers!), my family and friends hand them out, etc." The most important distribution method, he says, is sending them out with books: "People who buy books have already said (with their Visa card) that they like the stuff, so I give them something to help spread the word."

MAIL AND FAX PRESS RELEASES

Most publications are online to some degree. Most journalists have e-mail addresses these days; but the problem with e-mail is e-mail overload. We're reaching the stage where people ignore a huge proportion of their e-mail because they simply don't have time to deal with it all. That doesn't mean trying to contact someone by e-mail is a waste of time, but it does mean that you may want to supplement e-mail contact with mail and fax. Also, as all good marketers know, hitting someone with your story from multiple directions can often help push your story to the front.

In Chapters 16 (*Reaching Journalists Online*) and 17 (*Electronic Press Releases*) we discussed how to send out press releases across the Internet. You can also find help on the Internet for sending real-world press releases. Peter sent a release about one of his company's books (*The CDnow Story: Rags to Riches on the Internet*) to 344 journalists via fax, for a total cost of $86; that included the cost of the list of fax numbers and the faxing process. Within a few hours of transmission, he got his first response. *Boardwatch Magazine*, a well-known and well-respected magazine devoted to the online world, planned to run a story about the book.

One of the most convenient methods for sending out fax press releases is **ImediaFax** (http://www.imediafax.com/). This is a great little system. You begin by picking the type of media you want to fax to—newspapers, magazines, and broadcast media—and how you want to select the contacts: by industry, editor, classification, media name, state, metro market, or circulation. For instance, you might choose to contact magazine editors. You would first choose which types of magazines you're interested in (advertising, banking, jewelry, law, and so on). Then you select the type of editors you want to contact at each magazine—the Book Review editors, the Feature editors, the New Product Review editors, and so on. You can even see a list of the magazines that ImediaFax has found for you and omit certain magazines from the list.

In this manner you can drill down the list until you've made your selections according to various criteria and omitted the contacts you're not interested in, until you end up with your final list. You can now choose to send a press release by fax, or you can get all the names in a text file so you can import them into a database and send a press release by mail. This really is a great way to build a contact list quickly and get the press releases sent out in a matter of hours. And at 25 cents a page it can be affordable. You could also set up your own fax system, of course, using your computer or a broadcast fax machine. At around a minute per page, you could probably fax out the releases for nine cents each, perhaps less.

You might also want to send press releases by snail mail (that's Internet jargon for the post office), though this can get a little expensive and time consuming—around 45 cents per press release, plus plenty of folding and stuffing. Many of the directories and listings we mentioned in Chapters 16 and 17 also include snail-mail addresses.

ARE FOLLOW-UPS ESSENTIAL?

Many PR people will tell you that follow-ups are essential; in other words, after mailing something out, you should call. There's no doubt that follow-ups can make your marketing campaign much more effective. Calling journalists and trying to keep your products and services in their minds can make a big difference; but it's still possible to carry out an effective PR campaign with a pretty low level of follow-up. PR guru Marcia Yudkin believes that follow-up calls are not necessary, that it's quite possible to market your products without follow-up calls, though "if you're especially effective on the phone and have the time, follow-up calls might be worth a try." The problem for many small-business people is finding the time, and you may find it a more effective use of your time and money—which, you'll remember, are much the same thing—to send out a follow-up press release, or the same press release to another couple of thousand contacts, than to call and talk with people. You should probably limit calls to high-profile publications, the sort of places that will give you a large payback if they do run your story. Also, bear in mind that doing a follow up call may alienate the journalist and ruin any chance you have of getting coverage. Be conservative about follow-up calls.

ANOTHER FORM OF CYBERSPACE—RADIO

Cyberspace really began around 150 years ago with Samuel Morse's first telegraph transmission in 1844. After all, that was the beginning of electronic communications, crude as it may have been. Since then we've seen the development of a variety of electronic forms of communication—systems that create an imaginary space where electronic communications take place, as cyberspace is sometimes defined. These forms of communication include telephones, television, radio, computer bulletin board systems, the online services, and the Internet.

There's one area of cyberspace with a truly enormous number of users, an area that's cheap and easy to use for the marketing of products: radio. There are around 12,000 radio stations in the United States, and hundreds of different talk shows play on these stations or are syndicated to multiple stations.

One way to promote your site is to promote yourself as a talk-show guest. If you have something worth saying, you can easily get on a radio talk show. As Joe Sabah, author of *How to Get on Radio Talk Shows All Across America*, points out, radio talk shows need guests. As an example, his book discusses a radio station in Pittsburgh, PA, which has five hosts, each with an average of about 65 guests a month—or almost 4,000 guests a year.

People buy products they hear mentioned on talk radio; Joe Sabah has been on well over 600 talk shows and has sold more than $330,000 worth of the books he promotes on those shows. TV shows are even more productive; popular TV talk shows can launch bestsellers and celebrity careers.

Radio is a relatively efficient way to get the word out about your Web site. You generally don't have to go anywhere; you do the show at home or your office using the telephone, and you can track down the talk shows through a variety of radio-show databases. Joe Sabah (jsabah@aol.com, 303-722-7200) sells a database of 700 talk shows, along with his book, for around $200. Bradley Communication's Publicity Blitz database includes thousands of radio stations and talk shows, as do the Gebbie Press directories. Peter used some of these directories and e-mailed hundreds of radio stations asking for an invitation, and indeed appeared on scores of radio shows, some big, some small.

You could also use some of the media-interview services discussed in Chapter 16 (*Reaching Journalists Online*): **GuestFinder** (http://www.guestfinder.com/), **Radio Tour** (http://www.radiotour.com/), and Radio-TV Interview Report. And here's yet another of these services: **HotTopics** (http://www.bookpromotions.com/hottopic.htm).

ADVERTORIALS

Do you know the term *advertorial*? It refers to a newspaper ad that is camouflaged as an article. Many papers carry advertorials—it's a way for a newspaper to fill space, with what appears to be editorial content, at a low cost. Free, actually. Here's how this all works.

Companies pushing their products pay an advertorial company to carry an article for them. The company may provide the text, or it may pay more and have the advertorial company write the article. Either way, the text has to read like a newspaper article rather than an ad. The advertorial company then lays out the article to look just like a newspaper article, and prints it along with scores of other advertorials in a large newspaper-like publication, which it sends to thousands of newspapers. The newspapers receive this and can run the articles for free; the advertorial companies make their money from the companies providing the articles.

Now, there's a bit of a gamble involved here. If you create an article newspapers are interested in, it may be run in many newspapers across North America. If you don't…it won't. On the other hand, advertorial companies often have guarantees. Metro Creative Graphics, for instance, will rerun your article, perhaps even with changes, if it doesn't appear in at least 100 papers. (Note, however, that it assumes that for every newspaper clipping it finds, it has missed three, so it is actually guaranteeing to send you 25 newspaper clippings of your article.) You can easily spend $2,000 or $3,000 or more.

Will advertorials work for you? That's hard to say. It depends on the product you're writing about, the quality of the article, whether the article is suitable for the time of year, and so on. Peter's experience was mixed; he created an advertorial for *Poor Richard's Web Site*, and although it did appear in dozens of small papers around the country, he's not really sure how much business he received from it. On the other hand, a number of companies swear by advertorials—a publisher of books about antiques and another publisher selling books about real estate use advertorials effectively. If you'd like to look into this form of publicity, contact these companies:

Metro Creative Graphics
http://metrocreativegraphics.com/

News USA
http://newsusa.com/

Family Features Editorial Services (Specializes in the food and lifestyle sections of newspapers)
http://www.culinary.net/

MORE THAN WE CAN COVER

Of course there's far more to learn about real-world marketing and promotions than we can cover here. Tens of millions of words have been written about real-world, low-cost marketing, so we suggest you get out and read a few good marketing books, and then consider how to use the ideas online, and how to use the ideas offline to promote your products online.

Here are a few books to get you started:

Guerrilla Marketing, by Jay Conrad Levinson, who has written about a zillion Guerrilla Marketing books: *Guerrilla Marketing, Guerrilla Marketing Attack, Guerrilla Marketing Excellence, Guerrilla Marketing Online*, and so on. They're well known and well respected.

Six Steps to Free Publicity, by Marcia Yudkin, Plume/Penguin. From a well-known publicity guru.

1001 Ways to Market Your Books, by John Kremer, **Open Horizons** (http://www.bookmarket.com/). You may not be publishing books, but nonetheless this is a great primer on marketing. Kremer comes up with many ideas that can be applied to all sorts of products. Flick through this book at a bookstore and see if you can apply any suggestions to your situation…then buy the book.

Grassroots Marketing : Getting Noticed in a Noisy World, by Shel Horowitz, Chelsea Green Publishing Company.

CHAPTER NINETEEN

Sales Basics—
Not *All* the Rules Have Changed

The Internet has provided a remarkable impetus to new businesses. Thanks to media hype, and the fact that in many ways the Internet really does provide a new sales channel that makes it easier to reach customers, a lot of people with little or no business experience (and even less sales and marketing experience) have started new enterprises.

Under the misapprehension that the rules have changed, and that the Internet means nothing will be the same again, these people are attempting to sell products online without understanding the first thing about sales. There's a slight arrogance here, too. Many people with more technical skills than business skills think that their time has come, that sales skills are no longer necessary, that technology is now king.

Technology is just a tool, though. Human nature remains the same as it was before 1994, so although the manner in which you can reach people has changed, all the basic principles of sales remain the same. What are those principles? That's what we're going to touch on in this chapter.

Peter learned these sales techniques the hard way—selling encyclopedias door to door (back in the days when encyclopedias were books rather than plastic disks). He also sold telecommunications equipment, photographic business cards, and burglar alarms. Later he sold his technical-writing services, then he sold books as publisher of Top Floor Publishing, and today he's selling ebusiness services with BizBlast.com.

So to save you some time (and some shoe leather), here's a primer in sales, the basic techniques you need to understand if you want to succeed in selling your products and services.

IT'S A NUMBERS GAME

Marketing and sales are not easy and the work just never ends. Inexperienced marketers don't realize how much work it takes to promote a product.

Furthermore, they often equate sales leads with sales. (A *lead*, in sales terminology, is a contact with a *prospect*, someone you believe may become a customer.) They get excited when they make contact with prospects, and excited when they feel that they are close to making a sale. Having made a contact, they often slack off a little; they take a rest while they wait for the inevitable sale. What they don't realize is that there's "many a slip twixt cup and lip." Most leads will not turn into sales, however close the sale may appear. You need many, many leads.

This is a double-edged sword. Understand the numbers and you can see the road to success. As sales people in training are told many times, the real secret to success in the sales business is not sneakiness or smooth talking; it's hard work. You must make contact with prospects over and over again. Sales really is a numbers game, and once you know the numbers you can plan what it takes to meet your goals.

On the Internet, making contact is relatively easy; but the ratio of contacts to sales is even worse than in the real world. You may have to make contact with 100 people to make a sale, and may need to get your message in front of 10,000 people to find those 100.

Salespeople "don't get no respect" among the general public. Most people have the idea that the truly successful salespeople are somehow too slick for their own good. In fact, many of the really top sales people are not like this at all; their secret is that they are persistent and work very hard. Sales is quite simple: the more leads you get, the more prospective clients you contact, the more sales you'll make! You may have heard Woody Allen's claim, "80 percent of success is turning up." Eighty percent of sales success is turning up...again, and again, and again.

BELIEVE IN YOUR PRODUCT

If you don't believe in your product, how can you sell it? You can't; at least, you can't do so well. If you sell a product that you know is not very good, you'll do so only halfheartedly. You'll never really be able to push the product hard, because in the back of your mind there'll be a little voice saying, "well, that's not *quite* true, now, is it?"

It sometimes seems that the Internet has turned into a vast get-rich-quick seminar. We receive scores of get-rich-schemes in our e-mail inboxes every day. Most of these schemes are based on this simple principle: 'Here's this great product you can buy from us; you can then sell it to other people, and you'll make a fortune.' Of course in most cases, the touted product is not particularly good (if it even exists at all). Nonetheless, thousands of people are signing up to sell these products, and most will ultimately fail. One major reason for their failure is that it's hard to sell bad products. It's hard because people don't *want* bad products, and it's hard because you won't be able to put all your energy into a product you don't believe in.

If you know your product is good, you'll feel comfortable trying to convince people to buy it; and you'll be able to handle the rejection that's an occupational hazard of any sales or marketing job.

LEARN TO HANDLE REJECTION

If sales is a numbers game, with far more losses than wins, then it follows that you're going to experience a lot of rejection. Most people who go into sales cannot handle this and eventually leave the profession. A salesperson spending all day on the phone, or all day knocking on doors, experiences a huge number of rejections. Until you've done this sort of job you can't imagine the effect it has on you—being told *No*, over and over, scores or hundreds of times a day.

Luckily for you, selling products on the Web is not the same. You're not going to experience the same type of personal rejection; but your product will be rejected, far more often than it's accepted, and that can be depressing. You'll see from your logs, for instance, that 300 people arrived at your site today…yet you only sold three or four products. *What's wrong*, you want to know; *why did all those people turn you down?*

Successful salespeople understand that rejection is all part of the numbers game, so they don't let it get them down. They know that if, on average, 99 people out of 100 are going to reject their product, then all they have to do is find 100 people to make a sale. The cup isn't half empty; it's half full (or perhaps the cup isn't 99 percent empty, it's 1 percent full). Rejection is no longer something to be feared, but something to be accepted as a normal part of the sales and marketing process.

TELL PROSPECTS WHAT YOU WANT THEM TO DO

Here's another principle that sales trainers drum into their students: you have to *ask for the sale!* This principle was put into verse by Elizabethan poet Robert Herrick over 300 years ago:

To get thine ends, lay bashfulness aside
Who fears to ask, doth teach to be denied

(Herrick was actually talking about seduction, but the principle is the same.) Herrick knew that to be successful in sexual conquests, one has to—at the right moment—make a move and ask the prospect to buy in to what one is selling. If you're too bashful to ask, what will happen? The prospect may be unsure, though ready to be swayed—but if you don't ask, the prospect isn't going to buy. Worse, someone else may ask the prospect first.

You have to tell prospects what you want them to do. Don't simply provide information and hope that people at your Web site will make the obvious choice. Don't write ads that present your products and then just hope that people will know what to do. You have to *tell them:* tell them to click here; tell them to visit right away to find out about the special offer; tell them to order right now! Then tell them to tell their friends.

GIVE A GUARANTEE

Don't be afraid to give a guarantee, and a good one at that. Remember that it's easy to set up store on the Web, and many people are understandably nervous about doing businesses with companies they've never heard of before; if anyone can set up a Web store with minimal expense, how can one be sure they're for real?

How can you convince prospects that doing business with you is safe? Even if they're fairly sure that you will ship what you're selling, they may not be sure that what you're selling is worth having. How can you convince them that it's safe to order from you?

Web-site owners should look at the way direct-marketing companies—mail-order companies—have handled this issue. (These companies have been dealing with similar problems for a hundred years, after all.) They clearly state their guarantee, often several times. The guarantee is usually a more than generous one, typically a 100 percent guarantee for a year. To inexperienced marketers this type of guarantee is somewhat frightening. They envision their products flooding back to them 11 months after they've sold them; but the secret is that if you have a good product, and you're selling at a fair price, few of your products will ever be returned to you, probably a small fraction of one percent. (Less than 0.3 percent of the books Peter's sold across his Web site have been returned.)

The guarantee can be a real encouragement to buy. You're saying, in effect, "go ahead, even if you're not sure you want this product, you can always return it." Once the product is in their hands, another sales technique takes over, something known in the sales business as the *puppy dog close:* Once buyers have a product in their possession, they're unlikely to return it. Imagine a family with children, shopping for a puppy. They find a small dog the kids seem to like—but they're not quite sure they want to buy. "Take the puppy home tonight," says the store owner. "If you change your mind you can always bring the puppy back tomorrow." Will the dog ever be returned? Not likely; and the same is true of your products. Despite the guarantee, buyers will almost never return a quality product.

THE SALES MESSAGE—IT'S AN ART

Writing sales messages presents two problems to most people. They often can't write well to begin with, and writing a sales message is more difficult than writing, say, a simple business letter. You're trying to persuade someone to do something for you, and that's not easy. Writing a sales message is an art. To learn this art, you have to change your mindset a little. It's worth reading a few books on this subject. You might look at *Cash Copy*, for instance, by Dr. Jeffrey Lant (ISBN: 0940374234). This book is sold mainly by mail order, and though bookstores can order it for you, it may take a while to get. (Search for *cash copy* at **Google**, http://www.google.com for places selling it so you can get it more quickly.) This is an excellent introduction to writing sales pieces. In the meantime, consider the following points.

Benefits, Not Features

"Nobody wants a quarter-inch drill," the sales maxim goes, "they want a quarter-inch hole"—a subtle, yet important difference. When you're selling a product, think about what *benefit* the buyer will gain. You'll often see Internet companies blaring various technical details about their products—in particular, it seems, companies selling computer products, hardware and software, seem to have no idea of the concept of customer benefit. They focus on all the little intricacies of their products, forgetting that nobody cares; customers want to know what the product actually does for them.

When you're writing sales pieces—e-mail ads, sales information at your Web site, even banner ads in which you have only a few words worth of space to work with—you must remember this concept. Try to forget about the technical details, and focus on what your product actually *does*.

Also, inexperienced marketers often are unable to put themselves in their clients' shoes. They always look at the product from the point of view of their own company. This, of course, is similar to focusing on features rather than benefits. Step into your prospects' shoes, and think about what they want. Forget what *you* want to achieve, and think instead about how you can help your clients achieve what *they* want. If you can't do this, you can't write effective sales pieces.

Cut the Jargon—Write Simply

Yet another problem for many people on the Internet is that they often find it difficult to write simply and directly. They're too wrapped up in the jargon of their business and the jargon of the Internet. Sometimes that's okay. If you're sure the people you're selling to are as conversant with the jargon as you are, you might get away with it; but why risk it? Why write using jargon when it's quite possible to write in plain English and be understood by far more people?

Do not overestimate the knowledge of your prospects, especially Internet and computer knowledge. The personal computer may have been around 25 years, and if you believe the media, everyone and his dog uses the Internet day in and day out. However the fact is that most people are fumbling around with technology they don't really understand. If you throw too much computer and Internet jargon into your sales messages, you'll just confuse most people.

Bring Objections into the Open

An important technique taught to salespeople—and one that can be used, carefully, when writing sales pieces—is to bring objections into the open. (By *objections* we mean reasons that a prospective client may have for not wanting to buy from you.)

Let's say that your product has an inherent problem, one that prospects are likely to be concerned about and see quite clearly. You could ignore the problem, of course, and hope your prospects don't think too much about it; but they will. On the other hand, you can bring the objection out into the open, deal with it, and move on.

For instance, let's say you're selling kites, and let's say that it's clear that your kites are a little on the expensive side, and that you often hear objections from people about the price. It's clear that price is holding people back from buying. You could write a sales piece that doesn't mention price until the end, when you ask for the sale. Or you can start talking about the price early on. You point out that this kite isn't for everyone, that this isn't some toy-store kite selling for five bucks. No, the customer's paying for quality here, one of the world's best kites, a real work of art...and that doesn't come cheap.

Don't try to hide problems and avoid objections that you know are going to arise anyway. Deal with them head on and early, and perhaps even turn them into advantages.

Everything's a Sales Piece

Don't forget that when you're selling, everything's a sales piece. Every bit of business communication, everything that carries a message from you to prospective clients, can carry information that may help sell your products. That's not to say that you have to turn every communication into a long sales pitch, or that you have to beat people over the head with your sales message; but think of little ways in which you can reach people. The signature block in your e-mail message can be used to carry a sales message, a sidebar or a copyright footer in your Web pages, your business cards, your search-engine listings; all these can be little sales messages.

FIND A WAY TO STAY IN TOUCH

Finding prospects and getting sales is a lot of hard work; but you can make it a little easier by finding a way to stay in touch. Just because you can't convert a prospect to a buyer today, doesn't mean you can't do so next week or next month; and if some people buy from you today, they might do so again later if you present them with something else they'd be interested in.

The Internet provides an easy way to keep in touch with people—e-mail. Try to persuade visitors to give you their e-mail addresses. Sign them up for new-product bulletins and newsletters, for instance. Keeping in touch with them costs a fraction of the price of real-world mailings, so it's a big mistake not to tap into this potential market.

READ A FEW SALES BOOKS

What are most new Internet marketers reading? They're reading mostly geek stuff. Sure, they read a few books about Internet marketing like this one; but they also read books on setting up Web sites, on creating Web pages, on HTML and Web design, on Internet basics. All of this reading is okay, but it's like auto mechanics spending all their time learning about how to use tools, and little or no time learning about how to fix cars.

Read a few books about selling. Take a trip to your local bookstore, or browse through the categories in an online bookstore and see what you can find. There's no lack of books on the subject, so pick one or two bestsellers and read them. Learn a little about the mail-order business, too—about the methods used to convert catalog recipients to buyers, for instance. As we've mentioned elsewhere in this book, Web sites have a lot in common with mail-order catalogs. In many ways, they are closer to catalogs than to stores, in fact.

Yes, yes, you may find the idea of selling rather distasteful; but if you're reading this book, then we can be fairly sure you're trying to sell something. It may be your products and services, or perhaps your ideas and beliefs. Whatever you're up to on the Internet, if you're trying to convince people to take some kind of action, you're *in the sales business*! Learn about the business, not just the tools. When you fully understand the principles, you'll be able to use the tools to put the principles into action.

INDEX

POOR RICHARD'S WEB SITE

Geek-Free, Commonsense Advice on Building a Low-Cost Web Site, 2nd Edition

Poor Richard's Web Site is the *only* book that explains the entire process of creating a Web site, from deciding whether you really need a site—and what you can do with it—through picking a place to put the site, creating the site, and bringing people to the site. It is full of common-sense advice that Amazon.com called an "antidote to this swirl of confusion" and "straightforward information." Praised by *BYTE magazine*, *Publisher's Weekly*, and *USA Today*, *Poor Richard's Web Site* can save you thousands of dollars and hundreds of hours.

❝Poor Richard's Good Advice. With all great new things comes a proliferation of hucksters and snake-oil salesmen, and the Internet is no exception. The antidote to this swirl of confusion lies in Peter Kent's *Poor Richard's Web Site.* The analogy to Ben Franklin's volume is appropriate: the book is filled with the kind of straightforward information the Founding Father himself would have appreciated."

—Amazon.com

❝We highly recommend that you get a copy."

—Marketing Technology

❝Very well written."

—Library Journal

❝Poor Richard's offers clear advice to help you defend against jargon-happy sales people and computer magazines."

—Fortune.com

Poor Richard's Web Site is available in bookstores both online and offline, and at http://www.TopFloor.com/

Poor Richard's Web Site, Second Edition
by Peter Kent   ISBN: 0-9661032-0-3

POOR RICHARD'S E-MAIL PUBLISHING

Creating Newsletters, Bulletins, Discussion Groups, and Other Powerful Communication Tools

E-mail publishing is a powerful communications medium that anyone with Internet access can use. It's cheap, effective, and very easy to use once you learn the tricks of the trade. Electronic publishing is one of the most efficient ways to promote your products or services online, as well as being an excellent way to drive traffic back to your Web site.

Poor Richard's E-mail Publishing is your complete, step-by-step, guide to the nuts and bolts of creating newsletters and discussion groups via e-mail. Whether you're an e-mail novice or a seasoned professional, this resource belongs on your shelf.

You'll find answers to questions such as:

- How do I set up an HTML newsletter?

- Why is e-mail better than a Web site for distributing information?

- How can I communicate via e-mail without spamming?

- What is the proper e-mail etiquette?

- Where do I find subscribers and then how can I manage them?

- Where can I find a high-powered list service?

- What are the insider's tricks to hosting a successful e-mail discussion list?

- How can I generate income through advertising or ancillary product sales?

Poor Richard's E-mail Publishing is available in bookstores both online and offline, and at http://www.TopFloor.com/

Poor Richard's E-mail Publishing
by Chris Pirillo   ISBN: 0-9661032-5-4

POOR RICHARD'S BUILDING ONLINE COMMUNITIES

Create a Web Community for Your Business, Club, Association, or Family

Anyone with Internet access can set up an online community—you don't have to be a rocket scientist or spend thousands of dollars. In fact, you probably already have the programs you'll need. But to have a successful Web community where members actively participate you'll need a bit more information. *Poor Richard's Building Online Communities* explains everything you'll need to know, such as:

- What programs are involved and how to manage them

- Where to promote your community so others can find it

- How to protect the privacy of your members

- Ways of dealing with dissension and needless arguments

- How to provide information that people can use

- How to foster a sense of trust and belonging with your members

You'll also learn about the types of systems you can use (mailing lists, usenet newsgroups, Web-based message boards, etc.). The authors explain the advantages and disadvantages of each system as well as how to create and manage each type of community.

If you decide to host a community that is open to everyone, you'll need to invite people to join. This book offers several ways to promote your community.

Finding and getting to know people who share your interests is one of the most interesting and useful things you can do on the Internet. So start building your online community now!

Poor Richard's Building Online Communities is available in bookstores both online and offline, and at http://www.TopFloor.com/

**Poor Richard's Building Online Communities
by Margaret Levine Young and John Levine   ISBN: 0-9661032-9-7**

POOR RICHARD'S
INTERNET RECRUITING

Easy, Low-Cost Ways to Find Great Employees Online

One of the most challenging and dreaded tasks for any manager or human resource professional is finding and hiring qualified employees. Recruiting is time consuming and expensive, and a poor decision can devastate the health of a company. But with the advice in this book and an Internet connection, you can find *great* employees faster and cheaper than ever before!

Did you know that one of the first documents new users post on their personal Web site is their résumé? And that you can use search engines like AltaVista to immediately locate people seeking employment in your industry—*all without spending a dime*?

Poor Richard's Internet Recruiting contains lots of other clever ideas for finding employees online, including:

- Participating in Internet forums (excellent vehicles for networking and branding). You'll discover not only how to find your targeted forums, but the appropriate ways to participate.

- Perusing industry niche sites. Learn how to find sites for your specific industry and why these sites are one of the best places for finding the qualified candidates you need.

- Maintaining an employment section on your Web site. This seems like a no-brainer, but many companies don't take advantage of their Web site's traffic.

- Posting jobs at state and city job banks. If you're hiring locally, why pay for national exposure?

- Searching colleges and universities. Find out how to take advantage of one of the easiest Internet recruiting methods available.

Poor Richard's Internet Recruiting is available in bookstores both online and offline, and at http://www.TopFloor.com/

Poor Richard's Internet Recruiting
by Barbara Ling   ISBN: 0-930082-01-0

POOR RICHARD'S HOME AND SMALL OFFICE NETWORKING

Room-to-Room or Around the World

Today's businesses have multiple offices, mobile workers, telecommuters, and virtual offices. How do they all keep in touch, share information, and collaborate? This book offers an easy-to-understand explanation of the technology available for connecting employees.

You'll learn about inexpensive networking alternatives, software, installation, types of connections, security, and administration. The book also discusses how to use the Internet to communicate with instant messaging and file sharing. With the geek-free advice in this book, you will discover the most economical and efficient way to keep in touch with your employees and business contacts.

Poor Richard's Home and Small Office Networking
by John Paul Mueller   ISBN: 1-930082-03-7

POOR RICHARD'S CREATING EBOOKS

How Authors, Publishers, and Corporations Can Get into Digital Print

The ebook business—everyone wants to know more. What does the future hold? Why publish electronically? After deciding to enter the market, how should content be formatted and how should this content be marketed, sold, and protected? These are just some of the questions that *Poor Richard's Creating eBooks* will address.

The economics of epublishing (including Print On Demand) vs. print publishing are discussed and contractual issues-copyright, security, and encryption are dissected. The future of ebooks is uncertain. But it is clear that the industry needs more information to make decisions on how they will participate. *Poor Richard's Creating eBooks* will lead the way in educating publishers, authors, booksellers, corporate communication departments, and industry pundits.

Poor Richard's Creating eBooks
by Chris Van Buren and Jeff Cogswell   ISBN: 1-930082-02-9

ORDER FORM

TOP FLOOR
PUBLISHING

Order Direct from the Publisher and Get a 15% Discount!

To order copies of any of the *Poor Richard's Series* using a credit card, visit http://www.TopFloor.com or call 877-693-4676. You can also copy and mail/fax this form to: Top Floor Publishing, 8790 W. Colfax #107, Lakewood, CO 80215 USA, fax 305-675-8531.

	retail	special	TOTAL
Poor Richard's Web Site	$29.95	$25.46	_____
Poor Richard's Internet Marketing and Promotions	$29.95	$25.46	_____
Poor Richard's E-mail Publishing	$29.95	$25.46	_____
Poor Richard's Building Online Communities	$29.95	$25.46	_____
Poor Richard's Internet Recruiting	$29.95	$25.46	_____
Poor Richard's Home & Small Office Networking	$29.95	$25.46	_____
Poor Richard's Creating eBooks	$29.95	$25.46	_____

Shipping: Add $5.95 for Priority Mail or $8.95 for Global Priority. If you need additional shipping information, please call 877-693-4676 or visit http://TopFloor.com

Name: _____
Address: _____
City: _____
State: _____
Country: _____
Zip/Postal Code: _____
Email: _____
(We will not sell or use your contact information for any other purpose.)

Payment: ____Check or ____Credit Card (Visa, MasterCard, Amex, Discover)
Card Number: _____
EXP date: _____
Name on Card: _____
Signature: _____

FREE INFORMATION ABOUT SETTING UP AND PROMOTING A WEB SITE

http://www.TopFloor.com/

If you are setting up a Web site, or if you have a Web site and you want marketing and promotions advice that really works, visit http://www.TopFloor.com/.

You'll find free information of all kinds: questions to ask a hosting company, the top 10 mistakes to avoid when setting up a Web site, 8 reasons why you should create your own online community—plus links to hundreds of Web sites with services that will help you set up and promote your site, several chapters from each book in the *Poor Richard's Series*, and much more.

Also, sign up for the free e-mail newsletter, *Poor Richard's Web Site News*. With more than 48,000 subscribers in over 80 countries, this is one of the most respected newsletters on the subject.

You can read back issues and subscribe to the newsletter at http://www.PoorRichard.com/newsltr/, or to subscribe by e-mail, send an e-mail message to subpr@PoorRichard.com.

The Main Page:
http://www.TopFloor.com/

The Newsletter:
http://www.PoorRichard.com/newsltr/

E-mail Subscriptions:
send a blank e-mail message to subpr@PoorRichard.com

(Continued from the back cover)...

Poor Richard's Internet Marketing and Promotions provides techniques that really do work—techniques the authors have actually *used* successfully. For instance, Peter Kent has used low-cost e-mail newsletter advertising (no, not spam!), to attract people to his site, affordably and effectively. (You'll learn how to do it yourself in Chapter 12.) Tara Calishain has used press releases "over the wires" very successfully—a $75 press release, if written well and properly targeted, can buy the equivalent of tens of thousands of dollars of advertising. (Check out Chapter 17 to try it for yourself.)

In *Poor Richard's Internet Marketing and Promotions* you'll learn:
- How to prepare your Web pages to make sure they're properly registered in the search sites
- Where else you should be registering your site, and why search sites probably *won't* send a flood of traffic your way
- Why banner advertising is a good way to lose money, and how to test it without spending too much
- How to find low-cost alternatives to banner advertising
- How to create an e-mail newsletter, using your own e-mail program, a free service, or a high-powered newsletter server
- Why affiliate programs are a great way to promote your products, and how to set up an affiliate system without spending a ton of money

These are not expensive systems that only large companies can use. The techniques in this book can be used by anyone, including individuals and small companies on tight budgets. Many of the ideas are free grass-roots techniques that take time, not money. Others are very low-cost procedures that are well within the budget of most people.

More importantly, these techniques have been used in the real world. Top Floor Publishing, publisher of this book, is a small company founded by best-selling author Peter Kent. Without the clout and budget of a large publisher, Peter Kent was able to use these techniques to push *Poor Richard's Web Site*, the first book in this series, onto the Internet Business best-seller lists. He was able to push it so far, in fact, that it became one of the most widely reviewed titles in computer-book history. He and Tara Calishain describe the techniques he used, along with many others, such as these: